D0217038

Puerto Rican Studies in the
City University of New York:

THE FIRST 50 YEARS

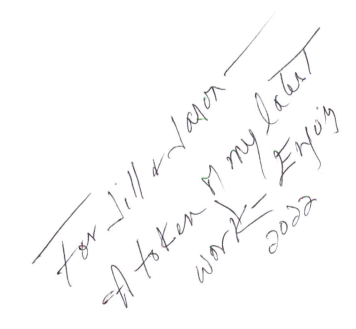

For Jill & Jason —
A token of my latest
work — Enjoy
2022

Puerto Rican Studies in the City University of New York:

THE FIRST 50 YEARS

EDITORS

María Elizabeth Pérez y González
and Virginia Sánchez Korrol

CEN
TRO
PRESS

Copyright © 2021 by Centro Press, Center for Puerto Rican Studies. All rights reserved. No part of this publication may be reproduced, distributed, or transmitted in any form or by any means, including photocopying, recording, or other electronic or mechanical methods, without the prior written permission of the publisher, except in the case of brief quotations embodied in critical reviews and certain other non-commercial uses permitted by copyright law.

ISBN: 978-1-945662-49-2 (paper); 978-1-945662-50-8 (ebook)
Library of Congress Control Number (LCNN): 2021948909

Printed in the United States of America

Centro Press
Center for Puerto Rican Studies
Hunter College, CUNY
695 Park Avenue, E-1429
New York, NY 10065
centrops@hunter.cuny.edu
http://centropr.hunter.cuny.edu

DEDICATIONS

Para mis abuel@s, parents, husband (Rev. Dr. Fr. Belén), children (Jesús—RIP;
Daniela and Lavender Alexander), familia (por sangre, matrimonio, y Espíritu),
Veronica and Elsie;
and Lisa (RIP)—love you mucho!

To generations quienes lucharon for me to be able to write/right
some of our collective story

To people of good will: may we unite to overcome adversities as a human race

Para Borikén y su gente por doquier

—MEPyG

AND

For all the scholars and pioneers who teach and promote
Puerto Rican Studies in the academy and beyond,

and especially for my husband, Dr. Charles R. Korrol,
who has stood beside me at every step of this extraordinary journey

—VSK

AND

To all PRS/PRLS students—you give us hope

—MEPyG and VSK

Puerto Rican Studies in the City University of New York: The First 50 Years

EDITORS: María Elizabeth Pérez y González and Virginia Sánchez Korrol

TABLE OF CONTENTS

FOREWORD

50 years of Puerto Rican Studies at CUNY

Félix V. Matos Rodríguez, Chancellor

It is a great honor and a source of personal pride to commemorate the first 50 Years of Puerto Rican Studies at the City University of New York (CUNY). I say this not only as the first Puerto Rican and Latino to serve as chancellor of the nation's largest urban university, but also as a scholar who has dedicated most of my academic life to studying the Puerto Rican experience.

Starting when I was a graduate student in New York City, I was always attracted to CUNY because of its longstanding commitment to the field of Puerto Rican studies. A few similar Puerto Rican Studies programs had also developed in other parts of the country, but CUNY has always been in the lead of creating and institutionalizing those spaces. When I first joined the CUNY system in 2000 as part of the Black and Puerto Rican Studies Department at Hunter College, I was delighted to become a proud member of that community.

One of my fondest experiences in Hunter was serving as director of the Center for Puerto Rican Studies. Centro, as it is commonly referred to, was created in part to serve as a key component of the academic, methodological, and archival infrastructure to Puerto Rican Studies departments across the CUNY system. Centro has always stood up as a vital repository in its field: an unparalleled intellectual space to produce scholarship thanks to its vast library and archive, and an indispensable resource to serve the academic departments throughout the system and throughout the country, and the community outside academia as a whole. It was a dream for me as a historian to have the opportunity to help curate what is the most important collection of historical and archival materials on the Puerto Rican experience in the United States. It also allowed me to be a participant of the collective effort of rescuing materials and records from a diverse array of individuals and organizations.

I loved the opportunity it afforded me to talk and interview Puerto Rican pioneers and agents of change who had sometimes been neglected by the history books. I could tell a number of stories about elected officials, artists, or labor and community-based organization leaders who I engaged with as we were building that collection. That's how I met *la Doctora* Antonia Pantoja, the founder of ASPIRA and, at the time, the first and only Puerto Rican to get the Presidential Medal of Freedom, and convinced her that her papers belonged at Centro. During my time we also finalized the donation of the massive archives of *El Diario/La Prensa*, the oldest Spanish-language daily newspaper in the U.S. To this day, it is an ongoing source of joy for me to see those materials being used by everyone from graduate students to academics, journalists, TV producers, or filmmakers getting information for a documentary, or retired individuals digging into their own family's history.

The academic, intellectual, and social infrastructure for Puerto Rican Studies that CUNY provides has continued to anchor and nurture my career over the years, as president of Eugenio María de Hostos Community College—which was created as a result of the activism of the Puerto Rican community to create a higher education space in the South Bronx,—as president of Queens College, and currently as Chancellor.

I feel that, in many ways, the role that I have now leading the system and its 25 campuses is directly connected to the investment that CUNY has made in Puerto Ricans and other Latino groups. Those are investments that, as a chapter in this book documents, didn't always come without contestation, and in some instances there were spaces that were fought against institutionally before being fully embraced. Fortunately, over time that activism has created a much more nurturing environment and a space for institutionalization and growth.

Puerto Rican Studies started as a grassroots movement to educate our community, to encourage civic engagement, and to provide information to advance national, state and city policies. As we celebrate its first 50 years in CUNY, I personally feel that we need to continue to enhance and advance the original mission while we make sure that the field remains grounded on the current Puerto Rican experience. Moving forward, we will keep thinking how to fulfill the mission in the light of new times, while reassessing what are the right methodological tools that we need and what we can learn from in other disciplines and fields of study.

One significant development over the past decades has been the strengthening of relationships and partnerships with a growing universe of ethnic and racial groups nationwide, owing in part to the evolution of the Puerto Rican community here in New York and in the U.S. While those exchanges will certainly continue, we will always examine when we need to focus exclusively or primarily on things Puerto Rican and when it is appropriate to be part of a broader lens. The focus will depend on resources and circumstances at the time: Puerto Rico's economic crisis, Hurricane María, or the Puerto Rican bankruptcy, for example, were on-the-ground events that we could not predict, and which made us reconsider how we could be more connected with the Island.

Also, as the Puerto Rican diaspora becomes more complex by becoming on the one end multigenerational, and on the other end receiving fresh waves of migrants from the Island, we need to be attentive to the new chapters in history that are constantly opening up. The increasing presence of the Puerto Rican community in Orlando and Central Florida is one prime example. The people there are beginning to tell their stories and build a place in the larger Puerto Rican diasporic experience. Still, we also need to keep looking at the evolving stories of our more 'historical' communities such as New York, Hartford, or Chicago.

Looking into the future, it's clear to me that there is a vibrant new generation of scholars trying to redefine the field, and my experience tells me that there is always some disruption when that happens. But that is the nature of innovation. We need to have on-going dialogues between different generations who experience their Puerto Ricanness in different and new ways that need to be reflected in the field of Puerto Rican Studies. These are exciting but not always easy conversations, so we need to continue to create and nurture the intellectual and civic infrastructure that will make those conversations flourish, and then we need to turn them into action that will help advance the quality of life of all Puerto Ricans.

We have the good fortune that CUNY has created a fertile environment for that conversation to continue well into the future. As chancellor, I am pleased that I was recently able to secure a $10 million grant by The Andrew W. Mellon Foundation that will be a boost for what should be the next phase not only of Puerto Rican and Latino studies, but all the ethnic and racial studies in the CUNY system.

It has been a long and joyful journey that has also had its share of struggles, but I'm more confident than ever that we have laid a solid foundation for another 50 Years of Puerto Rican Studies in CUNY.

¡Pa'lante!

Félix V. Matos Rodríguez
November 2021
New York City

PREFACE

This volume marks the 50th anniversary of Puerto Rican Studies in CUNY, focusing on the senior colleges, of which there are 11 in total among its 25 campuses, graduate center, and professional schools. Seven of these senior colleges originally housed either a department or program of PRS and continue to do so in 2021, albeit in differing forms. While the community colleges were enthusiastically involved in activism that resulted in PRS in CUNY, the fact that PRS departments and programs materialized in the senior colleges as degree-granting entities is what distinguishes them from the community colleges, some of which initially established PRS programs, and several of which still have distinct PRS courses as part of their curriculum. The editors deemed it best to highlight the senior colleges because of their cumulative experience in PRS at that level of the bifurcated CUNY system. The nuanced nature of PRS in community colleges is best examined from among its own scholar-practitioners and students. Of particular significance deserving of further study is the naming of Eugenio María de Hostos Community College in September 1969, which was a direct response to student outcry for equity.

The original concept of this volume called for the CUNY senior colleges who had established departments and programs of PRS to contribute essays on the history of their origins to date, the current state of affairs, and future projections in light of reaching its 50-year milestone in the academy. The editors spent ample time reaching out to scholars who might contribute to this important work. Over the course of a year, the volume took another direction leaning toward the legacy of PRS rather than solely a department-based focus. It also expanded its portfolio to include retrospectives as a way to reflect on the growing pains and evolution of PRS—its curriculum, students, faculty, and institutional constraints. This approach allowed for senior colleges to be more widely represented and for an opportunity to include the distinct experiences of PRS practitioners and students. Having exercised due diligence, yet due to circumstances beyond our control, two of the seven PRS units established early on in CUNY—Hunter College and John Jay College of Criminal Justice— are not featured in, but neither are they absent from, this volume. Likewise, PRS literature is an area of expertise that would have been an ideal addition to round out the expanse of knowledge herein. In all, this volume is a tribute to all who put themselves on the line to advocate for a more inclusive curriculum and university setting in CUNY—one that includes Puerto Rican Studies and Black Studies, which ultimately unlocked the doors of the academy for Dominican, Mexican, Latinx, Asian American, and Judaic Studies, as well as for peoples of all backgrounds.

The editors, Drs. María Pérez y González and Virginia Sánchez Korrol, share long careers as professors in PRS at Brooklyn College. They also share a combined total of 32 years as chairpersons of the department. María Pérez y González is a first-generation college graduate of CUNY's John Jay College of Criminal Justice B.A./M.A. Program (Class of 1987) and a professor in PRLS (since 1992). Because of what Puerto Ricans and their allies accomplished by establishing PRS in the academy over half a century ago, she stands as a living testament of their efforts. This book project gave her the opportunity to delve into rich archival records. She would have approached her time in PRLS differently, had she been armed with this newfound knowledge. "I took some PRS courses at John Jay College with Ricardo Campos and read the then newly released *Industry and Idleness: Labor Migration Under Capitalism* (1986). Migdalia DeJesús Torres de García was chairperson then, but I was unaware that it was a relatively new field." María's father gave her the first book she read about Puerto Rico; it was about its "discovery" by Christopher Columbus. An *independentista,* her father knew the history therein was inadequate, but it was the only book of its kind in English that existed for children at the time. That sparked a curiosity that continues to burn bright. Born and raised in Brooklyn, she spent much time in her maternal grandparents' home in Coney Island. When they returned to Puerto Rico in 1975, she spent summers with them, and grew to understand the umbilical cord that draws her back to her ancestral homeland.

As early as 1968, Virginia Sánchez Korrol understood that the field of Puerto Rican Studies would become the core of her academic and activist career. As a prelude to her enrollment in the M.A./Ph.D. program in History at the State University of New York at Stony Brook, she posed one question to the Latin American/Caribbean Studies faculty at the interview. "Can your program prepare me to specialize on Puerto Rico and U.S. Puerto Ricans? I'm a working mom, and I don't have time to waste." She was accepted into the program with a grant and the opportunity to teach in the fledgling PRS program. Her strong motivation was born from the frustration of reading about the student demands for PRS at Brooklyn College, her alma mater, and not being part of the struggle. As she began to write a dissertation on the Puerto Rican migrant community in New York, 1917 to 1947, years that reflected her family's migration from Puerto Rico to New York, her own education was further enhanced under the mentorship of Dr. Frank Bonilla and the scholars and archival resources of the Center for Puerto Rican Studies. To date, her scholarship on PRS has been incorporated into a myriad of educational, academic, and advisory venues at the national, state, and local levels.

Based on their shared DiaspoRican experiences, in conjunction with their longevity as faculty in the field of PRS, the editors embraced the opportunity to honor the past half century of PRS and its protagonists, including the critical role it has played in broadening the intellectual boundaries of academia. In this volume, the editors have respected the writers' varied historical uses of the terms in each essay referring to what is now commonly known as the pan-ethnic and pan-racial group of Latinxs/Latines; they include the terms Hispanics, Latinos, Latinos/as, Latinas(os), and Latin@s. Unless specified otherwise by the writer, these terms are used interchangeably throughout this volume.

ACKNOWLEDGMENTS

We wish to express our gratitude to the exceptional writers represented in this volume. Their commitment to documenting the development and impact of Puerto Rican Studies is an homage to the pioneers and current practitioners in the field, as it sets the record straight on the evolution of knowledge about disenfranchised communities in institutions of higher education. We thank our Brooklyn College colleagues, Prudence Cumberbatch, Chairperson of Africana Studies, who first suggested a 50th anniversary tribute to PRS, and Antonio Nadal, whose invaluable treasure chest of memories and information was placed at our disposal, and our meticulous Centro Press Editor, Xavier Totti. Appreciation also goes to Matilda Nistal (Secretary/Administrative Assistant) and Gisely Colón López (alumna and current Graduate Teaching Fellow) of PRLS for their unwavering support throughout this labor of love. We thank everyone who in some way contributed to this volume with information, suggestions, good intentions, and encouraging words. Above all, the caring support of our families and friends enabled us to complete this work.

To the future students and practitioners of PRS in all its iterations, we leave you with the following: if the essays herein resonate with your experience of instinctively knowing you are more than what others say and have the potential to achieve what seems out of your grasp, we hope you see yourself in these pages. It is our hope that you also see how alliances forged with people of good will from all walks of life are invaluable to creating a better world for us all. Finally, for those of you who are Puerto Rican, we hope you see that being Puerto Rican echoes in your blood and is imprinted on your soul, not limited by your birthplace, race, or language. ¡Pa'lante!

INTRODUCTION

Virginia Sánchez Korrol and María Elizabeth Pérez y González

Just over fifty years ago, the City University of New York was rocked to the core when an intrepid band of activist students and faculty clamored at the gates for a seat in the academy and representation in the curriculum. How their demands changed the university and became an important component of knowledge in collegiate education forms the core of this collection of essays, as it assesses more than a half century of Puerto Rican Studies, and beyond. The essays present a history of the radical movement that set the record straight; they describe a Puerto Rican struggle for justice and equity in a nation that often relegated them to second class citizenship. It weaves a story of visionaries who embraced the belief that their heritage and experiences were equally as valuable as anyone else's; and that it counted toward a more realistic and comprehensive history of the United States and, in the process, applied its principles and ideals in creating a just and better nation.

The idea to institutionalize an area of academic inquiry labeled Puerto Rican Studies (PRS) took root during the insurgency of the Civil Rights movements, buttressed by an unpopular Vietnam War that indiscriminately destroyed the futures of a generation of able-bodied minority youth. Strident grassroots movements mobilized a multitude of disenfranchised communities of color to redress their erasure from access to equal opportunity and civil rights.

Among these, the struggle for Puerto Rican and Black Studies was led by a generation of *barrio* activists, future leaders in the making, many of whom formed a critical mass of "first in the family" college students. The movement called for a revised agenda, as well as institutional reforms that would carve a path into the city's colleges and higher education, endowing students with the requisite knowledge to help the neglected communities from which they came. Armed with the outrage of the aggrieved at institutional racism, which denied them access and opportunity, the student activists interrogated the contradictions of their condition in a nation where even their citizenship posed perplexities among privileged U.S. Americans whose collective narrative claimed "We the people" but failed to include them. In response, the student activists began to assert their rights to self-definition and self-determination (see Reed in this volume).

The community also played a critical role in radicalizing the student activists. As Puerto Rican parents and community leaders raised alarm over the failure of an unresponsive school system unwilling or unable to reverse an appalling dropout rate among the *barrio's* youth, ASPIRA (1961) opened its doors and created high school student clubs to staunch the hemorrhage. ASPIRA aimed to instill "uplift," a sense of pride in young people about their Puerto Rican heritage to counteract the ways they were depicted in the schools, media, and society at large. Honing student interest in the history, culture, and the politics of the Puerto Rican archipelago, ASPIRA reinforced critical thinking along with basic skills, and coined the slogan of the three A's—awareness, analysis, and—action as its guiding principle. Ultimately, ASPIRA sought to create a cadre of educated leaders, pillars of the community who would exercise decision-making power in the multi-layered spheres of American society. Wherever their graduates were to be found, in state, local, or federal government, or in higher education or the public schools, or in business or health care, ASPIRA's tactics would prove to be highly successful (see Nadal and Morales Nadal in this volume).

Thus was the training of the *Aspirantes* who were well represented among the student activists demanding Puerto Rican Studies, and other non-traditional programs, in the university. In urban areas where Puerto Rican/Latinx communities concentrated, dissatisfied youth rose in unofficial alliance, organizing like-minded comrades into a national reformative coalition that harbored nascent programs in Chicano/a, Mexican American, Puerto Rican, African American, and Cuban Studies throughout the nation. They took their cues from the militant Black Panthers' (1966) proactive social service engagement, along with civic affirmations of equity spawned from the political leanings of progressive community organizations. Inspired by the Young Lords, first in Chicago (1968), and then in New York (1969), Black and Puerto Rican activists joined or created dozens of groups like the Lords in New York, or the Chicano Brown Berets in East Los Angeles (1966). All shared a common agenda: equitable inclusion, a nationalist identity, and an urgent, long overdue need to understand their people's reality within the broader confines of American society.

Militant activists demanded proportional representation in the colleges of New York City, as well as recognition of their historical roots as correctives to a negative, but dominant, national narrative. In response, they specifically centered the creation of departments of Black and Puerto Rican Studies with faculty specialists to teach the Puerto Rican and Latinx experience in the United States in newly created courses. Such audacity was not far removed from that of their working class community and clearly reflected the maturation of Puerto Rican and other Latinx enclaves that protested over segregation versus neighborhood schools; control of community school boards; the Voting Rights Act and the elimination of the literacy test; labor unions and human rights; and police brutality. All served as textbook case studies for the activist generation.

In 1969, the Board of Higher Education of the City of New York (BHE) resolved, in its minutes of July 9th, that due to the attention received by the "Five Demands" at City College, Black and Puerto Rican Studies programs, departments, centers, and institutes should be developed and given priority funding in CUNY. Furthermore, it stated that CUNY's goal should be to achieve a stellar reputation of national leadership in these fields. Thus, Ethnic Studies became an official part of CUNY's academic mission. Among the CUNY campuses, Lehman College held the distinction of being the first to receive approval on June 30th of that year to establish Departments of Puerto Rican and Black Studies.

The underrepresented, "powerless" black and brown students had stormed the citadel, the symbolic ivy-covered towers of the senior colleges and the community colleges,[1] transforming higher education in ways the activists could not then imagine. Their story held the drama of making the impossible possible and has become the stuff of legend. Still, while the hard-won resolution sealed a gripping impasse that had paralyzed the system's institutions of higher education, in meeting the demands of the protesters, the BHE set into motion the evolution of a totally untested academic field.

Between 1968 and 1972, new academic departments and programs of PRS were established at Lehman, Hunter, City, Brooklyn, John Jay, and Queens Colleges.[2] Under a new policy of the BHE, Open Admissions attracted a flood of students to the university—among them, women and other applicants who previously failed to meet the entrance requirements. How would scholars of the Puerto Rican experience, faculty, and staff, hired to administer newly minted academic units, remain committed to the urgent demands and mandates of the fiery activist generation, while negotiating entrenched practices of traditional institutions, and still deliver a legacy? What would be the price of institutionalization? (See Cabán and González in this volume.)

In less than a decade, the New York City fiscal crisis of 1976 led CUNY to impose undergraduate tuition for the first time ever, resulting in a steady decline in the student population and non-reappointment of faculty. Budget cuts quickly followed, underscoring the imminent danger of departmental or program restructuring and mergers. These events combined to weaken the status quo of the often small, non-traditional departments. Indeed, an ongoing struggle to save the first and only bilingual (Spanish-English) community college, Eugenio María de Hostos, from a merger with Bronx Community College (1973-1978),[3] had already sent a well-justified wakeup call throughout the system, raising concerns for the future of PRS departments. Undoubtedly, small departments and the recently established community college in the Bronx were vulnerable. What had Puerto Rican Studies accomplished in an inaugural decade of implementation and development that could validate its continued existence and growth in the academy? And how long would temporary reprieves save departments from extinction?

Since its inception, PRS battled negative stereotypes in the academy labeling the discipline as an un-American, non-rigorous collection of disparate courses designed to promote identity politics. Given a professoriate that came of age during the period of the "Greatest Generation," the idealistic American values of the Second World War era inculcated assimilation—to create one people, one culture out of many (E Pluribus Unum)—and acculturation. In their view, a curriculum that demanded representation of the experiences of ethno-racial minorities, albeit U.S. citizens, was unwarranted.

In the ten short years of forging an academic enterprise within a highly bureaucratic structure, itself dependent on the vicissitudes of a state budget, an aura of illegitimacy not only clouded the achievements of PRS, but its significance as well. In academic circles, the discipline's grassroots origins were never far removed from its existence as a political expediency in response to a growing and vocal ethnic minority population. Were these departments academic enough or merely service oriented; intellectually rigorous or watered-down entities for fomenting anti-American nationalist ideologies? Were they products of Affirmative Action? That federal policy promulgated under the Kennedy administration aimed to improve the hiring of women and underrepresented minorities, but it raised issues for many professorial gatekeepers who questioned the academic preparation of Puerto Rican/Latinx faculty (see Vázquez in this volume).

Although the field of PRS steadily produced a body of research literature challenging the status quo and expanding the knowledge base, its importance had yet to be recognized, partly because there were no representative professional academic organizations or peer-reviewed journals for intellectual dissemination and discourse, as was the practice in other academic disciplines. Moreover, it took longer to develop and tenure a productive and published faculty in the small, under-resourced PRS departments often called upon to diversify its standing committees, assist in faculty recruitment efforts, represent colleges in the geographic community of the college, and to serve as personal as well as academic advisors to students.

In response to the questions and practical academic issues impacting the evolution of Puerto Rican Studies, the First International Conference of Puerto Rican Studies took place at Brooklyn College on April 3-4, 1981. The Brooklyn College PRS Department had agreed to mount a broad-reaching conference on its tenth anniversary that would submit the field to scholarly scrutiny. The conference offered a unique opportunity for introspection, a time to analyze the strengths and weaknesses, and to evaluate the overall state of the field. Future directions became a pervasive concern underscoring the urgent need for action and revitalization of interdisciplinary course offerings in light of projected demographic changes and budgetary constraints that were sure to cripple all PRS units. Ultimately, the conference would take stock of the field, secure its intellectual moorings in academia, and produce for posterity the first assessment of the state of the discipline based on the expert analysis of practitioners in the field.

Christened *Toward a Renaissance of Puerto Rican Studies,* the conference brought together an invitation-only confluence of influential academics conversant in the study, teaching, and dissemination of the best practices of interdisciplinarity, Africana Studies, the Humanities, Social Sciences, Media, and Education. Established scholars and pioneers who were breaking ground in their respective fields took part as presenters of seminal papers, or as respondents. Among the participants were professors of Chicano/a Studies from the University of California and the University of Texas systems, as their experiences and areas of expertise closely reflected those of PRS. Faculty came from Fordham University, University of Massachusetts, the State University of New York at Stony Brook, the University of Puerto Rico, Interamerican University of Puerto Rico-San Germán, the University of Connecticut, and the strongest research institution in the field of PRS at CUNY, the Center for Puerto Rican Studies (Centro).

For two days the congregants debated and discussed the ideas expressed in the series of seminal papers. Comparative study and cultural pluralism, for example, became topics of concern primarily because the discrete Puerto Rican focus might be reduced, but an overall assessment of the origins, advances, and future projections for the maturation of the field was essential to develop a curricular blueprint for the continued growth of PRS. This roadmap would take into consideration the recommendations of the conference participants as well as a student perspective based on a series of questionnaires. Ultimately, a consensus for future directions encouraged forging alliances, collaborative work across disciplines, and joint participation in professional conferences, particularly the Latin American Studies, Caribbean Studies, and American Studies Associations, where the new scholarship in PRS would be welcomed and disseminated. Recognizing the historical importance of the ten-year conference, the papers were collected in a publication, *Toward a Renaissance of Puerto Rican Studies* (see Sánchez and Stevens-Arroyo 1987 in Pérez y González's essay in this volume).

It is in the constructive spirit of the Renaissance Conference that the editors of this volume committed to produce a scholarly review of the field of PRS as it marks its first fifty years. Throughout this period, transformative changes have taken place in the discipline of PRS, in the field of Puerto Rican and Latinx Studies overall, and within the institutions of higher education. At this fifty-year mark, Ethnic Studies has been approved or is being proposed for curricular inclusion in public school education,[4] signaling a critical turning point in the coming of age of PRS within its varying iterations in the academy. Indeed, the contributions of PRS to critical scholarship on (im)migration, ethnicity, race, gender, and class have never been so important in understanding U.S. American diversity. The influence of PRS on the emergence of such new areas of academic inquiry as Latinx Studies, Women's and Gender Studies, U.S. Caribbean Studies, Afro-Latinx Studies, and LGBTQIA Studies is indisputable (see Acosta-Belén in this volume). As significant, the intellectual concepts introduced in PRS have led to transformations in the traditional disciplines, particularly in the study of diasporic communities, intersectionality, and coloniality (see Bose in this volume).

Our intention in the pages that follow is to document the fifty-year evolution of a field, contested in its beginnings, but having emerged as a vital area of study in the academy. In this quest we were fortunate to join forces with some of the most eminent scholars in the field, as well as a group of younger academics at the threshold of their careers. Their outstanding, informative work becomes even more significant when we consider that much of the documentation relevant to the evolution of individual departments and programs throughout CUNY is incomplete, has been lost, or destroyed.[5] Additionally, since many of the pioneers in the field are no longer with us, we discovered that current faculty did not often have an experiential recollection or historical memory of the evolutionary record. Thus, in the interest of gathering primary sources to tell this story as broadly and accurately as possible, the editors have established an archival PRS depository for personal papers and memorabilia, to which we invite contributions at <50YEARSofPRS-CUNY@brooklyn.cuny.edu>.

BOOK MAPPING

The twelve essays in this collection are grouped into two categories. **LEGACY** provides a historical overview of the development of PRS—its changing relationship and influence on academia, the traditional curriculum, scholarship, pedagogy, and allied fields. Focusing broadly on PRS provides analytical perspectives on the impact of the field in creating or influencing knowledge and as a transformative resource in the disciplinary areas of the Humanities, Social Sciences, Pedagogy, and Media Studies. An expansive investigation of the trajectory of PRS beyond the colleges of CUNY adds an important dimension to the volume.

IN RETROSPECT: Voices from the Field elicits individual experiences, remembrances, and departmental histories of PRS through the lens of two pioneer academics, a relative newcomer to the field, and a doctoral student on the cusp of becoming a full-time practitioner in the discipline.

In all, this collection follows the evolution of PRS from its origins to its various iterations, and to its dispersal across the nation where it begins to take shape in conversation with other Ethnic Studies.

LEGACY

In his provocative article, "Remaking Puerto Rican Studies at 50 Years," Pedro Cabán rethinks the contemporary field of PRS as it relates to, and is distinct from, the study of Puerto Rico and its expansion of a research agenda that is not bound by disciplinary limitation. He explores the evolution of PRS from the period of marginalization to its production of original research, and to its role in expanding the knowledge base in the academy. He brings us back to an essential mission of the discipline, that of empowering the community, offering a more inclusive perspective for a future iteration of PRS in light of current events in the archipelago, as well as in the United States.

In "Puerto Rican Studies: A Legacy of Activism, Scholarship, and Collective Empowerment," Edna Acosta-Belén explores in depth the scholarship produced in the field of PRS over the past fifty years. Highlighting its originality and its impact on shaping the overall socio-political consciousness of diasporic Puerto Ricans, she details the ways the scholarship debunks the hegemonic narratives that produced subaltern "otherness." Along with a focused agenda of activism and collective action, the authoritative nature of the new research and its ultimate challenge to the traditional disciplines helped reassess the heretofore colonized or racialized experiences of Puerto Ricans and other marginalized communities. Acosta-Belén's extensive references reinforce the imprint of a significant scholastic legacy, correctives to the notion of identity politics, as well as the founding of the Puerto Rican Studies Association.

In "Bilingual Education and Puerto Rican Studies: From Vision to Reality," Antonio Nadal and Milga Morales Nadal dissect the notion that the United States is a conglomerate of ethno-racial, (im)migrant, and religious backgrounds. What follows is a systematic historical overview of the oppression, suppression, exclusion, and conflict faced by non-English speaking communities in the United States, among them, disenfranchised U.S. citizens such as Puerto Ricans. The organic relationship between PRS in the creation of bilingual and bicultural education, multicultural studies, and the struggles to implement a pedagogy of language diverse communities of learners is rarely acknowledged. Yet, the field of PRS became the entryway for bilingual education in the CUNY system and contributed to new approaches and policies, academic achievement, and educational equity.

Since its emergence as an academic discipline, Puerto Rican Studies' interdisciplinary and intersectional approaches to scholarship have influenced the field of Sociology and the Social Sciences, as Christine Bose posits in her essay, "Five Decades of Puerto Rican Studies: Influences on Sociology and Allied Social Sciences." In addition to presenting a compelling analysis that supports the intellectual contributions of PRS and Ethnic Studies to the Social Sciences, Bose interrogates the research subjects highlighted in the leading journals in the field from the 1940s to the 1960s, the 1970s to the 1980s, and the 1990s to the present. Searching for research topics on Puerto Rican issues, it was not until the 1970s that studies on topics such as segregation and educational advancement began to appear in journals. By the 1990s, PRS research on a variety of subjects was accepted in key journals including *The American Sociological Review* and *The American Journal of Sociology*. Nonetheless, PRS research in the Social Sciences and allied fields appeared regularly in the journals that arose from the field—*CENTRO Journal, Latino Studies Journal*, and *Latino(a) Research Review*.

Conor Tomás Reed vibrantly documents a turbulent period in "The Evolution of Puerto Rican Studies at City College" from its inception to the present, detailing the militant role of student activists, the multiethnic coalitions of community leaders and other stakeholders, and the faculty who shaped the department from its beginnings to the present day academic unit. While based on a "chronicle of archives," including an analysis of newspaper accounts, oral histories, flyers, college bulletins, and the minutes of student organizations to relate the steps in departmental evolution, Reed also fleshes out this history within the broader events that took place in New York City. Among these, Reed connects the public school boycotts of 1964, led by Black and Puerto Rican parents seeking the long overdue integration of the public schools, to the student and faculty leaders of PRS. With roughly one million youngsters participating in the boycott, parents and teachers organized Freedom Schools where students were taught the histories of their ancestors by those who lived and researched it.

While the contentious push for PRS at Brooklyn College was also led by coalitions of student activists, its conception differed from that of the other campuses of CUNY. The department emerged from the Institute of Puerto Rican Studies, which student and faculty activists had founded a year before. In her finely detailed essay, "How a Few Students Transformed the Ivory Tower: Puerto Rican Studies and its (R)evolution at Brooklyn College," María E. Pérez y González illuminates four distinct milestones in the evolutionary trajectory of the department: from the establishment of the Institute and its overriding influence on shaping the mission of PRS to the struggle for administrative autonomy; and from an era of academic legitimacy and national and international recognition to college-wide leadership and full curricular and administrative integration. Rich in its extensive archival documentation, the history of PRS in Brooklyn College reflects the field's changes and continuity over the past fifty years.

In "Puerto Rican Studies: Transitions, Reconfigurations, and Programs Outside of the CUNY System," Edna Acosta-Belén addresses the misconception that PRS is limited to New York City by providing an expansive array of information about its evolution and the leading scholars in the field at university centers in New York State, New Jersey, Illinois, Connecticut, and Massachusetts. The first programs in Chicano/a Studies established at several university centers in California, including the University of California at Santa Barbara and at Berkeley, motivated institutions of higher education throughout the Southwest to create similar programs. Beyond its institutional base, PRS in CUNY played much the same role in the northeastern U.S. Taking into account the spread, scope, mission, academic milestones, and the highly profiled pioneering faculty who established PRS departments and programs in private and public institutions throughout the Northeast,

Acosta-Belén delves into the intellectual contributions of the faculty at the helm of these new academic units. She further delineates the transformations and reconfigurations over five decades that ultimately result in the institutionalization of the field of PRS.

In what might serve as the capstone essay for this section, and a transition to IN RETROSPECT: Voices from the Field, Juan González writes, "So Much Knowledge and We Still Ain't Free: Puerto Rican Studies Fifty Years Later." From his vantage point as an organizer in the New York City Young Lords, a journalist in print and broadcast media, and an academic researcher, González reviews the history of PRS, searching the past for lessons for the future. Interrogating how we reconcile the fact that after decades of scholarship on this subject the American people remain woefully uninformed about Puerto Ricans and Puerto Rico, the author's perceptions of the problem cover a broad spectrum of possibilities.

IN RETROSPECT: Voices from the Field

In "Past is Prologue: A Look Back at the Evolution of Puerto Rican Studies in the Academy," Jesse M. Vázquez describes the ongoing frustrations of directing a program on limited resources at Queens College (CUNY) and the struggle for academic legitimacy. He recalls the continuously looming uncertainty about creating departments and programs that could be eliminated with one stroke of an administrative pen. Yet, the commitment of the pioneer scholars in the field, who sought to change the status quo by empowering their community through education, never wavered.

Regina A. Bernard-Carreño relates her faculty experiences in "Puerto Rican Studies at Baruch College." Seeking a unique position that would allow her to introduce students to her own research interests in African American Studies, and encompass as well Puerto Rican Studies, the formerly named Department of Black and Hispanic Studies at Baruch College (CUNY) was ideal. In this retrospect, Bernard-Carreño provides a look at PRS as told through interviews with the faculty that helped build the department.

"Camuyana en Brooklyn: Reflecting on My Journey Through Puerto Rican and Latino Studies" relates the experiences of Gisely Colón López, a doctoral student in CUNY's Graduate Center. She relates her journey from insecure student to becoming an activist, teacher, and filmmaker. In all, her inspirational journey in higher education as an undergraduate student, staff member of the Center for Puerto Rican Studies, adjunct in CUNY Puerto Rican/Latinx Studies (PRLS) units, and a graduate student in PRLS, reflects the experiences of countless students whose stories are seldom told.

In "Reflections on a Return to Lehman College," Andrés Torres compares his role as a young activist professor in the early decades of PRS at Lehman College (CUNY) with the department to which he returned as a Distinguished Lecturer. Torres bears first-hand witness to the ways in which the field has changed over decades but still delivers that sense of awe for each new generation of students who encounter their history for the first time.

CONCLUSION

The work of the scholars represented herein underscores how the struggles of Puerto Rican activists to claim their civil rights and forge inroads to opportunity in a nation built by the sweat of their ancestors, (im)migrants, and laborers, ultimately benefits us all. Through research and copious scholarly production, the field of PRS has established its academic legitimacy. PRS has challenged, corrected, created, and expanded knowledge, while simultaneously propagating anti-racist and decolonial ideologies, curriculum, and practices. At an individual level, the achievements of PRS can best be found among the scores of students whose lives have been transformed and enriched because of what they learned in PRS classes that can be utilized in future endeavors. They are a living testament to what PRS founders and pioneers intended.

Collectively, in its various iterations in the academy, Puerto Rican Studies (and Ethnic Studies) continues to promote the paradigm of equity and justice for all people in the U.S., as it similarly promotes the study of the intersectionalities of the U.S. American experience from the perspective of those who have been marginalized. The legacy of Puerto Rican Studies opens an opportunity to absorb a more comprehensive history of this nation and challenges the myths that perpetuate facts favoring the ideology of a select few. Overall, this volume on the first fifty years of Puerto Rican Studies in CUNY, and nationally, elucidates a legacy of individual and collective agency in the midst of relentless challenges and goals for the future of Puerto Rican Studies in the next half century.

NOTES

[1] Student activism was documented in the Borough of Manhattan, Bronx, and Queensborough community colleges (see CUNY Digital History Archives): <https://cdha.cuny.edu/coverage/coverage/show/id/23/>; <https://cdha.cuny.edu/solr-search?q=Bronx+community+college/>; and <https://cdha.cuny.edu/collections/show/91/>.

[2] Baruch established a Program of Black and Hispanic Studies (not PRS), although its focus was largely Puerto Rican Studies.

[3] The broad community coalition formed as part of this long struggle is captured in a documentary available to the public at: <https://www.youtube.com/watch?v=0_hSi6IzRFk/> by Jiménez, Ramón J. and Félix Romero, Producers. 2006. *Hostos: The Struggle, The Victory*. Directed by Félix Romero. South Bronx Sez, Inc. Documentary. 18 minutes.

[4] A cursory search of state boards of education in regions with a significant Puerto Rican population reveals the following are either implementing or in the planning stages of including Ethnic Studies in the high school curriculum: California (2021), Connecticut (2020), Illinois (2021), Indiana (2018), Massachusetts (2019), New York (2018), and Texas (2020).

[5] In one instance at Queens College, CUNY, the archives were removed and discarded during a period of office sharing (Jesse M. Vázquez 2021, pers. comm.).

LEGACY

CHAPTER 1

REMAKING PUERTO RICAN STUDIES AT 50 YEARS

Pedro Cabán

In 1969, Puerto Rican students, faculty, and staff rebelled against a major urban public university and demanded an education that was responsive to their needs. The beleaguered City University of New York (CUNY) administration was shaken by the militance of the protests and abashed by accusations that it was complicit in perpetuating a racist educational policy that demeaned the experiences and accomplishments of black and brown people. Unapologetic university officials relented and grudgingly established the first Puerto Rican Studies departments and institutes in the CUNY system. In July 2019, a popular uprising in Puerto Rico upended the political order in the archipelago. The uprising was the culmination of a series of tribulations that have plagued Puerto Rico for over fifteen years. Puerto Ricans endured a financial crisis, radical austerity measures, devastating hurricanes and earthquakes, thousands of deaths, and massive outmigration before their collective indignation exploded the political landscape. Puerto Rico's popular uprising over 50 years after the establishment of the first departments of Puerto Rican Studies creates an opportune moment to evaluate how and why the research priorities of Puerto Rican Studies (PRS) and the study of Puerto Rico have at moments coalesced, while at other moments they have diverged. In addition, this essay will trace the evolution of PRS, noting its growing epistemological diversity, varied analytical concerns, and conceptually challenging explication of colonialism's enduring impact on the Puerto Rican experience.

Four features corresponding to different moments in the evolution of Puerto Rican Studies make this interdisciplinary field distinctive. The first to be addressed is the moment in the early 1970s when both PRS and Puerto Rico studies advanced a radical critique of university-sanctioned scholarship. The second to be discussed is how PRS became increasingly defined by its research on the Puerto Rican experience in the United States; the salience of the archipelago as a focus of study declined as the diaspora continued to grow. As this reorientation of the field was taking place, PRS departments came under increased pressure by university administrators to adapt its curriculum and instruction to appeal to a rapidly diversifying urban Latinx population. PRS departments were required to expand their curriculum to be inclusive of the experiences of other populations. University administrators called for merging PRS with race and ethnic studies units. Some administrators proposed eliminating their departmental status (Cabán 2003). The reconfiguration and dismantlement of Puerto Rican Studies departments led to a third feature of contemporary PRS; its scholarship moved from a position of relative academic isolation and marginalization to one of growing institutional acceptance. Accusations that PRS catered to the provincial interests of academically unprepared students diminished as PRS scholarship was viewed more favorably when it became clear it contributed to the university's newfound multicultural and diversity missions; pressures were growing for educational institutions to be more inclusive. These changes in PRS can be described as *dispersion, differentiation,* and *dialogue.* Fourth, the crises that have consumed Puerto Rico for the last fifteen years have generated new forms of collaboration between scholars and activists in Puerto Rico and the United States. At the moment, PRS scholars and intellectuals in the diaspora are joining their colleagues in the archipelago in action-oriented research and analysis that advance social justice in Puerto Rico.

1. THE PARTICULARITY OF PUERTO RICAN STUDIES

Puerto Rican Studies scholarship has expanded rapidly in part because it is not bound by the epistemological constraints that delineate the parameters and methods of knowledge production constitutive of the traditional disciplines. Freed from disciplinary limitations, scholars have embarked on original research on the varied dimensions and manifestations of the

Puerto Rican experience. There is no distinctive Puerto Rican Studies epistemology, a unique theory of knowledge creation or consensus about which research methods are distinctive to the field. Yet, PRS is unique among race and ethnic studies. Puerto Ricans in the archipelago are positioned as colonial subjects with a diminished U.S. citizenship status. They are also racialized subjects in the U.S.; their material and social conditions correspond to that of other marginalized populations of color. Where Puerto Ricans reside fundamentally alters their positionality and redefines their relationship to power. Puerto Ricans' binary attributes as racialized citizens and colonial subjects invests their experience with a layer of complexity that distinguishes them from other Latinx populations. Since 1898, Puerto Ricans have been in a state of coloniality imposed by the United States. A key task of the early PRS scholarship was to challenge and undermine university-sanctioned knowledge that is used to normalize colonialism and the racial subordination of Puerto Rico. Josephine Nieves, the inaugural chairperson of the Department of Puerto Rican Studies at Brooklyn College when it was founded half a century ago, observed that the efforts to build the field of PRS "involved, in particular, a critique of the way social science theory and methods had served to legitimize our colonial history" (Nieves 1987, 5).

Nieves was a major intellectual force in the elaboration of PRS as an interdisciplinary field of study. Along with her colleagues, she conceived and effectively advocated for the establishment of the Centro de Estudios Puertorriqueños (Center for Puerto Rican Studies, Centro).[1] In the 1970s and 1980s, Centro researchers Frank Bonilla, Ricardo Campos, and Juan Flores collectively helped forge an interpretive paradigm grounded in historical materialist and critical cultural theory. Rafael Ramírez, one of the founders of CEREP (Centro de Estudios de la Realidad Puertorriqueña), was recruited by Bonilla to Centro and was instrumental in building the Culture Task Force.[2] Led by Centro's staff and researchers, Marxist theory gained prominence in the young field of PRS. Centro also created Task Forces on History, Migration, Language Policy, Cultural Studies, Higher Education, and Film (Ortíz Márquez 2009). Later, the Oral History Task Force was established. Centro encouraged researchers to theoretically interrogate the continuities and ruptures in the racialization of Puerto Ricans living in the colony and Puerto Ricans living in the United States. An early Centro project entailed exploring the relationship between foreign-financed capitalist development and population displacement in the colony during the immediate post-World War II period. Centro also published path-breaking studies on the cultural production and language practice of the diaspora.

In Puerto Rico, CEREP, formed by Angel G. Quintero Rivera, Marcia Rivera, Lydia M. González García, and Gervasio L. García, among others, questioned the accepted historical narratives that trivialized the complexities of economy and culture under colonialism, and denied the salience of race and class in the construction of agrarian capitalism. Although Centro and CEREP set about on different research projects, they collectively influenced the field's research priorities. PRS, from its inception, and Puerto Rico studies driven by CEREP's revisionist project of historical rediscovery, were emancipatory and critical, and contested the portrayal of Puerto Ricans as passive victims unable to resist their oppression. For these activist intellectuals, "the ones living in the island as well as the ones established in New York City, the main objective became to defy and question the traditional concepts that guided Puerto Rican society" (Vázquez Valdés 2010).[3] Indeed, according to Josephine Nieves, "the reality of the movement of Puerto Ricans between the Island and the United States was an important point of reference" for interrogating the university "for its role in distorting our history" (Nieves 1987, 3).

2. THE SALIENCE OF THE DIASPORA IN REPOSITIONING PRS SCHOLARSHIP, PEDAGOGY, AND THE RADICAL CRITIQUE OF WHITE SUPREMACY

Despite the common analytical affinities and embrace of historical materialism and critical historiography, Centro, with its focus on the diaspora, and CEREP, with its focus on the colony, had embarked on two different political projects. This was not unexpected since Centro was the product of community-based struggles to expose the university's duplicity in legitimizing the racial order and perpetuating social inequities. The U.S.-based PRS movement demanded academic enclaves for independent knowledge production that would be deployed to empower the Puerto Rican community. As a result of Puerto Rican student activism, a "variety of sheltered spaces were won, where creative experiments with new modalities of academic management, instruction, group study, and the organization of research and its dissemination have taken place" (Bonilla 1992).

Puerto Rican Studies was part of a much larger project to democratize the university and deploy its resources for community empowerment. Puerto Rican Studies launched a systematic and sustained critique on how university knowledge was created and how it was deployed to preserve and rationalize the economic oppression and political exclusion of the Puerto Rican community, even as the university celebrated the presumed superiority of whiteness. A new knowledge was vitally necessary to repudiate denigrating portrayals of our people (Cabán 2004).

Centro was a critically important achievement in the struggle to democratize CUNY. Centro became a locus of scholarly activity where faculty, students, and staff coordinated academic programming and collectively developed research agendas. Freed from the tyranny of the traditional disciplines' canonical orthodoxies, Centro, and the scholars who relied on its resources, could construct a new scholarship that lay bare the corrosive bias of university-sanctioned knowledge. In a seminal article, Carmen Whalen explored the "radical context" that established Centro. She notes that Centro was not merely the product of the radical times; in fact, it "created another 'radical context' by providing physical space, alternative approaches, and support for the scholarship that laid the foundations for Puerto Rican Studies as a field of research today" (Whalen 2009, 222). In addition, Centro was a strategic focal point where the community devised action plans to counter CUNY's relentless campaign to hobble PRS departments.[4]

In contrast, university-based revisionist scholars in Puerto Rico critically studied the processes and structures of colonialism. CEREP employed the academic resources of the university to discredit the established historical narratives and expose them as ideological tools to inculcate colonial subservience. According to Quintero Rivera, CEREP provided a counter narrative to "apologetic discourses of our social and political reality...presented as social science or history" (Asociación Estudiantes Graduados de Historia 2016).[5] Moreover, as Marcia Rivera noted, "CEREP took as its challenge to investigate the history of those without a history: workers, women and blackness in Puerto Rico" (Asociación Estudiantes Graduados de Historia 2016).[6] CEREP sought to dismantle the university-sanctioned narratives of Puerto Rico's early history under U.S. colonial rule. CEREP was a project led by professional intellectuals to decolonize the university by exposing its role in perpetuating a colonial mindset. CEREP exposed the university as an instrument of colonialism for disseminating and validating the knowledge produced in the metropolis, as it failed to acknowledge anti-colonial narratives produced by Puerto Rican scholars. While these were important episodes in a long history of intellectual opposition to colonialism, CEREP did not seek the systemic transformation of the university.

This stands in contrast to the radical educational and political agendas of Centro and PRS during this formative period. Working class Puerto Rican students and faculty led the initial attack against the public university, primarily the institutions of the City University of New York (CUNY). But, Rutgers University and some institutions of the State University of New York (SUNY) were also fiercely contested sites. These agendas included disrupting the public university's capacity to perpetuate white supremacy. Urban working-class Puerto Ricans braved arrests, police abuse, suspension, and expulsion in their tireless campaign to democratize the university by ending the systematic exclusion of the racialized working class. Institutional transformation required racial democratization. The thought that a racialized working-class movement could turn the university on its head, that is to say, to promote racial justice rather than operate on behalf of white supremacy, was revolutionary (Cabán 2007, 7).

But, Centro and PRS were also engaged in a campaign to expose the university's role in the production and dissemination of knowledge that perpetuated and reinforced notions of Puerto Rican inferiority and fatalism. The conceptual lynchpin of the Puerto Rican Studies movement "was its analysis of the relationship between university-sanctioned forms of knowledge and racial power" (Cabán 2007, 6). The students were fiercely insistent and unrelenting in their demands for programs and departments because it was essential to counter university-sanctioned knowledge that was deployed to legitimize the subordination of the Puerto Rican diaspora. Students, faculty, community leaders, activists, and artists were determined to expose the epistemological dimensions of university-sanctioned knowledge, which normalized racial oppression and demarcated the diaspora's subservient role in the rapidly expanding post-World War II urban economy. In effect, the diaspora community fought to decolonize the university and, through praxis, organically developed a critique of the university as constitutive of the coloniality of power.

Fundamental differences in the social contexts influenced the respective research agendas of Centro and CEREP. The experience of migrant Puerto Ricans as racialized displaced surplus labor compelled to negotiate a new positionality in an alien environment differed from that of the Puerto Rican colonial subject. The metaphorical assault on the public university system in the metropolitan New York area was part of a larger campaign to democratize those institutions of the state that held such sway over Puerto Rican lives. This contrasted with the work of scholars in Puerto Rico who sought to demystify the practice and ideology of colonial subordination. Colonialism, dehumanizing and exploitative as it was, positioned Puerto Ricans on the archipelago as subjects of empire. The colonial state, whose function is to advance the geopolitical and economic interests of the empire, orchestrated the veritable expulsion of surplus labor to counteract the disruptive consequences of post-World War II capitalist development. The vast majority of the hundreds of thousands of Puerto Ricans who were relocated to the U.S. lived a precarious existence. Yet, their expectation of returning became increasingly unrealistic with each passing year given the intractable persistence of high unemployment levels. The post-World War II labor migrants who were deceived into believing their dislocation was temporary would form the core of the Puerto Rican diaspora. While the lived experiences of Puerto Ricans in the colony and in the United States were different, both were the product of capitalist development in a colonial social formation.

Despite the auspicious beginnings, a long-term radical collaborative project never materialized. Instead, scholars established two separate spheres of intellectual labor: Puerto Rican Studies and Puerto Rico studies. However, since PRS is characterized by an expansive embrace of all matters *puertorriqueñidad*, it is not surprising that the knowledge produced in the archipelago is considered constitutive of PRS. Moreover, the study of Puerto Rico as a colony subject to the dictates of a decaying empire was from the beginning an important area of PRS research and its teaching mission. In the last decade, PRS scholars in the diaspora have written extensively about the crises that have engulfed Puerto Rico. Such preoccupation demonstrates that the study of colonialism is an important part of the Puerto Rican Studies research agenda. There is a certain irony to the effort, well intentioned as it is, to encompass the study of Puerto Rico in the field of PRS. Puerto Rican Studies scholars, particularly those whose intellectual labor takes place outside of Puerto Rico, and who employ historical materialism, positivist social science, or any of the litany of conceptual and analytical armaments derived from Western epistemic schemas might be criticized as producing studies about the colonial subject, rather than studies from and with the colonial subject's perspective.

3. RETHINKING PUERTO RICAN STUDIES

The contemporary Puerto Rican Studies field is *dispersed, differentiated,* and in *dialogue* with other fields. *Dispersal* denotes that PRS scholars have faculty appointments in a variety of academic units throughout the university. This contrasts with the early history of Puerto Rican Studies when scholars did their intellectual work in relative isolation in small, politically vulnerable academic departments that were interspersed throughout the CUNY colleges. Before CUNY established PRS departments, relatively few scholars of the Puerto Rican experience worked in colleges and universities outside the Northeast. Now PRS scholars have appointments in colleges and universities throughout the United States. They have appointments in traditional academic departments, as well as race and ethnic studies, including Chicana/o or Mexican American Studies. This is a measure of the import of PRS scholarship to the academic mission of the university and its contributions to diversifying the university's knowledge base.

PRS scholarship is also highly *differentiated*. PRS scholars are expanding the knowledge base in the humanities that either did not exist or were in their formative stages when CUNY established PRS departments. Scholars have diversified the research agenda of PRS to include sexuality and gender studies, women's studies, racial and Afro-Latino identities, music, performance, and media (often defined as cultural and lifeworld studies). This new scholarship challenged the materialist, determinist, and male-centric underpinnings of some of the early scholarship. During its formative stage, PRS was heavy on historical materialism and positivist historiography and was faulted for dismissing cultural studies. The cultural was often dismissed as derivative of the material. Consequently, the "classical approaches" in the early phase of

PRS may not have anticipated the significance of cultural and lifeworld studies to transformative political processes. Although Centro is known for the application of a Marxist conception of history, it was also deeply engaged in research to comprehend how the diaspora preserved its cultural identity. In Bonilla's words, Centro wanted "to understand how a people have managed to maintain a common culture, language, aesthetic and collective identity in a most hostile and destructive milieu" (Bonilla and González 1973).

PRS has undergone a paradigmatic shift and is almost unrecognizable from its origins over a half century ago. Over the course of the last ten years, the *CENTRO Journal* and *Latino Studies*, the lead journals for PRS scholarship, have published original, often transformative, research on the Puerto Rican experience in the diaspora and the archipelago.[7] Prominent PRS scholars were engaged in planning the *Latino Studies Journal*, which emerged as the single most important scholarly journal in the field and in the process has contributed to the institutionalization of the field. Both journals have a good record of identifying emerging areas of research.

Pérez Jiménez in her insightful review of the history of *CENTRO Journal* observed:

We encounter a greater diversification of the theoretical frames employed to analyze Puerto Rican experiences. Advances in the fields of Latino studies, comparative ethnic and race studies, critical race theory, queer studies, colonial and postcolonial studies, as well as diaspora, migration, and globalization studies all became reference points for the journal's articles, reflecting the broader conceptual shifts reconfiguring Puerto Rican studies itself. (2017, 45)

The *CENTRO Journal* understood the shifting scholarly terrain and provided a venue which "amplified the range of voices, writing styles, and genres that could take part in a scholarly journal, an orientation consonant with Centro's foundational aims to establish broader networks of intellectual dialogue and social conversations" (Pérez Jiménez 2017, 45). In fact, Centro's research agenda in the 1970s was ground-breaking because it embodied the nexus between distinct intellectual traditions and analytical frameworks. The Centro Task Forces were conceived to promote collective research and to transgress the boundaries between and among policy areas and research modalities usually claimed as the domain of a single discipline. Article titles in *Latino Studies* over the same period also show the growing scholarly production of these innovative and expanding sub-fields of Puerto Rican Studies. In contrast, history, colonialism, the political economy of Puerto Rico, as measured by published articles in these journals, appear to have lost their place of prominence in these journals. Gender, race, and sexuality studies have emerged as vibrant and critically important research areas. This scholarship has expanded the knowledge base and theoretical scope of Puerto Rican Studies.[8]

While cultural studies, defined broadly, has a marked presence in the preferred journals for PRS, scholars have continued to publish important books in the social sciences and history. The subjects addressed include state-sponsored migration, law and colonialism, the particularities of Puerto Ricans' statutory citizenship, the civil rights movement and political participation, surveillance and policing, the political and economic dynamics of the Florida Puerto Rican population, and others (Lebrón 2019; Meléndez 2017; Thomas and Lauria-Santiago 2019). Recent scholarship explores how marginalization, exploitation, and racial and gender violence are also constitutive of empire (Godreau 2015; Muzio 2017; Rodríguez-Silva 2012). Comparative explorations situate Puerto Rico within a matrix of colonial and neocolonial social formations and help elucidate the nature of Puerto Rican exceptionalism (the complicated dynamics generated by racism, capitalist colonialism, and population displacement) (Alamo-Pastrana 2016; Dinzey-Flores 2013; García-Colón 2020). In the century-long project of building the American empire, Puerto Ricans are but one segment among vast populations of racialized peoples whose centrality to capital accumulation and U.S. global prominence cannot be dismissed.

The valorization of the cultural has not only contributed to a rich differentiation of knowledge in the field, but also redefined the nature of its *dialogue* with Chicano/a studies. PRS has been in *dialogue* with Chicana/o Studies since at least 1971 with the founding of the Center for Chicano-Boricua Studies of Wayne State University. In the same year, Samuel Betances edited *The Rican: Una Revista de Pensamiento Contemporáneo Puertorriqueño.* The journal was an important source of path-breaking essays on the status and intersections of Puerto Rican and Chicano Studies. Indiana University Northwest began publishing the *Revista Chicano-Riqueña* in 1973, under the editorship of Nicolás

Kanellos and Luis Dávila. The Chicano-Riqueña Studies program was established in the University of Indiana in 1974.

In 1983, the Inter-University Program for Latino Research (IUPLR) was established. The IUPLR was the first funded national organization for interdisciplinary collaboration among university-based Latina/o research centers. Centro, under Frank Bonilla's leadership, was the driving force in establishing this consortium, which was a precursor to developing nationally based research agendas that conceptualized Mexican Americans/Chicano/as and Puerto Ricans in the diaspora as racialized minorities. Initially, Latina/o scholars working under the auspices of IUPLR studied the structural forces that shaped the economic and social conditions of the Latina/o working class. But, over the years with the ascendance of cultural studies, and cognizant of the importance of the visual arts to identify formation and political education, the IUPLR established the Digital Research Project and annually convenes the Latino Art Now! Conference (Inter-University Program for Latino Research).

Latinx Studies is the culmination of the gradual transformation of a political project that implicated the university in legitimizing the inequities inherent in capitalist economy, into a moderately disruptive academic project that is engaged in "decolonizing" the university and the traditional disciplines. PRS has been intrinsic to the development of a unified field of Latinx studies and has established itself as one of the key knowledge fields in race and ethnic studies (Cabán 2003). PRS scholars, alongside scholars who study the experience of Mexican Americans, U.S. resident Central Americans, and other people of Latin American and Caribbean descent, have created Latina/o sections within the major professional associations. Scholars trained in these disciplines, primarily female scholars, have established Latina/o sections to promote Puerto Rican-based research in Sociology (the Latina/o Sociology Section) and Anthropology (The Association of Latina and Latino Anthropologists). Latina/o Sections have also been established in the American Political Science Association-Latino Caucus and the Latin American Studies Association (LASA).

Recently, PRS scholars established the Puerto Rico section in LASA. The seven-member executive committee is composed of young scholars based in Puerto Rico, the United States and Great Britain. Shortly after the 2019 summer uprising, LASA/Puerto Rico released an "Urgent Communiqué About the

Situation in Puerto Rico." The section expressed deep concern, noting that its members not only "have academic and intellectual interests in the archipelago" but have family there as well. The section affirmed that "Puerto Rico, Puerto Ricans, and Puerto Ricanness are not merely objects of study, they are an integral part of our own positionalities within academia" (Latin American Studies Association (LASA)/Puerto Rico Section (PR) 2019). LASA/Puerto Rico evokes an earlier history of collaboration between scholars in the diaspora and archipelago. PRS scholars played a prominent role in establishing the Latina/o Studies Association (https://latinxstudiesassociation.org/home/mission-statement/). They have served as officers in the Caribbean Studies Association and the Association of Caribbean Historians. In 2003, Nelson Maldonado-Torres was among the founders of the Caribbean Philosophical Association and served as president. Other notable professional associations with a strong PRS representation are the National Latinx Psychological Association and the American Society of Hispanic Economists.

It is important to emphasize that while PRS is an inclusive and interdisciplinary field, it is almost exclusively located in the traditional liberal arts and sciences colleges. There is substantial and varied scholarly literature in legal studies, education and education policy studies, labor studies, public health and health disparities, and environmental justice in the Puerto Rican experience.[9] The labor of scholars in these fields helps fulfill part of the promise of the early PRS movement to create new knowledge in service of disenfranchised sectors of the Puerto Rican community. More can be done to acknowledge the centrality of this research to the PRS field.

The vibrant academic dispersal, creative differentiation, and sustained dialogue of PRS with other fields of study accelerated in the aftermath of the virtual elimination of PRS departments and programs in the CUNY system. Only Hunter College (1969) and Brooklyn College (1970) have academic departments that include Puerto Rican Studies in their title. A decade ago, I wrote that "in contrast to the waning importance of Puerto Rican Studies academic units, Puerto Rican Studies scholarship has gained acceptance in some academic fields and disciplines" (Cabán 2009). From its early decidedly insurrectionary beginnings, PRS scholarship has extended the bounds of inquiry and theorizing beyond the early work on capitalist development under colonialism and the racialized history of the diaspora. The growth and diversity of PRS scholarship is also a testament to the success of the Puerto Rican academic community in forging alliances and building networks to secure a presence in the university. The current moment, marked by heightened Puerto Rican activism in the archipelago and the United States, affirms that through their collective intellectual labor Puerto Ricans have developed the skills and insights to withstand a relentless campaign to deny their common humanity. While establishing common ground with other Latinx populations, PRS resists the subsumption of Puerto Rican specificity under constructed ethnic labels.

Many PRS departments have been reconfigured as Latinx Studies departments or as Latin American and Latina/o academic units. PRS departments, which once played an important role in building academic community, have been supplanted by professional associations. In addition to the conferences and symposia these associations convene, they are also the focal point of online chat communities and serve as social media sites. Professional associations have also become significant venues for the dissemination of PRS scholarship, building academic communities, and fostering collaboration.

The Puerto Rican Studies Association (PRSA) is one of the most consequential and enduring achievements of the Puerto Rican Studies movement. PRSA's first organizational meeting was held in White Plains, New York, in 1992. Since that time, the organization has evolved into the preeminent venue for disseminating the interdisciplinary scholarship that is the hallmark of PRS. PRSA has helped forge a robust professional identity for PRS scholars and has been an advocate for PRSA scholars wrongfully denied tenure and supported PRS departments and programs under budgetary assault. With the demise of academic departments, PRSA became indispensable for sustaining the dispersed PRS academic community. Through its conferences and seminars, PRSA promoted greater acceptance of Puerto Rican Studies scholarship. The research presented at PRSA conferences reflects the state of the field. By honoring the exceptional and enduring academic accomplishments of PRS scholars, the association has been pivotal in institutionalizing the field. Because of the activism of PRSA, apprehension that the closing or remaking of PRS departments into hybrid race and ethnic studies would lead to the demise of PRS scholarship has waned.

Yet, despite this achievement, some of the goals of the PRS movement were never fully realized. The goal of decolonizing the university and appropriating its resources to empower racialized and marginalized communities proved an unattainable quest. The ardent advocates of PRS surely underestimated the capacity of the university to resist efforts to erode the centrality of Western canon in higher education. But, PRS did make modest, yet profoundly important, changes to the university culture. PRS scholars gained the university's belated acceptance that their field of study was not a shambolic academic indulgence. PRS developed into a viable academic field. PRS's early project to rewrite a distorted history that had reduced the Puerto Rican experience to an accident of empire has expanded to embrace a much larger and richer spectrum of inquiry and theorizing.

Judged in this light, the Puerto Rican community did not fail in its disruptive project to transform the university. It confronted the university's most regressive features and staked the claim that the study of the Puerto Rican experience is inviolable. Moreover, if we envision PRS as including the professions, we can better gauge the transformative legacy of this upstart academic field. During the current neoliberal moment, the institutional viability of PRS has ironically been strengthened. To the extent that PRS, and literally all race and ethnic studies, are able to attract students from a national population that is becoming increasingly brown, the less likely the university is to eliminate courses on racialized communities from the curriculum. The public universities and colleges, where Latina/o Studies predominate, are cash-strapped, enrollment-driven educational enterprises that have shown an impressive alacrity in adjusting their mission to respond to shifting market demands. Ironically, as the university administrations attempt to promote a "multicultural educational experience," race and ethnic studies are under-resourced and are portrayed as marginal to the university's academic mission.

With the substantial reductions of state support in public higher education, universities have had to depend on student tuition as the primary source of revenue. Long forgotten are fervid battles between administrators and students over the academic value of race and ethnic studies. As universities fiercely compete for a diminishing number of students willing to take on debt, administrators are more concerned about the monetary value, rather than the academic value, of race and ethnic studies. Graduates of market-oriented academic programs, who acquire a functional knowledge of America's racialized communities, are particularly attractive to employers who want a competitive edge in selling their services and products to a young and growing "minority population." This is indeed one of the ironies of PRS on its fiftieth anniversary. In their radical quest to transform the university and decolonize the production and dissemination of knowledge, the militant proponents of PRS helped the university respond to the demographic change and economic challenges that have transformed New York in the last half century. The university has adopted a market-oriented strategy to enhance its bottom line. This is a paradoxical, but not small, achievement.

4. PUERTO RICAN STUDIES AND PUERTO RICO IN CRISIS

PRS is marked by a conceptual tension along two fault lines. In the previous section, I discussed the seemingly divergent research agendas among cultural, gender, and sexuality studies (which valorize the non-material dimensions of the political sphere), and political economy, politics, and history, in both their historical materialist and positivist epistemological forms. In the last decades, scholars have analyzed and theorized important dimensions of Puerto Rican identity that were relegated to the margins of the field. Research on racism in Puerto Rico and in the diaspora, the experiences of Afro-Boricuas/Afro-Latinxs, queer and transgender persons, and feminist critiques of the male-centric research priorities, have redefined the scope of Puerto Rican Studies.[10] Yet, these need not be mutually exclusive framings as Centro attempted to demonstrate when it established the Task Forces in the early 1970s. Despite different methodologies and theoretical framings between cultural studies and political economy, Centro scholars attempted to align these two forms of knowledge creation through praxis. Notwithstanding this initial and farsighted vision, the conceptual divides, and analytical priorities, between "cultural studies" and "political economy" have become more extensive and challenging to bridge. But, events that have transpired since Hurricane María, including the exodus of Puerto Ricans, the collapse of the colonial state's legitimacy, the formation of diaspora organizations in solidarity with the archipelago, and the rise of grassroots resistance and advocacy collectives (AgitArte and Colectiva Feminista en Construcción) create novel opportunities to promote a nexus at the organizational level between these alternative paradigmatic approaches. The critical reappraisal of PRS that is taking place in the wake of the rejuvenation of the Puerto Rican Studies Association may also spur a conceptual reassessment of the constructive intersections of cultural studies and political economy.

The second fault line, also introduced above, concerns the distinctive modalities used to represent and interpret the Puerto Rican experience in the diaspora and the archipelago. Here, I am referring to the distinction between Puerto Rican Studies and Puerto Rico studies discussed earlier. The early attempts by the CEREP in Puerto Rico and Centro in New York to develop research agendas to explore the continuities and commonalities between the Puerto Rican experience in the diaspora and the archipelago did not yield the hoped-for collaboration.[11] This may change. The Republican Party's relentless drive to fortify white supremacy and establish a polity ruled by plutocrats, has fostered solidarity among all racialized populations. These recent radical political developments are eroding distinctions between Puerto Ricans in the diaspora and the archipelago, as well as among racialized and economically vulnerable populations. Puerto Rico's endless economic and humanitarian crises, and the resurgence of a campaign of hate against Latinx immigrants, are transforming the research agenda and modes of academic collaboration in PRS. It is a politically urgent moment to envision a holistic Puerto Rican Studies paradigm that is based on a conceptual and spatial unity (e.g., cultural and political economy/diaspora and diaspora-archipelago).

Since 2005, but especially after the archipelago's financial collapse of 2008-09, virtually every aspect of the Puerto Rican people's existence has been disrupted by the misfortunes that have befallen the archipelago. Puerto Rico has been afflicted by debt, destruction, displacement, and dissent. Puerto Rico's massive debt to the municipal bond market and hedge funds is without historical parallel. The systemic defunding of the public employees' pension was fraudulent and at a scale that is incomprehensible. The ruling political parties, the pro-commonwealth Popular Democratic Party and the pro-statehood New Progressive Party, have been exposed as inherently corrupt patronage operations detached from the people and unmoved by their plight. The Puerto Rico Oversight Management and Economic Stabilization Act of 2016 (PROMESA) stripped the Puerto Rican government of the limited autonomy it enjoyed for almost six decades. Puerto Ricans have been victimized by heartless austerity measures imposed by both the colonial state and a technocratic and unaccountable financial control board created by PROMESA.

Puerto Rico had barely recovered from the damage caused by Hurricane Irma when Hurricane María struck the archipelago on September 20, 2017. Hurricane María rained more destruction and death on Puerto Rico than any other hurricane in modern history. The hurricane claimed over 4,600 lives (Kishore 2018). Property damage was estimated at $95 billion (Disis 2017). Hurricane María destroyed the electrical grid, thousands of homes were made uninhabitable, and the health care infrastructure was severely damaged. In the aftermath of Hurricane María, migration reached unprecedented levels. From 2017 to 2018 about 133,500 Puerto Ricans migrated to the United States, and about one-third settled in Florida (Glassman 2019). The 3.9 percent decline of population in 2018 was the largest single year decline since 1950, the first year that annual data were collected (Flores 2019). Puerto Ricans were displaced by the collapse of society in numbers that were unimaginable at the start of the millennium. The scale and pace of exodus resembles the mass migration of refugees fleeing an active war zone.

The public institutions, federal as well as insular, responsible for safeguarding the well-being of the population, utterly failed. Puerto Ricans were abandoned by their government to fend for themselves in a denuded and devastated landscape. The people had reached a limit with the prolonged period of collective suffering and government malfeasance. The political class's blithe contempt for their fellow Puerto Ricans, who were shell shocked at the visible collapse of their society, provoked the massive uprising of summer 2019. Nearly a million people, almost a third of the archipelago's population, roared their collective indignation at the abuse of their humanity.

The despised Governor Ricardo Rosselló Nevares was forced to resign on August 2. Key members of his cabinet also resigned. The Puerto Rico Supreme Court ruled that Rosselló violated the constitution when he appointed Pedro Pierluisi as his successor on August 5. Wanda Vázquez Garced, Secretary of Justice and third in the line of succession, was appointed governor on August 7. Her administration has been marked by the incompetence and lack of transparency that were hallmarks of the Rosselló administration. Vázquez Garced and her administration have been condemned for their ineffectual response to the devastating earthquake that inflicted much damage to southwestern Puerto Rico. Thousands have protested, demanding her resignation.

Puerto Rican Studies is most vibrant, creative, and relevant when the Puerto Rican community in the diaspora and the colony is under threat. Collaboration becomes more compelling and vigorous during periods of genuine crisis (Hurricanes Irma and María, the summer 2019 uprising, the Navy out of Vieques movement, the anti-PROMESA campaign, the anti-coal ash protests, the student strikes at the University of Puerto Rico, and the December 2019 and January 2020 earthquakes). Puerto Rican Studies scholars, public intellectuals, and activists in the diaspora and the archipelago directed much of their research and intellectual labor to documenting and evaluating the litany of traumas that had transformed the Puerto Rican experience. PRS scholars in the U.S. were instrumental in disseminating information, providing analysis, and creating venues for PRS scholars and activists from the archipelago to share their work. Puerto Rican researchers were invited to conferences and offered short research appointments at universities in the U.S. Most prominent among these was Princeton University's Program in Latin American Studies that established the Princeton Task Force on Puerto Rico; Arcadio Díaz Quiñones was actively engaged in this initiative.

The impact of the shocks that befell Puerto Rico has had an effect on Puerto Rican Studies. In particular, it is leading to a reappraisal of the two faulted lines I described above; the divide between cultural studies and political economy and rethinking the intersections between Puerto Rican Studies and Puerto Rico studies. The massive, ongoing exodus of Puerto Ricans, many of whom see themselves as forced to embark on a peregrination they fear will be permanent, has strengthened the links between Puerto Ricans in Puerto Rico and the United States. In addition, the connection between research and activism, which was a defining goal of the early PRS movement, has been regenerated. Increasingly, the boundary between knowledge production and political empowerment of disenfranchised communities, which academia valorizes, is under scrutiny by a generation of young scholars steeped in the legacy of the insurrectionary period of the Puerto Rican students' movement of the 1960s and 1970s.

There is little doubt that the study of Puerto Rico is gaining prominence in PRS. Scholars, activists, journalists, and organizers in the diaspora and the archipelago published hundreds of articles and essays in a wide array of online periodicals, newspapers, magazines, podcasts, and blogs about Puerto Rico's protracted crisis. They published incisive analysis and illuminating commentary on events and actors that are remaking Puerto Rico. The reports of Centro de Periodismo Investigativo (Center for Investigative Journalism) and the Centro para la Nueva Economía (Center for a New Economy), both in Puerto Rico, exposed the incompetence, corruption, and confabulations of the colonial government. They are bulwarks against the highly concentrated corporate media in Puerto Rico, which filter and sanitize news in an insidious "commercialization of public discourse," thus seeking to normalize colonialism and citizen passivity (McChesney 1998).

This abundance of information armed scholars and activists with the vital insights that are necessary for informed and effective analysis and action. *The Washington Post, New York Times, Huffington Post, El Nuevo Día, CENTRO Journal, Jacobin, NACLA, The Guardian, The Hill, New Politics, Conversation.com, Latino Rebels, The Nation, The Intercept, Dissent, 80 grados, Democracy Now!, Atlantic, New Yorker, Hedge Clippers, NOTICEL,* and other sources published reports and commentary by scholars, policy makers, organizers, lawyers, health care providers, and activists. The critical popular writing revealed the mechanisms of colonial subjugation, and the perfidy of multinational banks and hedge funds in their schemes to impoverish Puerto Rico, and exposed the institutionalized corruption that permeated virtually all of government. But, it also documented the resistance and resilience of humble Puerto Ricans as they struggled to rebuild their devastated society and protested to bring down Rosselló's administration.

Puerto Ricans also creatively used the arts in a campaign of cultural resistance that was disseminated in a variety of media. AgitArte was among the most creative and daring activist groups deploying art and performance to challenge the authorities and build solidarity. Music had a vital and energizing presence at every protest event. The woman's collective, Plena Combativa, is well known for performing original compositions at protest events and was ever present at the uprising of summer 2019. The visual arts and music were indispensable mediums to educate, mobilize, organize, and to ridicule and discredit corrupt and incompetent government officials.

This unity of diverse forms of resistance (academic and journalistic writing, and performative and physical action) is nicely captured in *Aftershocks of Disaster* (Bonilla and LeBrón 2019). This ground-breaking and original anthology, edited by Yarimar Bonilla and Marisol LeBrón, is a collection of essays written by academics and journalists, activists and community organizers, artists and poets, arranged into a sweeping and contemplative portrait on the transformative physical and emotional impact of Hurricane María on Puerto Rico. Arcadio Díaz Quiñones, an emeritus professor from Princeton University, eloquently described the Rutgers University conference on which *Aftershocks* was based as a demonstration "of the strength of the ethos of solidarity among diverse diasporic communities and the institutions they have created as well as the moral sensibility of their allies at universities and research centers" (Díaz Quiñones 2019). *Aftershocks* shows how politically progressive individuals are dismantling a metaphorical border that was devised by the colonial state to discourage transnational community building.

Valor y Cambio, created by Frances Negrón Muntaner and Sarabel Santos Negrón in 2019, is described as "a story-telling, community-building, and solidarity economy project." *Valor y Cambio* combines technology, culturally appropriate material incentives, graphic art, and history to provoke "a broad conversation about what is a just economy and how to foster collective empowerment" under conditions of severe austerity (Negrón Muntaner and Negrón 2019). *Valor y Cambio* was installed in economically vulnerable communities in Puerto Rico and New York, and furthers the evolving Puerto Rican transnational identity. The *Puerto Rico Syllabus*, conceived by Yarimar Bonilla, Marisol LeBrón, Sarah Molinari, and Isabel Guzzardo, is another creative project which fosters a link between research and activism, and which blurs the boundaries between cultural studies and political economy (Bonilla et al.). It promotes and sustains an ongoing exchange of knowledge between scholars and activists in the diaspora and in Puerto Rico on the origins and repercussions of the debt crisis. It is an accessible digital resource that offers the general public a variety of information sources on Puerto Rico. The goal of the *Puerto Rico Syllabus* "is to contribute to the ongoing public dialogue and rising social activism regarding the debt crisis by providing historical and sociological tools with which to assess its roots and repercussions" (Bonilla et al.).

Many colleges and universities, particularly those in CUNY and SUNY, participated in Puerto Rico's recovery process and provided humanitarian assistance. The *Listening to Puerto Rico* Teach-Out is an innovative program developed by the University of Notre Dame and the University of Michigan to create an archive of "film testimonies from Puerto Ricans of all walks of life." Described as "an engaged digital learning project," *Listening to Puerto Rico* aims to deepen awareness and comprehension of the "urgent multidimensional crisis" that Puerto Rico faces and to "learn of successful organizations, strategies and solutions that are contributing" to its recovery (*Listening to Puerto Rico*). *Listening to Puerto Rico* and *Puerto Rico Syllabus* have given joint presentations at academic conferences to discuss digital projects and solidarity work. Both are exploring strategies to expand the use of "digitally engaged scholarship." According to Sarah Molinari, Ph.D. Candidate in the CUNY Graduate Center Anthropology Program and one of the participants, both groups are looking at contrasting interpretations and new knowledge that the "mainstream media and academic accounts" are unable to provide. Their collaborative initiative also responds to the "growing public interest in alternative learning methods" (Molinari 2019).

The Centro de Estudios Puertorriqueños has undergone a sea change since its origins. It has established an expansive social media and video presence, and through its *Puerto Rican Nation* program helps promote community solidarity. While researchers continue to generate timely analysis on political and economic conditions of Puerto Ricans in the U.S. and Puerto Rico, Centro has embarked on an ambitious schedule of summits, symposiums, and conferences. Some of the conferences are network and community building events, while others are designed to promote coalitions and partnerships among an array of Puerto Rican community-based organizations, service agencies, and corporate stakeholders. Through its Diaspora Summits, Centro has taken a leadership role in promoting a dialogue among academics, public officials, community organizations, and "multimedia makers" with the aim of setting "policy priorities and focusing on stateside-led rebuilding efforts for Puerto Rico in the aftermath of Hurricanes Irma and María" (Centro de Estudios Puertorriqueños 2019). Conferences have been organized in Puerto Rico, the Northeast, Washington, and Orlando and regularly include scholars and activists from Puerto Rico. The Centro also launched the *Rebuild Puerto Rico* initiative, which is described as "an online information clearinghouse for the stateside Puerto Rican community and other allies to support disaster relief and recovery efforts" (https://centropr.hunter.cuny.edu/events-news/rebuild-puerto-rico). Centro operates an ambitious program to promote the arts and culture and creates accessible spaces for community education and dissemination of the latest PRS scholarship.

There is an undeniable urgency to deploy social media, digital communication technologies, and web-based platforms to create and disseminate new knowledge and to build opportunities to expand the scope of solidarity work. The use of social media and other digital technologies has been instrumental for building scholarly communities, solidarity groups, and community-based movements following Hurricane María and *#RickyRenuncia*.

CONCLUSION

PROMESA, Hurricane María, and the summer uprising of 2019 have transformed Puerto Rico and created a bond of activist solidarity between Puerto Ricans in the diaspora and the archipelago. The Navy out of Vieques movement is the only comparable event, but the protesters' goal was to reclaim territory and expel an occupying force from a Puerto Rican island. The 2019 summer uprising was different. Protesters challenged a corrupt political class and the *junta*, the despised agency the federal government deployed to impose austerity. However, before the uprising, few Puerto Ricans were aware of the explosive groundswell of opposition and affirmation that was percolating after years of colonial abuse. The relentless resistance against the junta, the self-reliance and human dignity shown in the aftermath of the hurricane, and the outrage and courage of those protesting the degeneracy of the political class awakened the world to the fact that after 121 years of colonialism and remorseless attacks against all who fought for self-determination, Puerto Ricans are not cowed. The colonizer and the colonial state had failed to strip Puerto Ricans of their dignity and humanity. Many PRS scholars, activists, teachers, and intellectuals in the diaspora clearly understood they had a responsibility to support the collective cry of indignation. Many of them fought battles to establish Puerto Rican Studies, protested police brutality, marched for Puerto Rican independence, and participated in the Navy out of Vieques protests.

Young scholars continue to be drawn to Puerto Rican Studies. This in itself is a revolutionary act considering that, despite PRS's heightened academic standing, the field is not immune from criticism. Its detractors label PRS, as well as Black Studies, as identity politics, lacking academic rigor and as nothing more than an updated version of angry demands of the 1970s by individuals whose presence in the university should be contested. Yet, the more cosmopolitan and progressive faculty, many of whom are of color, acknowledge the importance of the scholarship that marks the current state of the field. Paradoxically, as Puerto Rico appeared on the verge of deteriorating into a Caribbean dystopia, Puerto Rican Studies scholarship regained the vibrancy, urgency, and critical properties that marked its origins in the turbulent 1960s.

Puerto Rican Studies has come full circle. PRS was the product of urgent and persistent student demands for the university to cede a space for Puerto Ricans to control the narrative; to create new knowledge of their reality, and in the process to expose the racist underpinning of university-sanctioned scholarship. This knowledge was to be deployed in service of marginalized and precarious communities. The task, then as now, is for Puerto Ricans to acquire an education that will empower them to lead a life with dignity and economic security, as they effect positive social change. Today, Puerto Rican Studies is on much firmer academic grounds than 50 years ago; there are far more scholars who can draw on the expansive knowledge that has been produced about the Puerto Rican experience in the diaspora and the archipelago.

PRS has created new knowledge and deployed new technologies to challenge the institutions and agents who enforce a neoliberal agenda on an impoverished colony. PRS scholars are also studying the demographic reconfiguration of Latinx communities resulting from successive waves of Puerto Rican migrants who started fleeing the archipelago with the onset of the 2005 depression. PRS researchers are focusing on the lives of these economic exiles and their impact on the communities in which they settle. The economic, social, linguistic, and cultural challenges the new migrants face are simultaneously similar to, but different from, the experience of post-World War II Puerto Rican migrants. Fifty years after Puerto Rican Studies was established with a clear social justice agenda, it continues to pursue the same quest. However, this time PRS does so with substantial institutional experience and the academic capacity gained by its enduring struggle to create a secure academic presence in the American university.

ACKNOWLEDGMENTS

I want to acknowledge and thank Aldo Lauria Santiago, Sarah Molinari, Charles R. Venator Santiago, Xavier Totti, Edna Acosta Belén, and the editors, María E. Pérez y González and Virginia Sánchez Korrol, for their comments and assistance in providing information for this chapter.

NOTES

[1] See Vázquez and Otero (2017) on the origins of Centro and *CENTRO Journal*.

[2] My thanks to Xavier Totti for this information.

[3] Author's translation.

[4] See Ortíz Márquez (2009) for an analysis of Centro's impact on the development of Puerto Rican Studies.

[5] Author's translation.

[6] Author's translation.

[7] See Vázquez and Otero (2017) for an insightful essay on the history and personal reflections by the long-standing editor of the *CENTRO Journal* on "the creation of the Center for Puerto Rican Studies" in 1973 and its journal. The essay traces the history of the *CENTRO Journal* as she guided its development from a modest newsletter into the leading academic journal in the field of Puerto Rican Studies.

[8] Turmoil in the Puerto Rican Studies Association in mid-2020 was partially attributable, according to a sizeable portion of the membership, to the inability of the organization's executive board to "address the current needs of the field of Puerto Rican Studies: one that foregrounds Black, feminist and queer perspectives" (Open Letter to the PRSA 2020).

[9] A very partial list includes the following: Anthony DeJesús, Milga Morales Nadal, and Sonia Nieto (Education); Juan González (Environmental Justice); Jodie Roure, Juan Cartagena, Tanya Hernández, and Natasha Lycia Ora Bannan (Law); Judith Aponte and Urayoán Colón Ramos (Health Disparities); and the late Angelo Falcón (Policy Analysis). See Lloréns and Stanchich (2019) for a discussion on environmental degradation, climate change, and the environmental justice movement in post-Hurricane María Puerto Rico.

[10] See the essay by Mario Mercado-Díaz on anti-Blackness in Puerto Rico and the diaspora (Mercado-Díaz 2020). For a discussion on racism in the archipelago, see Franco Ortíz, et al. (2019).

[11] Indeed, the signatories of the Open Letter on PRSA criticize the association for "the displacement of the diasporic origins of the association" (*Open Letter to the PRSA* 2020). Eric Kelderman (2020) discusses the turmoil in the Puerto Rican Studies Association that resulted in the mass resignation of the Executive Board and the election of a new board.

REFERENCES

Alamo-Pastrana, Carlos. 2016. *Seams of Empire Race and Radicalism in Puerto Rico and the United States.* Gainesville: University Press of Florida.

Asociación Estudiantes Graduados de Historia. 2016. Reflexionando sobre CEREP y la Nueva Historia Puertorriqueña: A 28 años del final de un proyecto historiográfico. <https://aeghcea.files.wordpress.com/2016/03/20-reflexionando-sobre-cerep3.pdf>.

Bonilla, Frank. 1992. Circuits and Cycles: A Century of Puerto Rican Migration. Connecticut Humanities Council.

Bonilla, Frank and Emilio González. 1973. New Knowing, New Practice: Puerto Rican Studies. In *Structures of Dependency*, eds. Frank Bonilla and Robert Henríquez Girling. 224–34. Stanford, CA: Stanford University.

Bonilla, Yarimar and Marisol LeBrón, eds. 2019. *Aftershocks of Disaster: Puerto Rico Before and After the Storm.* Chicago: Haymarket Books.

Bonilla, Yarimar, Marisol Lebrón, Sarah Molinari and Isabel Guzzardo. *Puerto Rico Syllabus.* <https://puertoricosyllabus.com>.

Cabán, Pedro. 2003. Moving from the Margins: Three Decades of Latina/o Studies. *Latino Studies* 1(1), 5–35.

———. 2004. Presidential Welcome. 6th Biennial Conference of the Puerto Rican Studies Association. New York.

———. 2007. Black and Latino Studies and Social Capital Theory. *Latin American, Caribbean, and U.S. Latino Studies Faculty Scholarship.* 36. <https://scholarsarchive.library.albany.edu/lacs_fac_scholar/36>.

———. 2009. Puerto Rican Studies: Changing Islands of Knowledge. *CENTRO: Journal of the Center for Puerto Rican Studies* 21(2), 256–81.

Center for Puerto Rican Studies. 2019. Diaspora Summit. <https://centropr.nationbuilder.com/prsummit4>.

———. 2019. Rebuild Puerto Rico. <https://centropr.hunter.cuny.edu/events-news/rebuild-puerto-rico>.

Díaz Quiñones, Arcadio. 2019. Foreword. In *Aftershocks of Disaster: Puerto Rico Before and After the Storm*, eds. Yarimar Bonilla and Marisol LeBrón. ix-xiii. Chicago: Haymarket Books.

Dinzey-Flores, Zaire Zenit. 2013. *Locked in, Locked Out: Gated Communities in a Puerto Rican City.* Philadelphia: University of Pennsylvania Press.

Disis, Jill. 2017. Hurricane María could be a $95 billion storm for Puerto Rico. *CNN Money* 28 September. <https://money.cnn.com/2017/09/28/news/econo-

my/puerto-rico-hurricane-maria-damage-estimate/index.html>.

Flores, Antonio and Jens Manuel Krogstad. 2019. Puerto Rico's population declined sharply after hurricanes Maria and Irma. *Pew Research Center* 26 July. <https://www.pewresearch.org/fact-tank/2019/07/26/puerto-rico-population-2018>.

Franco Ortíz, Mariluz, Hilda Lloréns, María I. Reinat-Pumarejo, Bárbara I. Abadía-Rexach and Gloriann Sacha Antonetty Lebrón. 2019. Conversación justa sobre racismo y privilegios de raza y género en Puerto Rico. *80grados* 29 March.

García-Colón, Ismael. 2020. *Colonial Migrants at the Heart of Empire: Puerto Rican Workers on U.S. Farms.* Oakland: University of California Press.

Glassman, Brian. 2019. More Puerto Ricans Move to Mainland United States, Poverty Declines: A Third of Movers from Puerto Rico to the Mainland United States Relocated to Florida in 2018. United States Census Bureau. 26 September. <https://www.census.gov/library/stories/2019/09/puerto-rico-outmigration-increases-poverty-declines.html>.

Godreau, Isar P. 2015. *Scripts of Blackness: Race, Cultural Nationalism, and U.S. Colonialism in Puerto Rico.* Chicago: University of Illinois Press.

Inter-University Program for Latino Research. n.d. Latino Art Now! <https://iuplr.org/latino-art-now>.

Kelderman, Eric. 2020. How a Fight Over a Black Lives Matter Statement Transformed an Academic Association. *Chronicle of Higher Education* 28 September.

Kishore, Nishant, Domingo Marqués, Ayesha Mahmud, Mathew V. Kiang, Irmary Rodríguez, Arlan Fuller, Peggy Ebner, Cecilia Sorensen, Fabio Racy, Jay Lemery, Leslie Maas, Jennifer Leaning, Rafael A. Irizarry, Satchit Balsari and Caroline O. Buckee. 2018. Mortality in Puerto Rico after Hurricane María. *The New England Journal of Medicine* 379(July 12), 162–70.

Latin American Studies Association (LASA)/Puerto Rico Section (PR). 2019. Urgent Communiqué about the Situation in Puerto Rico. <https://www.docdroid.net/2MDa4lk/comunicado-lasa-pr-situacion-pr.pdf - page=2>.

LeBrón, Marisol. 2019. *Policing Life and Death: Race, Violence, and Resistance in Puerto Rico.* Oakland: University of California Press.

Listening to Puerto Rico. <https://listeningtopuertorico.org>.

Lloréns, Hilda and Maritza Stanchich. 2019. Water is Life, but the Colony is a Necropolis: Environmental Terrains of Struggle in Puerto Rico. *Cultural Dynamics* 31(1-2), 81–101.

McChesney, Robert. 1998. Making Media Democratic. *Boston Review* Summer. <https://bostonreview.net/archives/BR23.3/mcchesney.html>.

Meléndez, Edgardo. 2017. *Sponsored Migration: The State and Puerto Rican Postwar Migration to the United States.* Chicago: The Ohio State University Press.

Mercado-Díaz, Mario. 2020. To My Fellow BoriBlancos: When We Say 'Down with White Power,' We Also Mean Our White Power. *Latin American Perspectives* 2 October. <https://nacla.org/puerto-rico-white-supremacy>.

Molinari, Sarah. 2019. Personal communication. 12 November.

Muzio, Rose. 2017. *Radical Imagination, Radical Humanity: Puerto Rican Political Activism in New York*. Albany: State University of New York Press.

Negrón Muntaner, Frances and Sarabel Santos Negrón. 2019. *Valor y Cambio*. <https://www.valorycambio.org/abouttheproject>.

Nieves, Josephine, et al. 1987. Puerto Rican Studies: Roots and Challenges. In *Toward a Renaissance of Puerto Rican Studies: Ethnic and Area Studies in University Education*, eds. María E. Sánchez and Antonio M. Stevens Arroyo. 3–12. Highland Lakes, NJ: Atlantic Research and Publications.

Open Letter to the PRSA. 2020. *Puerto Rican Studies Obituary*. 13 August. <https://sites.google.com/view/prsaletter>.

Ortíz Márquez, Maribel. 2009. Beginnings: Puerto Rican Studies Revisited. *CENTRO: Journal of the Center for Puerto Rican Studies* 21(2), 177–97.

Pérez Jiménez, Cristina. 2017. *CENTRO Journal*: Three Decades of Struggle and Scholarship in Support of Puerto Rican Studies. *Diálogo* 20(2), 33–45.

Rodríguez-Silva, Ileana. 2012. *Silencing Race: Disentangling Blackness, Colonialism, and National Identities in Puerto Rico*. New York: Palgrave Macmillan.

Thomas, Lorrin and Aldo Lauria-Santiago. 2019. *Rethinking the Struggle for Puerto Rican Rights*. New York: Routledge.

Vázquez, Blanca and Néstor Otero. 2017. Origins of the *Centro Journal*, Arts and Politics. *Diálogo* 20(2), 107–16.

Vázquez Valdés, Leyda. 2010. Algunos apuntes sobre el Centro de Estudios Puertorriqueños (CUNY) y el Centro de Estudios de la Realidad Puertorriqueña (CEREP) en la historia de los estudios culturales puertorriqueños. *Cuarto Propio* 6. <https://xdoc.mx/documents/algunos-apuntes-sobre-el-centro-de-estudios-puertorriqueos-cuny-5e7fb35928a19>.

Whalen, Carmen Teresa. 2009. Radical Contexts: Puerto Rican Politics in the 1960s and 1970s and the Center for Puerto Rican Studies. *CENTRO: Journal of the Center for Puerto Rican Studies* 21(2), 221–55.

CHAPTER 2

PUERTO RICAN STUDIES: A LEGACY OF ACTIVISM, SCHOLARSHIP, AND COLLECTIVE EMPOWERMENT

Edna Acosta-Belén

INTRODUCTION

Galvanized by civil rights, racial, social, and political struggles, and the cry for equality and freedom that also inspired the upheavals of the late 1960s and early 1970s at numerous U.S. colleges and universities, Puerto Rican students, faculty, and other members of disenfranchised communities of color joined together to stake their claims for equal access and representation in higher education and for the establishment of Puerto Rican and other ethnic and racial studies academic programs. This essay analyzes the impact of Puerto Rican Studies in fostering interdisciplinary and intersectional critical approaches, and in advancing scholarship, teaching, and advocacy focused on multiple aspects of the history and socioeconomic, political, and cultural experiences of Puerto Ricans as a colonized and racialized diasporic population. It also provides a synopsis of the main theoretical and critical currents influencing the evolution of Puerto Rican Studies, and those issues and theoretical approaches that framed the substantive body of new scholarship about stateside Puerto Ricans produced throughout the course of their five-decade development. Since its inception, Puerto Rican Studies and other emerging programs of that era were particularly instrumental in efforts to integrate new research and teaching perspectives about their respective populations into the curriculum of the mainstream disciplines and professional fields, and in fostering multicultural learning and diversifying educational institutions.

Moreover, the aforementioned educational battles contested long-standing Anglo-conforming notions of "melting pot" assimilation and "American exceptionalism," since their fundamental egalitarian and freedom precepts were far from reflecting the deeply rooted unequal treatment and exclusion of populations of color in U.S. society (Glazer and Moynihan 1963; Noble 2002). They exposed a generally ignored long history of systemic racism endured by disenfranchised "minority groups" that deprived them of the same rights and opportunities for socioeconomic and educational advancement afforded to the white majority population. At the elementary and secondary school levels, segregation and the dire conditions of public schools in low-income neighborhoods were visible signs of the pervasive neglect by city and state governments. When compared to whites, the lack of representation among teachers and administrators of color was self-evident, as was the inability of schools to provide adequate instruction to all students, including (im)migrant learners with limited English proficiency.[1] The magnitude of these deficiencies and unequal conditions resulted in substantial numbers of students of color dropping out before completing high school, or having limited access to a college education. For stateside Puerto Ricans, in particular, their underprivileged socioeconomic and educational status was at the center of a 1976 U.S. Commission of Civil Rights study forecasting a gloomy "uncertain future" (U.S. Commission of Civil Rights 1976).

The insurgent origins of Puerto Rican Studies and other ethnic and racial studies programs and departments (i.e., Black/Afro- or African American, Chicano/a, Native American, Asian American) of the late 1960s and early '70s, and the battles for their legitimacy and institutionalization at most of the U.S. colleges and universities where they were based, were part of their evolution. Slightly over half a century after their inception, some programs are still bound to justify or fight for their existence. Only a fraction of those higher education institutions responding to demands to create these programs have been supportive in maintaining or fortifying them, although usually at a steady level, rather than propelling them into significant growth. In general, during periods of budgetary cuts, some universities still view these areas of study as non-essential to their academic missions; either they eliminate them, reduce their size, or merge them with other existing administrative units. Nevertheless, enough institutions throughout the country invested the resources that eventually brought recognition to the intellectual legitimacy and scholarly output generated by Puerto Rican Studies and other trailblazing interdisciplinary fields of academic inquiry of that period, a tribute to their importance and ability to reinvigorate and reconceptualize their missions during the last five decades. According to Acuña, 139 U.S. institutions have programs focused on Chicanos/as, Puerto Ricans, and other Latinos/as (2011, 273–98).

Arising from student and community-based activism, Puerto Rican Studies was pivotal in subsequent decades in sustaining an academic critique of canonic knowledge and of the recycled implicit biases, erasures, and gaps within the traditional disciplines regarding the study of ethnic and racial minorities, women, and LGBTQ populations.[2] Another important aspect of the push for overarching educational changes was incorporating new and previously ignored knowledge, about what were then sorely neglected populations, into research, teaching, and service endeavors. Learning about their largely hidden histories, cultures, and experiences as ethnic and racial minorities, as well as about the structural and other underlying sources of pervasive inequalities and the underprivileged status of their communities, was also central to their mission.

In due course, Puerto Rican Studies and other non-traditional fields played a significant role in contesting the circumscribed Eurocentric perspectives, paradigmatic modernity-rationality precepts, and "universal" claims that for centuries have dominated the production of knowledge and liberal education. Another key aspect of their initial efforts was to deconstruct the privileged hegemonic narratives and faulty generalizations of Western thought and the power relations and ideologies that reinforced the subaltern "otherness" generally attributed to populations of color (Puerto Ricans included) in the scholarship of the traditional academic disciplines. In general, this undertaking was of critical importance for the ethnic and racially diverse populations from Latin American, Caribbean, African, and Asian countries, formerly colonized by Western European powers or the United States.

DECOLONIZING KNOWLEDGE AND CONSTRUCTING
DECOLONIAL IMAGINARIES

Over three decades ago, Frank Bonilla succinctly captured the fundamental flaw of most scholarship about Puerto Ricans prior to the emergence of Puerto Rican Studies, and some of the lingering effects of that preceding body of knowledge:

[...] we have set out to contest effectively those visions of the world that assume or take for granted the inevitability and indefinite duration of the class and colonial oppression that has marked Puerto Rican history. All the disciplines that we are most directly drawing upon—history, economics, sociology, anthropology, literature, psychology, pedagogy—as they are practiced in the United States are deeply implicated in the construction of that vision of Puerto Ricans as an inferior, submissive people, trapped on the underside of relations from which there is no foreseeable exit. (1987, 17)

Less than a decade after the burgeoning of Puerto Rican Studies as an academic field and the establishment of over a dozen programs/departments, the great majority found in the New York metropolitan area at CUNY and SUNY institutions, the growth in scholarly productivity and the number of specialists in this field at a wider range of U.S. institutions was becoming more apparent (see Acosta-Belén in this volume). As a rule, Puerto Rican Studies departments were able to hire a small number of core faculty, while programs relied mostly on faculty with suitable expertise based in traditional departments at their corresponding institutions. Collectively, they represented an important catalyst in producing a substantive body of new scholarship on the Puerto Rican diaspora during ensuing decades that gradually influenced the work of other faculty in the social sciences and humanities disciplines, as well as professional and applied fields. Prior to the advent of Puerto Rican Studies, research on stateside Puerto Ricans was generally more limited in terms of quantity, quality, and scope. For the most part, this previous research was being done by non-Puerto Rican scholars. In contrast, five decades later there is a vigorous and continuous level of scholarly productivity focusing on the Puerto Rican diaspora and a significantly larger number of stateside and island-based academic researchers.

Before the 1970s, a considerable portion of the research output on stateside Puerto Ricans was focused on the Great Migration to New York, the "problems" that their mass migration brought to the city, and the poverty conditions that overwhelmed their lives. Stereotyped portrayals of the Puerto Rican people were often based on flawed generalizations and entrenched notions about preconceived racial and social deficiencies of impoverished populations. Added to these characterizations were catchy concepts that proclaimed an ostensible "culture of poverty" (Lewis 1966)—which turned into a metaphor of Puerto Rican life ("La Vida") on the island and in New York—along with reiterated discourses about what was branded "the Puerto Rican problem." The latter ascribed characterization was widely used by numerous scholars, policy makers, and the media to describe the mass "invasion" of migrants from Puerto Rico to New York City (Meléndez 2017).

Besides the prevalence of "problem-focused" and "blaming the victim" community portraits, there were some obvious gaps in studies about the diaspora. Part of that void was the scarcity of research about the longstanding presence of Puerto Ricans in the United States dating back to the mid-nineteenth century and the forces that propelled different generations to migrate, both before and after the U.S. invasion of Puerto Rico and prior to the post-World War II migrations. The paucity of research is illustrated by the fact that, during the mid-twentieth century Great Migration, scholars mostly viewed Puerto Ricans as "newcomers" to New York City (Handlin 1959; Mills, Senior and Goldsen 1950; Senior 1965), even though there were around 70,000 Puerto Ricans in the United States in 1940 and 301,375 in 1950—the majority of them living in the city and a few other nearby states (Acosta-Belén and Santiago 2018, 98–106). By 1970, the U.S. Puerto Rican population was almost five times as large (1,442,774), and over 80 percent was concentrated in three states: New York, New Jersey, and Illinois. New York City, the primary Puerto Rican migration destination, was at the time the focal point for the great majority of research studies about the community, even though many Puerto Ricans also settled in nearby cities in New Jersey (e.g., Paterson and Newark) and in other large cities like Chicago and Philadelphia. It was not until the decline of New York's manufacturing industries, and its ensuing fiscal crisis of the 1970s, that Puerto Ricans began to move out of New York City to several other cities and states. By 2015, slightly over 14 percent of stateside

Puerto Ricans resided there, although they still represented about 30 percent of the total Latina/o population of New York state (Acosta-Belén and Santiago 2018, 96–105; Centro Data Brief 2016).

The greater part of prior migration studies also paid scant attention to the multiple ways in which generations of Puerto Rican migrants built their lives and contributed to the economy as well as the political and cultural life of New York City and other parts of the country. The latter omission is not entirely surprising since, in general, the enduring centricity of mainstream U.S. historical narratives rarely delved into the particular histories and contributions of the vast array of non-Anglo populations of different racial and ethnic backgrounds that brought their labor, creative imaginations, and aspirations to the making of the United States (Takaki 1993). In most cases, the bulk of migration research also failed to address adequately the impact of U.S. colonialism on Puerto Ricans and the island's limited power to steer the course of its own socioeconomic and political life, including the formulation of policies that, during the post-World War II period, impelled the mass migration of Puerto Rican workers. These migrants became an important source of low-wage labor for U.S. manufacturing, agriculture, and service industries. Although some migration of Puerto Ricans had occurred under the Spanish colonial regime, prompted either by political persecution or economic reasons, after the U.S. invasion and throughout the twentieth century, migration became a major way of Puerto Rican life, and to this day continues to be a viable and frequent alternative for island residents.

The rapid pace of the ongoing New Millennium Migration (1990s-2010s) shows that the stateside influx of Puerto Ricans is now reaching levels comparable to those of the postwar Great Migration, and, concomitantly, causing a serious decline in Puerto Rico's population (Acosta-Belén and Santiago 2018; Meléndez and Vargas-Ramos 2014). However, prior to the 1970s, except for some policy makers, urban planners, and technocrats who viewed migration as a safety valve to reduce poverty and unemployment in Puerto Rico, only a handful of island scholars paid much attention to the history of Puerto Ricans in the United States or to the lives these migrants forged away from their homeland (Hernández Cruz and Muschkin 1994; Nieves-Falcón 1975; Maldonado-Denis 1976; Seda Bonilla 1977; Vázquez Calzada 1979). Up to that point, there was an obvious research separation between the study of island and stateside Puerto Ricans. Stateside scholars, writers, artists, and musicians—some of whom had been born or had strong personal and professional ties in Puerto Rico—were particularly instrumental in beginning to bridge that separation (Mohr 1989).

Under the leadership of Frank Bonilla, the founding of the Centro de Estudios Puertorriqueños (Centro) [Center for Puerto Rican Studies] in the academic year 1973-74 was a catalyst in stimulating research, teaching, and community outreach endeavors of Puerto Rican Studies scholars and community activists, and in narrowing the existing divide between the island and its diaspora. Some island-based academics were also receptive to strengthening the connections with Centro and Puerto Rican Studies faculty. Researchers gradually began to go beyond the dichotomized island-mainland approaches and gave increased attention to the transnational interconnections between Puerto Ricans in both geographic locations (Duany 2002). Most of the new research on the diaspora focused on previously understudied areas. Among those that stood out the most were efforts to unveil and document early migrations of Puerto Ricans to the United States before and after the U.S. invasion (History Task Force 1979, 1982). Reconstructing mid-nineteenth century and early twentieth century Puerto Rican presence in New York and seeking a more nuanced understanding of the socioeconomic conditions, cultural lives, and activism of *los/as pioneros/as* (migrant pioneers), prior to and during the civil rights struggles that inspired both the Chicano/a and Puerto Rican movements (Torres and Velázquez 1988), were of particular interest to researchers. During the decades that followed the publication of an edited version of the *Memorias de Bernardo Vega* [*Memoirs of Bernardo Vega*, (1984)] in 1977,[3] new studies began to document in more detail the presence and toils of the *tabaqueros/as* (tobacco workers) and other working-class Puerto Ricans during the formative years of Spanish Harlem (El Barrio), the Lower East Side, the Brooklyn Navy Yard, and other parts of the city (Matos-Rodríguez and Hernández 2001; Ortiz 1986; Pérez y González 2000; Rodríguez 1989; Sánchez Korrol 1983, 1994; Sánchez Korrol and Hernández 2010). These scholarly endeavors brought to light some of the most notable community leaders and organizations, along with writers, artists, journalists, and *cronistas* (columnists) writing for New York City's Spanish-language periodicals (Acosta-Belén 1993; Acosta-Belén and Sánchez Korrol 1993;

Burgos 1997; Colón 1982; Colón López 2002; Kanellos 1990, 2011; Kanellos and Martell 2000; Padilla Aponte 2001; Sánchez González 2001, 2013; Sánchez Korrol 1994, 2018; Thomas 2010; Vera Rojas 2010, 2010-2011, 2018).

A noticeable growth in microhistories and ethnographic studies of Puerto Rican communities in other U.S. cities and states gradually shifted the focus away from New York City where, up to recent years, most Puerto Ricans had resided. Centro's early work began to expand the geography of Puerto Rican migrations (History Task Force 1979, 1982). Prior studies on Puerto Rican migrant communities, other than those in New York, were few in number and limited to early migrations from Puerto Rico to Hawaii that occurred after the U.S. invasion of the island (Camacho Souza 1984, 1983; López 2005; López and Forbes 2001; Rosario Natal 1983). Since the 1980s, the most notable growth has been in historical, demographic, and ethnographic studies about Puerto Ricans in Chicago, a city that until the late 2000s held the second largest Puerto Rican population (Cruz 2004; Fernández 2012; Padilla 1985, 1987; Pérez 2004; Ramos Zayas 2003; Rúa 2012; Toro-Morn 2005). By 2010, Chicago was trading its second place with Philadelphia (Vázquez-Hernández 2017; Whalen 2006, 2001). Subsequent scholarship brought more attention to the changing demographics of Puerto Rican migration. The geographic dispersion of Puerto Ricans from New York City to other cities and states that started in the mid-1970s accounts for the growing scholarly interest on a wider range of migration destinations. Worthy of mention are those studies focused on Hartford, Connecticut (Cruz 1998; Glasser 1997, 2005); Lorain, Ohio (Rivera 2005); Morristown, New Jersey (Jiménez de Wagenheim 2005); Boston, Massachusetts (Matos-Rodríguez 2005), and other New England states and cities (Torres 2006). After almost two decades, projected increases in the Puerto Rican population in Florida—a growth pattern that began in the 1990s—became a reality. Recent population estimates show that this state's Puerto Rican population now surpasses that of New York. Thus, it is expected that new research focused on Orlando and other areas in Central and South Florida will continue adding to already available work (Duany and Matos-Rodríguez 2006; Duany and Silver 2010; Silver 2019). As a whole, the body of work on a larger spectrum of stateside Puerto Rican communities allows researchers to engage in comparative approaches and analyses of their changing socioeconomic and educational status, their levels of political participation, and the various similarities and differences that contribute to past and current migration trends, including those of more recent arrivals to old and new places of settlement.

The burgeoning of Puerto Rican Studies must be seen as a part of a more encompassing Puerto Rican civil rights movement and the ethnic and racial revitalization drive embraced by stateside Puerto Rican communities during the 1970s and '80s. This was a period of social and political engagement and creativity that led to the founding of valued cultural institutions (e.g., the Nuyorican Poets Cafe, Museo del Barrio, Taller Boricua, Taller Puertorriqueño) (Acosta-Belén 1992, 2009; Flores 1993; Torres and Velázquez 1998). Education activism generated the transformative agendas that led to the emergence of Puerto Rican Studies and bilingual/multicultural education programs, and brought centrality to what was, up to that point, the peripheral study of ethnicity and race in academic teaching and research. Other important educational outcomes included the founding of Aspira, Centro, Hostos Community College, and Boricua College in New York City. Numerous manifestations of ethnic and racial pride and the creative imagination of writers, artists, and performers were evident during those years. Different forms of cultural expression provided Puerto Rican Studies scholars and teachers with opportunities to highlight a vast array of issues (e.g., cultural and racial identities, assimilation, and class, gender, racial, and sexuality-based forms of oppression). Through fictional and non-fictional writings and performances, a multiplicity of new voices revealed what it meant to grow up Puerto Rican in a racialized and segregated white Anglo-American society (Acosta-Belén 1992, 1993, 2009; Flores 1993). The cultural affirmation of *la puertorriqueñidad* (Puerto Ricanness) within the communities of the diaspora was somewhat surprising to many island residents, due in part to the presumed cultural and linguistic assimilation of those Puerto Ricans born or raised in the United States. Ironically, while a consciousness of nationality was being celebrated by stateside Puerto Ricans, U.S. and Puerto Rican government officials and law enforcement agencies on the island were complicit in the systematic persecution, surveillance, and incarceration of pro-independence supporters and militants, and in suppressing nationalistic sentiments, a practice that started in earnest in the 1930s (Acosta 1987; Bosque Pérez and Colón Morera 1997).

The performing poetry movement galvanized by the founding of the Nuyorican Poets Cafe (1972), and the public murals and sculptures of several Puerto Rican visual artists in New York, Chicago, and other urban neighborhoods were indicative of the cultural effervescence of those years. Numerous novelists, short story fiction writers, poets, and playwrights began to publish their works, be recognized by critics, and were included in various major anthologies of Latina/o literature that made their way into the universities (Kanellos 2002; Stavans 2011). A select number of them were represented in general anthologies of U.S. literature. The legacies of old and new generations of Puerto Rican authors are now one of the most prolific and recognized areas of cultural production within the diaspora. Several prominent writers and artists served as adjunct or visiting faculty in Puerto Rican Studies departments/programs. These multiple manifestations of ethnic pride and cultural creativity validated the struggles and resilience of Puerto Ricans against colonialist historical erasures and gave voice to some of the social and racial prejudices they endured in U.S. society.

In Chicago, New York, Philadelphia, and other nearby cities, the social and political activism of the Young Lords stood out because of their grass-roots-oriented "serve the people" (Morales 2016, 17) endeavors—among them, breakfast programs for school children, improvement of community hospitals and health services, women's equal rights and reproductive health initiatives, and social, political, and educational consciousness raising (Enck-Wanzer 2010; Fernández 2020; Guzmán 1998; Meléndez 2005; Morales 2016; Torres and Velázquez 1998; Wanzer-Serrano 2015; Young Lords and Abramson 2011). A few of the most obvious manifestations of the nationalistic tenor of those years were t-shirts with catchy slogans, such as "I'm proud to be Puerto Rican," "¡Palante, siempre palante!" (Move forward, always forward!), "Black is Beautiful," "¡Despierta Boricua, defiende lo tuyo!" (Wake up Boricua, defend what's yours!), and "¡Viva Puerto Rico Libre!" (Long live a free Puerto Rico!); the popularity of the Afro hair style; and the use of berets bearing the Puerto Rican flag, such as those worn by the Young Lords.

Musical trends included the salsa craze popularized internationally by the Fania All Stars (i.e., Johnny Pacheco, Ray Barreto, Willie Colón, Celia Cruz, Larry Harlow, Héctor Lavoe, Tito Puente, Richie Ray), and influenced other generations of Puerto Rican musicians and performers

(Aparicio 1997; Flores 2016). Subsequent musical genres such as rap, hip-hop, and reggaeton were embraced by both stateside and island Puerto Rican performers, and those from other nationalities, eventually reaching both U.S. mainstream and international audiences (Flores 2000; Rivera 2003; Rivera, Marshall, and Pacini Hernández 2009).

Since Centro's founding, facilitated by CUNY and major grants from the Ford Foundation and other sources, this institution has been central to the overall process of documenting and advancing scholarship on Puerto Rican migration and the formation and evolution of a diaspora in New York City and other stateside communities. Today, Centro is regarded as the premier repository of archival materials that unveil the political, social, cultural, and educational legacies of stateside Puerto Ricans. Its invaluable archival and library resources include collections of personal papers of prominent community members, records of various community organizations, periodicals, photographs, visual art, documentaries, and video and audio interviews (Hernández 2011-2012). The process of digitizing these collections was initiated under the leadership of former Centro director Edwin Meléndez, who stepped down from his position at the end of June 2021. During his 13 years of dedicated service to Centro, he also launched numerous other innovative research and community outreach initiatives. Several of Centro's digitized archival collections are now more accessible to researchers, teachers, students, community activists, and the general public.[4] Centro's online data briefs about stateside and island Puerto Ricans keep the public abreast of current demographic and other statistical data trends, and issues of import to all Puerto Ricans. Annual Centro-sponsored Diaspora Summits represent one of the most sustained effective ways for getting island and stateside Puerto Rican Studies scholars, other professionals, students, community activists, policy makers, and public officials together to discuss a myriad of issues faced by their respective communities. Besides their continuing role in producing, publishing, and disseminating new research and scholarship through *CENTRO Journal*, *Centro Voices*, and Centro Press, other community outreach initiatives include educational projects and tools to enrich all levels of the teaching and learning process. One of those educational projects is the *Puerto Rican Heritage Poster Series* and *Study Guide*, a pictographic introduction to the history and contributions of the Puerto Rican diaspora (Acosta-Belén 2012-2013).

As Puerto Rican Studies faculty and Centro researchers were challenging the shortcomings of previous scholarship about the diaspora, a "new Puerto Rican historiography" was emerging among island scholars. These research endeavors were stimulated in part by the establishment of the Centro de Estudios de la Realidad Puertorriqueña (Center for the Study of Puerto Rican Reality—CEREP) in 1970. Recognizing the importance of their respective efforts in decolonizing scholarship on stateside and island Puerto Ricans, Puerto Rican Studies, Centro, and CEREP researchers opened the door to increased collaborations and exchanges that progressively contributed to bridging the previous knowledge gap that had separated the island from its diaspora. In doing so, scholars from both geographic locations have been contributing to the process of restoring a *memoria rota* (truncated memory)—those dispersed or hidden parts of the history of the Puerto Rican people erased, suppressed, or misrepresented by their experiences of coloniality and migration and by official repression or cultural exclusion (Díaz-Quiñones 1993).

Another important research and scholarship milestone was the *Recovering the U.S. Hispanic Literary Heritage Project* (also known as the *Recovery Project*) in 1991, initiated by Puerto Rican literature scholar Nicolás Kanellos. Currently Brown Foundation Professor of Hispanic Studies at the University of Houston, Kanellos, a renowned author of groundbreaking research on U.S. Hispanic theater and immigrant literature (Kanellos 1990, 2011), is also editor of the first comprehensive anthology about the rich Hispanic literary heritage of the United States (Kanellos 2002)—a legacy that originated when the Southwest was still part of the Spanish empire and subsequently the nation of Mexico. Also worthy of recognition is his role as founder and Director of Arte Público Press, a pioneer in publishing and promoting Puerto Rican, Chicana/o, and other Latina/o literatures of the United States. Arte Público has published over 600 books since it was established.

Through the *Recovery Project*, unpublished writings of several Puerto Rican authors or those previously published and rescued from neglected Spanish-language periodicals in New York City dating back to the latter part of the nineteenth and the first half of the twentieth centuries, were collected and reprinted in edited volumes by Arte Público Press. Among these edited collections are the writings of community activist and columnist Jesús Colón (Acosta-Belén and Sánchez Korrol 1993; Padilla Aponte 2001); those of his brother Joaquín Colón López (2002); an unpublished novel, *Firefly Summer* (1996) by librarian and folklorist Pura Belpré; two historical novels, one each about the lives of Inocencia Martínez and Emilia Casanova, both nineteenth-century feminists, abolitionists, and members of the New York City expatriate movement to liberate Cuba and Puerto Rico from Spanish rule (Sánchez Korrol 2018, 2013); a Spanish and English translation edition of Guillermo Cotto-Thorner's 1951 classic novel *Trópico en Manhattan* (Manhattan Tropics) (2019); and the reprinting of out-of-print editions of the creative writings of numerous stateside Puerto Rican authors. Additionally, before he joined the University of Houston, Kanellos was co-founder and co-editor (with Luis Dávila) of the *Revista-Chicano Riqueña* in 1972 (in later years, the *Americas Review*). Until it ceased publication in 1999, this journal was instrumental in stimulating the growth of these literatures and the emergence of a new generation of Latina/o writers, mostly ignored by mainstream publishers until the 1980s. Many of these authors first were introduced to readers by the *Revista* or published their early works with Arte Público Press.

The founding of the Puerto Rican Studies Association (PRSA) in 1992 was a momentous accomplishment in advancing and disseminating new scholarship on the diaspora, and in bringing together stateside and island academics and activists to share their research, creative works, and other educational and community-focused endeavors. Since 2013, in addition to the biennial PRSA conference, a one-day symposium is held during intermittent years, allowing scholars, writers, artists, teachers, students, and advocates from different parts of the country and Puerto Rico to have an added opportunity to engage in scholarly dialogue and networking (Sánchez Korrol 2011-2012). As the founding president of PRSA, Virginia Sánchez Korrol and other Puerto Rican feminist scholars fought for equal representation of women in the leadership of the organization. Since its inception, PRSA has been central to the process of disseminating multidisciplinary knowledge about Puerto Ricans that informs multiple undertakings in the research, teaching, service, and advocacy areas. The impressive body of Puerto Rican Studies scholarship by preceding and more recent generations of researchers, and the aforementioned research entities, attests to the vitality of the field during the last five decades and their enduring contributions in transforming and expanding knowledge about stateside and island Puerto Ricans.

THEORETICAL AND CRITICAL APPROACHES

As early as the 1950s, major critiques of the history and nature of colonialism and the experiences of colonized peoples made the writings of Franz Fanon, Albert Memmi, Aimé Césaire, and others indispensable reading for progressive Puerto Rican scholars of the 1960s and '70s. After World War II, decolonization efforts were driven by the liberation struggles being carried out in many of the colonial territories and by the United Nations' recognition of the fundamental right of peoples to self-determination and the independence of their respective homelands. For the populations of most of these territories, achieving sovereignty was the first step in freeing themselves from the dehumanizing effects of colonial domination and racialization on their minds and identities; that is, the subaltern "otherness" attributed to them by the colonizer. Doing so involved a process of individual learning and collective self-renewal to see themselves through a less distorted mirror. Ashis Nandy (1983) referred to the history of colonialism in India as an "intimate enemy" and a system of domination that involves "the loss and the recovery of self" for both the colonized and the colonizer. For Puerto Ricans, however, envisioning a path to dismantling the political structures of colonial domination in their homeland remains unrealized and is still fraught with hurdles and uncertainties, and far from any clear resolution.

This reality did not deter Puerto Rican scholars from trying to understand their own "loss and the recovery of self" under U.S. colonialism, along with reclaiming the erasures and exclusions in their colonized and diasporic history, and articulating new definitions of self. In fact, during the late 1960s and '70s, those aims became part of a reinvigorated intellectual undertaking for both stateside and island Puerto Ricans. Despite the estrangement that up to that point existed between Puerto Rico and its diaspora, academics, writers, and artists from both sides were gradually able to bridge this gap in subsequent decades. This was due in part to significant growth both in migration from the island and the U.S. Puerto Rican population after the 1970s, but also to the increased levels of productivity and visibility of Puerto Rican Studies scholarship among stateside researchers.

All Puerto Ricans, whether born in Puerto Rico or stateside, are holders of U.S. citizenship and are able to move freely between the island and the colonial metropolis; thus, migration continues to be a persistent and routine occurrence in their lives. The early years of the new millennium began to show how continuing increases in out-migration from Puerto Rico to the United States account for an ongoing decline in the island's population, along with other contributing factors. The latter include Puerto Rico's aging population, the increased life expectancy of its residents, and a decline in fertility rates (Acosta-Belén and Santiago 2018, 134–5). Their combined effect accounts for a new demographic portrait of Puerto Ricans with implications and challenges that will keep researchers and policy makers engaged for the foreseeable future. In the year 2000, Puerto Rico's population was slightly over 3.8 million; by 2019 it had declined to less than 3.1 million. This means that, currently, 5,828,706 (or over 65 percent) of all Puerto Ricans reside stateside (U.S. Census 2019). Behind these population figures and trends is the more conspicuous diasporic condition of old and new generations of Puerto Ricans and what can be learned from their histories of migration and settlement, including their past and present ties to the island and their evolving relationship with U.S. society. As in the Puerto Rican case, "Movement between cultures, languages, and complex configurations of meaning and power have always been the territory of the colonized" (Mohanty 1992, 89).

Throughout the course of its development, a good portion of Puerto Rican Studies scholarship incorporated influences from a substantive corpus of theoretical work. Classic Marxist theory and subsequent contributions to it by twentieth century critical theorists focused primarily on the analysis of class in shaping socioeconomic structures, modes of production, division of labor, and ideologies. Of particular interest were the relations between industrial capitalist nations and previously colonized developing nations, and the presence of (im)migrants of color in their former colonial metropoles. From the 1960s to the present, Marxist, development, world systems, postmodern, postcolonial, feminist, subaltern, queer, cultural, critical race, and decoloniality studies and theoretical paradigms have been among the most prevalent in researching and analyzing the histories, conditions, identities, and subjectivities of populations of color, including women and LGBTQ populations. By and large, these critical theories further advanced the critique of the limitations of Western intellectual traditions and production of knowledge, and the subaltern "otherness" attributed to colonized populations and women. Deconstructing the hierarchical power structures and sources of oppression allowed Puerto Ricans and other subaltern groups to raise their consciousness about the factors that accounted for their marginal status in U.S. society and, in doing so, reconceptualize their stigmatized identities found repeatedly in previous scholarship and the media. For Puerto Ricans and other U.S. populations of color, a crucial aspect of this process was "decolonizing identities, historiographies, and epistemologies" (Pérez 1999; Vélez 2019).

Part of this undertaking was to engage in sustained critiques of the theoretical and methodological deficiencies of prior scholarship, and the analysis of the power structures and relations that shape the production of knowledge at different historical times. The multifaceted body of Puerto Rican Studies research has been critical in uncovering some important historical erasures and exclusions, and in pursuing decolonized knowledge and constructing new imaginaries about the Puerto Rican people. This scholarly output was shaped by an increased consciousness of different forms of oppression that enabled Puerto Ricans (and other subaltern populations) to break away from seeing themselves through the eyes of the colonizer, but rather through a different prism, as historical agents and members of U.S. society with the ability to envision their own strategies of survival and resistance, and pursue their own struggles for social justice. In looking at ways in which the aforementioned critical theories have influenced scholarship in the humanities and social science disciplines during the 1970s and subsequent decades, it is no surprise that a large number of these researchers are, or have been, connected to the interdisciplinary field of Puerto Rican Studies and affiliated fields.

In the early 1980s, a vanguard of Chicana and Puerto Rican feminist writers "came out" in order to relate their individual oppressive experiences as lesbians within the context of their respective social and cultural milieus and as part of families and their communities (Anzaldúa 1987; Moraga and Anzaldúa 1981; Acosta-Belén and Santiago 2018, 250–2). Subsequent pioneering work by Puerto Rican scholars (Asencio 2002; García and Torres 2009; La Fountain-Stokes 2009; La Fountain-Stokes and Martínez-San Miguel 2018; Martínez-San Miguel 1997; Negrón-Muntaner 1994; Ramos 1987; Torres 2002, 2009) focused on how different LGBTQ identities influence the personal, family, and community lives and migration experiences of Puerto Ricans. Initiatives to incorporate the perspectives and contributions of women of color into research, teaching, and the curriculum of ethnic and racial studies programs were also carried out by Puerto Rican feminists. Research and curriculum transformation projects to integrate Puerto Rican women into Puerto Rican Studies were undertaken by feminist researchers stateside and in Puerto Rico (Acosta-Belén 1986; Acosta-Belén and Bose 1991; Acosta-Belén, Bose and Sjostrom 1991; Fiol-Matta and Chamberlain 1994). By and large, most academic disciplines eventually began to adopt mainstream intersectional approaches that viewed class, ethnicity, race, gender, and sexualities as interconnected socially constructed subjective categories of analysis, shaping individual and collective experiences and identities.

During the early stages of Puerto Rican Studies, its interdisciplinary perspectives and approaches to teaching, research, service, and advocacy were molded by the battles against the socioeconomic, racial, educational, and political disparities that led to their implementation. Pivotal to their academic mission was addressing recurrent omissions, implicit biases, and flaws in the basic assumptions of research paradigms used in prior scholarship about Puerto Ricans and other populations of color. Another part of this challenging undertaking was the need to construct and adopt new critical frameworks that more accurately addressed the distinct colonial realities, suppressed histories, and experiences of Puerto Ricans as a socioeconomically marginalized and racialized diasporic population. Eventually, ethnic and racial studies, feminist and LGBTQ studies, and multicultural education initiatives faced a sustained backlash from mainstream Anglo-American educators and pundits making pronouncements about the advent of "the culture wars" and "political correctness," or viewing these programs as divisive and a threat to hegemonic narratives of a presumably unified U.S. nation. Such assertions, however, also carried the enduring implicit denial of the country's long history of unequal treatment, white supremacy, and racial and gender violence against Puerto Ricans and other populations of color.

Theoretical work of recent decades, in the areas of decolonial studies and the construction of decolonial imaginaries, continues to focus on transcending the Euro-centered epistemologies and intellectual traditions and delinking the production of knowledge from Western epistemic authority and its self-proclaimed "civilizing" colonialist role. Additionally, these theoretical approaches give due attention to counter-hegemonic and insurgent knowledges and discourses produced by historically neglected subaltern populations. These approaches have engaged Latin American, Caribbean, and stateside Puerto Rican/Latina/o scholars since the 1990s (Pérez 1999; Negrón-Muntaner and Grosfoguel 1997). What differentiates these critical approaches from previous postcolonial thinking is their focus on lingering dominant power structures and relations introduced by the European colonizing enterprise in the Americas. These included a legacy of social and racial hierarchies imposed upon conquered indigenous and African enslaved populations. Another important difference is an increased reliance on geopolitical locations and local histories in understanding subaltern epistemologies, suppressed modes and practices of producing knowledge, and the ways in which coloniality still impacts the lives of a wide range of these populations.

Decolonial theoretical concepts such as *la colonialidad del poder* [the coloniality of power] (Quijano 1992, 2000, 2014), *la colonialidad del ser* [the coloniality of being] (Mignolo 2000, 2007, 2012; Maldonado-Torres 2007; Mignolo and Walsh 2018), and "the modern colonial gender system" (Lugones 2007) have been influential among academic researchers and activists of color in the United States and other countries of the hemisphere. This is due primarily to the relevance of decolonial thinking to the analysis of the interrelated nature of modernity and coloniality, and their enduring presence in the dominant power structures of contemporary capitalist societies. For those organic intellectuals seeking transformative alternatives to the universality claims of Western epistemologies, it means an exploration of pluriversal decolonial modes of knowledge that transcend traditional academic intellectual circles and validate the collective nature of formulating strategies and projects aimed at advancing social and political change. It also means, as Quijano argues, engaging in a sustained project to contest and subvert those power structures by *vivir adentro y en contra todo el tiempo* [living inside and against at all times] and striving for a constant *revolución epistémica* [epistemic subversion] (2014, 296). Along similar lines, Mignolo (2007) envisions an "epistemic reconstitution" that delinks from "the modern/colonial academic epistemology that permeates our lives beyond the university" (Mignolo and Walsh 2018, 246).

Clearly, the concepts of "coloniality/decoloniality" are of particular import to the production of knowledge and the critical analysis of the contemporary realities of Puerto Ricans, other populations of color, and, in particular, historically neglected sectors such as indigenous and Afro-descendant populations in the United States and the Americas. The importance of decolonial studies to Puerto Ricans and other U.S. ethnic and racial populations was first underscored by Grosfoguel (2008, 2010, 2012) almost a decade ago. At the time, he warned scholars about the dangers of reproducing the "Western Eurocentric fundamentalist epistemology" that could lead to "the disciplinary colonization of ethnic studies" (Grosfoguel 2012, 88). He also introduced an intellectually challenging proposal to redefine ethnic studies as "transmodern decolonial studies." Although Grosfoguel evidently recognized the value of ethnic studies departments/programs and the importance of preserving them, he also envisioned the more transformative possibilities of decolonial thinking:

It would be a different story if ethnic studies departments or programs proposed to open themselves up to transmodernity, that is, to the epistemic diversity of the world, and redefine themselves as "transmodern decolonial studies," offering to think "from" and "with" those "others" subalternized and inferiorized by Eurocentered modernity, offering to define their questions, their problems, and their intellectual dilemmas "from" and "with" those same racialized groups. (2012, 88)

Only time will tell the extent of the influence of decolonial thinking on Puerto Rican Studies. What is clear is that new generations of scholars and activists are intent on creating new alternative spaces and forms of critical engagement, more attuned to and inclusive of other community voices, in addressing issues and conditions that influence or imperil the quality of life of all Puerto Ricans.

CONCLUDING REMARKS

The substantive body of Puerto Rican Studies scholarship and pedagogy focused on the diaspora over the last five decades reveals enduring measures of progress and spirited determination in dealing with past and current challenges. Fifty years ago, the U.S. Puerto Rican population was 1.3 million and there were only about 3.3 percent of Puerto Ricans with some college education or a completed degree. Based on 2018 estimates, the stateside Puerto Rican population has increased since then to about 5.8 million, and about 30.5 percent of Puerto Ricans had some college or AA degree, with 20 percent holding at least a BA degree, and 6.5 percent a graduate or professional degree (Krogstad 2014; U.S. Census 2019). Although this educational progress might be relatively modest when compared to the U.S. white majority population, it also shows that stateside Puerto Ricans are better equipped today to mobilize for collective action towards social and political change than they were in the past. This is true in terms of sheer population growth, which has resulted in a more visible presence in higher education and other spheres, and the continuing research, teaching, and advocacy being done by larger numbers of Puerto Rican Studies faculty and other scholars—whether they are based in the remaining Puerto Rican/Latina/o Studies academic units, or in numerous other disciplinary or interdisciplinary areas found at an array of U.S. universities and in Puerto Rico. Equally important is the increased consciousness and historical memory of the empowering legacies of struggle and survival that Puerto Ricans have forged throughout the course of their long-lasting presence in the United States. Hence, one can only imagine the potential for more encouraging outcomes that these changing realities could eventually bring to the educational, socioeconomic, and political progress of Puerto Ricans.

For Puerto Rican students, and those from other underrepresented cultures and races, the burgeoning of Puerto Rican Studies was their introduction to learning about the understudied or suppressed histories of their respective populations and their particular experiences in and contributions to the nation. In doing so, these programs generally played a critical role in engaging students of all races and cultures. Along with expanding knowledge about their historical roots and identities, and learning what motivated their families and other Puerto Ricans to migrate and settle in the United States, the new field provided students of different backgrounds with opportunities to develop the critical tools to engage in neglected, but necessary, conversations about colonialism, migration, the analysis of class, race, ethnicity, gender, and sexualities, and the intersecting nature of these socially constructed categories.

Of similar importance was enhancing their understanding of the power structures and hierarchies that perpetuated racism, white supremacy, and the inequalities and injustices that contribute to the less privileged status of their communities. In multiple ways, Puerto Rican Studies marks the beginning of a continuing teaching and learning process about the complex and uneasy relationship of Puerto Ricans with U.S. society. The field also became a creative space for Puerto Ricans to see themselves as part of a diaspora that, paradoxically, is to varying degrees connected to and disconnected from both the homeland that their migrant families left behind, and the society they live in. As part of the academy, Puerto Rican Studies added to broader efforts to document and validate the U.S. nation's multicultural and racial diversity, and the study of the histories and cultures of, what were before, mostly overlooked populations. Increased knowledge about the multicultural, racially diverse, and conflictive U.S. history, and the damaging effects of socioeconomic exploitation, systemic racism, and persistent inequities have been crucial in moving forward the quest for social change and the yet to be realized goals of equal rights and justice for all groups. Thus, for Puerto Rican Studies, the significance of their original and evolving mission is still as meaningful today as it was half a century ago.

Meanwhile, the empowering nature of knowledge in strengthening the social and political consciousness of Puerto Ricans is linked to their own legacies of activism against all forms of unequal treatment and ongoing strides for meaningful social, political, and educational changes. In general, during the last five decades, numerous Puerto Rican Studies scholars have produced and continue to revitalize a substantial body of decolonized and decolonial knowledge about stateside and island Puerto Ricans. With their research, they are preserving a long history of prior and current educational, social, and political battles, some of which have yielded emboldening outcomes. Their expanding legacy includes the creation of enduring educational, cultural, and service institutions and establishing vibrant communities in various U.S. cities and states. They continue to document changes and progress within our communities, without ignoring the numerous obstacles and challenges that still persist for a significant number of less privileged Puerto Ricans. Collectively, the survival struggles and accomplishments of the Puerto Rican diaspora now stand as important sources of inspiration for new generations to give continuity to the prior work of researchers, educators, other professionals, and community activists in what is still the unfinished business of moving closer to more equitable achievements in higher education and several other areas. Mindful of protecting the described gradual gains while continuing to surpass them, stateside Puerto Ricans are now more empowered to confront setbacks and persist in moving forward. Passing this burning torch to present and future generations remains an important component of the enduring mission of Puerto Rican Studies.

NOTES

[1] The creation of bilingual education programs was a major outcome of the Puerto Rican and Chicana/o civil rights movements. Congressional approval of the Bilingual Education Act of 1967 made available Title VII federal grants for teacher training and curriculum development projects in this field. Many of the bilingual education teacher training programs were located at higher education institutions that had established Puerto Rican Studies and were the precursors of the multicultural education movement of later years (see Nadal and Morales Nadal in this volume).

[2] Variations of the LGBTQ acronym since its initial use in the mid-1990s have remained fluid through the years. Other sexuality and gender-based identities have been added to this acronym in order to be more inclusive of emerging categories. More recently, the letters I (intersex), A (asexual), and the + sign (to encompass other gender identities and sexual orientations) have been added to a new LGBTQIA+, but the expanded acronym is not yet used with any regularity. As of this writing, most academic publications continue to use the LGBTQ version.

[3] The original Vega manuscript, entitled La familia Farallón, has been in the custody of the Centro de Investigaciones Históricas (CIH) at the University of Puerto Rico for close to a decade. As of this writing, the manuscript is only accessible to CIH affiliated researchers and not available to the general public.

[4] Yarimar Bonilla, a Professor in the Department of Africana, Puerto Rican/Latino Studies at Hunter College and in the Anthropology doctoral program at CUNY's Graduate Center, has been appointed as Centro's Interim Director. She is the first woman to occupy this position.

REFERENCES

Acosta, Ivonne 1987. *La Mordaza: Puerto Rico, 1948-1957*. Río Piedras, PR: Editorial Edil.

Acosta-Belén, Edna, ed. 1986. The *Puerto Rican Woman: Perspectives on Culture, History, and Society*. First edition 1979. New York: Praeger.

_____. 1992. Beyond Island Boundaries: Ethnicity, Gender, and Cultural Revitalization in Nuyorican Literature. *Callaloo* 15 (4), 979–98.

_____. 1993. The Building of a Community: Puerto Rican Writers and Activists in New York City, 1890s-1960s. In *Recovering the U.S. Hispanic Literary Heritage*, eds. Ramón Gutiérrez and Genaro Padilla. 179–95. Houston: Arte Público Press.

_____. 2009. *Haciendo patria desde la metrópoli*: The Cultural Expressions of the Puerto Rican Diaspora. *CENTRO: Journal of the Center for Puerto Rican Studies* 29(2), 49–83.

_____. 2012-2013. *Puerto Rican Heritage Poster Series* and *Study Guide*. New York: Centro de Estudios Puertorriqueños.

_____. et al. 2000. *Adiós, Borinquen Querida: The Puerto Rican Diaspora, Its History, and Contributions*. Albany: CELAC.

Acosta-Belén, Edna and Christine E. Bose. 1991. *Albany PR-WOMENET Database: An Annotated Bibliography on Puerto Rican Women*. Albany: CELAC/IROW.

Acosta-Belén, Edna, Christine E. Bose and Barbara R. Sjostrom. 1991. *An Interdisciplinary Guide for Research and Curriculum on Puerto Rican Women*. Albany: CELAC/IROW.

Acosta-Belén, Edna, and Virginia Sánchez Korrol, eds. 1993. *The Way it Was and Other Writings by Jesús Colón*. Houston: Arte Público Press.

Acosta-Belén, Edna and Carlos E. Santiago. 2018. *Puerto Ricans in the United States: A Contemporary Portrait*. First edition 2006. Boulder: Lynne Rienner Publishers.

Acuña, Rodolfo F. 2011. *The Making of Chicana/o Studies: In the Trenches of the Academy*. New Brunswick, NJ: Rutgers University Press.

Anzaldúa, Gloria. 1987. *Borderlands/La Frontera: The New Mestiza*. San Francisco: Aunt Lute.

Aparicio, Frances. 1997. *Listening to Salsa: Latin Popular Music and Puerto Rican Cultures*. Middletown, CT: Wesleyan University Press.

Asencio, Marysol. 2002. *Sex and Sexuality Among New York's Puerto Rican Youth*. Boulder: Lynne Rienner Publishers.

Belpré, Pura. 1996. *Firefly Summer*. Houston: Arte Público Press.

Bonilla, Frank. 1987. Puerto Rican Studies and the Interdisciplinary Approach. In *Toward a Renaissance of Puerto Rican Studies: Ethnic and Area Studies in Education*, eds. María Sánchez and Anthony Stevens-Arroyo. 15-20. Highland Lakes, NJ: Atlantic Research and Publications.

Bosque Pérez, Ramón and José Javier Colón Morera. 1997. *Las carpetas: persecución política y derechos civiles en Puerto Rico*. Río Piedras, PR: CIPDC.

Burgos, Julia de. 1997. *Song of the Simple Truth: The Complete Poems of Julia de Burgos*. Compiled and translated by Jack Agüeros. Willimantic, CT: Curbstone Press.

Camacho Souza, Blase. 1983. *Boricua Hawaiiana: Puerto Ricans of Hawaii: Reflections of the Past and Mirrors of the Future, A Catalogue*. Honolulu: Puerto Rican Heritage Society of Hawaii.

_____. 1984. Trabajo y Tristeza--"Work and Sorrow": The Puerto Ricans of Hawaii 1900-1902. *Hawaiian Journal of History* 18, 156–73.

Centro Data Brief. 2016. Puerto Ricans in New York, the United States, and Puerto Rico, 2014.<https://centropr.hunter.cuny.edu/sites/default/files/PDF/

STATE%20REPORTS/4.%20NY-PR-2016-CentroReport.pdf>.

Colón, Jesús. 1982. *A Puerto Rican in New York and Other Sketches*. First edition 1961. New York: International Publishers.

Colón López, Joaquín. 2002. *Pioneros puertorriqueños en Nueva York, 1917-1947*. Houston: Arte Público Press.

Cotto-Thorner, Guillermo. 2019. *Trópico en Manhattan/Manhattan Tropics*. Translated by J. Bret Maney. Houston: Arte Público Press.

Cruz, José E. 1998. *Identity and Power: Puerto Rican Politics and the Challenges of Ethnicity*. Philadelphia: Temple University Press.

_____. 2019. *Liberalism and Identity Politics: Puerto Rican Community Organizations and Collective Action in New York City*. New York: Centro Press.

Cruz, Wilfredo. 2004. *Puerto Rican Chicago*. Charleston, SC: Arcadia Publishing.

Data USA. 2019. Puerto Rico/Data USA. <https://datausa.io/profile/geo/puerto-rico/>.

Díaz-Quiñones, Arcadio, 1993. *La memoria rota*. Río Piedras, PR: Ediciones Huracán.

Duany, Jorge. 2002. *The Puerto Rican Nation on the Move: Identities on the Island and the United States*. Chapel Hill: University of North Carolina Press.

Duany, Jorge and Félix Matos-Rodríguez. 2006. *Puerto Ricans in Orlando and Central Florida*. New York: Center for Puerto Rican Studies.

Duany, Jorge and Patricia Silver, eds. 2010. *Puerto Rican Florida*. Special issue of *CENTRO Journal* 22 (1).

Enck-Wanzer, Darrel, ed. 2010. *The Young Lords: A Reader*. New York: New York University Press.

Fernández, Johanna. 2020. *The Young Lords: A Radical History*. Chapel Hill: University of North Carolina Press.

Fernández, Lilia. 2012. *Brown in the City: Mexicans and Puerto Ricans in Postwar Chicago*. Chicago: University of Chicago Press.

Fiol-Matta, Liza and Mariam K. Chamberlain, eds. 1994. *Women of Color and the Multicultural Curriculum: Transforming the College Classroom*. New York: Feminist Press.

Flores, Juan. 1993. 'Qué assimilated, brother, yo soy asimilao': The Structuring of Puerto Rican Identity. In *Divided Borders: Essays on Puerto Rican Identity*. 182–95. Houston: Arte Público Press.

_____. 2000. *From Bomba to Hip-Hop: Puerto Rican Culture and Latino Identity*. New York: Columbia University Press.

_____. 2009. *The Empire Strikes Back: Caribeño Tales of Learning and Turning*. New York: Routledge.

_____. 2016. *Salsa Rising: New York's Latin Music of the Sixties Generation*. New York: Oxford University Press.

García, Lorena and Lourdes Torres. 2009. New Directions in Latina Sexualities. *NWSA Journal* 21(3), vii-xvi.

Glasser, Ruth. 1997. *Aquí me quedo: Puerto Rican Connecticut*. Middleton, CT: Connecticut Humanities Council.

_____. 2005. From 'Richport' to Bridgeport: Puerto Ricans in Connecticut. In *The Puerto Rican Diaspora: Historical Perspectives*, eds. Carmen T. Whalen and Víctor Hernández-Vázquez. 174–99. Philadelphia: Temple University Press.

Glazer, Nathan and Daniel P. Moynihan. 1963. *Beyond the Melting Pot*. Cambridge: MIT Press.

Grosfoguel, Ramón. 2008. Latin@s and the Decolonization of the US Empire in the 21st Century. *Social Science Information* 47(4), 605–22.

_____. 2010. "Colonialidad del poder y dinámica racial: Notas para la reinterpretación de los latino-caribeños en Nueva York." In *Lugares descoloniales: espacios de intervención en las Américas*, eds. Ramón Grosfoguel and Roberto Almanza Hernández. 125–59. Bogotá: Pontificia Universidad Javeriana.

_____. 2012. The Dilemmas of Ethnic Studies in the United States: Between Multiculturalism, Identity Politics, Disciplinary Colonization, and Decolonial Epistemologies. *Human Architecture: Journal of the Sociology of Self-Knowledge* 10(1), 81–90.

Guzmán, Pablo. 1998. La Vida Pura: A Lord of the Barrio. In *The Puerto Rican Movement: Voices of the Diaspora*, eds. Andrés Torres and José E. Velázquez. 155–72. Philadelphia: Temple University Press.

Hernández-Cruz, Juan L. and Clara Muschkin. 1994. *Corrientes migratorias en Puerto Rico/Migratory Trends in Puerto Rico*. San Germán, PR: Universidad Interamericana.

Hernández, Pedro Juan. 2011-2012. The Evolution of Centro's Archives of the Puerto Rican Diaspora, 1973-2012. *Latino(a) Research Review* 8(1-2), 85–100.

History Task Force, Centro de Estudios Puertorriqueños. 1979. *Labor Migration Under Capitalism: The Puerto Rican Experience*. New York: Monthly Review Press.

_____. 1982. *Sources for the Study of Puerto Rican Migration, 1879-1930*. New York: Centro de Estudios Puertorriqueños.

Jiménez de Wagenheim, Olga. 2005. From Aguada to Dover: Puerto Ricans Relived Their World in Morris County, New Jersey. In *The Puerto Rican Diaspora: Historical Perspectives,* eds. Carmen T. Whalen and Víctor Vázquez-Hernández, 106–27. Philadelphia: Temple University Press.

Krogstad, Jens Manuel and Mark Hugo López. 2014. Hispanic Nativity Shift. Pew Research Center, *Hispanic Trends*. <https://www.pewresearch.org/hispanic/2014/04/29/hispanic-nativity-shift>.

Kanellos, Nicolás. 1990. *A History of Hispanic Theater in the United States: Origins to 1940*. Austin: University of Texas.

_____, ed. 2002. *Herencia: The Anthology of Hispanic Literature of the United States*. New York: Oxford University Press.

_____. 2011. *Hispanic Immigrant Literature: El Sueño del Retorno*. Austin:

University of Texas Press.

Kanellos, Nicolás and Helvetia Martell. 2000. *Hispanic Periodicals in the United States: Origins to 1960*. Houston: Arte Público Press.

La Fountain-Stokes, Lawrence. 2009. *Queer Ricans: Cultures and Sexualities in the Diaspora*. Minneapolis: University of Minnesota Press.

La Fountain-Stokes, Lawrence and Yolanda Martínez-San Miguel, eds. 2018. *Revisiting Queer Puerto Rican Sexualities/Revisitando las sexualidades puertorriqueñas queer*. Special issue of *CENTRO: Journal of the Center for Puerto Rican Studies* 30(2).

Lewis, Oscar. 1966. *La Vida: A Puerto Rican Family and the Culture of Poverty-San Juan and New York*. New York: Random House.

López, Iris. 2005. Borinquis and Chop Suey: Puerto Rican Identity in Hawai'i, 1900 to 2000. In *The Puerto Rican Diaspora: Historical Perspectives,* eds. Carmen T. Whalen and Víctor Vázquez-Hernández. 43-67. Philadelphia: Temple University Press.

López, Iris and David Forbes. 2001. Borinqui Identity in Hawai'i: Present and Future. *CENTRO: Journal of the Center for Puerto Rican Studies* 13(1), 110–27.

Lugones, María. 2007. Heterosexualism and the Colonial/Modern Gender System. *Hypatia* 22(1), 186–209.

Maldonado-Denis, Manuel. 1976. *Puerto Rico: A Socio-Historic Interpretation*. New York: Random House.

Maldonado-Torres, Nelson. 2007. On the Coloniality of Being: Contributions to the Development of a Concept. *Cultural Studies* 21(2-3), 240–70.

Martínez-San Miguel, Yolanda. 1997. Deconstructing Puerto Ricanness through Sexuality: Female Counternarratives on Puerto Rican Identity (1894-1934). In *Puerto Rican Jam: Rethinking Colonialism and Nationalism,* eds. Frances Negrón-Muntaner and Ramón Grosfoguel. 127–39. Minneapolis: University of Minnesota Press.

Matos-Rodríguez, Félix V. 2005. Saving the Parcela: A Short History of Boston's Puerto Rican Community. In *The Puerto Rican Diaspora: Historical Perspectives,* eds. Carmen T. Whalen and Víctor Vázquez- Hernández. 151–73. Philadelphia: Temple University Press.

Matos-Rodríguez, Félix V. and Pedro Juan Hernández. 2001. *Pioneros: Puerto Ricans in New York City: 1892-1948*. Charleston, SC: Arcadia Publishing.

Meléndez, Edgardo. 2017. *Sponsored Migration: The State and Puerto Rican Postwar Migration to the United States*. Columbus: Ohio State University Press.

Meléndez, Edwin and Carlos Vargas-Ramos, eds. 2014. *Puerto Ricans at the Dawn of the New Millennium*. New York: Centro Press.

Meléndez, Miguel "Mickey." 2005. *We Took the Streets: Fighting for Latino Rights with the Young Lords*. First edition 2003. New Brunswick, NJ: Rutgers University Press.

Mignolo, Walter D. 2000. The Geopolitics of Knowledge and the Colonial

Difference. *South Atlantic Quarterly* 101(1), 57–96.

————. 2007. The Rhetoric of Modernity, the Logic of Coloniality, and the Grammar of De-Coloniality. *Cultural Studies* 21(2-3), 449–514.

————. 2012. *Local Histories/Global Designs: Coloniality, Subaltern Knowledges, and Border Thinking.* Princeton, NJ: Princeton University Press.

Mignolo, Walter D. and Catherine E. Walsh. 2018. *On Decoloniality: Concepts, Analysis, Praxis.* Durham, NC: Duke University Press.

Mills, C. Wright, Clarence O. Senior and Rose Kohn Goldsen. 1950. *The Puerto Rican Journey: New York's Newest Migrants.* New York: Harper Brothers.

Mohanty, Chandra Talpade. 1992. Feminist Encounters: Locating the Politics of Experience. In *Destabilizing Theory: Contemporary Feminist Debates*, eds. Michele Barrett and Anne Phillips. 74–92. Redwood City, CA: Stanford University Press.

Mohr, Nicholasa. 1989. Puerto Rican Writers in the U.S., Puerto Rican Writers in Puerto Rico: A Separation Beyond Language. In *Breaking Boundaries: Latina Writings and Critical Readings*, eds. Asunción Horno-Delgado, Eliana Ortega, Nina M. Scott and Nancy Saporta Sternbach. 111–6. Amherst: University of Massachusetts Press.

Moraga, Cherrie and Gloria Anzaldúa, eds. 1981. *This Bridge Called My Back: Writings by Radical Women of Color.* Watertown, MA: Persephone Press.

Morales, Iris. 1996. ¡*Palante, Siempre Palante!: The Young Lords.* POV American Documentary Series.

————. 2016. *Through the Eyes of Rebel Women: The Young Lords, 1969-1976.* New York: Red Sugarcane Press.

Nandy, Ashis. 1983. *The Intimate Enemy: Loss and Recovery of Self Under Colonialism.* Delhi: Oxford University Press.

Negrón-Muntaner, Frances. 1994. *Brincando el charco: Portrait of a Puerto Rican* (film). ITVS.

Negrón-Muntaner, Frances and Ramón Grosfoguel, eds. 2008. *Puerto Rican Jam: Rethinking Colonialism and Nationalism.* First edition 1997. Minneapolis: University of Minnesota Press.

Nieves, Falcón, Luis, ed. *El emigrante puertorriqueño.* 1975. Río Piedras, PR: Editorial Edil.

Noble, David. 2002. *Death of a Nation: American Culture and the End of Exceptionalism.* Minneapolis: University of Minnesota Press.

Ortiz, Victoria. 1986. Arthur Schomburg: A Biographic Essay. In the *Legacy of Arturo Alfonso Schomburg: A Celebration of the Past, a Vision for the Future.* 18–117. New York: Schomburg Center for Black Culture.

Padilla Aponte, Edwin Karli, ed. 2001. *"Lo que el pueblo me dice": Crónicas de la colonia puertorriqueña en Nueva York.* Houston: Arte Público Press.

Padilla, Félix. 1985. *Latino Ethnic Consciousness: The Case of Mexican Americans and Puerto Ricans in Chicago.* Notre Dame, IN: University of Notre Dame Press.

_____. 1987. *Puerto Rican Chicago*. Notre Dame, IN: University of Notre Dame Press.

Pérez, Emma. 1999. *The Decolonial Imaginary: Writing Chicanas into History*. Bloomington: Indiana University Press.

Pérez, Gina M. 2004. *The Near Northwest Side Story: Migration, Displacement, and Puerto Rican Families*. Berkeley: University of California Press.

Pérez y González, María E. 2000. *Puerto Ricans in the United States*. Westport, CT: Greenwood Press.

Quijano, Aníbal. 1991. Colonialidad, Modernidad/Racionalidad. *Perú Indígena* 13(29), 11–29.

_____. 2000. Coloniality of Power, Eurocentrism, and Latin America. *Nepantla: Views from South* 1(3), 533–80.

_____. 2014. Presentación de libro *Cuestiones y horizontes* del Dr. Aníbal Quijano. *Yuyaykusun* 7, 279–98.

Ramos, Juanita, ed. 1987. *Compañeras: Latina Lesbians*. New York: Latina Lesbian History Project.

Ramos-Zayas, Ana. 2003. *National Performances: The Politics of Class, Race, and Space in Puerto Rican Chicago*. Chicago: University of Chicago.

Rivera, Eugenio. 2005. La colonia de Lorain, Ohio. In *The Puerto Rican Diaspora: Historical Perspectives*, eds. Carmen T. Whalen and Víctor Hernández-Velázquez. 151–73. Philadelphia: Temple University Press.

Rivera, Raquel Z. 2003. *New York Ricans from the Hip-Hop Zone*. New York: Palgrave.

Rivera, Raquel Z., Wayne Marshall and Deborah Pacini Hernández, eds. 2009. *Reggaeton*. Durham, NC: Duke University Press.

Rodríguez, Clara E. 1989. *Puerto Ricans Born in the USA*. Boston: Unwin Hyman.

Rosario Natal, Carmelo. 1983. *Éxodo puertorriqueño (Las emigraciones al Caribe y Hawaii)*. San Juan: n.p.

Rúa, Mérida M. 2012. *A Grounded Identity: Making New Lives in Chicago Puerto Rican Neighborhoods*. New York: Oxford University Press.

Sánchez González, Lisa. 2001. *Boricua Literature: A Literary History of Puerto Rican Literature*. New York: New York University Press.

_____. 2013. *The Stories I Read to the Children: The Life and Writings of Pura Belpré, the Legendary Storyteller, Children's Author, and New York Public Librarian*. New York: Centro Press.

Sánchez Korrol, Virginia. 1994. *From Colonia to Community: The History of Puerto Ricans in New York City: 1917-1948*. First edition 1983. Berkeley: University of California Press.

_____. 2011-2012. The Birth of an Institution: Multifaceted Prisms of PRSA's Early Years. *Latino(a) Research Review* 8(1-2), 60–72.

_____. 2013. *Feminist and Abolitionist: The Story of Emilia Casanova*. Houston: Arte Público Press.

_____. 2018. *The Season of Rebels and Roses*. Houston: Arte Público Press.

Sánchez Korrol, Virginia and Pedro Juan Hernández. 2010. *Pioneros II: Puerto Ricans in New York City, 1948-1998*, Bilingual Edition. Charleston, SC: Arcadia Publishing.

Seda Bonilla, Eduardo. 1977. Who is a Puerto Rican: Problems of Socio-Cultural Identity in Puerto Rico. *Caribbean Studies* 17(1-2), 105–21.

Senior, Clarence. 1965. *Puerto Ricans: Strangers—Then Neighbors*. Chicago: Quadrangle Books.

Silver, Patricia. 2020. *Sunbelt Diaspora: Race, Class, and Latino Politics in Puerto Rican Orlando*. Austin: University of Texas Press.

Stavans, Ilan, ed. 2011. *Norton Anthology of Latino Literature*. New York: W.W. Norton.

Takaki, Ronald. 1993. *A Different Mirror: A History of Multicultural America*. Boston: Little, Brown Back Bay Books.

Thomas, Lorrin, 2010. *Puerto Rican Citizen: The History and Political Identity in Twentieth-Century New York City*. Chicago: University of Chicago Press.

Toro-Morn, Maura I. 2005. Boricuas in Chicago: Gender and Class in the Migration and Settlement of Puerto Ricans. In *The Puerto Rican Diaspora: Historical Perspectives*, eds. Carmen T. Whalen and Víctor Vázquez-Hernández. 128–50. Philadelphia: Temple University Press.

Torres, Andrés. 2006, ed. *Latinos in New England*. Philadelphia: Temple University Press.

Torres, Andrés and José E. Velázquez, eds. 1998. *The Puerto Rican Movement: Voices of the Diaspora*. Philadelphia: Temple University Press.

Torres, Lourdes. 2002. Becoming Visible: US Latina Lesbians Talk Back and Act Out. *Counterpoints* 169, 151–62.

_____. 2009. Queering Puerto Rican Women Narratives: Gaps and Silences in the Memoirs of Antonia Pantoja and Luisita López Torregrosa. *Meridians* 9(1), 83–112.

U.S. Census Bureau. 2019. Hispanic Heritage Month 2019. Detailed Profile. 2019: ACS 1-Year Estimates Selected Population Profiles, Puerto Ricans. <https://www.census.gov/newsroom/facts-for-features/2019/hispanic-heritage-month.html>.

U.S. Commission of Civil Rights. 1976. *Puerto Ricans in the Continental United States: An Uncertain Future*. Washington, DC: The Commission.

Vázquez Calzada, José L. 1979. Demographic Aspects of Migration. In *Labor Migration Under Capitalism: The Puerto Rican Experience*, ed. History Task Force, Centro de Estudios Puertorriqueños. 223–36. New York: Monthly Review Press.

Vázquez-Hernández, Víctor. 2017. *Before the Wave: Puerto Ricans in Philadelphia, 1910-1945*. New York: Centro Press.

Vega, Bernardo. 1977. *Memorias de Bernardo Vega: Contribución a la historia de la comunidad puertorriqueña en Nueva York*. Edited by César Andreu Iglesias. Río Piedras, PR: Ediciones Huracán.

_____. 1984. *Memoirs of Bernardo Vega: A Contribution to the History of the Puerto Rican Community in New York*. Translated by Juan Flores. New York: Monthly Review Press.

Vélez, Emma. 2019. Women in Philosophy: Why the Decolonial Imaginary Matters for Women in Philosophy. *Blog of the American Philosophical Association* 16 January. Ed. Adriel Trott. <https://blog.apaonline.org/2019/01/16/women-in-philosophy-why-the-decolonial-imaginary-matters-for-women-in-philosophy>.

Vera-Rojas, María Teresa. 2010. Polémicas feministas, puertorriqueñas y desconocidas: Clotilde Betances Yaeger, María Mas Pozo y sus 'charlas feministas en el *Gráfico* de Nueva York, 1929-1930. *CENTRO: Journal of the Center for Puerto Rican Studies* 22(2), 4–32.

_____. 2010-2011. "Alianzas transgresoras: Hispanismo, feminismo y cultura en *Artes y Letras. Latino(a) Research Review* 8(1-2), 175–8.

_____. 2018. *"Se conoce que usted es 'moderna'": lecturas de la mujer moderna en la colonia hispana de Nueva York*. Madrid: Iberoamericana-Vervuert.

Wanzer-Serrano, Darrel. 2015. *The New York Young Lords and the Struggles for Liberation*. Philadelphia: Temple University Press.

Whalen, Carmen T. 2001. *From Puerto Rico to Philadelphia: Puerto Rican Workers and Postwar Economies*. Philadelphia: Temple University Press.

_____. 2006. *El Viaje: Puerto Ricans of Philadelphia*. Charleston, SC: Arcadia Publishing.

Whalen, Carmen T. and Víctor Vázquez-Hernández, eds. 2005. *The Puerto Rican Diaspora: Historical Perspectives*. Philadelphia: Temple University Press.

Young Lords Party and Michael Abramson. 2011. *Palante: Voices and Photographs of the Young Lords, 1969-1971*. First edition, 1971. Chicago: Haymarket Books.

CHAPTER 3

BILINGUAL EDUCATION AND PUERTO RICAN STUDIES: FROM VISION TO REALITY

Antonio Nadal and Milga Morales Nadal

INTRODUCTION

This chapter provides a general overview of the socio-historical events and challenges associated with the struggle for educational equity, language rights, bilingual education, and, shortly thereafter, the fight for the establishment of university programs in the Northeast and Chicago focusing on the U.S., Puerto Rico, and, subsequently, the Puerto Rican and Latinx diasporic communities' history and culture. Within that context, the emphasis will be on policies and practices related to language rights and teaching and learning. The point of departure includes a brief historical summary of the confluence of factors including colonization, immigration, and xenophobia as these have impacted education and language diverse learners[1] in public school systems, in communities, and/or in universities in the U.S. and Puerto Rico.

Through research, advocacy, militancy, transformational teaching, and policy development and implementation, Puerto Rican scholars, community organizers, and activist students played a significant role in developing and fighting to institutionalize bilingual programs as part of a progressive movement where the cultures and histories of the respective language diverse communities would be appreciated, valued, and included in curricula and daily instruction, both in schools and in the universities, through Puerto

Rican Studies. Emerging from the civil rights events of 1968, the organic relationship between bilingual programs and Puerto Rican Studies contributed significantly to new approaches and policies impacting academic achievement and educational equity in our language diverse communities, yet little of this history has been acknowledged or credited to those who fought for these rights for all language diverse children in the U.S. The following explores how the City University of New York (CUNY) served as a stage for the creation and implementation of various innovative academic programs, including: university level cutting edge social, historical, and community-based bilingual courses and instruction; bilingual teacher education and preparation; and bilingual teaching methods and approaches offered by Puerto Rican Studies programs and departments as part of the bilingual teacher preparation and bilingual education programs in U.S. schools.

While more is yet to be done, through bilingual teacher education programs focused on the preparation of prospective educators, and through preparation in a variety of careers where bilingualism is viewed as additive by the broader community via Puerto Rican and Latinx Studies academic units, new and vibrant areas of study, teaching, and learning will continue to contribute to the development of the overall identity, strength, and empowerment of language diverse communities.

THE "MELTING POT" AS A TOOL OF SUPPRESSION OF NATIVE AMERICAN AND OTHER INDIGENOUS LANGUAGES AND CULTURES IN THE UNITED STATES

A widely held perception about the U.S. is that it is a nation of immigrant peoples representing the ethnicities, races, nationalities, and religious backgrounds of the entire world. The concept of the American "melting pot," attributed to an immigrant playwright named Israel Zangwell in 1892, purports to blend, under a common language and a derivative common American culture, the lives and histories of this country's designated "minorities." This ideal belies a history of racial, national, linguistic, religious, and ethnic suppression and conflict that is more characteristic of U.S. development and civilization since its founding (Loewen 1995). There is little mention in archetypical history texts, for example, that prior to the arrival of an Anglo-Saxon population of pilgrim settlers, in what is now the

Northeastern U.S. in the early seventeenth century, who are portrayed as founders of this nation, there already existed a broad array of Indigenous (Native American) and Mexican communities with distinct languages and cultures in various geographic regions in this country. The early settler population was predominantly English speaking, but would subsequently include Dutch, German, and French groups, among others.

In the U.S., the development of the concept of dominant languages evolved and was cemented within religious institutions and utilized as an assimilative tool in public school educational systems stressing English as a *lingua franca* or language of wider communication. Subsequent generations of language diverse communities indigenous to the U.S. and new immigrant and migrant groups have challenged and continue to challenge the "English only" milieu under the banner of language rights as oppressive, discriminatory, and as a denial of educational equity. Educators and some historians have characterized the history of language rights in the U.S. as alternating episodes of benign intolerance and periods of fierce intolerance as this country sought to incorporate and assimilate large numbers of immigrants and migrants through enslavement, conquest, exploitation, and colonization (Baker and Wright 2017). It has been through education, informal and formal schooling, that success in assimilation to an "American" culture, and a corresponding development of a dominant social and cultural ethos of the U.S. as the offspring of Western European values and traditions, has been claimed, and even attained (Baker and Wright 2017). In this respect, education/schooling has played a continuous role in testing the notion that "education is the great equalizer" (Swick 2018).

To that end, the archetypal narrative of American history textbooks has portrayed the U.S. as a land of opportunity for sojourners from other lands, many of whom eventually would be forced to shed their national, cultural, and linguistic ties to their countries of origin while undergoing a process of settlement, acculturation, and assimilation to the integrationist and developing mythology of the so-called American "melting pot" (Loewen 1995). In the early 19th century, religious persecution and economic deprivation in Europe of Protestant sects, and the expansion of trade with the "New World," contributed to an influx of European immigrants from Italy, Germany, Holland, France, Poland, Czechoslovakia, Ireland, and Wales, among other countries.

These immigrants entered a country where more than 300 separate Native American languages and Spanish were already spoken and used for communication. Nevertheless, English was the language gradually substituted as the lingua franca and would eventually be offered as a common linguistic glue purported to facilitate unity among the newly arrived European groups in the expanding northern industrial and manufacturing urban centers of the country. In that early period, extant European languages, such as Spanish, were tolerated as a crutch for quick assimilation.

It was not solely immigrants but also original inhabitants of the North American continent, including those who claimed Indigenous and Native American languages and cultures, who were held to these stipulations. Moreover, the denial of maintaining the language of origin extended to utilizing the acquired English literacy only for purposes of reading religious literature; such was the case in mission schools in the southwest. In the areas of the South, Midwest, and Southwest of the U.S., under the rule of a Catholic Spanish monarchy, church-sponsored and forced conversion by Jesuit and Franciscan sects was the common practice and preferred method to attempt to assimilate the Indigenous youth in mission schools (Baker and Wright 2017). Other missionaries in more localized communities (e.g., Dutch Reform and German Moravian) also utilized their respective languages to promote Christian conversion and teaching (McCarty 2004).

European immigrants entered the initially, and seemingly, tolerant setting of the late 18th and early 19th centuries. Acceptance of school instruction in languages other than English was allowed in several public and private venues, such as in the religious and congregational German-English schools set up by German communities in Ohio, Pennsylvania, Missouri, Minnesota, North and South Dakota, Wisconsin, and Texas. The German-English bilingualism of this period was accepted as a matter of expediency (Crawford 2004) and was not an isolated example, as ethnic mother tongue and English instruction existed in other ethnic-based communities among the Dutch, Danish, Norwegian, Swedish, Hungarian, Italian, Polish, Spanish, French, Russian, and Czech communities (Kloss 1998). The exceptions to this were Benjamin Franklin's anti-German stance in the 1750s, a California state legislature's law mandating English only instruction in 1855, and the ruthless language suppression policies of the Bureau of Indian Affairs in the 1880s.

With U.S. expansion through war, purchase, and occupation during the 19th century, newly acquired territories that would eventually become semi-sovereign entities of the union and referred to as "free" and "slave states," schooling and education came within the purview of a "states' right doctrine," that is, a right granted to the state government to authorize and implement as it saw fit. The issue of a national language did not prevail despite English's growing unofficial status as the nation's lingua franca. This was partially due to factors such as lack of interest by school administrators, isolated schools in rural areas, and ethnic and linguistic homogeneity within an area enabling a permissive attitude to instruction in the immigrant's mother tongue (Baker and Wright 2017).

The U.S. underwent a radical change in the first two decades of the 20th century with regard to language. The apparent permissiveness gave way to the desire to assimilate great masses of diverse communities into that "cauldron" where out of many would come one (*E Pluribus Unum*). The rise in numbers of immigrants whose native language was not English, around the turn of the 20th century, affected a dramatic, persistent change toward language diversity, particularly in the public school systems. Confronted with a teeming enrollment of immigrant children whose first language and cultural identity differed from the Anglo norm, prior tolerance was replaced by xenophobic attitudes. This fear of new foreigners raised the call for greater integration of these new "diverse" immigrants and, most of all, greater assimilation of these newcomers under the banner of Americanization. The results included demands that English be instituted in public and private schools as the sole medium of instruction.

U.S. involvement during the First World War fueled an antipathy toward the German people residing as naturalized citizens of the U.S., and the German language and culture as well. The Nationality Act of 1906 had already required immigrants to speak English as a prerequisite for becoming a naturalized citizen (Baker and Wright 2017). Adding to this social and political environment was a renewed adherence once again to previous legislation and policies such as the Monroe Doctrine of 1823 and the Doctrine of Manifest Destiny, declaring the U.S. as the entitled and hegemonic power of the Western hemisphere, precluding the influence and intervention by any European power in this part of the world.

NATIVISM PROMOTED, AND ENGLISH USED TO AMERICANIZE THE NEW DIVERSE IMMIGRANT POPULATIONS

The end of the 19th century (1898) saw the U.S. exercise its new hemispheric and imperial might in a war against Spain for the occupation and control of the islands of Cuba and Puerto Rico in the Caribbean Sea and the Spanish colonies of Guam and the Philippine islands in the Pacific. Although most of the Spanish-American War was fought in Cuba, with a revolutionary movement led by Cuban rebels against Spain over a thirty-year span, the U.S. wrested military control from the insurgents and took credit for Cuba's liberation. With the signing of the Treaty of Paris in December of 1898, Spain formally recognized a U.S.-brokered Cuban independence and the ceding of Guam and the Philippine islands as U.S. possessions. Puerto Rico was thrown in as war booty by Spain to compensate for U.S. losses in the war (2010). The Puerto Rico situation was significant because the territory had gained a Charter of Autonomy from Spain in November of 1897, which declared it virtually independent from its 400 years of Spanish colonization (Wagenheim and Jiménez de Wagenheim 1996). This short-lived period of political sovereignty has not been overlooked by anti-colonialists. Till this day, many of the Island's residents and many living in the U.S. diaspora continue to advocate for independence despite the U.S. reach into every sector of the economy, culture, and life of the people of Puerto Rico. The American government's influence is felt at every level, regardless of the Island's so-called commonwealth status, or as it is known, Estado Libre Asociado (Free Associated State). Most notably, the Jones Act of 1917, declaring its residents as U.S. citizens, would limit even further the Island's autonomy (Vargas 2002).

The beginning of the 20th century would place the U.S. as an imperial power in the Atlantic and Pacific oceans; simultaneously, an American nativism took hold, strengthening the will to impose a social and cultural vision that could be transmitted by linguistic imposition, within and beyond its borders. By 1923, 34 states of the U.S. had decreed that English must be the language of instruction in all elementary schools, public and private.

Puerto Rico, as a colonial territory of the United States, was a case in point, as it, too, was the focus of a pervasive assimilative thrust impugning its use of Spanish as the native language (Aponte Vázquez 2012). The

Foraker Act (1900) established a civilian government in Puerto Rico and ended a two-year military occupation by the United States. As early as 1901, under the provision of the Supreme Court's *Downes v. Bidwell* case, the decision declared Puerto Rico as belonging to, but not a part of, the United States. This set the pattern for the existing colonial status of the Island under the control of the U.S. Congress and the U.S. presidency. A 1902 colonial policy motivated by the American intention of complete control of the educational system of Puerto Rico purported to make the Island "bilingual" as it conferred "equal" status to the Spanish and English languages (Acosta-Belén and Santiago 2010). The social and cultural firestorm that ensued among Puerto Rico's defenders of a 400-year Spanish language heritage, and an entrenched American educational bureaucracy of U.S. commissioners of education appointed by the president of the United States, would be partially addressed almost fifty years later. With the first ever election of a Puerto Rican governor, Luis Muñoz Marín in 1948, Spanish was formally recognized as the lingua franca and medium of instruction in the Island's schools, and a Puerto Rican commissioner of education was appointed by the Island's governor. An important concession to American authorities was giving English the official and mandatory status of a second language, required from elementary school through university study. Because it constituted a bilingualism enforced by U.S. colonial policy and not developed organically with the consent of the Puerto Rican people, the teaching of English became a major social issue, denounced by many, including the political historian Pedro Aponte Vázquez, as *bilingüismo a la cañona* [bilingualism at gunpoint] (Aponte Vázquez 2012).

Along with the enduring controversy of Puerto Rico's political status, the imposition of English as a language of instruction, with the U.S.' expectation of having it become the language of wider communication, a fierce nationalism of linguistic and cultural resistance in defense of Puerto Rico's Spanish-speaking and literary legacy emerged. A plethora of writings from the Island's intellectuals and cultural critics arose following the post–WWII attempts at modernization, such as the mostly economic initiatives, sponsored by the U.S. government and the Island's colonial leadership, known as Operation Bootstrap. Most notable among the responses to linguistic encroachment on the Island are a collection of award-winning short stories titled *Terrazo* (Homeland), challenging the cultural, political, and colonial presence of the U.S. in Puerto Rico.

In two of the stories, the author, Abelardo Díaz Alfaro, introduces the character of Peyo Mercé, an avuncular and highly esteemed country school teacher assigned to teach English in Puerto Rico's *jíbaro* (peasant) highlands to poverty-stricken children of the area's barrios. Peyo was no friend of the policies and practices of the American educational bureaucracy overseeing the supervision of hastily trained, underpaid teachers, overburdened with teaching English with overly repetitive instructional drills devoid of any meaning and lacking a relationship to the cultural context of the children they were supposed to turn into fluent English speakers of the American idiom (Díaz Alfaro 1947). In the short story, "Peyo Mercé enseña inglés" (Peyo Mercé Teaches English), the character of Peyo is tasked with teaching the children the sounds of common farm animals, such as a rooster. Díaz Alfaro describes the pained expression of the children, barely hiding the dislike of imitating an American rooster's crowing in the morning. "The rooster says cock-a-doodle-do." Amidst laughter and some snickering, the children attempt to imitate Peyo's cued version with their own fractured pronunciation. After an extended chorus of this nonsensical call and response drill, one child tells Peyo in impeccable Spanish, "Maestro, the American rooster may say 'cock-a-doodle-do,' but my Puerto Rican rooster responds 'Qui-quiri-quí.'" The unrestrained laughter of the children at that response, and Peyo's acknowledgement of their clever recognition of an absurd situation, speaks volumes regarding the Spanish-English controversy in Puerto Rico persisting today. While much of the current population may utilize English, Island residents prefer and are often adamant in their preference for Spanish in their daily use of language. In fact, speaking Spanish has been viewed as a cultural stamp of authenticity to demonstrate allegiance to the Puerto Rican linguistic values of the Island's inhabitants.

THE U.S. MAINLAND "RECEIVES" PUERTO RICAN MIGRANTS TO ITS SHORES

The language controversy played out differently on the U.S. mainland during the 1950s and '60s. While economically related policies were instituted to promote a massive migration of Puerto Ricans to United States rural and urban areas, in order to complement Operation Bootstrap, Puerto Rican migrants were held responsible for that engineered displacement and often accused of having a lack of preparedness and willingness to integrate, and less likely to assimilate into the broader U.S. society. As vast numbers of Puerto Ricans crossed the ocean on ships and more so on planes, the fear of Puerto Rican migrants coming to the U.S. in large numbers set the stage for xenophobic attitudes and discrimination impacting their participation and overall success in the country's overwhelmed public school systems. Within largely urban school districts, researchers described a dire situation resulting in Puerto Rican children "put back in their classes so that they are with children who are two or three years younger than they are" (Cordasco 1976, 102). New York City, and its sprawling public education system, the largest in the nation, became the epicenter for the massive Puerto Rican migration to the U.S. post–WWII. The colonial government's creation of a Migration Division, known after 1952 as the Commonwealth Office and sponsored by Puerto Rico's Department of Labor, was an agency set up to both alleviate the social and economic hardships of a programmed displacement of Puerto Rican families and to provide cheap labor for American companies in mainland U.S. cities (Acosta-Belén, Santiago 2010). The brunt and impact of this social and economic policy was acutely felt by the children of migrants. They encountered an education system that was initially both not prepared with the necessary resources to meet their needs and unwilling to successfully advance their education.

American and colonial authorities, from former U.S.-appointed colonial governor Theodore Roosevelt to Muñoz Marín, identified the "problem" of Puerto Rican migrants as a language barrier and focused on Puerto Ricans' purported reluctance to learn English for the purpose of social integration and assimilation (Roosevelt 1937). Puerto Rican children in New York City were placed in what were then called Non-English Programs. The educational arena became an early battleground for a nascent Puerto Rican civic community seeking to right the impression that Puerto Rican children suffered from a language deficit, were immersed in a culture of poverty holding back their achievement, and promoting low school attendance and high drop-out rates (Totti and Matos Rodríguez 2009). The deficit theory was pre-eminent in the New York City Board of Education's *The Puerto Rican Study,* conducted over a five year period (1953-1957), documenting the educational failure of Puerto Rican children in the city's schools and submitting some recommendations for change. Most of the study's recommendations were not implemented at the time, except for the creation of a new teacher category known as the Substitute Auxiliary Teacher (SAT). This new position provided the presence of an additional and bilingual teacher in the "mainstream" classroom to aid Spanish-speaking children in the academic content areas, as well as the process of English language acquisition. While most of the recommendations were not implemented, the study included expert knowledge from professional social scientists and educators in its analysis of the socio-cultural, linguistic, and economic factors shaping the reality of Puerto Ricans in the U.S. (López 2007). The principal investigator and author of *The Puerto Rican Study*, J. Cayce Morrison, sought the advice and counsel of community activists, academicians, parents, and policy makers in formulating a more comprehensive view of the Puerto Rican community in New York and addressing the mistaken and biased expectations of the city's school system *vis à vis* Puerto Rican children. In ways not fully explored in the popular and academic literature on Puerto Ricans in the U.S. during the late 1950s, it set the stage for the intense and ensuing "school wars" of the 1960s and beyond regarding bilingual education, ethnic and racial integration, language rights, and equity in the city's schools. However, the seeds were also planted for some cooperative relationships with universities and communities addressing the preparation of teachers for language diverse students through participation in, for example, workshops with the University of Puerto Rico and with colleges and universities in metropolitan New York and elsewhere (Cordasco 1976).

Various progressive organizations emerged in the early 1960s and '70s. These organizations, with strong leadership, sought to address the neglect and miseducation of language diverse children, particularly of Puerto Ricans. These groups, such as ASPIRA ("aspire" in Spanish), the Puerto Rican Legal Defense and Education Fund (PRLDEF), and the United Bronx Parents, supported language rights and bilingual programs. They proposed policy initiatives designed to empower Puerto Rican children and their communities. Blending research and practice, Drs. Antonia Pantoja, Frank Bonilla, and Francisco Trilla founded ASPIRA, Inc. in 1961 (Reyes 2012). *Aspirantes,* as the student members of ASPIRA were called, "cut their teeth" as young political activists in the local clubs of the city-wide ASPIRA Club Federation. Most notably, these included Digna Sánchez, Fernando Ferrer, and the late Angelo Falcón, all recognized as dynamic, respected leaders in the Puerto Rican/Latinx communities. PRLDEF was founded in 1972 by three young attorneys—César Perales, Victor Marrero, and Jorge Batista—to protect the civil rights of Puerto Ricans. The United Bronx Parents (1966), led by Evelina Antonetty, ensured that the community was engaged in the decisions affecting Puerto Rican children, not only in the Bronx, but in New York City overall.

THE NEED FOR LINGUISTICALLY AND CULTURALLY APPROPRIATE EDUCATIONAL PROGRAMS FOR LANGUAGE DIVERSE CHILDREN IN U.S. SCHOOLS

Meanwhile, in a parallel development, the Cuban exile community founded a bilingual "dual language" model elementary school in Coral Way, Florida, in 1963 for Cuban children as a vehicle for the preservation of their Spanish language and Cuban culture while learning English. Staffed by largely middle-class emigré teachers, already educated and experienced teachers in Cuba, the school served as a model for early bilingual education initiatives in the United States. It also underscored the importance of teacher preparation in the area of native language literacy for successful second language (English) acquisition. Eventually, the authorized federal funding was directed at developing mostly transitional bilingual education programs; federal and state funding for these programs became contingent on the promotion of English language acquisition to the detriment of maintaining native language and literacy. The foremost bilingual educator and author of several multicultural education-centered texts, Sonia Nieto, has suggested that it behooves us to apply a political lens to the contextual development of bilingual education programs, not only with reference to the Cuban experience in bilingual education program development in Florida, but also to the disparate treatment of language diverse communities of color in the U.S., including Native American, Asian, Caribbean, and other Latinx groups (Nieto 1991).

Building on the established legal framework related to language rights and the needs of language diverse children, within the context of the powerful civil rights movements in the 1960s, the Puerto Rican community asserted its presence in the struggles for empowerment and social justice in the forms of demanding bilingual-bicultural education programs, as well as access and equity in the university. Many Puerto Rican activists, and allies from other language diverse communities, in addition to civil rights activists and educators, favored a position in support of learning English while maintaining native language fluency. Two very important court decisions became harbingers of this modern movement toward bilingual education ultimately flowering in the 1960s and '70s. The first took place, decades earlier, in California--the *Méndez vs. Westminster* landmark case of 1947; the other involved the Supreme Court decision in *Brown vs. the Board of Education of Topeka, Kansas* in 1954. In the former case, a federal circuit court held that school segregation itself is unconstitutional and violates the 14th amendment. The rulings in the Méndez case, in addition to other cases, were used as building blocks for challenging the "separate but equal" doctrine previously enshrined in the Supreme Court's decision in *Plessy vs. Ferguson* of 1896 (Strum 2010). Significant in both cases was the involvement of organizations across racial and ethnic lines, such as the National Association for the Advancement of Colored People (NAACP), and the League of United Latin American Citizens (LULAC) founded in 1929 to represent the civil rights of Mexican-American citizens in the South and Southwest.

These community-based efforts would serve as a prelude to the rise of Mexican-American student groups in the 1960s, focusing mainly on schooling and identity, but also on economic and political self-determination. The creation of Young Citizens for Community Action evolved into the Brown Berets in Los Angeles in 1966 as a powerful and organized force within the Chicanx movement. Their 13-point political program encompassed issues such as housing, land return, open borders, environmental preservation, and, of paramount importance, bilingual education, among others. "To the extent that 'El Movimiento' (The Movement) espoused bilingual education, it was always with connection to the broader race radical political economic project of self-determination as tied to alleviating inequality, exclusion, segregation, racism, and poverty. Bilingual education was never meant to be isolated from the structural racism and material oppression that needed to be alleviated in the larger U.S. society, as well as in schools. The same was true for the other large Latino community of the 1960s–Puerto Ricans in New York" (García and Ka Fai Sung 2018, 5).

Organized groups, such as NAACP and LULAC, mentioned earlier, helped to foster more radical organizations, such as the Black Panther Party in Oakland, California (1966); the Young Lords Organization in the Midwest and the Northeast (1968-1969); La Raza Unida Party in the Southwest (1970), and student activist groups throughout the U.S. Within the context of a highly radicalized anti-Vietnam War movement, and the newly energized civil rights struggle of African-Americans throughout the 1960s and '70s, the movement for Puerto Rican independence from the United States was also embraced by many young college students, particularly in the Northeast.

Recognition of the dearth of academic literature and socio-historical information regarding language diverse communities created a new aware-ness in the Latinx community with respect to the civil and human rights of Puerto Rican and Chicanx communities. Concomitant to the unleashing of these developing social forces and movements were legislative government initiatives responding to citizens' demands for educational equality under the law. Education once more became a focus, particularly among college age activist youth and communities of color throughout the country and gave way to the struggle for open admissions (accessibility to senior colleges in the CUNY system). Organizations such as ASPIRA, United Bronx Parents, the Puerto Rican Legal Defense and Education Fund, and the Mexican-American Legal Defense and Education Fund (1973) contributed to the artic-ulation of demands focused on educational equity in the Puerto Rican and other language diverse communities. These community-based advocates, along with researchers from academia, and progressive activists, worked in collaboration with leaders from the Black community and were joined by allies from different racial and ethnic backgrounds. They were instrumental in the modification of the Elementary and Secondary Education Act (ESEA) of 1965, leading toward the adoption of the federal Bilingual Education Act (1968) (BEA) under Title VII. The BEA itself was preceded by Senator Ralph Yarborough's amendment to the ESEA in 1967 with the intent "to provide assistance to local educational agencies in establishing bilingual American education programs, and to provide certain other assistance to promote such programs" (Cordasco 1976, 63). His initiative served to recognize the educational neglect of both Mexican-American and Puerto Rican children in U.S. schools, which was pivotal to the legislation since the children were a by-product of conquest and made U.S. citizens without prioritizing the teaching of the English language. While Yarborough was a Democrat from Texas, the bill was co-sponsored by Senators Jacob Javits and Ted Kennedy from New York. Nonetheless, it was a reluctant Congress that supported funding for the program. The funding focus was on schools with a high concentration of children of limited English-speaking ability and family income of less than $3,000 a year. Activities supported by the funding were to include "history and culture related to the student's background, parental involvement, and provision for pre-school and adult education programs related to bilingual education" (Cordasco 1976, 65).

Of critical importance to the growing activism, particularly in New York communities, was the impact of civil rights legislation, such as Title VI of the Civil Rights Act of 1964, which prohibited the denial of federal assistance on the grounds of race, color, or national origin (Ochoa 2016). Other court battles throughout the U.S. gave rise to an even stronger advocacy for providing educational opportunities to language diverse students. In the Supreme Court's ruling of 1974, known as *Lau vs. Nichols*, the court affirmed the government's authority to support and provide meaningful programs to language diverse students. The Lau decision involved a class action suit filed in California by 1,800 Chinese students claiming they did not understand the instruction of their English-speaking teachers, therefore denying them equal educational opportunity (Ochoa 2016). *The Lau Remedies* of 1975 spelled out approaches and methods for the teaching of English language acquisition skills and the assessment of language diverse children. While there were several other court cases pending throughout the country focusing on the language rights of language diverse children in school systems, it was in the 1974 case of *ASPIRA of New York, Inc.* and *ASPIRA of America, Inc. vs. the New York City Board of Education,* where PRLDEF sued and won a ruling resulting in a mandated Consent Decree to address related issues of assessment, instruction, and resources for students who spoke predominantly Spanish. In addition to identifying students by their surnames and a Home Language Survey, instructional materials in their native language were to be provided. Specific approaches and programs were to enhance the academic performance of language diverse children, in addition to addressing high levels of truancy and drop-out rates.

EDUCATIONAL PROGRAMS DESIGNED WITH LANGUAGE DIVERSE CHILDREN AND ADULTS IN MIND

Additional bilingual school models emerged out of the late 1960s and early '70s, calling for fundamental change in educational programs for language diverse students and a more equitable approach to their teaching and learning. P.S. 25 in New York's Bronx School District 7 was led by a Puerto Rican principal, Hernán La Fontaine, who included innovative curriculum developers and bilingual multicultural scholars and practicing teachers in his administration. Among them were Professors Sonia Nieto and the late Herminio Vargas, who together with Carmen Dinos and the former Chairperson of Puerto Rican Studies, the late María Sánchez, contributed to the development of the Bilingual Teacher Education Program at Brooklyn College, CUNY. The program continues to this day, shared by the School of Education and the Department of Puerto Rican and Latino Studies (PRLS), and produces about 75 percent of the bilingual education teachers in the borough of Brooklyn.

This bilingual program model was purposefully comprehensive, as its advocates sought to contribute to a strong national Puerto Rican and Latinx identity and the educational success and empowerment of future generations of Latinx students. It was inspired and initially led largely by a steering committee of activist students and faculty within the Brooklyn College Institute of Puerto Rican Studies, and sought to address the instructional needs of language diverse children by supporting language teaching in the native language (Spanish) and in the target language (English), while ensuring a culturally relevant environment through music, art, and food. Stressing the value of two languages as a benefit to the development of the children, community members were engaged and provided a familial atmosphere affirming the children's language and histories.

As part of the Institute of Puerto Rican Studies' stated mission to extend its work on education, culture, and language, the Centro de Educación Para Adultos (Center for Adult Education) was created in 1972 to provide training for the acquisition of the Spanish version of the high school equivalency diploma for migrant and immigrant adults who were dominant Spanish speakers. This program was staffed by bilingual Puerto Rican and Dominican Brooklyn College students, mostly education majors, under the direction of the Institute's assistant director, Antonio Nadal, who developed the curricular structure, lesson plans, and assessment instrument. Funds for the student teachers/tutors came largely from the college's Federal Work-Study Program. The Institute, with the collaboration of the faculty of the newly formed Department of Puerto Rican Studies (PRS) in 1970, under the leadership of its founding chair, Josephine Nieves, and the curriculum advisor, program developer, instructor, and long-time community activist, Julio Morales, addressed the needs of student parents of young children by opening a bilingual day care center (La Escuela Infantil Bilingüe) in 1973, the first in the CUNY system. It would service children of preschool age (3-5 years old) with a bilingual curriculum, inclusive of the teaching and learning of both Spanish and English and of the history and culture of the students. The curriculum was developed primarily by Sonia Nieto, a full-time faculty member of the Department of PRS. The native language and culture of children and adults in these programs were viewed as underpinnings of culturally responsive and relevant academic content that was being developed by local educators and scholars from Puerto Rico, living/working in the U.S., committed to the early demands of student activists for strong academic programs that integrated the students' native language; the culture and history of Puerto Rican and Latinx students; commitment to activist service in the community; and a conscious effort to create awareness of the issues of race, class, ethnicity, and gender. Taken together, the implementation of programs along these lines was expected to raise awareness about individual and collective identities of youth from diverse linguistic backgrounds.

THE ROLE OF PUERTO RICANS IN BILINGUAL EDUCATION: ACHIEVEMENTS AND CHALLENGES

The battleground of New York City's schools was characterized by issues of racial and ethnic integration, as well as language rights, as they pertained to models of bilingual education within the spectrum of federally mandated transitional versus native language maintenance approaches. The issue of bilingual education and mother tongue maintenance was buttressed by the creation and research of the CUNY Center for Puerto Rican Studies at Hunter College (El Centro founded in 1973) via its Language Policy Task Force. Its pioneering research uniting the efforts of local school districts with nascent bilingual (Spanish-English) programs focused on language use in its sociocultural, sociolinguistic, and psycholinguistic realms (Pedraza 1987). El Centro's work gave additional impetus to the study of bilingualism and bilingual education in various Puerto Rican Studies departments/programs in CUNY during the early 1970s. The decade of the 1980s would see the development of a CUNY Bilingual Council led by Professors Ofelia García and Ricardo Otheguy. Several colleges in the CUNY system, such as Hostos and Kingsborough Community Colleges and Lehman and Brooklyn Colleges, among others, had developed programs of university level bilingual course instruction in Spanish with an English as a Second Language component (ESL) for a burgeoning population of Spanish dominant undergraduates enrolled under CUNY's Open Admissions and other college access programs, such as College Discovery, SEEK (Search for Elevation, Education, and Knowledge), and EOP (Educational Opportunity Program). However, continued vigilance over hard-won language rights has required ongoing stalwart advocacy and monitoring, not only at the university level, but also with regard to the implementation of the ASPIRA Consent Decree with its impact on school-age children within New York City schools.

Among the pioneers who continue to express commitment to bilingual education as a tool for educational advancement for language diverse communities, and as an asset for careers in local and international spheres, is Luis Reyes, currently a Member-at-Large for the New York State Department of Education Board of Regents, and founder and chairperson of the NYC Board of Education's Latino Commission on Educational Reform (1990). Along with attorney César Perales, co-founder of PRLDEF (now renamed Latino Justice-PRLDEF) both have been ceaseless in their determination to ensure the civil and human rights of language diverse communities.

The intersectionality of race, class, gender, sexual orientation, ethnicity, and language serve as prisms to observe and study the implementation of educational initiatives and programs related to the Puerto Rican community. It is within Puerto Rican and Latinx studies, as well as other ethnic studies programs, that language rights and educational equity have been protected (Nieto 1987). The challenges to bilingual education policies and programs continue as the nativist and xenophobic flames of intolerance toward diverse communities are fueled by present governmental policies and practices encouraging walls instead of open roads and paths to success for all, regardless of differences.

Bilingual educators and activists in the decades-old struggle for language rights and its relevance to academic success and achievement cannot underestimate the impact that the Puerto Rican community, and all who have actively committed to programs of native language maintenance in schools, has had on the development of the research literature, programs, and policies, which undergird many of the bilingual-bicultural curricular innovations at the various levels of the educational ladder. Whether at the preschool level, in adult education programs, or in teacher preparation at the university level, the offering of these kinds of programs throughout the Northeast and Chicago grew out of the lived experiences, knowledge, activism, and commitment of Puerto Rican and other activist students, as well as progressive educators and community members, who understood Frederick Douglass' oft-quoted phrase, "Power concedes nothing without a demand."

Student diversity, reflecting communities of color in the universities, resulted from activist organizing. It was through the articulation of demands that the universities began programs to recruit people of color and to address the educational needs of Puerto Ricans and other Latinx students. One particular demand from students at City College of New York and Brooklyn College was that the Spanish language and Puerto Rican culture and history courses become part of the curriculum for education majors who would be working with Puerto Rican children in the NYC Board of Education system (Biondi 2012; City University of New York Board of Higher Education 1969). Without the demands for change, the qualitative changes and reforms, as well as the academic units emanating from them, would not have been achieved. This is a result of the efforts of Black, Puerto Rican/Latinx, Native American, Jewish, and Asian civil rights activists and communities, as well as Anglo allies. Since then, while public universities and other institutions claim to support and advocate for human and civil rights, experience has shown that they will retract that support and resources as funding priorities are set by those who are at the table.

In recent times, the COVID-19 pandemic; high levels of unemployment; lack of compassionate concern by a neglectful and, oftentimes, hostile federal administration; and climatic disasters have contributed to a complicated period of struggle where issues of race and racism have finally been brought to the forefront, causing for a much needed focus on how this impacts the normal state of affairs in educational institutions in the U.S. and in Puerto

Rico. However, a competing narrative has arisen. Backlash to ethnic studies and bilingual programs has recently come from the Executive Branch of the U.S., which in September 2020 called for a Commission on Patriotic Education. The critical and authentic research among bilingual and multicultural educators often continues to be criticized or sidelined as contributing to linguistic "balkanization" or divisiveness, contrary to the goals of assimilation or Americanization (Fishman 2014). It is not yet clear if a new federal administration may address the contending narrative.

As the Puerto Rican community recognizes and affirms the leadership of African Americans in the struggle for civil and human rights in the U.S., and continues its support and development of ethnic studies programs, including those focused on Latinx, Native American, Mexican-American/Chicanx, and Asian students, there is ongoing suppression of earlier gains. These gains include voting rights, gender-related policies, policing reforms, educational equity and integration, and language rights. With respect to language rights, whereas middle- and upper-class Anglo-Americans support the cognitive benefit of raising their children bilingually, this support is not always present in the provision of tax dollars that would enhance the education of poor and first-generation immigrant children and lead to their empowerment (Nadal 2018). To that end, current school demographics tell the story of an even more diverse population. As departments of Puerto Rican Studies have intentionally adapted curricula to reflect the histories and cultures of the large numbers of other Latinx and language diverse students from other countries, so have bilingual programs. Despite a national educational system that is not necessarily geared to accept or accommodate the intersections of language, race, class, gender, sexual orientation, and ethnicity that students represent, the interdisciplinarity of Puerto Rican and Latinx Studies, bilingual studies research, and bilingual teacher education programs are evident in their present-day articulations across the multi-layered system.

Changes in the Latinx population of the U.S. and its relevance to the dynamics of language usage and interaction in a diverse and multifaceted form of emerging bilingualism have led to new and innovative research in not only how language is learned and acquired, but how language is done in daily interactions by communities of speakers. Since inception, bilingual teacher education personnel in Puerto Rican and Latinx programs and departments have advocated for a philosophy of bilingual maintenance. This is evident in the more recent socio-linguistic research literature regarding varieties within standardized languages. While school systems adopt and utilize Standard American English as the preferred and privileged language to be acquired among recent immigrants for whom English is the target language, Latinx researchers have posited that what is called for is a newer approach of translanguaging which takes into account how languages interact in the emergent bilingual.

This perspective was described by Latinx researchers as a "unitary linguistic competence—that is, the two languages of a bilingual are not separate linguistic systems but manifestations of acts of deployment and suppression of linguistic features (words, sounds, rules) that society assigns to one or another language. Their language practices are never just additive but inherently dynamic, as bilingual learners use their developing unitary linguistic repertoire to make meaning and adapt to their socio-linguistic context" (Sánchez, García and Solorza 2017, 2; García 2009; Otheguy, García and Reid 2015). This would serve to highlight the particular and idiosyncratic language use of our children. Inherent in this newer research is our communities' thrust in favor of ensuring that language diverse children are appreciated and valued for their linguistic and cultural knowledge and skills as they seek to integrate equitably into the current educational system.

Dual language programs are often offered as a promising way for language diverse children to interact with English-speaking monolingual children, and sometimes are considered "boutique" programs. These programs have been offered to families whose children are English dominant with the promise of developing young bilingual speakers. However, Latinx researchers have posited that the bilingual aspect has been left out, as the assessment of success in these programs is generally geared toward Standard American English language acquisition within the language diverse population at the expense of the native language.

With regard to the changing demographics of language diverse students, including the lower numbers of Puerto Rican students in the public schools of New York City, the attitude and practice towards inclusiveness already implemented in the bilingual-bicultural programs sharing the progressive original goals of the educators and activists of the 1960s will prevail. There are movements evolving in the U.S. and in Puerto Rico from an ongoing dialogue and actions taken among the caretakers of the original Puerto Rican Studies and bilingual education programs for which the goal continues to be the empowerment of language diverse communities. Nonetheless, challenges persist.

Presently, the Latinx population of the U.S. surpasses 60 million (Noe-Bustamante, López and Krogstad 2020). Two thirds are of Mexican origin; the remaining third is mainly Puerto Rican, Central and South American, and a growing number of Dominicans and Haitians from the Caribbean. These are viewed as posing an enormous challenge to large, urban educational districts that are not pedagogically nor financially supported by state budgets. Puerto Rican and Latinx bilingual educators and advocates continue to raise equality and equity in education as part of the civil rights of the newer populations. In fact, there continue to be efforts to roll back the gains of community activists, educators, and liberal politicians of the reformist era of the 1960s. Yet, the voices of our younger population of language diverse students have been expressed in recent demonstrations, including Black Lives Matter, and calls have been made for greater resources afforded to PRLS and ethnic studies in general. CUNY's first chancellor of color, Félix Matos-Rodríguez, was appointed in 2019. Among his set of priorities is a focus on ethnic studies. Along those lines, in 2020, CUNY received a $10 million Mellon grant, the largest ever to CUNY, advancing its programs in Black, race, and ethnic studies and the humanities. Although experience has shown it is unlikely to be sustained, perhaps ethnic studies and bilingual teacher education programs will gain some traction even in the midst of a fiscal crisis.

CONCLUSION

At the moment of this writing, the U.S. is undergoing a period of social transformation fomented by a global pandemic that has shaken fundamental civic and political institutions, as they pertain to racial, ethnic, gender, sexual orientation, language representation, and the empowerment of the most vulnerable in a persistently racially and economically stratified U.S. society. Social institutions continue to be undergirded by an economic, social, and political system that disproportionately excludes and disenfranchises communities of color. Indeed, the educational issues of multiculturalism and diversity that ensued in the political narrative of the 1960s, counterposed to the "melting pot" metaphor of assimilation into a unified *E Pluribus Unum* American culture, ruled the civic and educational dialogue of the time. In many ways, this narrative has once more come to bear on the events being portrayed by activists of a renewed civil rights movement, questioning the very foundations and language of the "founding fathers" credited with forging an American republic. The advent of almost instant communication via social media and a more informed populace, cognizant of the successful actions of past leaders and organizers, have given impetus to this new generation. Building on past achievements of the elders and no longer willing to accept intolerance, mythical assimilation, and the status quo, a multiethnic and multicultural activist cohort has arisen. Mostly under the banner of Black Lives Matter, and despite the pandemic, young, progressive activists have taken to the local streets and into the voting booths around the country. The elders are finally witnessing the realization of the intersectionality of race, ethnicity, gender, class, sexual orientation, and language coalescing in a new movement. The more than half a century existence of bilingual education programs and Puerto Rican Studies has evolved. However, the original values and goals inclusive of committed research, advocacy, militancy, transformational teaching and learning, and the organic links with community are evident within the current discourse. The struggle for the language rights of all, but particularly the Spanish language diverse communities, continues.

While some may question whether or not bilingual education programs and PRLS will prevail, it appears the answer is in the affirmative.[2] The persistent need for bilingual education and the qualitative differences effected by the Puerto Rican community, scholars, authors, and activists of more than 50 years ago, and the persistence of Puerto Rican Studies' original values and goals, have impacted new generations from kindergarten through the university who are ready to take the reign of areas of study that are critical to the social well-being and educational success of current language diverse students and the larger community. Scholar-activists, focused on the juncture of bilingual education and the role of Puerto Rican Studies to prepare the bilingual educators of the future, appreciate the great commitment made by the elders and are encouraged by the work of the current generation, which has come to understand the essentiality of how the dynamics of language, history, and culture converge to define and empower language diverse communities.

ACKNOWLEDGMENTS

The authors want to acknowledge the comments and suggestions contributed by Dr. Deborah Norat, a retired bilingual educator and administrator in the NYC Department of Education, to this chapter.

NOTES

[1] Children for whom English is considered a second language and the language to be acquired, will be referred to as "language diverse". This term includes students labeled as emergent bilinguals.

[2] The founders of the Bilingual Teacher Education Program at Brooklyn College (see "Educational Programs Designed with Language Diverse Children and Adults in Mind" earlier in this essay), including activist students, understood the significance of ensuring that all students be required to be taught what is being referred to as a culturally and linguistically responsive and sustaining curriculum that affirms their cultural identities. To that end, they developed it in partnership with PRLS so that the cultural, historical, and linguistic needs of the students would be met. Currently, the impetus for including ethnic studies in secondary school curricula (many states have moved in this direction, including Arizona, California, Connecticut, Illinois, Massachusetts, New York, Rhode Island, Texas, and Washington) has been met with approval by some and disinterest or controversy by others. However, relevant literature and corresponding research supporting the inclusion of ethnic studies in the high school is already extant, particularly as it relates to policies and practices in California, Texas, and New York. It appears that the ongoing need for preparing teachers to implement new curricula will center ethnic studies and give rise to new materials and resources required to prepare educators to implement the new courses. Within the CUNY system, a cursory review of CUNY bilingual teacher education programs reveals that most campus teacher education programs already require credit in ethnic studies.

REFERENCES

Acosta-Belén, Edna and Carlos Santiago. 2010. *Puerto Ricans in the United States: A Contemporary Portrait*. New York: Lynne Rienner Publishers.

Aponte Vázquez, Pedro. 2012. *Bilingüismo y lucha de clases: análisis de la enseñanza del inglés en Puerto Rico*. San Juan: Publicaciones René.

Baker, Colin and Wayne E. Wright. 2017. *Foundations of Bilingual Education and Bilingualism*. UK: Short Run Press, Ltd.

Biondi, Martha. 2012. *The Black Revolution on Campus*. California: University of California Press.

Cordasco, Francesco. 1976. *Puerto Rican Children in Mainland Schools: A Source Book for Teachers*. New York: Barnes & Noble.

City University of New York Board of Higher Education. 1969. Minutes of 9 May.

Crawford, James. 2004. *Educating English Learners: Language Diversity in the Classroom*. Fifth edition. Los Angeles: Bilingual Education Services, Inc.

Díaz Alfaro, Abelardo. 1947. *Terrazo*. Rio Piedras, PR: Editorial Edil.

Fishman, Joshua A. 2014. Three hundred Plus Years of Heritage Language Education in the U.S. In *Handbook of Heritage, Community, and Native American Languages in the United States: Research, Policy, and Educational Practice*, eds. Terrence G. Wiley, Joy Kreeft Peyton, Donna Christian, Sarah Catherine K. Moore and Na Liu. 36–44. Washington D.C. and New York: Center for Applied Linguistics and Routledge Press.

García, Ofelia. 2009. *Bilingual Education in the 21st Century: A Global Perspective*. Malden, MA: Whiley/Blackwell.

García, Ofelia and Kenzo Ka Fai Sung. 2018. Critically Assessing the 1968 Bilingual Education Act at 50 Years: Taming Tongues and Latinx Communities. *Bilingual Research Journal* 41(4), 318–33.

Kloss, Heinz. 1998. *The American Bilingual Tradition*. Washington, DC: Center for Applied Linguistics and Delta Systems.

Loewen, James W. 1995. *Lies My Teacher Told Me*. New York: New Press.

López, Madeleine E. 2007. Investigating the Investigators: An Analysis of the Puerto Rican Study. *CENTRO: Journal of the Center for Puerto Rican Studies* 19(2), 61–85.

McCarty, Teresa L. 2004. Dangerous Difference: A Critical Historical Analysis of Language Education Policies in the U.S. In *Medium of Instruction Policies: Which Agenda? Whose Agenda*, eds. James W. Tollefson and Amy B.M. Tsui. 71–93. Mahwah, NJ: Lawrence Erlbaum.

Nadal, Antonio. 2018. Not a White Paper. Contributor to unpublished manuscript. Alliance for Puerto Rican Education and Empowerment (APREE). <https://www.apree.org/publications/>.

Nieto, Sonia. 1987. Puerto Rican Studies and Bilingual Education. In *Toward a Renaissance of Puerto Rican Studies: Ethnic and Area Studies in University Education*, eds. María E. Sánchez and Antonio M. Stevens-Arroyo. 37–41. Highland Lakes, NJ: Atlantic Research and Publications, Inc.

Nieto, Sonia. 1991. *Affirming Diversity: The Socio-Political Context of Multicultural Education*. Philadelphia: Routledge Press.

Noe-Bustamante, Luis, Mark Hugo López, and Jens Manuel Krogstad. 2020. U.S. Hispanic Population Surpassed 60 Million in 2019, but Growth Has Slowed. Pew Research Center 7 July. <https://www.pewresearch.org/fact-tank/2020/07/07/u-s-hispanic-population-surpassed-60-million-in-2019-but-growth-has-slowed/>.

Ochoa, Alberto. 2016. Recognizing Inequality and the Pursuit of Equity Framework. In *Latino Civil Rights in Education: La lucha sigue*, eds. Anaida Colón Muñiz and Magaly Lavadenz. 24–46. New York: Routledge Press.

Otheguy, Ricardo, Ofelia García and Wallis Reid. 2015. Clarifying Trans-languaging and Deconstructing Named Languages: A Perspective from Linguistics. *Applied Linguistics Review* 6(3), 281–307.

Pedraza, Pedro. 2016. Memoirs of *El Centro*: The Impact of the Civil Rights Movement in Higher Education. In *Latino Civil Rights in Education: La lucha sigue*, eds. Anaida Colón Muñiz and Magaly Lavadenz. 88–99. New York: Routledge Press.

Pedraza, Pedro and Melissa Rivera. 2005. *Latino Education: An Agenda for Community Action Research*. National Latino Education Research and Policy Project. Mahwah, NJ: Lawrence Erlbaum Associates.

Reyes, Luis. 2012. Minding/Mending the Puerto Rican Pipeline in New York City. *CENTRO: Journal of the Center for Puerto Rican Studies* 25(2), 140-59.

Roosevelt, Theodore. 1937. *Colonial Policies of the United States*. Garden City, NY: Doubleday, Doran and Company, Inc.

Sánchez, María Teresa, Ofelia García and Cristián Solorza. 2017. Reframing Language Allocation Policy in Dual Language Bilingual Education. *Bilingual Research Journal* 41(1), 37–51.

Strum, Phillipa. 2010. *Mendez vs. Westminster: School Desegregation and Mexican-American Rights*. Kansas: University Press of Kansas.

Swick, David M. 2018. *The Great Equalizer*. New York: Hachette Audio.

Totti, Xavier and Félix V. Matos Rodríguez. 2009. Activism and Change Among Puerto Ricans in New York, 1960's and 1970's. *CENTRO: Journal of the Center for Puerto Rican Studies* 21(3), 1–7.

Vargas, Herminio. 2002. *Language and the American Education of Puerto Ricans*. San Juan: Ex Libris Corp.

Wagenheim, Kal and Olga Jiménez de Wagenheim, eds. 1996. *The Puerto Ricans: A Documentary History*. Princeton, NJ: Markus Wiener Publishers.

CHAPTER 4

FIVE DECADES OF PUERTO RICAN STUDIES: INFLUENCES ON SOCIOLOGY AND ALLIED SOCIAL SCIENCES

Christine E. Bose

INTRODUCTION

Puerto Rican Studies has influenced the discipline of sociology and allied social sciences. This essay begins by describing the importance of interdisciplinary contributions to sociological research, emphasizing how the concept of intersectionality has furthered sociology's connections with various interdisciplinary studies. The next several sections are organized chronologically beginning with the nascent linkages between sociology and studies about Puerto Ricans, covering the 1940s through the 1960s. The subsequent section focuses on the 1970s through the 1990s, primarily reviewing feminist and gender-focused studies in Puerto Rico and stateside. Then, as the links between sociology and Latino/a research expanded from the 1990s forward, subsections discuss the sociological specialty areas and briefly address the allied social sciences that best reflect these burgeoning connections, in addition to noting the influences on sociological theory. Since the intertwining of Puerto Rican Studies and sociology extends beyond academic research, the final substantive section examines public sociology, as well as professional organizations and journal publications.

INTERSECTIONALITY AND INTERDISCIPLINARY CONTRIBUTIONS

Since their emergence, Puerto Rican and Latino/a Studies, along with Africana Studies, Asian American Studies, LGBTQ Studies, and Women, Gender, and Sexuality Studies, have helped prod sociologists and other social scientists into interdisciplinary research and intersectional analyses. This happens, in part, because interdisciplinary work is of particular interest to some sociologists, especially those involved in the sociology of race and ethnicity or gender and sexuality, but also because some sociology faculty have joint positions within interdisciplinary programs/departments. The results of such linkages become visible in the following sections where examples of intersectional and interdisciplinary research are cited.

Intersectional approaches began flourishing in the early 1990s, fostered by writings of women of color, most notably sociologist Hill Collins (1990) and legal scholar Crenshaw (1991). While originally derived from research on African American women, intersectionality has become the most important paradigm or critical approach for understanding aspects of people's multiple marginalizations and the interconnected systems, or matrix of domination, based on race, ethnicity, gender, class, sexuality, citizenship, and other axes. It proposes that in different situations, one or more of these factors come to the fore in shaping a person's experiences and outcomes. As a framework, it fosters interdisciplinary connections as well as an understanding of the diversity of experiences among women of color and others. However, it is frequently applied to Black women and "other women of color," prompting sociologists Baca Zinn and Zambrana (2019) to write specifically on how "Chicanas/Latinas Advance Intersectional Thought and Practice." Among other points, they note the importance of the early edited volume, *This Bridge Called my Back: Writings by Radical Women of Color* (1981), by Moraga and Anzaldúa. One goal of this chapter is to begin uncovering the ways that Puerto Rican Studies also has advanced intersectional thought.

Finally, Puerto Rican Studies and the social sciences are linked through their overlapping interests in international studies, especially in Latin America and the Caribbean (see Acosta-Belén in this volume), and in decolonial studies (Mignolo and Walsh 2018).

PUERTO RICAN STUDIES AND SOCIOLOGY: INITIAL MODELS

The impact of Puerto Rican Studies on sociology and allied social sciences has grown over time, both in its substance and in the depth of its impact, differentially influencing various subfields and theories within the discipline.

As Hernández (1996) indicates, most early publications about Puerto Ricans were written by non-Puerto Ricans and the social science research concepts and explanatory models they used were frequently both inadequate and deficient. These early writings tended to focus on the impacts that mass migration of working class Puerto Ricans to New York City and other stateside locations had on U.S. society, rather than paying attention to their importance for the regional manufacturing and service economies, their particular needs, or the effects of racism, discrimination, and segregation on them. Some mainstream sociologists, such as Mills, Senior, and Goldsen (1950), were not optimistic about the potential social mobility of the stateside Puerto Rican rural and semi-skilled labor community. Indeed, much early sociological research tended to blame Puerto Ricans for their plight, using concepts like the purported "culture of poverty" (Lewis 1966). In addition, Glazer and Moynihan (1963) suggested Puerto Ricans and other New York City groups were unable or unwilling to conform to the (mythical) U.S. "melting pot" assimilation paradigm and instead chose to maintain distinct identities that melded traditional values with aspects of their new communities. Importantly, as Hernández (1980) argued, the best way to enhance this flawed scholarship was to increase the numbers of Puerto Rican social scientists—something encouraged as part of the development of Puerto Rican Studies. In line with this suggestion, several Puerto Rican scholars, including Andrés Torres (1995), have challenged the relevance of the still-used concept of the melting pot.

One way to see the shifts in the predominant framing of Puerto Rican-related issues is to examine the changing article topics appearing in the leading sociological journals, the *American Sociological Review* (ASR) and the *American Journal of Sociology* (AJS). During the 1940s and 1950s and through the 1960s, articles mainly focused on fertility, family planning, intermarriage, and bilingualism. The first two topics reflected an incorrect assumption that the Post-World War II Great Migration of Puerto Ricans to New York City and other Northeastern areas was instigated by extreme poverty and over-population on the island. Instead, there was an actual loss of the means to make a livelihood when the island's economy shifted from an agricultural one to industrial manufacturing, spurred by Puerto Rico's economic development program, Operation Bootstrap, but functionally controlled by U.S. corporate capital. In fact, the Puerto Rican government created policies to promote migration as an escape valve from the job losses created by this economic shift.

Then in the 1970s and 1980s, published articles in these two journals shifted to issues related to community building in the United States such as residential and school segregation, and educational mobility. The displacement of communities due to urban renewal, activism around forced student busing to out-of-neighborhood schools (used as a response to residential segregation), and other inner-city uprisings of the late 1960s and early 1970s partially prompted this changed focus. Yet, as early as 1981, *Daedalus*, the journal of the American Academy of Arts and Sciences, published a special issue on American Indians, Blacks, Chicanos, and Puerto Ricans that included articles by Frank Bonilla, Ricardo Campos, Juan Flores, and Pedro Pedraza about Puerto Ricans; and starting in the late 1990s, articles began to appear in *ASR* and *AJS* on different topics, especially on definitions of race and racial classifications, racism, racial-ethnic wage inequalities, and housing discrimination, and on a diversity of subjects like health, the military, or "street language." Puerto Rican-generated concerns finally made it into the lead journals—although there are many more book reviews than articles on Puerto Ricans. Cabán (2009) agrees that, despite any economic or political struggles affecting U.S. higher education—which had an impact on institutional funding for Puerto Rican Studies programs or departments—scholarship in the field had gained acceptance in some academic disciplines beginning in the 1990s and a new cohort of Puerto Rican scholars was advancing scholarship in emerging fields and traditional disciplinary departments.

In contrast, publications growing out of the Puerto Rican and Latino/a Studies movements during the same period have hundreds of articles found by using the key search word "Puerto Rican," many of them written by sociologists and other social scientists. Among these important journals are *CENTRO Journal* (founded in 1987), the *Latino Review of Books* (founded in 1995 and transformed into the *Latino(a) Research Review* in 1999), and *Latino*

Studies (founded in 1999). Since disciplinary journals accept comparatively few articles on Puerto Rico or Puerto Ricans, these refereed journals and others like them offer authors an excellent outlet for their research. They also bring together interdisciplinary and multidisciplinary Puerto Rican Studies research in one place that social scientists from many fields read.

FEMINIST AND GENDER-FOCUSED STUDIES IN PUERTO RICO AND STATESIDE: 1970s-1990s

Feminist social scientists writing about island or stateside Puerto Rican women, during the years spanning the 1970s through the 1990s, were not only influenced by Puerto Rican Studies, but were helping to create or expand the field.

Writing on "Puerto Rico: Feminism and Feminist Studies," sociologist Colón Warren (2003) reviews many of the main contributions and contributors of social science analyses, from the 1970s through 2002, that focused on women's unequal status in Puerto Rico and documented their socioeconomic and political struggles. This literature review is so extensive that there is insufficient space here to incorporate the many significant researchers she cites. Colón Warren argues that feminist research in Puerto Rico during the late twentieth century viewed women's situation in the context of the island's macroeconomic, political, and social processes, as well as its colonial relations, and that most studies had a strong relationship with feminist groups and activists fighting for their rights in the private and public spheres. Colón Warren describes in detail four areas that represent the recurring topics between 1970 and 2000, and notes that the vast majority of these studies are qualitative rather than quantitative. The first research area is intersectional analyses that focus on interactions among subsets of colonial, national, class, racial, gender and/or sexual identity dynamics. Some of this research was motivated by mobilizations among Black women or LGBTQ groups in Puerto Rico at the time, but all of it reflects a diversity of interests among groups of women, rather than a unified movement. The second area is economic development, women's work, and poverty. Here, Colón Warren reviews publications on the differing labor conditions of white collar, industrial, and home workers and points to the need for more research on occupational segregation by race among women and on family poverty (which later was addressed by Colón-Warren 1998; Nieves-Rosa and Thomas-Breitfield 2002; and others).

The third area is family relations and violence against women, as well as resistance to it. Colón Warren argues that the domestic sphere is not only one of reciprocal support and affection but also is shaped by internal power relations and gender hierarchies. In this section, she examines class and gender intersections in the family, as well as women's resistance to violence. The fourth area is sexual and reproductive rights, including debates over birth control, which was viewed by some as a method of individual and national social mobility as well as giving women control of their families, but by others as a form of population control and genocide forced on the island from the outside. (The latter view was popularized by the 1982 documentary *La Operación*, dealing with the sterilization of Puerto Rican women.) Colón Warren's review is a "must read" due to its extensive coverage of Puerto Rico, but she herself also published extensively on Puerto Rican women both in Puerto Rico and in the northeastern U.S. (e.g., Santana Cooney and Colón Warren 1979).

In another sociological review essay, spanning the years from 1950 to 1980, Bose (1986) describes parallel research about the status of stateside Puerto Rican women (e.g., Santana Cooney 1979; Santana Cooney and Ortiz 1983). Bose gathers considerable data comparing Puerto Rican women with three groups (Mexicans, Cubans, and other U.S. Latinas), examining topics that were of particular concern at the time (e.g., migration, region of residence, employment and unemployment, occupational segregation and type of job, income, education, language proficiency, family composition, marital status, and fertility rates). She finds that stateside Puerto Rican women had higher labor force participation than those on the island. They were increasing their average educational level, had higher rates of professional employment than other U.S. Latinas, were becoming more geographically dispersed, and entering better labor markets including white collar (instead of operative) jobs. On the other hand, Puerto Rican household income was still low, partly due to the increasing numbers of female-headed households. Some of the income-determining factors (e.g., education and number of children) concerned individuals. Nonetheless, Bose concurred with Ríos (1985), that many more of the determinants were structural or demand-side features, like region of residence (especially concentration in New York City), residential segregation, the ratio of men to women (determining marriage opportunities), and government policies.

In a later study, Bose (1992) challenged the sociological discussions of poverty current at the time using Latinas as an example. Research on men's poverty focused on the concept of the underclass and stressed the role of industrial restructuring, especially in the inner cities of the Northeast and Midwest (Wilson 1987). This approach decomposed poverty by race or ethnicity, yet it treated the existence of female-headed households as an outcome of men's unemployment, rather than a direct cause of women's poverty. In contrast, the feminization of poverty, which stressed women's own characteristics, tended to ignore the experiences of racial-ethnic groups. Bose (1992) developed a gender-unified approach to predict women's poverty by testing the importance of geographic variation, individual characteristics, and household structure using comparisons among Latinas, while also considering individual characteristics and household structure. She discovered that living in a female-headed household indeed was a major predictor (along with age) of Cuban, Mexican, and Puerto Rican women's poverty, as expected by the feminization of poverty approach. Yet, Puerto Rican women were statistically different in the predictive model from Cuban and Mexican women, supporting earlier criticisms of feminization of poverty research for failing to take account of racial-ethnic differences. Nonetheless, regional economic characteristics played a smaller, but significant, role for Latinas, especially in terms of the jobs available in any given labor market. These opportunities were not linked to sunbelt-rustbelt divisions as they were for men, and as the industrial restructuring perspective had predicted for Blacks. Ironically, all three Latina groups often fared better when they lived outside of their usual region of concentration, possibly because they could migrate to better jobs. In sum, merging men's and women's models of poverty determination, using diverse Latina examples, enhanced sociological understanding of how gender and ethnicity intersect.

SOCIOLOGY SPECIALTY AREAS AND ALLIED SOCIAL SCIENCES: 1990s AND BEYOND

Since the 1990s, Puerto Rican and Latino/a Studies have had a profound impact on many specialty areas within sociology and particularly helped to shape research on migration; socioeconomic status; housing segregation; race-ethnicity and racialization; and the media. In addition, partially due to Puerto Rican Studies, some theoretical sociological paradigms have shifted. While research on Puerto Ricans is found in other sociological subfields (e.g., religion, demography, and criminology), the impact has been largest in the following areas. Furthermore, the authors are so numerous, that only a few samples are mentioned herein.

Migration: Influential and ground-breaking works on migration include *Labor Migration Under Capitalism* (History Task Force 1979) and Ricardo Campos and Frank Bonilla's (1976) "Industrialization and Migration: Some Effects on the Puerto Rican Working Class," especially important for their conceptualization of circular migration patterns.

A decade later, Alicea (1990) reframes discussions of Puerto Rican migration around the concept of "dual home bases," one in the U.S. and one in Puerto Rico, each with a set of psychological attachments and relatives who can help. In parallel, Aranda (2006) more recently writes about the two-way emotional links that migration creates for families split between island and stateside populations. In another book, Aranda and her co-authors (2014) compare various Latin American and Caribbean immigrant groups in Miami, examining the factors that pushed them to emigrate and the structural and emotional challenges of creating a community in Miami. On a related topic, and in a frequently reprinted article, Toro-Morn (1995) looks at how gender relations within families can mediate migration to Chicago, and how this connects to their choice between paid and reproductive labor.

Research by political scientist Edgardo Meléndez (2017) adds an additional, structural dimension to stateside analyses by looking at the role of the post–WWII Puerto Rican government in managing mass migration to the U.S. and helping workers find employment there. Many stateside community-focused studies by a variety of social scientists address migration outcomes in specific U.S. destination cities or regions. These cover both earlier settlements such as New York City (e.g., Díaz-Stevens 1993; Haslip-Viera et al. 2004), Philadelphia (Whalen 2001), Hartford (Cruz 1998), Lorain, Ohio (Rivera 2005), and Chicago (e.g., Fernández 2012; Padilla 1987), among others, as well as newer destinations in Florida (e.g., Duany and Matos-Rodríguez 2006; Duany and Silver 2010) or parts of the South (Lippard and Gallagher 2010).

Socioeconomic Status: Research on stateside Puerto Ricans' socioeconomic status is plentiful and covers a broad range of topics, making it impossible to cover more than a fraction of these investigations. Many studies focus on specific aspects of employment and unemployment, informal economy, or reproductive work; outcomes such as wages, poverty, and unemployment; or predictors of success, such as education levels or language ability. Among the important works on changing economic outcomes is Rivera-Batiz and Santiago's *Puerto Ricans in the United States: A Changing Reality* (1994). In addition, several classic socio-historic texts, roughly from the 1990s, provide wide-ranging national overviews of stateside Puerto Ricans' socioeconomic status as it changed over time. These include Rodríguez's *Puerto Ricans: Born in the USA* (1989) and Pérez y González's *Puerto Ricans in the United States* (2000). The two most recent and comprehensive volumes are Acosta-Belén and Santiago's *Puerto Ricans in the United States: A Contemporary Portrait* (2006, second edition 2018) and economist Edwin Meléndez and political scientist Vargas-Ramos's edited collection *Puerto Ricans at the Dawn of the New Millennium* (2014). Written at different points in time, these comprehensive publications cover Puerto Rican communities created by different waves of migrants, geographic population shifts or dispersion from the Northeast and Midwest to new settlement areas, unexpected economic improvements in stateside communities during the 1980s, and the effects of the current economic collapse in Puerto Rico, Hurricane María, and the impact of the New Millennium Migration on island and stateside Puerto Ricans.

Housing Segregation: Housing ownership and residential segregation are less obvious indicators of economic status than other measures. They are important because high levels of housing segregation often are associated with under-funded schools and fewer local job opportunities.

Latino/a sociologists are finding that as Puerto Rican communities become more geographically dispersed, levels of housing segregation across the United States show more variation. For example, in a comparison of New York and Orlando, Villarrubia-Mendoza (2007) finds that Florida-based Puerto Ricans live in neighborhoods with lower percentages of blacks and less residential segregation from non-Hispanic whites than in New York. This is associated with higher household incomes, levels of college attainment, and homeownership compared to blacks—showing that Puerto Ricans seem better off in some Sunbelt cities than in many Rustbelt ones. In a parallel study of 72 counties nationwide, each with 3,000 or more Puerto Rican residents, Vélez and Burgos (2010) also find that geography matters. Their study shows that Puerto Ricans are moving away from urban areas and into suburban ones with higher proportions of whites, which has a positive effect on wages.

Pointing to a different aspect of residential segregation, de Jesús and colleagues (2014) focus on its relationship to marriage choices, in part because stateside Puerto Ricans have higher rates of out-group intermarriage than do other Latinos/as. In their national study, the authors find that Puerto Ricans living in highly segregated counties are considerably less likely to marry whites than Puerto Ricans who live in less segregated counties, which is important because segregation is a significant factor affecting the socioeconomic mobility of persons of color. In addition to these specific studies, information on residential segregation often is part of broader Puerto Rican community studies and demographic studies.

Race-Ethnicity and Racialization: Turning to the issue of race and racialization, sociological work on the definitions and fluidity of racial categories by Rodríguez (2002) examines how Latinos/as report race and ethnicity to the U.S. Census and on how skin color stratifies Latinos/as. Similarly, Landale and Oropesa (2002), compare island and stateside Puerto Rican definitions of race, finding that stateside residents are very likely to resist U.S.-based racial definitions and tend to identify by ethnicity. Looking at systematic racialized social systems, Bonilla-Silva (2003) makes widely recognized theoretical contributions, especially focused on "colorblind racism," that are further described below.

For those seeking a comprehensive overview of contemporary social science perspectives on race and Puerto Ricans, Vargas-Ramos' (2017) anthology, *Race, Front and Center: Perspectives on Race Among Puerto Ricans*, pulls together a wide range of articles from *CENTRO Journal* drawn from history, sociology, and anthropology, as well as language/literature. For those seeking a historical and multidisciplinary perspective, Jiménez Román and Flores's (2010) anthology, *The Afro-Latin@ Reader*, illustrates how the categories of Black and Latino/a are not exclusive; in fact, they expand discussions about the complex intersections between blackness and *Latinidad*.

Media: Puerto Rican studies has significantly influenced research in media studies and cultural studies within sociology. In this realm, Clara Rodríguez has brought a more intersectional understanding of stereotyping and racial constructions as they appear in diverse media formats. Important books by Rodríguez include *Latin Looks: Images of Latinas and Latinos in the U.S. Media* (1997), *Heroes, Lovers, and Others: The Story of Latinos in Hollywood* (2004), and *America as Seen on TV: How Television Shapes Immigrant Expectations around the Globe* (2018). Indeed, such research on societal racial constructions has significantly influenced broad level theories within sociology, resulting in non-binary paradigm shifts in analyses of race, as described next.

Sociological Theory and Race-Racism: By the 1990s, sociological theory began to move away from discrimination-based frameworks and to focus on institutionalized racism and its effects on persons of color (Bonilla-Silva 2003; Feagin 2006; Feagin and Sikes 1994; Omi and Winant 1994). A major figure in this shift, among others, is Puerto Rican sociologist and 2018 President of the American Sociological Association, Eduardo Bonilla-Silva.

Bonilla-Silva's early work (1997, 1999) demonstrates how prior social science understandings of race-ethnicity were limited by simplistic theories that framed racism as a prejudicial and "incorrect" attitude. Consequently, racism was studied as an individual characteristic and a phenomenon that was only reflected in overt behavior. Bonilla-Silva offered an alternative structural theory of racism based on his concept of hierarchical "racialized social systems," arguing that racism is both an attitude and a "social fact" (1999) maintained by varying institutional conditions, but always characterized by differing black and white economic opportunities.

Bonilla-Silva elaborates these ideas in *Racism without Racists: Color-Blind Racism and the Persistence of Racial Inequality in America* (2003), currently in its fifth edition. He argues that a new racial ideology, labelled "colorblind racism," became dominant among whites starting in the 1960s. Whites rationalize non-whites' contemporary status as being the product of (natural) market dynamics and imputed cultural limitations (cultural racism), by believing there is no white hostility that maintains white privilege (thus minimizing racism by seeing it only as an attitude), and proclaiming we now live in a post-racial society. This form of racism allows whites to criticize persons of color, thus indirectly supporting aspects of white supremacy and maintaining the U.S. racial order, while society as a whole appears to have "racism without racists."

Bonilla-Silva (2002) also popularized the concept of a "Latin Americanization of racial stratification" in sociology. He argues that the former bi-racial, black-white U.S. optic is being replaced by a tri-racial stratification system using color gradations that is comprised of Whites (traditional and "new Whites"), Honorary Whites (including light-skinned Latinos/as and most multi-racial people, among others), and the Collective Black (Blacks, dark-skinned Latinos/as, etc.). Bonilla-Silva sees multiple reasons for the emergence of this system. Demographically, the percentage of persons of color in the U.S. is rising, and some whites fear losing power. Similarly, the increase in interracial marriages and of multiracial children has pushed the U.S. Census to allow individuals to identify as multiple races, broadening racial categories and moving away from a black-white binary optic. Economically, some racial-ethnic groups match or exceed the socio-economic status of whites, threatening white supremacy. Finally, there is a "new racism" that maintains white privilege through institutional practices in less overt ways. Bonilla-Silva argues that the intermediate "Honorary White" group serves as a buffer to racial-ethnic conflict. He and others contend that this certainly occurs in some Latin American and Caribbean countries when, with the racial blending of a nation, a strategy to increase white power is to create a class of Honorary Whites, while assigning most persons of color to the category of Collective Black. Overall, the popularity of Bonilla-Silva's concepts of colorblind racism, racism without racists, and the Latin Americanization of racial stratification have significantly helped shift sociological paradigms to institutional, rather than individual, approaches and to refocus on racism, rather than race.

Allied Social Sciences

Puerto Rican Studies scholars who work in allied or applied social sciences have influenced sociological specialties as well as their own disciplines. The following are just a sampling of these important figures drawn from the fields of history, political science, urban planning, and social psychology or mental health.

History and Media Endeavors: Sánchez Korrol, writing about history, public education, and for the media, is the author of several volumes documenting the history and socioeconomic profile of the early New York Puerto Rican communities including *From Colonia to Community: The History of*

Puerto Ricans in New York City (1983, Second edition 1994). In *Pioneros II: Puerto Ricans in New York City 1948-1998* (2010), Sánchez Korrol and Hernández offer a photographic narrative of these communities during the Great Migration and the following decades. Among her useful reference texts, Sánchez Korrol co-edited a biographical volume on *Latina Legacies* (2005) with Chicana historian Vicki Ruiz, as well as their three-volume encyclopedia on *Latinas in the United States* (2006). Furthermore, Sánchez Korrol has done considerable "public history" that reaches out to non-academic audiences, such as her text for public school teachers (1999) and consulting on a revision of the New York State social studies curriculum. She also has been consulted about, and commented on, documentary films and movies, chaired the library and archives advisory group for the Center for Puerto Rican Studies, Hunter College, CUNY, and conferred with multiple New York museums about various exhibits.

Political Science: José Cruz has helped extend the sociological field of social movements with his works on stateside Puerto Rican politics, community organizations, and different forms of collective action. His research, grounded in early sociological writings about power and elites in cities, has critically examined ethnic identity and political power in northeastern urban environments. Cruz's first book was on Hartford, Connecticut (1998), and recently he has authored two volumes on changes in Puerto Ricans' political incorporation and participation in New York City over time, entitled *Puerto Rican Identity, Political Development, and Democracy in New York, 1960-1990* (2017) and *Liberalism and Identity Politics: Puerto Rican Community Organizations and Collective Action in New York City* (2019).

Urban Planning and Development: Focusing on another form of power, economist and urban planner Edwin Meléndez has contributed to urban sociology and political economy with his research on economic development, labor markets, and poverty. In his edited volume, *Communities and Workforce Development* (2004), he and other contributors look at the role of community organizations in changing the employment services industry that now tries to meet the needs of both workers and employers, using the facilities of community colleges, technology centers, union-sponsored projects, and other methods.

Social Psychology and Mental Health: Sociologists who work in social psychology often interact with scholars in psychology, educational psychology, counseling psychology, and others addressing mental health issues. For example, Lloyd Rogler is a Puerto Rican sociologist who carried out groundbreaking work in the areas of social psychiatry and the social psychology of poverty and human migrations. He was the founding director of the Hispanic Research Center at Fordham University, and garnered NIMH grants that resulted in training for mental health counselors in the area of cultural sensitivity. In addition, he authored multiple articles and books on Hispanic and Puerto Rican mental health. A significant example is his co-authored book on New York Puerto Rican families' intergenerational processes (Rogler and Santana Cooney 1984), focused on the transmission of sociocultural traits among first- and second-generation Puerto Ricans.

Similarly, in the field of counseling psychology, Azara Santiago-Rivera co-authored an important book on counseling Latinos/as, especially as related to family issues (Santiago Rivera, et al. 2002). She has published two other books and many articles on topics ranging from counseling and diversity, Latinos/as and depression, the impact of racism, and the effects of sociocultural and economic stressors on the psychological well-being of recent Latino/a immigrants. Among her other contributions, Santiago-Rivera is past president of the National Latinx Psychological Association (NLPA) and was founding editor of their *Journal of Latina/o Psychology* (renamed the *Journal of Latinx Psychology*).

These allied social sciences are significant both for their relevant published research and, perhaps, more importantly, for their applied aspects, that help improve the lived conditions and well-being of stateside Puerto Ricans and other U.S. Latinos/as, promote equity and social justice, and generally bring research to wider professional and public audiences. The next section discusses similar public sociology efforts, as well as outreach through academic organizations and journals.

PUBLIC SOCIOLOGY, ACADEMIC ORGANIZATIONS, AND JOURNALS

Public Sociology: Public sociology involves engaging non-academic audiences and uses sociology to address public issues such as social policies or social change movements. It is not the same as established applied fields like clinical psychology, demography, or social work, but rather intends to address contemporary or community concerns. Public sociology activities often are situated in policy-related institutes created by scholars or in other forms of community-engaged scholarship. Two important examples follow.

When CUNY and the Ford Foundation funded a proposal to create the Center for Puerto Rican Studies (Centro) at Hunter College, CUNY, sociologist Frank Bonilla became the founding Director in 1973. Over 23 years, Bonilla was central in defining Centro's research agenda by organizing research teams or task forces focused on the needs of the Puerto Rican community itself—including History, Education, Migration, Language, and on topics like prison reform and combating racism. The Task Forces produced groundbreaking books such as *Labor Migration under Capitalism* (History Task Force 1979) and *Industry and Idleness* (Bonilla and Campos 1986), covering the evolving patterns of Puerto Rican migration, persistent unemployment and high poverty rates. In addition, Bonilla joined and spoke for many community-based, policy advocacy organizations and coalitions. He also co-created the Inter-University Program for Latino Research (1983), a national consortium of university-based research centers that serves as a model for others doing interdisciplinary research in Latino/a Studies.

The University at Albany, SUNY, provides another model of public social science that reached a wide audience. In 1984, Acosta-Belén created the Center for Latino, Latin American, and Caribbean Studies (CELAC), which worked closely with the Department of Puerto Rican, Latin American, and Caribbean Studies (or PRLACS, currently the Department of Latin American, Caribbean, and U.S. Latino Studies or LACS). CELAC sponsored the *Latino(a) Research Review* (LRR), and, under its auspices, Acosta-Belén and Carlos Santiago co-founded the New York Latino Research and Resources Network (NYLARNet), subsequently directed by José Cruz. CELAC and the University's Institute for Research on Women (IROW), founded by Christine Bose, also provided the infrastructure to receive multiple Ford Foundation grants on "Integrating Puerto Rican Women into the Curriculum and Research" (from 1990-92), "Internationalizing Women's Studies: Cross-Cultural Approaches to Gender Research and Teaching" (from 1995-98), and "Gender Studies in Global Perspective" (from 1998-2002), among others. Such funding supported conferences and workshops, as well as created resources for research (Acosta-Belén and Bose 1991) and teaching (Acosta-Belén et al. 1991). Meanwhile, NYLARNet, in collaboration with Centro and the Institute for Urban and Minority Education at Teachers College, Columbia University, brought scholars together to produce short reports on issues related to Latino/a health, education, immigration, and politics in New York—for example, on Latino/a voting in the 2004 election, housing status, city variation in Latino/a socioeconomic status, Puerto Rican faculty in the CUNY system, and Latino/a faculty and diversity in the SUNY system.

Sections and Journals within Academic Organizations: Another way that scholars can reach out to broader audiences is for academic professional organizations to have interest groups dedicated to Latino/a Studies. For example, the American Sociological Association (ASA) has a Latina/Latino Sociology Section that sponsors its own sessions at annual meetings and gives annual awards for distinguished careers, research publications, and teaching and service, bringing attention to their work. Similarly, the Association of Latina and Latino Anthropologists (ALLA) has been a section of the American Anthropological Association (AAA) since 1990, dedicated to supporting student and early career scholars, highlighting scholarship, and enabling diverse analyses of issues facing Latino/a communities. The Society for Latin American and Caribbean Anthropology (SLACA) also is a section of the AAA, which added "the Caribbean" to its name in 2005-2006. SLACA awards book and student paper prizes; and it publishes the *Journal of Latin American and Caribbean Anthropology* (JLACA) that includes a focus on diasporic populations. There also are specialized sociology journals, such as *Gender & Society*, published by Sociologists for Women in Society (an organization independent of the ASA), that encourages the publication of intersectional research, including writings on women of color. In addition, mentioned above, the NLPA sponsors the *Journal of Latinx Psychology*.

Similar to the ASA, the Latin American Studies Association (LASA) has a section on Latino Studies. Created in the early 1990s, the section's existence recognizes the connections between stateside Latinos/as and their long history of socioeconomic and civil rights struggles (including for ethnic studies) with migration from their respective home nations and the transnational connections they maintain with them, thus expanding Latin American area studies which, during its early decades, paid little attention to U.S. Latino/a conditions and experiences (Acosta-Belén and Bose 2000). Furthermore, LASA publishes the journal *Latin American Research Review*, and a simple search of the term "Puerto Rican" reveals several hundred articles, with over half of them mentioning sociology.

Other social science organizations, like the American Political Science Association (APSA), have a more general Section on Race, Ethnicity, and Politics, similar to the ASA Section on Racial and Ethnic Minorities. Of interest is the fact that both of these sections publish journals, respectively named *Race, Ethnicity, and Politics* (APSA) and *Sociology of Race and Ethnicity* (ASA), that include specific articles on Latino/a groups.

Finally, there are Latino/a-focused journals of long standing, that were discussed at this chapter's outset: *CENTRO Journal* (founded in 1987), the *Latino Review of Books* (founded in 1995 and transformed into the *Latino(a) Research Review* in 1999), and *Latino Studies* (founded in 1999). These are not affiliated with professional organizations, but rather with the specific universities where they were founded (Hunter College, CUNY, and University at Albany, SUNY, for the first two) or the institutional location of the current editor. Similarly, the *Revista de Ciencias Sociales*, published at the University of Puerto Rico, Río Piedras, is an important source of articles on Puerto Ricans, although most of them are written in Spanish and may have a limited impact on monolingual U.S. sociologists.

In sum, an important way that social science research interconnects with Puerto Rican and Latino/a Studies is through policy-related institutes, journals, and academic organizations that attempt to reach a new generation of young scholars through interest-group sections or Latino/a-focused organizations.

CONCLUSION

This chapter is not intended as an exhaustive bibliography. Indeed, the authors cited represent only a fraction of several decades of scholarship; but they are illustrative of the major trends or streams through which Puerto Rican Studies has had an influence on the discipline of sociology, as well as on some of the allied social sciences. These connections were tentative in the 1940s and 1950s, but they solidified and escalated in the 1990s and, since the new millennium, the volume of work has become prolific. Among the factors that facilitated this interdisciplinary work were: the increased number of Puerto Rican social scientists at U.S. universities; social movements seeking change on the island and stateside; the development and impact of the concept of intersectionality, which encouraged research bridging racial-ethnic and women-gender studies; the expansion of sociological interest areas to incorporate relevant journals and research sections; and other forms of public sociology, especially journals and research institutes connected to community needs. The threads of change (and some of the relevant authors) described here cover the sociological fields of migration, socioeconomic status and social mobility, housing segregation, race-ethnicity and racialization, media, and theories of race and racism. Due to space limitations, other areas, such as social movements, demography, or sociology of education, religion, or criminology, could not be included here, but the chapter does bring to light additional links between Puerto Rican Studies, sociology, and the allied social science areas of history, political science, urban planning, and social psychology and mental health, revealing their current extensive interconnections.

REFERENCES

Acosta-Belén, Edna and Christine E. Bose. 1991. *Albany PR-WOMENET Database: An Interdisciplinary Annotated Bibliography on Puerto Rican Women*. Albany: University at Albany, SUNY (CELAC and IROW).

_____ . 2000. U.S. Latina and Latin American Feminisms: Hemispheric Encounters. *Signs: Journal of Women in Culture and Society* 25(4), 113–9.

Acosta-Belén, Edna, Christine E. Bose and Barbara Sjostrom. 1991. *An Interdisciplinary Guide for Research and Curriculum on Puerto Rican Women*. Albany: University at Albany, SUNY (IROW and CELAC).

Acosta-Belén, Edna and Carlos E. Santiago. 2018. *Puerto Ricans in the United States: A Contemporary Portrait*. First edition 2006. Boulder: Lynne Rienner Publishers, Inc.

Alicea, Marisa. 1990. Dual Home Bases: A Reconceptualization of Puerto Rican Migration. *Latino Studies Journal* 1(3), 78–98.

Aranda, Elizabeth. 2006. *Emotional Bridges to Puerto Rico: Migration, Return Migration, and the Struggles of Incorporation*. Lanham: Rowman & Littlefield.

Aranda, Elizabeth, Sallie Hughes and Elena Sabogal. 2014. *Making a Life in Multiethnic Miami: Immigration and the Rise of a Global City*. Boulder: Lynne Rienner Publishers, Inc.

Baca Zinn, Maxine and Ruth Enid Zambrana. 2019. Chicanas/Latinas Advance Intersectional Thought and Practice. *Gender & Society* 33(5), 677–701.

Bonilla, Frank and Ricardo Campos, eds. 1986. *Industry and Idleness*. New York: Centro de Estudios Puertorriqueños, Hunter College.

Bonilla-Silva, Eduardo. 1997. Rethinking Racism: Toward a Structural Interpretation. *American Sociological Review* 62(3), 465–80.

_____ . 1999. Reply to Loveman: The Essential Social Fact of Race. *American Sociological Review* 64 (6): 899-906.

_____ .2002. We are all Americans!: The Latin Americanization of Racial Stratification in the USA. *Race & Society* 5, 3–16.

_____ .2003. *Racism without Racists: Color-Blind Racism and the Persistence of Racial Inequality in America*. First Edition 2003, Fifth Edition 2018. Lanham, MD: Rowman and Littlefield.

_____ .2019. 2018 Presidential Address, Feeling Race: Theorizing the Racial Economy of Emotions. *American Sociological Review* 84(1), 1–25.

Bose, Christine E. 1986. Puerto Rican Women in the United States: An Overview. In *Puerto Rican Women: Perspectives on Culture, History, and Society*, Second Edition, ed. Edna Acosta-Belén. 147–69. New York: Praeger Publishers.

_____ .1992. Labor Markets and Household Composition: Hispanic Women's Poverty in the U.S. In *Institutions and Gatekeeping in the Life Course*, ed. Walter Heinz. 99–119. Weinheim: Deutscher Studien Verlag.

Cabán, Pedro. 2009. Puerto Rican Studies: Changing Islands of Knowledge. *CENTRO: Journal of the Center for Puerto Rican Studies* 21(2), 257–81.

Campos, Ricardo and Frank Bonilla. 1976. Industrialization and Migration: Some Effects on the Puerto Rican Working Class. *Latin American Perspectives* 3(3), 66–108.

Colón-Warren, Alice E. 1998. The Feminization of Poverty among Women in Puerto Rico and Puerto Rican Women in the Middle Atlantic Region of the United States. *Journal of World Affairs* 5(2), 263–81.

_____ .2003. Puerto Rico: Feminism and Feminist Studies. *Gender & Society* 17(5), 664–90.

Crenshaw, Kimberly Williams. 1991. Mapping the Margins: Intersectionality, Identity Politics, and Violence against Women of Color. *Stanford Law Review* 46(6), 1241–99.

Cruz, José E. 1998. *Identity and Power: Puerto Rican Politics and the Challenge of Ethnicity*. Philadelphia: Temple University Press.

_____ .2017. *Puerto Rican Identity, Political Development, and Democracy in New York, 1960-1990*. New York: Lexington Books/Rowman and Littlefield.

_____ .2019. *Liberalism and Identity Politics: Puerto Rican Community Organizations and Collective Action in New York City*. New York City: Centro Press.

De Jesús, Anthony, Giovani Burgos, Melissa Almenas and William Vélez. 2014. Puerto Rican Intergroup Marriage and Residential Segregation in the U.S.: A Multilevel Analysis of Structural, Cultural, and Economic Factors. *Journal of Human Behavior in the Social Environment* 24(2), 156–78.

Díaz-Stevens, Ana María. 1993. *Oxcart Catholicism on Fifth Avenue: The Impact of the Puerto Rican Migration upon the Archdiocese of NY*. Notre Dame, IN: University of Notre Dame Press.

Duany, Jorge and Félix Matos-Rodríguez. 2006. *Puerto Ricans in Orlando and Central Florida*. New York City: Center for Puerto Rican Studies.

Duany, Jorge and Patricia Silver, eds. 2010. Puerto Rican Florida. Special Issue, *CENTRO: Journal of the Center for Puerto Rican Studies* 22(1), 4–31.

Feagin, Joe R. 2006. *Systemic Racism: A Theory of Oppression*. New York: Routledge.

Feagin, Joe R. and Melvin P. Sikes. 1994. *Living with Racism: The Black Middle Class Experience*. Boston: Beacon Press.

Fernández, Lilia. 2012. *Brown in the Windy City: Mexicans and Puerto Ricans in Postwar Chicago*. Chicago: University of Chicago Press.

García, Ana María, Director. 1982. *La Operación*. Video Documentary. Seattle, WA: IMDb.

Haslip-Viera, Gabriel, Angelo Falcón and Félix Matos-Rodríguez, eds. 2004. *Boricuas in Gotham: Puerto Ricans in the Making of Modern New York City*. Princeton, NJ: Markus Wiener Publishers.

Glazer, Nathan and Daniel Patrick Moynihan. 1963. *Beyond the Melting Pot: The Negroes, Puerto Ricans, Jews, Italians, and Irish of New York City*. Cambridge, MA: MIT Press and Harvard University Press.

Hernández, José. 1996 [1980]. Social Science and the Puerto Rican Community. In *Historical Perspective on Puerto Rican Survival in the United States*, eds. Clara E. Rodríguez and Virginia Sánchez Korrol. 13–21. Princeton, NJ: Markus Wiener Publisher.

Hill Collins, Patricia. 1990. *Black Feminist Thought*. New York: Routledge.

History Task Force, Centro de Estudios Puertorriqueños. 1979. *Labor Migration under Capitalism: The Puerto Rican Experience*. New York: Monthly Review Press.

Jiménez Román, Miriam and Juan Flores, eds. 2010. *The Afro-Latin@ Reader: History and Culture in the United States*. Durham, NC: Duke University Press.

Landale, Nancy S. and R. S. Oropesa 2002. White, Black, or Puerto Rican: Racial Self-Identification among Mainland and Island Puerto Ricans. *Social Forces* 81(1), 231–54.

Lewis, Oscar. 1966. *La Vida: A Puerto Rican Family in the Culture of Poverty—San Juan and New York*. New York: Random House.

Lippard, Cameron, D. and Charles A. Gallagher, eds. 2010. *Being Brown in Dixie: Race, Ethnicity, and Latino Immigration in the New South*. Boulder: First Forum Press/Lynne Rienner Publishers, Inc.

Meléndez, Edgardo. 2017. *Sponsored Migration: The State and Puerto Rican Postwar Migration to the United States*. Columbus: Ohio State University Press.

Meléndez, Edwin, ed. 2004. *Communities and Workforce Development*. Kala-mazoo, MI: Upjohn Press/Upjohn Institute for Employment Research.

Meléndez, Edwin and Carlos Vargas-Ramos, eds. 2014. *Puerto Ricans at the Dawn of the New Millennium*. New York City: Centro Press.

Mignolo, Walter D. and Catherine E. Walsh. 2012. *On Decoloniality: Concepts, Analytics, Praxis*. Durham, NC: Duke University Press.

Mills, C. Wright, Clarence Senior and Rose Kohn Goldsen. 1950. *The Puerto Rican Journey: New York's Newest Migrants*. New York: Harper and Brothers.

Moraga, Cherríe and Gloria Anzaldúa, eds. 1981. *This Bridge Called My Back: Writings by Radical Women of Color*. Watertown, MA: Persephone Press.

Nieves-Rosa, Limarie and Sean Thomas-Breitfield. 2002. Welfare reform 2002: Legislative Developments affecting Puerto Rico. National Council of La Raza 10 September.

Omi, Michael and Howard Winant. 1994. *Racial Formation in the United States: From 1960s to the 1980s*. Second edition. New York: Routledge.

Padilla, Félix M. 1987. *Puerto Rican Chicago*. Notre Dame, IN: University of Notre Dame Press.

Pérez y González, María E. 2000. *Puerto Ricans in the United States*. Westport, CT: Greenwood Press.

Ríos, Palmira. 1985. Puerto Rican Women in the United States Labor Market. Paper presented at the conference on The Changing Hispanic Community in the U.S. Albany, NY: State University of New York at Albany, March.

Rivera, Eugenio. 2005. La Colonia de Lorain, Ohio. In *The Puerto Rican Diaspora: Historical Perspectives*, eds. Carmen T. Whalen and Victor Vázquez-Hernández. 151–73. Philadelphia: Temple University Press.

Rivera-Batiz, Francisco L. and Carlos E. Santiago. 1994. *Puerto Ricans in the United States: A Changing Reality*. Washington, DC: National Puerto Rican Coalition, Inc.

Rodríguez, Clara E. 1989. *Puerto Ricans: Born in the USA*. Boston: Unwin Hyman.

_____.1997. *Latin Looks: Images of Latinas and Latinos in the U.S. Media*. Boulder: Westview Press.

_____.2002. *Changing Race: Latinos, the Census, and the History of Ethnicity in the United States*. New York: New York University Press.

_____.2004. *Heroes, Lovers, and Others: The Story of Latinos in Hollywood*. Washington, DC: Smithsonian Institution Press.

_____.2018. *America as Seen on TV: How Television Shapes Immigrant Expectations around the Globe*. New York: New York University Press.

Rogler, Lloyd H and Rosemary Santana Cooney. 1984. *Puerto Rican Families in New York City: Intergenerational Processes*. Maplewood, NJ: Waterfront Press.

Ruiz, Vicki L. and Sánchez Korrol, Virginia, eds. 2005. *Latina Legacies: Identity, Biography and Community*. New York: Oxford University Press.

_____, eds. 2006. *Latinas in the United States: A Historical Encyclopedia*. (Three volume set). Bloomington: Indiana University Press.

Sánchez Korrol, Virginia E. 1983. *From Colonia to Community: The History of Puerto Ricans in New York City, 1917-1948*. Second edition 1994. Berkeley: University of California Press.

————.1999. *Teaching U.S. Puerto Rican History*. Washington, D.C.: American Historical Association.

Sánchez Korrol, Virginia and Pedro Juan Hernández. 2010. *Pioneros II: Puerto Ricans in New York City 1948-1998 (Bilingual Edition)*. Charleston, SC: Arcadia Press.

Santana Cooney, Rosemary. 1979. Intercity Variations in Puerto Rican Female Participation. *The Journal of Human Resources* 4(2), 222–35.

Santana Cooney, Rosemary and Alice E. Colón Warren. 1979. Declining Female Participation among Puerto Rican New Yorkers: A Comparison with Native White Non-Spanish New Yorkers. *Ethnicity* 6(3), 281–97.

Santana Cooney, Rosemary and Vilma Ortiz. 1983. Nativity, National Origin, and Hispanic Female Participation in the Labor Force. *Social Science Quarterly* 64(3), 510–23.

Santiago-Rivera, Azara L., Patricia Arredondo and Maritza Gallardo-Cooper. 2002. *Counseling Latinos and la Familia: A Practical Guide*. Thousand Oaks, CA: Sage Publications.

Toro-Morn, Maura I. 1995. Gender, Class, Family, and Migration: Puerto Rican Women in Chicago. *Gender & Society* 9(6), 712–26.

Torres, Andrés. 1995. *Between Melting Pot and Mosaic: African Americans and Puerto Ricans in the New York Political Economy*. Philadelphia: Temple University Press.

Vélez, William and Giovani Burgos. 2010. The Impact of Housing Segregation and Structural Factors on the Socioeconomic Performance of Puerto Ricans in the United States. *CENTRO: Journal of the Center for Puerto Rican Studies* 22(1), 175–97.

Vargas-Ramos, Carlos, ed. 2017. *Race, Front and Center: Perspectives on Race Among Puerto Ricans*. New York: Centro Press.

Villarrubia-Mendoza, Jacqueline. 2007. The Residential Segregation of Puerto Ricans in New York and Orlando. *Latino(a) Research Review* 6, 119–31.

Whalen, Carmen Teresa. 2001. *From Puerto Rico to Philadelphia: Puerto Rican Workers and Postwar Economies*. Philadelphia: Temple University Press.

Wilson, William J. 1987. *The Truly Disadvantaged: The Inner City, the Underclass, and Public Policy*. Chicago: University of Chicago Press.

CHAPTER 5

THE EVOLUTION OF PUERTO RICAN STUDIES AT CITY COLLEGE

Conor Tomás Reed

Puerto Rican Studies at the City College of New York in Harlem, New York City, was born of a decolonial vision enacted just over fifty years ago to admit Puerto Rican students into the City University system and to include their experiences in the curriculum. These demands were animated by a broader insurgent movement to wrest the Island from United States control, and in the process, to cohere political power across the Puerto Rican diaspora (Fernández 2020; LeBrón 2019; Torres and Velázquez 1998). This vision was complicated by the institutionalization of Puerto Rican Studies in CUNY, which entailed both recognition and containment within an intellectual power structure that had been built by Euro-American colonial elites. One effect of this process was the alienation, subjugation, and ultimate reproduction of students as docile laborers, particularly those who did not belong to this privileged ethno-racial class. And yet, those who converged within Puerto Rican Studies at City College not only survived after much struggle, but vibrantly worked to dismantle the socio-economic conditions that hindered them. Altogether, this field was shaped as an intellectual and political response to colonialism (Bonilla 1972)—as well as a different way to do scholarship (History Task Force 1979)—having arisen from neighborhood struggles, campus occupations, transnational solidarities, and multi-ethnic interpersonal relationships.

This essay weaves together a chronicle of archives and oral testimonies on how Puerto Rican Studies at City College was formed in a multi-ethnic coalition, broadened in self-identification—changing into Latin American and Hispanic Caribbean Studies, and then Latin American and Latino Studies—to reflect the broader communities who converged within it, and despite administration attacks and malfeasance that turned the department into a program, continues to hold aloft a vision for decolonization in the present. The City College Cohen Library Archives contain only two slender archival boxes directly related to this institutional history. Notably, one of the boxes holds a 1975 dissertation by the first City College Puerto Rican Studies Chairperson Federico Aquino-Bermúdez, entitled Growth and Development of Puerto Rican Studies Departments: A Case Study of Two Departments at the City University of New York. Focused on City College and Lehman College, this work was born out of the struggle to create Puerto Rican Studies by an educator who helped to construct it.

This essay adds to Aquino-Bermúdez's record by combing through City College Course Bulletins; meeting minutes from the CUNY Board of Higher Education (BHE)/Board of Trustees (BoT); archives from the Schomburg Center for Research in Black Culture and the City College student newspapers The Campus, The Messenger, and The Paper; as well as the CUNY Digital History Archive and SLAM Herstory Project websites. This intricate history is also recovered by interviews conducted with three City College Puerto Rican Studies/Latin American and Latino Studies faculty: Sherrie Baver, Gabriel Haslip-Viera, and Iris López. Furthermore, because Puerto Rican, Caribbean, Latin American, and Latinx Studies are always more expansive than a college setting, this story also extends beyond the classrooms and campus gates to a range of autonomous studies that proliferated in social movements across the city, in the Puerto Rican diaspora, and transnationally. However, much remains to be amassed on the extraordinary array of syllabi, lesson plans, projects, student writing, and advocacy that emerged from these classrooms.[1]

PROLOGUES TO PUERTO RICAN STUDIES AT CITY COLLEGE

The study of Puerto Rican history and its colonial conditions long predates the formation of Puerto Rican Studies at City College. From the early 19th century, and then increasingly after 1898 when the United States seized colonial rule of Puerto Rico from Spain, Puerto Ricans transported their freedom learning to New York City, where they formed alliances with Cuban and African American organizations (Sánchez Korrol 2020, pers. comm.). They brought the tradition of *el lector*, designated men and women who read newspapers, political tracts, and literatures to rooms full of men and women rolling cigars (Tinajero 2010). Mutual aid organizations were formed like La Aurora, El Círculo de Tabaqueros, El Ejemplo, and La Razón, which hosted eclectic multi-lingual events (Sánchez Korrol 1994, 139). Perhaps the most famous Puerto Rican Studies architect, Pedro Albizu Campos (an *independentista*, or advocate of independence from U.S. colonial rule, who was known by his followers as El Maestro, "The Teacher"), graduated from Harvard Law School, and advanced anti-colonial causes of India and Ireland (including helping to draft the Irish Republican Constitution), before committing his life to the liberation of Puerto Rico (Denis 2015).

During the post-World War II period, at the height of the massive migration of Black southerners that transformed the communities and workplaces of multiple northern cities, another migration would begin with Puerto Ricans who also moved northwards from the Caribbean, especially to New York. The 1947-1952 implementation of Operation Bootstrap under colonial governor Luis Muñoz Marín—in which U.S. corporations set up tax-free low-wage factories on the Island, and courted Puerto Rican laborers, particularly women, for low-end blue-collar jobs in the United States—aided New York City's economic transition from manufacturing to finance, as it created an imbalance in traditional gender roles that greatly altered Puerto Rican society thereafter (Sánchez Korrol 2020, pers. comm.; Pérez y González 2020, pers. comm.). In 1950, Albizu Campos' Nationalist Party of Puerto Rico attempted to kickstart a revolution, which was violently crushed. Inequalities deepened on the Island, and hundreds of thousands of Puerto Rican migrants brought these memories to New York City, where they were huddled in overpriced tenements and under-resourced segregated schools alongside predominantly Black residents in the Bronx, Brooklyn, Lower East Side, and especially east Harlem.

Early 1960s New York City featured two significant developments in Black and Puerto Rican youth education initiatives. The 1961 formation of ASPIRA under community organizer Antonia Pantoja offered Puerto Rican students college preparation and neighborhood advocacy skills. As Louis Nuñez recalls, it was not a narrow strategy in which a select few would "individually overcome many obstacles to achieve some academic and career success," but a group process that began to involve hundreds and then thousands of Puerto Rican youth (2009). In addition, the sweeping impact of the 1963 March on Washington for Jobs and Freedom became harnessed several months later towards desegregating New York City public schools against the wishes of a recalcitrant Board of Education and local officials. Washington March co-organizer Bayard Rustin, along with school desegregation organizer Reverend Milton Galamison, the Congress of Racial Equality, and the National Association for the Advancement of Colored People coordinated two massive school boycotts in New York City on February 3 and May 18, 1964, which almost a million predominantly Black and Puerto Rican students joined. Simultaneously on these two dates, over two hundred bilingual freedom schools were hosted across New York City in churches and community centers. In the freedom schools, students performed skits about the life of Harriet Tubman, and heard historical lessons on Black abolitionists Frederick Douglass and Mary McLeod Bethune, as well as Puerto Rican *independentistas* Ramón Emeterio Betances and Eugenio María de Hostos. At the end of both days, students received a "Freedom Diploma" (Rustin 1964).

PUERTO RICANS ENTER AND TRANSFORM CITY COLLEGE

By the mid-to-late 1960s, the youth raised in these Black and Puerto Rican neighborhood campaigns began to trickle into a still-segregated CUNY to also agitate for changes. They would go up against a "color-blind meritocracy" with "CUNY's defenders, who refused to recognize the racial biases embedded within the institution, [and who] were typical of northern liberals who justified Jim Crow conditions even as they decried them below the Mason-Dixon Line" (Butt 2019, 189–92). The incoming Black and Puerto Rican student population was small but tremendously active at City College. They soon transformed campus anti-war sentiments to embrace the anti-colonial revolutions in Algeria, Cuba, and Vietnam, as they demanded changes in admissions, curriculum, hiring, and the college's relationship to Harlem from a culturally rooted and coalitional perspective.

Many of these Black and Puerto Rican youth entered through Search for Education, Elevation, and Knowledge (SEEK)—an experimental college preparation program that continues in the present—with a superb faculty roster that included organizers, poets, prose writers, and social critics like Aijaz Ahmad, Toni Cade Bambara, Barbara Christian, David Henderson, June Jordan, Audre Lorde, and Adrienne Rich (Reed 2019). In the Department of Romance Languages, the Puerto Rican Poet Laureate Diana Ramírez de Arellano also urged Puerto Rican SEEK students to excel (Medina 2014). Even so, Puerto Rican SEEK students lamented an absence in the otherwise ground-breaking SEEK program, as Eduardo Cruz reflects: "It was geared for Black students, not Puerto Rican students per se or Latinos. I know that I confronted the SEEK program in not having a Puerto Rican history class, leadership, or staff" (Jiménez 2009, 165). The SEEK learning methodology of diving into Black and Third World learning materials omitted in Eurocentric class-rooms encouraged students to revolutionize the entire college, as they also created student groups like Onyx Society, Puerto Ricans Involved in Student Action (PRISA), and eventually the Black and Puerto Rican Students Community (BPRSC) coalition, and later, the Puerto Rican Student Union (PRSU) (Reed 2019; Serrano 1998).

The Spring 1969 escalation campaign to expand access to City College reached a tipping point on April 22, when the student-led campus occupation shut down official business, and simultaneously constructed the University of Harlem for two weeks. The City College campus towers loomed atop a hill in west Harlem. Students consciously chose to take over the college as an act of intellectual and geo-political decolonization. Neighborhood residents, students of all ages, and various Black liberation organizers came to Harlem University's inaugural open-house event, including H. Rap Brown, Kathleen Cleaver, Emory Douglas, James Foreman, Adam Clayton Powell, and Betty Shabazz. This free college—suddenly under neighborhood control—hosted a walk-in clinic, tutorials, nightly community meetings, as well as a "free break-fast program for the children in the neighborhood, day care, [and] political education classes" (Ferguson 2012; Jiménez 2009). Campus buildings were renamed after Black and Third World revolutionaries like Che Guevara, Malcolm X, Pedro Albizu Campos, Marcus Garvey, Mao Tse-Tung, and Patrice Lumumba (Sasmor and Foty 1969). Puerto Rican City College SEEK students Henry Arce and Eduardo Cruz recall that twenty-five Harlemite parents brought "big pots of rice and beans and pork and *pasteles* [boiled green banana or cassava meat patties]," and the Lower East Side dispatched "a hundred parents to hold the gates" (Jiménez 2009, 170). By early May, City College's forty Black and Puerto Rican faculty all went on strike in support of the students' demands (Newt Davidson Collective 1974, 66).

Two of the most essential strike demands were the creation of a School of Black and Puerto Rican Studies/Third World Studies, and for the ethnic composition of incoming students to reflect the city's high school Black, Puerto Rican, and Asian student population. For Fall 1969, the CUNY Board of Higher Education approved the creation of a Department of Urban and Ethnic Studies (UES) at City College, starting with two courses: Afro-American Culture and Hispano-American Culture (City University of New York Board of Higher Education Minutes 1969, 201). They appointed as chairperson a U.S. military instructor named Osborne Scott over Wilfred Cartey, a faculty leader during the strike who the students and faculty had expressly demanded to head a Black and Puerto Rican Studies Department (City University of New York Board of Higher Education Minutes 1969, 238). Federico Aquino-Bermúdez was also appointed as faculty this semester to teach Puerto Rico-related classes, which by 1970 expanded to Puerto Rican Heritage, The Puerto Rican Community, The Puerto Rican Child in his Urban Setting, and Puerto Rican Folklore. Aquino-Bermúdez taught alongside Emilio Rivera, Migdalia de Jesús-Torres de García, Rex Serrano-Martel, and Benjamín Pacheco (City College of New York Course Bulletin 1970). Meanwhile, seven Black Studies classes in the department were taught by five faculty, and one Asian Studies class by one faculty member (City College of New York Course Bulletin 1970).

As the CUNY administration worked to implement but defang the curricular demand, they expanded entry in the University with the Fall 1970 creation of "Open Admissions"—allowing every New York City high school graduate a place in one of CUNY's two- or four-year colleges (City University of New York Board of Higher Education Minutes 1969, 187–9). Conrad Dyer writes about how "striking was the abruptness of the change: no major university system had ever moved, almost overnight, from a rigorously selective admissions standard to a policy of guaranteed admission for all high school graduates," a plan the Board of Higher Education (BHE) had initially set to implement by 1975 (Dyer 1990, 146). The creation of Open Admissions offered a historic opportunity for many more students to go to college, but the CUNY administrators did so unsustainably. They flooded the campuses with new students and did not increase resources, which overwhelmed faculty and staff workers and hindered the potential success of free substantive education for New Yorkers of all colors.

ADMISSIONS AND ETHNIC STUDIES: CONDITIONAL BREAKTHROUGHS

With the start of Open Admissions at CUNY, historically excluded New York City residents began to enter the university en masse with learning methods that their communities had been practicing all along. Meanwhile, various freedom schools and liberation projects continued to flourish around New York City. Puerto Rican Studies—while concurrently being institutionalized in CUNY—took several insurgent forms in New York City communities, as Puerto Ricans and other oppressed groups worked together to improve their lives. The Young Lords, a revolutionary youth group, coordinated direct actions around concrete issues like city garbage services, hospital care, housing lead safety, and ensuring that community spaces like churches were opened to people's needs. In early 1970, another Puerto Rican group on the Upper West Side, named El Comité—"made up of Vietnam veterans, factory and construction workers, the unemployed, and former gang members—took over a storefront on 88th Street and Columbus Avenue" (Muzio 2017; Velázquez 1998). By the summer, they co-coordinated "Operation Move-In," during which activists broke into and squatted in nine buildings on Columbus Avenue, as part of a resistance to the city "urban renewal" program that many Black and Puerto Rican neighborhood residents had deemed an "urban removal" of their families. Then in 1971, the Young Lords collaborated with the Puerto Rican Student Union (PRSU) to hold a conference at Columbia University that drew 1,000 students. They focused on creating "Free Puerto Rico Now Committees" in high schools and colleges, and that October they also coordinated a march of 10,000 from El Barrio to the United Nations to "demand the end of U.S. colonialism in Puerto Rico, freedom for Puerto Rican political prisoners, and an end to police brutality in our communities" (Morales and Oliver-Vélez 2010; Starr 2010). This emerging vision for Puerto Rican Studies offered models that could be formalized in public schools and higher education in New York.

In 1971, Aquino-Bermúdez drafted a proposal for a Department of Puerto Rican Studies that augmented the vision for how the college could be a Puerto Rican intellectual and political epicenter by developing a strong campus/community bond, a library of Puerto Rican materials, and regular trips to the Island (Aquino-Bermúdez 1971). He noted that the college's Education, History, and Romance Languages Departments refused to offer courses relevant to Puerto Rican Studies, and resisted when the UES tried to initiate them. Even so, the number of students who took courses on Puerto Rico jumped from 90 students in Fall 1969 to 250 students in Fall 1970, to 350 students in 1971—50 in each class (Aquino-Bermúdez 1975, 160). At this time, Puerto Ricans comprised about 9.3 percent (almost one million) of the city's population, 12.8 percent of Manhattan's population, but still only 4.6 percent of City College students (Aquino-Bermúdez 1971, 7-8). Aquino-Bermúdez framed some inherent antagonisms that Puerto Rican Studies had within settler-colonial U.S. universities which continue to resound today:

The department should assume an advocacy role in institutional and social change. The dilemma (and danger) become immediately evident that as the department or its students move into conflict roles and conflict issues, the pressures on the part of the University's administration as well as the political establishment will increase to diminish these activities. The department, however, has to constantly probe and push the limits to which such an activist role can be developed and sustained. (1971, 36–7)

As Aquino-Bermúdez pushed for the creation of a distinct Puerto Rican Studies Department, so, too, did his colleagues for Afro-American Studies, Asian Studies, and Jewish Studies Departments (City University of New York Board of Higher Education Minutes 1971, 106). By Spring 1971, UES Chair Osborne Scott argued, albeit as someone hired to de-escalate campus dissent, "the department has been committed to the task of transcending traditional academic disciplines, and forging a community of learning which pursues cross-cultural understanding, contacts, cooperation, and mutual support" (Wu 1971, 3). Presciently, he warned that the creation of these four new departments would increase "competition among the various ethnic groups for resources, faculty lines, and facilities" (Wu 1971). That semester, Charles V. Hamilton and Harold Cruse had been appointed by City College

President Marshak as outside advisors to review whether to create separate Black and Puerto Rican Studies Departments. They also assessed:

It would be far better not to create two separate departments of Black Studies and Puerto Rican Studies [that] would create unnecessary duplication and division which would be dysfunctional to the development of a sound academic curriculum. The study of materials relating to black people in Africa, the Caribbean and the United States should not be seen as isolated phenomena. (The Campus 1971, 4)

Even though, by this time, the 1969 strike's demand for the creation of a School of Black and Puerto Rican Studies had transformed into calls for a School of Third World Studies, the CUNY Board of Higher Education decided to approve an institutionalization process that fractured these entwined studies into more siloed, albeit inter-disciplinary, departments.

FORMATION OF PUERTO RICAN STUDIES

For the Fall 1971 semester, Aquino-Bermúdez chaired a new Puerto Rican Studies Department featuring eighteen faculty members and twenty-two courses, such as Ethnic Leaders, The Plastic Arts of Puerto Rico, The Impact of Puerto Rican Literature of Protest, and the Sociological and Psychological Impact of Colonialism on Puerto Rico (City University of New York Board of Higher Education Minutes 1971; City College of New York Course Bulletin 1972). Meanwhile, in each of the corresponding new departments, three Asian Studies faculty members taught over twelve courses, sixteen Afro-American Studies faculty members taught over sixty courses, and six Jewish Studies faculty members taught eleven courses. Although City College and the BHE refused to implement a Women's Studies Department, twelve faculty members from across disciplines offered fourteen cross-listed classes.

City College administrators housed Black Studies and Puerto Rican Studies in the Social Sciences Division, and Asian Studies and Jewish Studies in the Humanities Division, in an apparent attempt to create political divisions at the institutional level. It is worth speculating whether each of these new Departments felt compelled to adhere to some disciplinary methodologies over others that foregrounded certain categories of knowledge, while occluding historical links across these ethnic lineages. For example,

Afro-American Studies courses focused on African, Afro-American, and Anglophonic Afro-Caribbean histories and societies, with little analytic space dedicated to Afro-Puerto Rican and other Afro-Caribbean Spanish speakers, as well as Afro-Indigenous and Afro-Latin American histories—which was notably an earlier complaint against the UES Department under Osborne Scott (Haslip-Viera 2020, pers. comm.). Similarly, Puerto Rican Studies was not supposed to focus on African or Indigenous bridges, but instructors often ignored this limitation. Meanwhile, Asian Studies elided its Caribbean immigration lineages, and Jewish Studies apparently overlooked its long co-constitutive relationship to Black liberation. For example, the Fall 1972 semester featured a Black Studies course on the Prison and Concentration Camp and a Jewish Studies course on the Holocaust and Concentration Camps. Reading across the courses offered in each Department, we see potential comparative connections that were missed or impossible, given the college's preconceived structures.

By the end of the 1975-1976 academic year, after City College's Puerto Rican Studies Department expanded to offer thirty-four classes, CUNY communities were devastated by news that the Board of Higher Education would implement undergraduate tuition across the board, a decision which the federal government enforced as part of its agreement to ameliorate the state's fiscal crisis. In this same year, CUNY shifted from being a majority Euro-descended student body to a predominantly Black, Latinx, and Asian student body, in a newly achieved demographic reflection of New York City. The Fall 1976 imposition of tuition occurred with massive layoffs of many of the faculty who had helped usher in Open Admissions, as well as a drastic decline of students. CUNY and New York City punitive economic policies would soon bend the nation's cities and colleges towards privatization and sharpened inequalities (Phillips-Fein 2017).

This setback to educational access was coupled with news of a breakthrough in language justice at City College, in an example of conflicting messages of scarcity and abundance. Two days later, on May 7th, a *Campus* newspaper interview with Puerto Rican Studies Chairperson Aquino-Bermúdez announced his receipt of a $25,000 federal grant to implement bilingual education studies. He said, "There is a mentality of assimilation here in America, where the assumption is that people should speak English and nothing else," and yet "Puerto Rican Studies deals with bilingual elements, which include culture, land, and languages" (Knight 1976). While thirteen Black professors in the English Department were on a three-day hunger strike to protest tuition and major budget cuts, Puerto Rican Studies was finally getting support for a bilingual education demand that had been animated in the 1969 strike (Mahabeer 1976). The 1976-77 academic year was thus mired in massive layoffs, budget cuts, and universal tuition costs, alongside innovations in pedagogies for the multi-ethnic and multilingual communities that CUNY increasingly served.

Despite the gains in bilingual education, tuition imposition reduced the numbers of students in Puerto Rican Studies courses. As a result, the Puerto Rican campus community and its Department soon experienced a longing for cohesion amidst departmental setbacks. In a November 1977 open letter—"A Call to the Puerto Rican Student Body at CCNY"—student Franklin Velásquez warned, "If we cannot organize at City College, we will gradually be eliminated from this Institution. If we don't fight for any of our democratic rights, we will gradually lose Puerto Rican Studies and Bilingual Education.... If a Puerto Rican brother or sister has a problem with financial aid or a racist teacher, a Puerto Rican organization of concerned students should exist which can effectively defend that student's rights" (Velásquez 1977). The archival record is unclear on whether people on campus heeded his warning but demonstrates that the PRSU's visibility may have waned. More broadly, forty-eight City College faculty suffered job losses during CUNY's 1976 retrenchment, which slashed $64 million from its budget and laid off hundreds of faculty members (Wysoki 1976). By Fall 1977, only three Puerto Rican Studies professors were listed—Federico Aquino-Bermúdez, Adriana García de Aldridge, and Eduardo Irlanda—with an improbably huge list of forty-two courses to offer.

In this context, Gabriel Haslip-Viera was hired in 1977, and would remain at City College teaching Puerto Rican Studies for almost forty years. Haslip-Viera had taken night classes at City College in 1969, then daytime history courses in 1972. While a student, he also focused on community education and drug rehabilitation work with the Harlem Confrontation Program (Haslip-Viera 2016). Even though Haslip-Viera focused his doctoral studies on Mexican history, he was hired by the Puerto Rican Studies Department (Haslip-Viera 2019). Two years later, Sherrie Baver was hired by this Department, where she continues to teach at present in its current incarnation, the Latin American and Latino Studies (LALS) Program. Baver studied Latin American politics with a focus on Puerto Rico at Columbia University, where she also participated in the 1968 campus occupations. A non-Latina, Baver was hired as someone who had directly studied the Island's historical relationship to the United States. She recounts, "I came to a place that was interested in struggle" (Baver 2019).

The college's various ethnic studies departments fared differently in the first few years after universal tuition. In the Fall 1978 semester, Jewish Studies' enrollment dropped to three courses, two faculty members, and only one student majoring in the Department. In contrast, Black Studies had fifty-two courses and fourteen hundred students with eighteen faculty members, while Puerto Rican Studies had twenty-three courses and five hundred thirty-five students with eight faculty members (Tillman 1978). Baver and Haslip-Viera, alongside Aquino-Bermúdez, Irizarry, and other faculty like Adriana García de Aldridge, Luis Ortega, and Marcia Klugman brought in new classes like Cuban Transformations and the Urbanization of Puerto Rico, as well as a range of new scholarship on Puerto Rico, into the classroom.

From its inception, Puerto Rican Studies confronted a pre-existing array of disparaging texts that waged neocolonial arguments about a Puerto Rican "culture of poverty" and overpopulation as explanations for the conditions of Puerto Rican lives on the Island and in the diaspora. Instead of enacting pedagogical violence by introducing these texts to students, Puerto Rican scholars decided to create their own counter-canon (Whalen 2009). El Centro de Estudios Puertorriqueños (The Center for Puerto Rican Studies), founded in 1973 at Hunter College, produced research task forces, conferences, and *cuadernos* (notebooks) from which full-length books emerged, such as the History Task Force's *Labor Migration under Capitalism: The Puerto Rican Experience* (1979). City College Puerto Rican Studies faculty also brought in Manuel Maldonado-Denis' *The Emigration Dialectic: Puerto Rico and the U.S.A.* (1980), Arturo Morales-Carrión's *Puerto Rico: A Political and Cultural History* (1983), and various books on Puerto Rico published by Monthly Review Press (Haslip-Viera 2019).

By the early to mid-1980s, the New York City population continued to transform, with more Caribbean and Latin American families (in particular from the Dominican Republic) migrating to the city and thus altering the com-position of CUNY. At City College, from 1983-85, cultural historian Adriana García de Aldridge chaired Puerto Rican Studies. Sociologist Angelo Falcón also taught there while heading the Institute for Puerto Rican Policy, which he founded. In 1985, Haslip-Viera became the Department chairperson, and Federico Aquino-Bermúdez retired as Professor Emeritus. Iris López was wel-comed to join the faculty, where thirty-five years later she continues to teach and serve as Co-Director of the LALS Program with Baver. Born and raised in Brooklyn, with Puerto Rican parents who were factory workers, López had studied at Borough of Manhattan Community College and organized to create ethnic studies there in the early 1970s, and then studied at New York University and Columbia University. She explains, "I came to Puerto Rican Studies out of choice," bringing "critical thinking skills, understanding colonial history that has shaped us, and empowering students. My priority was to help the working class, especially racialized students," and to collaborate with the surrounding community of Dominicans and Puerto Ricans (López 2019).

By this time, courses on Cuban, Dominican, and Latin American his-tory were being regularly offered in the Department. Puerto Rican students were no longer the primary, let alone the majority, of Caribbean and Latin American students. Haslip-Viera recalls that the student composition in the Department was mostly Dominican, then Puerto Rican, then Mexican and Central American, and that even a cohort of Ghanaian (among other non-Caribbean and Latinx) students took classes. Accordingly, the Department consciously worked to amend its scope of studies. Despite opposition from Black Studies, International Studies, and Romance Languages (in particu-lar Argentine and Cuban professors), which argued that the Puerto Rican Studies faculty were not qualified to teach these broader fields, Haslip-Viera facilitated a "treaty of separation" (Haslip-Viera 2019). Black Studies agreed to teach courses on the Anglo- and Francophone Caribbean, and Puerto Rican Studies would teach the Spanish-speaking Caribbean. This further contributed to a formalized racialized and linguistic decoupling. For example, one would now need to take a Black Studies course on Haiti and a separate Latin American Studies course on the Dominican Republic to learn about the island of Ayiti/Hispaniola. Nevertheless, Latin American Studies instructors "were encouraged to ignore or violate these kinds of separation"

(Haslip-Viera 2020, pers. comm.). More broadly, major hemispheric changes—the fall and rise of dictatorships and U.S. military interventions across the Americas and the Caribbean—also informed this departmental re-focus.

LATIN AMERICAN AND HISPANIC CARIBBEAN STUDIES FORMED, THEN EMBATTLED

Thus, in the Fall 1986 semester, the Puerto Rican Studies Department changed its name and purpose to Latin American and Hispanic Caribbean Studies (LAHCS), chaired by Gabriel Haslip-Viera, with five faculty listed in the course catalog. Core classes now centered on the Heritage of the Spanish-speaking Antilles—Cuba, Dominican Republic, and Puerto Rico. By the late 1980s, department meetings discussed Central American solidarity initiatives. Closer to home, the faculty supported the emerging wave of students—including from their department—who led protests against tuition increases and budget cuts under Governor Mario Cuomo. This culminated in over a dozen campus occupations across CUNY in 1989, as well as the creation of the Guillermo Morales/Assata Shakur Community and Student Center at City College (created in part by LAHCS students and named after Puerto Rican and Black revolutionaries who had attended the college), followed by another wave of protests in 1991 (McKinley 1989; Nieves 1991; Schonberger 1991).

At this time in the Latin American and Hispanic Caribbean Studies Department (LAHCS), Baver served as Chairperson, and cultural studies scholar Juan Flores began to teach there before being invited to direct El Centro in 1994. In 1992, the Dominican Studies Institute (DSI) was founded at City College, where it began to assemble a major library, publications, and an archival collection of primary sources related to the Dominican Republic and its diaspora. With the creation of the DSI, what appeared first as an institutional breakthrough in further recognizing Caribbean and Latin American Studies soon became the opposite in late Spring 1996. At this time, City College President Yolanda Moses, the CUNY Chancellor, and the Board of Trustees used budget cuts under Governor Pataki and a vendetta against controversies in the Black Studies Department (namely accusations of anti-Semitism and reductive Afrocentric theories by its Chairperson Leonard Jeffries) as a pretext to demote all of the college's ethnic studies departments into programs (City University of New York Board of Higher Education Minutes 1996, 68-70).

As López recalls, "Moses had it in for Black Studies and Leonard Jeffries. This punitive sanction was a horrendous setback for all of us" (López 2019). Turning the Department into a program meant that all of the LAHCS faculty members were shifted to other departments, and thereafter depended on the discretion of their new chairpersons to hire people who specialized in Latin American Studies in order for the program to survive. From 1995 to 2005, no additional shared faculty lines were given to the LAHCS Program. This occurred at a moment when the faculty were publishing crucial works on Puerto Rico and Latin American migration, such as Baver's 1993 work *The Political Economy of Colonialism: The State and Industrialization in Puerto Rico* and Baver, Falcón, and Haslip-Viera's 1996 anthology *Latinos in New York: Communities in Transition*. In 1997, López chaired the program, with its faculty now based in Sociology, Political Science, and Bilingual Education. Haslip-Viera moved to El Centro and became its director in 1998, then returned to City College in 2000.

Akin to the rise of Puerto Rican Studies on the streets in the 1960s and '70s, City College students and the larger campus community responded to Moses' tenure with a range of actions that reflected the LAHCS program's vision of advocacy and study in the college and its surrounding transnational communities. As CUNY herstorian Suzy Subways recounts, the CUNY Student Liberation Action Movement (SLAM!), in which LAHCS students were involved, organized at City College to keep the campus "open and accessible to the surrounding neighborhoods" (Sigal 2012). In 1998, City College students were informed by the custodial staff that a smoke detector outside the Morales/Shakur Center was actually a surveillance camera aimed at the Center's door. Black Studies faculty member Herb Boyd reported, "In an adjoining room the students found a television monitor and an apparent listening device that was aimed at the student lounge" (*Democracy Now!* 1998). What kinds of activities were happening inside the Center? The Pre-University Program, also known as the Free University, gathered "hundreds of high school students from Harlem and Washington Heights to the campus each weekend for events and academic support" (Sigal 2012). Current New York City Councilmember Ydanis Rodríguez, at the time a LAHCS major who helped to lead the '89 and '91 campus occupations, was a part of the Dominican Youth Union that coordinated this weekly program.

AFTER OPEN ADMISSIONS

By the time Open Admissions was formally terminated as a policy at CUNY in 1999, the administration had been aiming for years to curb the entrance of Black and Latinx students who led many of the university's struggles for high-quality, affordable, public education that could be relevant to working New Yorkers of all colors. Then-Mayor Rudolph Giuliani's office released a report on "The City University of New York: An Institution Adrift" to justify this re-segregation policy. Incoming Chancellor Matthew Goldstein besmirched the student movement legacies of Third World liberation that had transformed the university's admissions three decades earlier, in an ostensible effort to make CUNY more academic and research oriented. He noted at the time, "The discussion has to move from the ill-preparedness of students and their dropout rates and all the other things that give the perception of CUNY as a *third world university*... we need to shift the focus" (Arenson 1999; Mayor's Advisory Task Force on the City University of New York 1999, emphasis added). Goldstein's use of the term was not merely coincidental. In order to erase both the radical legacy of Black and Latinx student struggles and the Open Admissions policy that had exponentially increased their presence at CUNY, the new chancellor framed the university as needing to be saved by using colonialist rhetoric to justify renewed discriminatory admissions practices.

Despite this institutional reform-as-counterinsurgency, the Latin American and Hispanic Caribbean Studies Program, now chaired by Baver, and the campus community maintained solidarity with the Dominican Republic, Puerto Rico, and broader Third World diasporas. A national conference called Dominicanos 2000 was hosted there, and sociologist Ramona Hernández (who had been a doctoral student of El Centro founding director Frank Bonilla) was invited to direct the Dominican Studies Institute, a post which she continues to hold today. Meanwhile, the struggle to oust the U.S. military from the Puerto Rican island of Vieques animated campus-wide solidarity efforts around the entwined themes of decolonization, environmental justice, and human rights (Baver 2019). This campaign was remarkably successful in 2003 as the U.S. was launching two new war fronts on false pretenses in Afghanistan and Iraq after the 9/11 attacks. Accordingly, the organizing momentum shifted to oppose these new imperial ventures.

Caribbean and Latin American students coordinated protests against military recruiters at City College, welcomed Iraq Veterans Against the War to speak on campus, and mobilized for countless anti-war demonstrations.

By 2007, the City College administration's course bulletins no longer listed the faculty for Latin American and Hispanic Caribbean Studies, as well as other ethnic studies programs, as it did for the rest of the college's programs and departments. As a result, the esteemed caliber of a range of ethnic studies faculty was under-recognized. Nonetheless, LAHCS faculty members continued to teach full course loads and publish books. In 2001, Haslip-Viera released *Taíno Revival: Critical Perspectives on Puerto Rican Identity and Cultural Politics*, and then in 2004 co-edited the volume *Boricuas in Gotham: Puerto Ricans in the Making of Modern New York City*. In 2006, Baver and Barbara Deutsch Lynch's book *Beyond Sun and Sand: Caribbean Environmentalisms* was released, followed by López's 2008 book *Matters of Choice: Puerto Rican Women's Struggle for Reproductive Freedom*. These works demonstrated the Program's ever-expansive interdisciplinary approach to linking Caribbean and Latin American Studies with environmentalism, late capitalist urban migration, reproductive autonomy, and ongoing debates on indigeneity and racialization.

From 2011 onwards, the CUNY Board of Trustees increased tuition almost every year and repressed efforts by campaigns to create more affordable access to the university (Alessandrini 2011). In 2013, Baver became the Director for the renamed Latin American and Latino Studies program, which was housed in the renamed "Colin L. Powell School for Civic and Global Leadership, formerly the Division of Social Sciences." Campus organizing efforts renewed to resist the militarization of CUNY—as evidenced by the return of the Reserve Officers' Training Corps (ROTC) and the hiring of former CIA Director General David Petraeus (Glück et al. 2014). CUNY responded with vehement campus repression and arrests of student leaders. Furthermore, in October 2013, the City College administration seized the Morales/Shakur Center and all of its belongings—including an invaluable trove of campus and community movement archives which are still in their custody, if not destroyed by now (Kaminer 2013; Merlan 2013). In the lineage of the University of Harlem in 1969, and the Free University in the late 1990s, the Center had been a vital resource for gathering people (including numerous LALS students) from the campus and community for organizing meetings, free textbook exchanges, and a community supported agriculture program. Both the administration and social movement participants recognized the significance of this semi-autonomous site of Third World Studies. Its closure was a chilling defeat for the campus community.

LATIN AMERICAN AND LATINO STUDIES IN THE PRESENT

For the last several years, funding contradictions and selective austerity measures have abounded. López and Baver have alternated chairing LALS (as did sociologist Norma Fuentes-Mayorga for one year). While teaching in the program, Haslip-Viera also chaired the Sociology Department from 2007 to 2013 before retiring in 2015, and López chaired Sociology from 2013 to 2016. By the end of 2016, as City College President Staiano-Coico suddenly resigned after being accused of embezzling almost $150,000 in college funds for personal use, Latin American and Latino Studies lost faculty lines as people retired and has operated without a program administrative assistant since 2017 (*The Ticker* 2016). López explains,

Every couple of years, since the 1990s, we've had different deans, revolving doors. You can't get help, then it's more difficult to create new curricula, new materials, to keep the door open to bring in students. I'm constantly trying to catch up and keep up. It's very hard to push ahead and create other things— events, activities, working with the community. Because of this austerity diet that we're all being fed, it's a stranglehold. (2019)

Baver notes that more broadly, "the University has become more neo-liberal, as neoliberalism has been pushed onto Latin America. Twenty-nine percent of CUNY is Latinx, and the college doesn't care. They say if you want money, fundraise" (Baver 2019). López agrees: "Our schools have become more corporatized, bringing in businesspeople to give talks. That's why people retire, it's now a foreign environment" (López 2019). Meanwhile, basic conditions at the college are exacerbated, with "no toilet paper, soap, paper towels, mouse infestation... Some departments are painted more frequently, with new rugs, but not for us" (López 2019).

Nonetheless, the program's 2020 roster illustrated its tenacious imaginative vision beyond these slow counter-insurgency austerity measures:

Deconstructing Dominican Identity; Caribbean Magic and Spirit; Art and Decolonization in Latin America; Afro-Latino Music and Cultures; Blancas, Negras, y Morenas: Gender and Race in Another America; and Latinas in Transition and Translation: The Latina in Latinx Studies. In addition to Baver, López, and Fuentes-Mayorga, the program includes faculty like Mariana Romo-Carmona, an editor with the hugely influential Kitchen Table: Women of Color Press, and Jessica González-Rojas, Executive Director of the National Latina Institute for Reproductive Health. They employ critical feminist classroom pedagogies to discuss race, class, gender, sexuality, and justice as conceptual and historical frameworks around which to advocate for freedom. In addition, the faculty work with students to critique prevailing discourses around cultures of poverty, disadvantages, the pressure to assimilate, and other ways that Caribbean and Latin American peoples and their diasporas continue to be dehumanized and underestimated (López 2019).

Meanwhile, in the office right next door, the Black Studies Program's new director is a longtime City College educator, Vanessa K. Valdés, who identifies as Black Nuyorican and seeks to reclaim Departmental status, in part by working closely with LALS. One example of collaboration is the Spring 2020 course Black Latina/x Feminisms that was cross-listed in both programs. Valdés explains,

I work alongside my colleague, Iris López, and respect the sovereignty of that program; we look for opportunities for collaboration... My focus remains firmly on the study of the global Black experience and on ensuring that the students and faculty (part-time and full-time) of this program, which is the largest of any of the Black Studies programs and departments within CUNY, continue to receive the courses and support that they need to succeed. (2019, pers. comm.)

At a December 2019 event on campus by the Free CUNY coalition called "Ourselves and the Academy: Ethnic Studies in CUNY," López, Romo-Carmona, and Valdés spoke with a room of undergraduate student organizers. While reflecting on the 1969 "Harlem University" campus takeover's lessons, Valdés framed the current moment as Black Studies and Latin American and Latino Studies respecting each other's autonomy, which is a notably different framing than how City College students and movements fifty years ago fought for Black and Puerto Rican Studies, Third World Studies, and Black and Third World Liberation.

This distinction opens up whether the politics of coalition-building in the university has transitioned into the politics of autonomy, which may risk continued erosion in an institutional context of struggling with scarce resources. Ethnic studies were formed out of entwined liberation movements, but then became isolated as embattled departments. However, as María Pérez y González (outgoing long-term Chairperson of Puerto Rican and Latino Studies at Brooklyn College) warns, in times of austerity administrators may wish to merge (and further downsize) these distinct programs or departments into one under the rubric of ethnic studies; she therefore argues "independence/departmental autonomy with strong solidarity among these ethnic studies groups and allies is more desirable and effective" (Pérez y González 2020, pers. comm.). To be sure, their future survival—and further, liberation—will be ameliorated through comparative studies and actions in conjunction with each other, as well as among larger coalitions like those that had achieved their initial founding. We will need to reconsolidate power across our differences to defend the studies that were enacted back then. But all the while, we must continue to demand that a Third World University and a broader liberated society is not only possible, but an inter-generational promise that we intend to keep.

Puerto Rican scholar Félix Matos Rodríguez was appointed on May 1, 2019, to become the first Chancellor of color in the university's history. Unlike many of the appointed members of the CUNY Board of Trustees, Matos Rodríguez is a longtime educator—particularly, a historian on the lives and work of Puerto Rican women—who previously served as President of Hostos Community College, Director of El Centro, and President of Queens College. A little-known fact is that Matos Rodríguez got his first teaching job at age twenty-three in LAHCS at City College under Haslip-Viera, who later served on Matos Rodríguez's doctoral committee. Those who know Matos Rodríguez's record of service and scholarship hoped that his leadership could restore and broaden ethnic studies across the university. However, since becoming Chancellor, Matos Rodríguez has presided over additional tuition increases that were approved in December 2019—during finals week, no less—that further pushed out the students who predominantly take ethnic studies classes. Furthermore, in spring 2020 after the onset of the Covid-19 pandemic, CUNY delayed and then stumbled to move classes fully online. Then 2,900 adjunct faculty, including in ethnic studies, were notified that they would not be rehired (and for some, lose healthcare access) for the subsequent fall semester. This situation is worsened by a $13 billion New York State budget deficit that refuses to prioritize public higher education. Baver surmises of the new chancellor, "His job is to run a gigantic bureaucracy; I don't see vast changes happening" (Baver 2019). However, Matos Rodríguez has inherited the leadership mantle in a moment when CUNY's faculty, staff, and students—as well as a wave of alumni and allies/accomplices in the city of New York—are ardently working to decolonize and transform the university and city, including revitalizing CUNY's Center ("El Centro") for Puerto Rican Studies, while fostering broader movement bridges between Puerto Rico, Palestine, the Philippines, Colombia, the Dominican Republic, Kashmir, and beyond (CUNY for Palestine 2021; Save Centro Coalition 2021; Strike MoMA 2021).

The timing and scope of efforts to transform CUNY matters well beyond our institutional history and immediate setting, even as we require the footing of our local histories of upheaval and reform. In Puerto Rico—one hundred fifty years after El Grito de Lares—the conditions for a 21st century decolonization struggle have emerged through recurring strikes at its public university, outrage at the 2016 U.S. Congressional Puerto Rico Oversight, Management, and Economic Stability Act (PROMESA), Hurricanes Irma and María, former island Governor Ricardo Rosselló's ouster, multiple earthquakes, and an ongoing pandemic. The disgraced Wanda Vázquez Garced-led government—now led by Pedro Pierluisi—confronted a populace that is increasingly turning to Mutual Aid Centers (Centros de Apoyo Mutuo), abandoned school reclamations like La Conde, Afro-Boricua LGBTQ initiatives like Espicy Nipples, feminist formations like Colectiva Feminista en Construcción, and cultural organizations like AgitArte in a new ecosystem of Puerto Rican direct democracy and liberation (AgitArte 2020; Colectiva Feminista en Construcción 2020; Díaz Ortíz 2020; Espicy Nipples 2020; La Conde 2020).

At CUNY, the fate of ethnic studies is once again at a crossroads, while campaigns to transform the university are gaining traction as the nation erupts in the most vibrant struggle for Black liberation and social transformations seen in two generations. If education is the practice of freedom, then where, how, and with whom we study is of the most profound significance. Over fifty years ago, a coalition of Puerto Rican, Black, and Asian students and teachers, with Euro-descended supporters, succeeded in altering the admissions criteria and curriculum of the largest public urban university in the nation, as part of a larger transnational metamorphic vision. Puerto Rican Studies advocates at CUNY can draw from these lessons as we strategize our future directions.

NOTES

[1] Readers are welcome to fill in more gaps to tell these stories of how our peoples transformed City College and CUNY by contributing to the online Puerto Rican Studies in CUNY archive that is linked to this volume: <50YearsofPRS-CUNY@ brooklyn.cuny.edu>.

REFERENCES

Alessandrini, Anthony. 2011. Our University: On Police Violence at CUNY. *Jadaliyya* 27 November. Accessed 20 January 2020. <https://www.jadaliyya.com/ Details/24707>.

Aquino-Bermúdez, Federico. 1971. Proposal for Department of Puerto Rican Studies, 1971-76. New York: City College of New York Cohen Library Archives.

_____. 1975. Growth and Development of Puerto Rican Studies Departments: A Case Study of Two Departments at the City University of New York. Ph.D. dissertation, University of Massachusetts.

Arenson, Karen W. 1999. Trustees Anoint CUNY Chief with a Pledge Not to Meddle. *The New York Times* 23 July. Accessed 20 January 2020. <https:// www.nytimes.com/1999/07/23/nyregion/trustees-anoint-cuny-chief-with-a-pledge-not-to-meddle.html>.

Baver, Sherrie. 1993. *The Political Economy of Colonialism: The State and Industrialization in Puerto Rico*. Westport, CT: Praeger.

_____. 2019. Interviewed by Conor Tomás Reed. 21 September.

Baver, Sherrie and Barbara Deutsch Lynch. 2006. *Beyond Sun and Sand: Caribbean Environmentalisms*. New Brunswick, NJ: Rutgers University Press.

Baver, Sherrie, Angelo Falcón and Gabriel Haslip-Viera, eds. 1996. *Latinos in New York:Communities in Transition*. Notre Dame: University of Notre Dame Press.

Bonilla, Frank. 1972. Cultural Pluralism and the University: The Case of Puerto Rican Studies. *Revista de Brooklyn College*. Revista del Instituto de Estudios Puertorriqueños de Brooklyn College 2(1), 9–15.

Butt, Tahir. H. 2019. 'You Are Running a de Facto Segregated University': Racial Segregation and the City University of New York. In *The Strange Careers of the Jim Crow North: Segregation and Struggle Outside of the South*, eds. Brian Purnell and Jeanne Theoharis, with Komozi Woodard. 189–92. New York: New York University Press.

CCNY Coalition. 1997. The Facts about CUNYCard. Philadelphia: SLAM! Herstory Project. Accessed 20 January 2020. <https://slamherstory.wordpress.com/2009/10/07/1997-the-facts-about-cunycard>.

Centros De Apoyo Mutuo: Centers of Mutual Support. 2020. *AgitArte* 21 January. Accessed 30 June 2020. <https://agitarte.org/centros-de-apoyo-mutuo-centers-of-mutual-support-4>.

Citibank: The Pawnbroker. 1998. *Spheric*. New York: CUNY Digital History Archive. Accessed 20 January 2020. <https://cdha.cuny.edu/items/show/341>.

College News in Brief. 1974. *The Campus* 24 January.

City College of New York Course Bulletins. 1968, 1969, 1970, 1973-74, 1974-75, 1975-76, 1978-79, 1981-83,1983-85, 1985-87, 1987-89, 1989-91, 1991-93, 1993-95, 1997-99, 1999-2001, 2001-2003, 2003-2005, 2005-2007, 2007-2009, 2013-2015, 2015-2017, 2017-2018, 2018-2019. New York: City College of New York Cohen Library Archives.

City University of New York Board of Higher Education Minutes. 9 July 1969; 22 July 1969; 29 September 1969; 24 May 1971; 28 May 1996. Accessed 6 March 2020. <http://policy.cuny.edu/minutes>.

Colectiva Feminista en Construcción. Instagram. Accessed 30 June 2020. <https://www.instagram.com/colectivafeministapr>.

CUNY for Palestine. Linktree. Accessed 15 June 2021. <https://www.linktr.ee/cuny4palestine>.

Denis, Nelson A. 2015. *War Against All Puerto Ricans: Revolution and Terror in America's Colony*. New York: Nation Books.

Díaz Ortíz, Jorge. 2020. Organizing Mutual Solidarity Projects as an Act of Resistance in Puerto Rico. *A Blade of Grass*. 16 June. Accessed 30 June 2020. <https://www.abladeofgrass.org/articles/organizing-mutual-solidarity-projects-act-resistance-puerto-rico>.

Dyer, Conrad. 1990. Protest and the Politics of Open Admissions: The Impact of the Black and Puerto Rican Student Community (of City College). Ph.D. dissertation, City University of New York Graduate Center.

Espicy Nipples. Instagram. Accessed 30 June 2020. <https://www.instagram.com/espicynipplez>.

Ethnic Error. 1971. *The Campus* 16 April.

Ferguson, Roderick A. 2012. *The Reorder of Things: The University and Its Pedagogies of Minority Difference*. Minneapolis: University of Minnesota Press.

Fernández, Johanna. 2020. *The Young Lords: A Radical History*. Chapel Hill: University of North Carolina Press.

Glück, Zoltan, Manissa McCleave Maharawal, Isabelle Nastasia and Conor Tomás Reed. 2014. Organizing Against Empire: Struggles over the Militarization of CUNY. *Berkeley Journal of Sociology* 20 October. Accessed 20 January 2020. <http://berkeleyjournal.org/2014/10/organizing-against-empire-struggles-over-the-militarization-of-cuny/>.

Haslip-Viera, Gabriel. 2001. *Taíno Revival: Critical Perspectives on Puerto Rican Identity and Cultural Politics*. Princeton, NJ: Markus Wiener Publishers.

_____. 2016. Interview with Gabriel Haslip-Viera on 16 December. Segment 7, Part 2. New York: Center for Puerto Rican Studies Library and Archives. Accessed 20 January 2020. <https://centropr.hunter.cuny.edu/digitalarchive/index.php/Detail/objects/3839>.

_____. 2019. Interviewed by Conor Tomás Reed. 10 September.

Haslip-Viera, Gabriel, Angelo Falcón and Félix Matos Rodríguez, eds. 2004. *Boricuas in Gotham: Puerto Ricans in the Making of Modern New York City*. Princeton, NJ: Markus Wiener Publishers.

History Task Force. 1979. *Labor Migration under Capitalism: The Puerto Rican Experience*. New York: Monthly Review Press.

Jiménez, Lillian. 2009. Puerto Ricans and Educational Civil Rights: A History of the 1969 City College Takeover (An Interview with Five Participants). *CENTRO: Journal of the Center for Puerto Rican Studies Journal* 21(2), 165–75.

Kaminer, Ariel. 2013. Protests as City Closes a Student Center. *The New York Times* 21 October. Accessed 20 January 2020. <https://www.nytimes.com/2013/10/22/nyregion/protests-as-city-college-closes-a-student-center.html>.

Knight, Angela. 1976. Bilingual Teaching Fights 'Assimilation Mentality.' *The Campus* 7 May.

La Conde. Instagram. Accessed 30 June 2020. <https://www.instagram.com/lacondepr>.

LeBrón, Marisol. 2019. *Policing Life and Death: Race, Violence, and Resistance in Puerto Rico*. Oakland: University of California Press.

López, Iris. 2008. *Matters of Choice: Puerto Rican Women's Struggle for Reproductive Freedom*. New Brunswick, NJ: Rutgers University Press.

_____. 2019. Interviewed by Conor Tomás Reed. 16 December.

Mahabeer, Pamela. 1976. 13 Black Profs Call Hunger Strike to Protest City U 'Resegregation.' *The Campus* 7 May.

Maldonado-Denis, Manuel. 1980. *The Emigration Dialectic: Puerto Rico and the U.S.A.* New York: International Publishers.

Mayor's Advisory Task Force on the City University of New York. 1999. The City University of New York: An Institution Adrift. New York: CUNY Digital History Archive. Accessed 20 January 2020. <https://cdha.cuny.edu/items/show/2421>.

McKinley, Jr., James C. 1989. CUNY Protests Spread to More Schools. *The New York Times* 28 April. Accessed 20 January 2020. <https://www.nytimes.

com/1989/04/28/nyregion/cuny-protests-spread-to-more-schools.html>.

Medina, Douglas. 2014. Oral History Interview with Henry Arce. New York: CUNY Digital History Archive. Accessed 20 January 2020. <https://cdha.cuny.edu/items/show/6842>.

Merlan, Anna. 2013. CUNY City College Students Protest After Morales-Shakur Center, Hub of Campus Political Activity, Is Abruptly Closed. *The Village Voice* 22 October. Accessed 20 January 2020. <https://www.villagevoice.com/2013/10/22/cuny-city-college-students-protest-after-morales-shakur-center-hub-of-campus-political-activity-is-abruptly-closed>.

Morales, Iris and Denise Oliver-Vélez. 2010. Why Read the Young Lords Today? In *The Young Lords: A Reader*, ed. Darrel Enck-Wanzer. ix-xiv. New York: New York University Press.

Morales-Carrión, Arturo. 1983. *Puerto Rico: A Political and Cultural History*. New York: W.W. Norton and Company.

Muzio, Rose. 2017. *Radical Imagination, Radical Humanity: Puerto Rican Political Activism in New York*. Albany: State University of New York Press.

Newt Davidson Collective. 1974. Crisis at CUNY. *CUNY Digital History Archive*. Accessed 20 January 2020. <https://cdha.cuny.edu/items/show/16>.

Nieves, Evelyn. 1991. Protests Are All but Over at CUNY. *The New York Times* 28 April. Accessed 20 January 2020. <https://www.nytimes.com/1991/04/28/nyregion/protests-are-all-but-over-at-cuny.html>.

Nuñez, Louis. 2009. Reflections on Puerto Rican History: Aspira in the Sixties and the Coming of Age of the Stateside Puerto Rican Community. *CENTRO: Journal of the Center for Puerto Rican Studies* 21(2), 33–47.

Phillips-Fein, Kim. 2017. *Fear City: New York's Fiscal Crisis and the Rise of Austerity Politics*. New York: Metropolitan Books.

Reed, Conor Tomás. 2019. CUNY Will Be Free!: Black, Puerto Rican, and Women'sCompositions, Literatures, and Studies at the City College of New York and in New York City, 1960–1980. Ph.D. dissertation, City University of New York Graduate Center.

Rustin, Bayard. 1964. *Freedom Schools Archives*. New York: Schomburg Center for Research in Black Culture. Microfilm reel.

Sánchez Korrol, Virginia. 1994. *From Colonia to Community: The History of Puerto Ricans in New York City*. Berkeley: University of California Press.

Sasmor, Ken, and Tom Foty. 1969. It May Not Be the Place You Knew. *The Campus*. 6 May.

Save Centro Coalition. Linktree. Accessed 15 June 2021. <https://www.linktr.ee/savecentrocoalition>.

Schonberger, Benjamin. 1991. Student Protests Over State Budget Cuts Spread to 8 CUNY Campuses. *The Chronicle of Higher Education* 17 April. Accessed 20 January 2020.<https://www.chronicle.com/article/Student-Protests-Over-State/86937>.

Secret Surveillance of Students. 1998. *Democracy Now!* 4 June. Accessed 20 January 2020. <https://www.democracynow.org/1998/6/4/secret_surveillance_of_students>.

Serrano, Basilio. 1998. ¡Rifle, *Cañón, y Escopeta!*: A Chronicle of the Puerto Rican Student Union. In *The Puerto Rican Movement: Voices from the Diaspora,* eds. Andrés Torres and José E. Velázquez. 124–43. Philadelphia: Temple University Press.

Sigal, Brad. 2012. Brad Sigal on SLAM! at City College from 1996 to 2000. Interviewed by Suzy Subways. Philadelphia: SLAM! Herstory Project. Accessed 20 January 2020. <https://slamherstory.wordpress.com/2014/04/07/first-audio-segments-from-the-oral-history-interviews>.

Starr, Meg. 2010. Hit Them Harder: Leadership, Solidarity, and the Puerto Rican Independence Movement. In *The Hidden 1970s: Histories of Radicalism,* ed. Dan Berger. 135–54. New Brunswick, NJ: Rutgers University Press.

Strike MoMA. Accessed 15 June 2021. <https://www.strikemoma.org>.

System-wide Investigation Uncovers Fund Misuse in CUNY Colleges. 2016. *The Ticker* 5 December. Accessed 20 January 2020. <https://theticker.org/archive/system-wide-investigation-uncovers-fund-misuse-in-cuny-colleges>.

Tillman, Linda. 1978. Jewish Studies Threatened. *The Campus* 29 September.

Tinajero, Araceli. 2010. *El Lector: A History of the Cigar Factory Reader.* Austin: University of Texas Press.

Torres, Andrés, and José E. Velázquez, eds. 1998. *The Puerto Rican Movement: Voices from the Diaspora.* Philadelphia: Temple University Press.

Velásquez, Franklin. 1977. A Call to the Puerto Rican Student Body at CCNY. *The Paper* 3 November.

Velázquez, José E. 1998. Another West Side Story: An Interview with Members of El Comité-MINP. In *The Puerto Rican Movement: Voices from the Diaspora*, eds. Andrés Torres and José E. Velázquez. 88–106. Philadelphia: Temple University Press.

Whalen, Carmen. 2009. Radical Contexts: Puerto Rican Politics in the 1960s and 1970s and the Center for Puerto Rican Studies. *CENTRO: Journal of the Center for Puerto Rican Studies* 21(2), 220–55.

Wu, Ernest. 1971. Scott Calls Proposal to Disband Dept 'Political Expedient.' *The Campus* 26 March.

CHAPTER 6

HOW A FEW STUDENTS TRANSFORMED THE IVORY TOWER: PUERTO RICAN STUDIES AND ITS (R)EVOLUTION AT BROOKLYN COLLEGE

María Elizabeth Pérez y González

Legend has it that in the Spring of 1969 Milga Morales stood on the desk of Brooklyn College's Vice President of Student Affairs and raised the Puerto Rican flag declaring, "Viva Puerto Rico!"—a rallying cry of unity for representation in the ivory tower.[1] She was a founding member of the year-old Puerto Rican Alliance, an organization consisting of a few first-generation college students, that actively demonstrated for inclusion of Puerto Ricans, their history and culture in the City University of New York (CUNY). This is just one moment in the struggle for Puerto Rican Studies during the tumultuous 1960s that successfully established the nation's first Institute of Puerto Rican Studies in September 1969, leading to a full-fledged department in 1970. Less than three decades later in 1998, sitting behind that same desk and in that same office, Morales became the first Puerto Rican/Latinx[2] Brooklyn College Dean of Students and in 2010 the Vice President of Student Affairs. Some might call that poetic justice. Activists call that vision, courage, audacity, sacrifice, and solidarity.

Alongside and inspired by non-Latinx Black activists, Puerto Ricans rose up in the midst of the Civil Rights movements in response to the dire situation their communities were experiencing. Teetering on despair, they found the inner power to declare, ¡Basta *Ya!* (Enough Already!). It was time to mobilize, organize, and push back against the abuse, neglect, racism, and injustices that were simultaneously obvious and obfuscated. Their *luchas* (struggles) brought forth historic achievements in U.S. academia, including the creation of the Brooklyn College (BC) Department of Puerto Rican Studies (PRS),[3] preceded by the Institute of Puerto Rican Studies.[4]

THE BIRTHING PANGS OF PRS: CHALLENGES AND ACCOMPLISHMENTS

When a few Puerto Rican students joined the campus anti-Vietnam War demonstration on April 27, 1968, it marked the beginning of numerous actions that ultimately resulted in PRS at BC. In May, student members of the W.E.B. DuBois Club[5]; Brooklyn League of Afro-American Collegians (BLAC)[6]; a handful of Puerto Rican students (some who identified as Black[7]); and the mostly white middle-class Jewish Students for a Democratic Society (SDS), including the President of the Student Government (College of Liberal Arts and Sciences), Michael Novick, disrupted the Faculty Council meeting and later engaged in a 16-hour sit-in at the Registrar's Office, demanding an increase in Black and Puerto Rican student enrollment, faculty, and courses. Numbering nearly 31,000 students, "1,002 were Negroes [a term used at the time referring to Black people] and 204 were Puerto Ricans"; there were "24 Negroes of the 767 full-time faculty"; no numbers were provided for Puerto Rican faculty members (Kihss 1968). Protesters were jeered and occasionally attacked by their counterparts. Although students were arrested and suspended in both incidents, they made some inroads. For example, Dean George Peck instructed academic departments to create such courses immediately. During this time, the Puerto Rican Alliance (PRA) was formed with a handful of Puerto Rican students, many of whom had entered college a few years earlier via the NYS-sponsored SEEK (Search for Education, Elevation, and Knowledge) and Educational Opportunity Programs. The Puerto Rican activists became aware that other student groups were demanding an Afro-American Studies Department and Institute and they became involved in similar efforts for Puerto Rican students. By Spring 1969, they joined BLAC, W.E.B. Dubois Club, and SDS in formulating and advocating "18 Demands"—opportunities and equity for Black and Puerto Rican students—to redress the status quo at Brooklyn College. Antonio "Tony" Nieves participated in the Central Committee of both BLAC[8] and PRA, consisting of six men and two women who designed a definitive platform for the allied students (Nieves 2019). The "18 Demands" had two guiding principles—"If Brooklyn College does not function for Black and Puerto Rican students, it should not function," and "These demands are non-negotiable" (Brooklyn College Department of Puerto Rican and Latino Studies Archives, n.d. circa 1969; Puerto Rican Alliance, n.d. circa 1970). The demands went public in April 1969 with 150 Black and Puerto Rican students and 40 white students occupying Acting President Peck's office.[9] In May, the activist campus groups engaged in various demonstrations: sit-ins, takeovers, the burning of a pig's head on the quad,[10] minor vandalism, pulling fire alarms, and small fires (Nieves 2019). As a result, in the pre-dawn hours of May 12th, 17 students were arrested in their homes across four boroughs plus two others shortly thereafter (Nieves 2019). They spent four days at Riker's Island, were each charged with 18 felonies and five misdemeanors that carried a cumulative sentence of 228 years and $15,000 bail (Biondi 2013, 168). The "BC 19"[11] bail was reduced to $6,500 since the students did not have any previous arrests, and only students of color were arrested even though there were white students from SDS involved. U.S. Representative Shirley Chisholm, a Brooklyn College alumna, helped raise money from local community and religious leaders (Biondi 2013, 169); some BLAC and PRA women also rallied to raise bail monies, and some supporters put up their homes as collateral (Nieves 2019). A year later, due to lack of evidence and with a letter from the newly appointed President John Kneller stating that he considered the case against the BC 19 closed and would rather have the students complete their educational goals, a deal was made to expunge the records after a short probationary period (Brooklyn College 1970). The heavy-handedness of law enforcement galvanized much fervor among the student body that continued to advocate for the 18 demands, as well as dropping the charges against the BC 19, and demanding that the NYPD vacate the campus (Biondi 2013, 170).

Students rallied for social and educational justice across CUNY and several emergency meetings of the CUNY Board of Higher Education (BHE) were held that May, calling upon the presidents of Borough of Manhattan Community and Bronx Community Colleges, and Brooklyn, City, and Queens Colleges to report on activities at their respective campuses, including lockdowns. It was during this time that a thorough review of university policies addressing admissions and university-wide faculty and student governance structures were undertaken (CUNY Board of Higher Education 1969a, 74–8). On July 9, 1969, the BHE sweepingly approved and called for the creation of Black and Puerto Rican Studies at the senior colleges "as interdisciplinary degree programs, institutes, or departments" (CUNY Board of Higher Education 1969b, 186).

In response to ongoing student activism, the creation of the Department of PRS at BC was announced at the Faculty Council meeting on March 17, 1970, by President Kneller and approved by the CUNY BHE in June effective September of that year (Brooklyn College Faculty Council Minutes 1970; CUNY Board of Higher Education Minutes 1970). Nonetheless, on April 30, 1970, about 50 PRA members took over a meeting between President Kneller and several deans to insist on 12 demands, three of which were non-negotiable. These spelled out the admission of an additional 1,000 students, the Black students to be new non-CUNY students, and no repercussions for demonstrators; all of which were ultimately agreed to (Horowitz 1981, 165). By spring commencement in 1970, many of the Brooklyn College graduates[12] wore a defiant fist of struggle or a peace sign on their gowns. Among them was PRA founding member Milga Morales, who was holding up a Puerto Rican flag (in itself an act of defiance because the flag was outlawed for nearly a decade in Puerto Rico). A funeral march proceeded, and "Taps" was played by a bugler, sounds that mimicked shots fired echoed, and "Revolution" by The Beatles was played as part of the commencement exercises; families applauded, argued, or walked out in response to the actions (Horowitz 1981,189; Milga Morales Nadal 2020, pers. comm.). Morales had experienced a college education the likes of which could not be found in textbooks. The tenacious activism of PRA had yielded fruits that would be harvested by those who would walk through the Brooklyn College gates for decades to come.

THE NASCENT DEPARTMENT OF PUERTO RICAN STUDIES

Both the Department of PRS and the Institute of PRS (IPRS) were led by Josephine Nieves. She and subsequent hires were appointed as faculty members in the Department of Sociology, and the majority on full-time lines were granted a Ph.D. waiver equivalency. Nieves was an alum of City College (CUNY), held a Master of Social Work from Columbia University, and was the highest-ranking Puerto Rican in the federal government. She was appointed by President Lyndon B. Johnson as regional East Coast Director of the Office of Economic Opportunity during the War on Poverty (Gil de la Madrid 1970; Nadal 2014). Nieves recruited Julio Morales as Deputy Chairperson/Assistant Director, and together they led and developed a cadre of programs and faculty that served students and the community. The challenge they faced, to create in academia that which was unprecedented, loomed large. The Puerto Rican Alliance, consisting also of Dominicans and Panamanians, remained active participants in PRS and students like Angel Delíz served from 1969 to 1973 as part of the Curriculum Committee to develop the courses for the new major (BC Department of PRLS Archives). During this period, faculty from Puerto Rico came as visiting professors, e.g., Blanca Córdova-Anderson, Luis Nieves Falcón, Francisca Pesquera Cantellops, and Juan Rodríguez Cruz. Many found refuge and employment in NYC because the anti-independence repression was in full force. Numerous Puerto Ricans from the U.S., who would later become well known, also lent their expertise, e.g., Miguel Algarín, Antonio Alvarado, Frank Bonilla, Sonia Nieto, Felipe Pedraza, Eduardo Seda Bonilla, Juan Angel Silén, and Herminio Vargas (BC Department of PRLS Archives).

Public engagement and place-based, experiential learning were key components of PRS. It was culturally expected that one could climb the proverbial social ladder but only while remaining committed to the advancement of one's community. Hence, the Adult Education Center, which offered a Spanish language high school GED program (General Equivalency Diploma) and the Escuelita Infantil Bilingüe (Bilingual Pre-School for Children), were formed in IPRS. Although the IPRS could not offer courses because it was not a department, it did so via the Departments of History, Sociology, Political Science, Economics, and Modern Languages, along with graduate courses beginning in the Fall of 1971 for use in the School of

Education. A six-credit community organization course was created that incorporated a theoretical framework similar to a conventional course plus an internship component partnering with community-based organizations. A six-credit study abroad summer course was also created offering students opportunities to travel to their heritage country, many for the first time, to encourage educational and cultural linkages with Puerto Rico and the Caribbean. Although short-lived, two other significant initiatives for IPRS were the bilingual *Revista del Instituto de Estudios Puertorriqueños de Brooklyn College*, published in spring 1971 and fall 1972,[13] that included academic, literary, and news pieces; and the Teatro Jurutungo,[14] a theater group dedicated to Puerto Rican culture founded and directed by Herminio Vargas. These served as vehicles of creative expression and knowledge.

Nieves' leadership was crucial during this nascent time in PRS. She knew departmental status was vital for autonomous decision-making within PRS to influence and vote in personnel actions and policymaking, thereby solidifying its future. Nieves also called on counterparts in CUNY and beyond, forming a "think tank" to respond to the need for resources in English about Puerto Ricans, to address a void in academia and consequently create teaching materials for the newly created PRS units. As Chairperson of the Committee on Puerto Rican Studies and Research (Colón López 2019, 24), Nieves presented the group proposal for the Centro de Estudios Puertorriqueños (Center for Puerto Rican Studies), a university-wide research center,[15] to Chancellor Kibbee that was approved by the CUNY BHE. Brooklyn College's Department of PRS was "thus identified as the locus for the Centro's creation" (Josephine Nieves 2020, pers. comm.). Frank Bonilla, a prolific political scientist, became the Centro's Founding Director in February 1973. Shortly after working to develop Centro programs, and perhaps in response to internal departmental issues, differing agendas and a faction that wanted a clear separation between the Institute and the Department,[16] Nieves took a special leave of absence and accepted a full-time research position at Centro,[17] thus closing one chapter and beginning another for Brooklyn College's Department of PRS.

In August 1973, Juan Rodríguez Cruz, a tenured professor on leave from the University of Puerto Rico, former Acting Director of the Institute of Caribbean Studies and Editor of the *Caribbean Review*, assumed the position as acting chairperson of PRS.[18] In November, a search committee was formed consisting of Dean Thomas Birkenhead and Professors Hyman Sardy, Sonia Nieto, Ricardo Pérez Shapiro,[19] and Carmen Dinos, a former PRS faculty member who transferred to the School of Education. In July 1974, the committee made its determinations known to the president; their choice was María E. Sánchez (Dinos, Pérez Shapiro, and Nieto 1974). However, on October 3, 1974, President Kneller appointed Elba Lugo de Luis Deza as Professor of PRS and Chairperson effective immediately.[20] This was deemed illegitimate by the PRS students and faculty since a majority of the search committee had voted for Sánchez. The president's appointee served as chairperson in name only as the students and allies, among them Vietnam War veterans Alex Boxill (Afro-Panamanian who coordinated the Veterans Organization) and Carlos Alejandro,[21] physically stood watch around the clock and blocked her entry into the 1205 Boylan Hall department office. The situation was exacerbated by the fact that the faculty and staff of PRS refused to work with her. The only chairperson they recognized was Sánchez, who had been teaching and working in PRS since the Fall of 1972. She was a well-respected educator with a stellar reputation among her peers and in the Puerto Rican community. As Co-Coordinator for what would soon become New York City's first widely acclaimed Bilingual Teacher Education Training Program, Sánchez held teaching licenses in regular and bilingual Spanish-English education and administrative supervisory certificates. She served as a principal with formal training in conflict resolution, which would be a fortuitous requisite for her career at Brooklyn College.

The refusal to appoint Sánchez as chairperson in July because she did not have a Ph.D.[22] mobilized a whirlwind of protests, initially via unproductive formal institutional protocols and soon thereafter through a massive campaign of petitions and letter-writing to inform the Puerto Rican community of the denial of departmental autonomy to choose its own leadership. It did not end there; demonstrations, strikes, rallies, and takeovers were the order of the day for over a year. To orchestrate these actions for a prolonged and concerted effort, while taking doctoral classes and running a department, was no easy feat for Sánchez. The protesters strategized via a PRS Department Steering Committee headed by the "General"—Sánchez—with point persons to handle critical aspects of a collective operation; its public face was the Committee for Self-Determination of the Department and Institute of PRS. Up to 25 people would gather every Tuesday evening, among them, faculty, staff, students, and community members, as well as representatives from Puerto Rican Alliance, Movimiento Estudiantil Dominicano, Veterans Organization, Partido Socialista Puertorriqueño (PSP),[23] Puerto Rican Revolutionary Workers Organization (PRRWO), Puerto Rican Student Union, and Federación Universitaria Socialista Puertorriqueña (FUSP).

Just two weeks after the Lugo de Luis Deza announcement, 100 students took over the president's office in Boylan Hall on a Friday, peacefully vacating early Monday morning after President Kneller agreed to meet with them later that day (Kalech 1974). At the meeting, the president declined to dismiss the security guards, and the students walked out chanting "Blacks, Latins, Asians, Whites, all the students must unite!" Over 50 students and faculty took over the Office of the Registrar and computer keypunch office. While the occupation was under way, there were rallies held on the quad in support of the students. Student Government was meeting to discuss whether they would lend their support. News articles appeared about Puerto Ricans fighting for self-determination and students' rights, and PRS put out a press release regarding administrative abuses and racist attacks against the Department, students, faculty, and staff—"We will not be coerced into accepting their puppet chairperson, because even worse than a lackey is a lackey of a lackey. We are not afraid of the Administration nor of their threats or tactics because we are organized and disciplined and do not bow to insane, authoritarian repression" (Brooklyn College: Puerto Rican Students Fight for Self-Determination 1974, 3–4, 21). The occupation lasted three days—students utilized the phones to make calls to their unsuspecting parents about their whereabouts and relative safety, assuring them they were acting in a sane manner; veterans would escort occupiers to the restrooms; food prepared by students' mothers made its way to protesters; and the premises were kept impeccably clean to avoid any excuse to characterize the takeover as anything other than a just cause (Antonio Nadal 2020, pers. comm.).

On October 24, 1974, the student-run WBCR-Brooklyn College Radio station issued a statement opposing the actions of the protesters, stating that President Kneller was within his rights to make academic decisions as these were not based on race. Nonetheless, they noted that peaceful demonstrators left the premises without damaging anything, no files or records had been tampered with, and that they had respected the confidentiality of student records. President Kneller resorted to using the legal system, ordering an injunction to vacate the office against the occupiers, subsequently calling in some 20-40 deputy sheriffs and 100-200 NYC police officers who ended the standoff at 4 am. They arrested those who remained behind after the leaders encouraged individuals who had any kind of criminal record to leave. As they were escorted to the police vehicles, they chanted "Blacks, Latins, Asians, Whites, for our rights we must fight!" They became known as the BC 44 (41 students of diverse backgrounds and three faculty) although the Supreme Court of the State of NY County of Kings record indicates that there were 53 charged, including pseudonyms John and Jane Doe as well as Richard and Roberta Roe.[24] The student strike was deemed limited in scope. Some news accounts indicated that the issues of race/racism had muddled the issue of student rights, causing a loss of support. Other news stories indicated it was successful, with an estimate of 75 percent of classes not held that day. A crowd of 2,500 gathered on the quad at midday to listen to those who had been arrested and released just that morning. The activists marched onto campus with the rallying cry of "BC 44! We've come back to give you more!" Their cause garnered support letters from the CUNY University Student Senate, University of Puerto Rico, Veterans Organizations on many CUNY campuses, and outside organizations and universities including Yale, Rutgers-Livingston, Harvard, Radcliffe, SUNY Stonybrook, and the Interracial Children's Books in NYC (Slater and Scalf 1974, 1). The *New York Times, New York Daily News, New York Post, City Star, Maceta* Newspaper of the Puerto Rican Student Union, and the *Kingsman* and *Spigot Magazine* student newspapers covered the story. After negotiations, the BC 44 were given a sixty-day suspended sentence as they all had clean records (Rodríguez 1974).

At the BHE meeting of November 1974, about 75 students took over the speaker's podium to demand the suspension of Lugo de Luis Deza pending an investigation into her qualifications and eligibility to serve as chairperson of PRS, including documentation that she had misinformation on her curriculum vitae and was on sabbatical leave from the University of Puerto Rico and expected to return the following summer (Siegel 1974). Chairman

Giardino indicated he had ordered President Kneller to investigate and ended the meeting abruptly. It was the first time the BHE had experienced such a disruption since the meetings went public in February of that year (Kline and Matthews 1974). At the December meeting, the PRS Steering Committee provided the BHE with the evidence they had collected, and Chancellor Kibbee was to follow up.

While peaceful activities continued in support of Sánchez's appointment as the official chairperson, in mid-April 1975, the Committee for Self-Determination called for a CUNY-wide demonstration to protest the fact that no PRS courses were listed in the summer schedule and in response to reports of pending personnel and programmatic cuts across PRS units due to NYC's fiscal crisis. On April 16th, during registration time, 60 members of the Committee for Self-Determination marched into the Registrar's Office and politely asked the staff to depart with their personal belongings as the students would be occupying the space. They wanted to meet with President Kneller and put forward 13 demands, including no reprisals against faculty, staff, and students; reversal of the administration's denial of tenure of Josephine Nieves; settlement of the renowned Puerto Rico historian Loida Figueroa's grievance regarding non-re-appointment in PRS; and implementation of the Justice Committee's demands, a broader-based coalition of the campus community to "combat racist administrative actions against members of the third world and poor white working class students" (Siegel 1975). The U.S. Department of Justice had an interest in the BC situation stemming from their Counterintelligence Program (COINTELPRO). An FBI agent had attempted to make his way into the office to retrieve the students' records for those who applied for federal jobs. This encounter was familiar to those involved in the PRS struggle since they knew there were undercover agents posing as students to keep track of their activities. The agent was quickly pushed back, causing the *Kingsman* student newspaper to claim "that flying karate kick at a man who carries a gun and a badge told you just how determined the protesting students are to get an education more substantial than a piece of paper" (Steier 1975a). The action was well planned with those willing to be arrested and those who supported them via security measures, food resources, and spokespersons to address the press and public. One of the students, José Ojeda, was quoted as saying, "We have so far been non-violent...we don't want a bloodbath in the Registrar's office... but you keep pushing our backs against the wall. I don't like sleeping in the Registrar's office, but we will sleep there, we will fight the police, we will do whatever is necessary to survive" (Steier 1975b).

ASPIRA's national President Luis Alvarez was asked by Brooklyn College to mediate the dispute between PRS and the administration; he ultimately sided with PRS, stating this was an outright attempt to divide the community (Siegel 1975). The newly renamed Africana Studies Department was also called in to help resolve the issue; after assessing the situation, they fully supported the right of self-determination for PRS over the objections of the president (Colón López 2019, 31). The *New York Daily News* and *New York Post*, as well as student newspapers covered the story; *Spigot Magazine*, a Student Government newspaper, had it on the front page plus a centerfold spread with numerous articles covering the varied aspects of the struggle (Seigel 1975).

The occupation lasted two nights until a written and signed agreement of 16 points was reached in the presence of constituencies from various interest groups—administrators, PRS, Student Government, the press, and community organizations. Overall, President Kneller reaffirmed his support of the Department and Institute of PRS regarding budgets and personnel; upheld Lugo de Luis Deza as Chairperson of PRS but conceded authority to Jorge Hernández, Assistant Director of the Institute of PRS, to sign off on any Department-related matters and would include PRS courses in the summer session; approved Figueroa as Professor for the following year; would make a decision regarding the tenure of Nieves; agreed that all photos taken of the demonstrators filed in CUNY central would be returned to the Committee for Self-Determination with no copies and that any alleged misuse of the photos would be investigated. Dialogue would continue in good faith on both sides, and the Committee would "continue to demonstrate peacefully and without disrupting the normal functions of the college" until their demands had all been met (Brooklyn College Department of Puerto Rican and Latino Studies Archives 1975).

Nieto would go on to pen an open letter, part of which she read during the April 28, 1975 meeting of the CUNY BHE, regarding the chronology of events, the wide-ranging support of their case, and the ensuing inaction of President Kneller on various significant issues, mainly the investigation of

Lugo de Luis Deza and the naming of Sánchez as the legitimate Chairperson of PRS. She indicated that while Lugo de Luis Deza initially supported the actions of PRS, she subsequently denounced them and was asking for early tenure and a letter of recommendation in the event that she had to leave BC: "The responsibility is yours. In order to avoid a very critical situation or even a dangerous clash in the near future, you must vote against the reappointment of Elba Lugo as Professor and Chairperson of the Puerto Rican Studies Department at Brooklyn College" (Brooklyn College Department of Puerto Rican and Latino Studies Archives 1975b). Despite the fact that 500 protesters gathered outside to show their support for PRS and condemn SEEK cutbacks, the Board unanimously reappointed Lugo de Luis Deza as a faculty member in PRS; the decision regarding the position of chairperson would be discussed by the Committee on Self-Determination and President Kneller in a forthcoming meeting.

In July 1975, Vice Chancellor David Newton announced that in the matter of Sánchez v. President (Brooklyn College), initially filed by PRS in December 1974 regarding the decision to appoint Lugo de Luis Deza over Sánchez, the Step Two grievance was denied on the basis that it was "a dispute over the correctness of academic judgment of the President and Board of Higher Education" (Brooklyn College Department of Puerto Rican and Latino Studies Archives 1975c).

In early October, the Department of PRS sent a detailed letter to President Kneller with 11 (some multi-part) demands in the interests of students, including the appointment of Sánchez as chair and her vacated position to be filled by another instructor; cessation of disciplinary charges against Carlos Alejandro and José Ojeda plus those arrested at the September 22, 1975 meeting of the BHE.[25]

The last documented actions for autonomy occurred on October 29, 1975, when PRRWO put forth its position paper, "The Fight to Defend PRS at BC," which addressed the attacks on PRS, SEEK, Africana Studies, and Open Admissions.[26] It also revealed internal ideological strife among supporters of PRS with the Maoist PRRWO stating the Marxist-Leninist PSP, FUSP, and other supporters were compromising too much (Brooklyn College Department of Puerto Rican and Latino Studies Archives 1975e). Simultaneously, the "BC Veterans Organization Urges You to Demonstrate" flyer was circulated decrying budget cuts during the time of a U.S. economic slowdown that resulted in a NYC fiscal crisis; violations of students' rights; and due process of law. That was witnessed by 200 students who attended the court hearing of Ojeda and Alejandro. The flyer condemned reprisals against students and faculty who dared to struggle for their democratic rights, ending with the familiar phrase of "Dare to Struggle! Dare to Win!" (Brooklyn College Department of Puerto Rican and Latino Studies Archives 1975f). Ideological differences aside, the supporters of PRS would continue to resist repression by presenting a public united front despite accusations of being willing to "sell out" or destroy the Department in the process (Fiske 1975); ultimately, this strategy proved effective.

On November 10, 1975, President Kneller officially named María E. Sánchez as Acting Chairperson, which was renewed annually through 1978 when she was finally appointed as Chairperson of the Department and Institute of PRS, four long and arduous years after her original selection for that position. Despite a myriad of campus and student issues, such as cutbacks to programming and the imposition of undergraduate tuition, PRS continued to serve as a critical mass for campus-wide mobilization and coalition-building against these measures, winning its greatest battle over self-determination.

Sánchez soon demonstrated that her capacity-building skills would engage PRS with the campus-wide community. This was made possible through much diligence and a weekly Friday three-hour meeting of faculty to plan and strategize. The results would bear the fruit of that labor.

In 1981, the Department organized a major international conference at Brooklyn College in honor of its tenth anniversary with a focus on the field of PRS—"Toward a Renaissance of Puerto Rican Studies: An Agenda for the Eighties," which resulted in *Toward a Renaissance of Puerto Rican Studies: Ethnic and Area Studies in University Education* (Sánchez and Stevens-Arroyo 1987), a classic in the field (see Sánchez Korrol and Pérez y González in this volume).

PRS served as part of the initial task force to create "Core Studies 9: Studies in African, Asian, and Latin American Cultures" (a comparative study of those parts of the world in a triad modular, multidisciplinary course via team teaching) through the curricular development efforts of Anthony Stevens-Arroyo. Virginia Sánchez Korrol, who served among its first rotating coordinators, taught the course, as did Nadal and Stevens-Arroyo, alongside faculty from other departments. The Caribbean Studies Program was created by Africana Studies along with PRS[27] (Proposal for Caribbean Studies Program 1982, 6; Department of Puerto Rican Studies Self Study Report 1988, 11; Brooklyn College Department of Puerto Rican and Latino Studies Archives n.d., 20). It was approved as a co-major, originally with no courses of its own. Sánchez Korrol served as its rotating coordinator (1982-1984), and Stevens-Arroyo remained an avid proponent of the program. The Spanish-English bilingual teacher education concentration was strengthened and grew with Antonio Nadal and Héctor Carrasquillo. PRS continued to work closely with the School of Education to develop grant proposals to support teacher training, create social studies paired courses, as well as some graduate courses for use in teacher education degree programs.

"Dubbed the 'plug and play' concept by curriculum planners in the early 90's, the Department of Puerto Rican and Latino Studies pioneered in the application of this practice since the department originated," but Sánchez helped solidify this during her leadership (Department of Puerto Rican and Latino Studies Self Study Report 1999, 17). PRS became an integral part of the campus-wide curricular offerings. It nestled itself into varied spaces of social institutions, where it helped to serve the Puerto Rican community and opened externship opportunities for students, aiding with career readiness. Its main vehicle for achieving this was through the Institute for PRS, later renamed the Center for Latino Studies (CLS).[28] Through the efforts of Carrasquillo, a sociologist, the Hispanic Young Peoples' Chorus was founded in 1981 as a community and student resource; it expanded in 1991 to a multi-service non-profit organization called Hispanic Young Peoples' Alternatives in Sunset Park, Brooklyn (Pérez y González 2000, 47).[29]

Sánchez's collaborative leadership model resulted in various important accomplishments. The formation of the PRS Alumni Association was a key vehicle for galvanizing much needed community support for the department.[30] It was through the close-knit collaborative network of alumni that PRS was able to move ahead and survive very difficult times after she was officially named Acting Chairperson. In the challenges of pursuing tenure and promotion to Associate Professor, she garnered strong support from alumni, fellow chairpersons, and faculty members whose respect and admiration she had earned because of her tireless work ethic in leading a team of faculty who had woven themselves into the fabric of campus life to advance the mission of BC.[31] PRS was successful on both counts—the struggle for Sánchez to be tenured from 1976-79 and for Associate Professor from 1985-1986.

By the time Sánchez stepped down as PRS Chairperson in 1989, the students, faculty, and staff had adeptly handled the fight for self-determination and internal ideological conflicts, while carving out disciplinary niches within the Core as well as other areas of the BC curriculum. Also, as noted in a PRS self-study report, "The idea was to foment a symbiotic relationship between our commitment to academic excellence and its translation into direct involvement in community issues" (Department of Puerto Rican Studies Self Study Report 1988, 2). Sánchez led the way in fulfilling that goal. She retired in the Spring of 1990 and was bestowed the honorary distinguished rank of Professor Emerita by President Hess. A $4,000 fund was set up in her name in the Center for Latino Studies (Sánchez Korrol 1990, 1-2). Under her leadership, a clear path was set for the department to build on a foundation of academic achievement.

The challenges regarding tenure and promotion, as well as a huge drop in student enrollment, and cutbacks to full-time faculty of PRS (and across CUNY) in response to the NYS and NYC policies implemented during the fiscal crisis were forthcoming, but the era for self-reflection and how the new interdisciplinary field would make its mark on and survive within the larger scheme of higher education would become the focus of PRS over the next decade (Department of Puerto Rican Studies Self Study Report 1988, 22).

ACADEMIC STRIDES AMIDST FISCAL AUSTERITY (1989-2004)

In the late summer of 1978, Virginia Sánchez Korrol[32] interviewed for an adjunct position and was convinced by Sánchez to apply for the recently vacated full-time position, which she began immediately. Sánchez Korrol then took up the mantle of chairing PRS in 1989. At the time, she had published her dissertation-turned-book, *From Colonia to Community: The History of Puerto Ricans in New York City, 1917-1948* (1983, 1994), which would become essential reading in the field of PRS, and had served as Co-Director of the Center for Latino Studies. Shortly thereafter, she spearheaded the formation of the Puerto Rican Studies Association (1992) which convened at a founding conference in White Plains, New York, where she became its Founding President. In 1994, she organized the first international biennial conference in Waltham, Massachusetts; BC remained intimately involved with PRSA, hosting it in 1998 (Department of Puerto Rican and Latino Studies Self Study Report 1999, 12). The PRSA was created as an academic organization that would bring together scholars, students, professionals, and community members studying and engaged in the Puerto Rican diasporic experience, including its deep-rooted connection to Puerto Rico.

There was a tenor of stability with the burgeoning of scholarship and curricular innovations. By then, PRS had experienced a measure of maturity and exercised its autonomy. It had become part of the academic landscape at all levels of the college despite its small number of five full-time, tenured faculty and a handful of adjuncts. While there was no ongoing battle with the administration per se, there were four CUNY-wide retrenchments during the 15 years with Sánchez Korrol at the helm. That meant joining PSC-CUNY union demonstrations at City Hall and at the State Capitol, while engaging in on-campus advocacy, and championing the stellar accomplishments of PRS to avoid dissolution and departmental mergers. This was the decade that PRS, and Ethnic Studies in general, at CUNY experienced numerous setbacks, including eliminations, consolidations, and departmental status reductions with no authority in personnel and curricular actions. These decisions made by those in power were bolstered by an anti-multicultural, and often racist, demagoguery at the national level to eliminate the academic gains of underrepresented communities. Despite the quality of Ethnic Studies units, administrators chose to eliminate or drastically reduce them due to budget shortfalls. It was under these threats that PRS at BC decided to grow and institutionalize the inclusion of Latino Studies.

In Spring 1996, PRS was set to meet with a Faculty Council Sub-Committee on Departmental Restructuring charged with assessing and recommending next steps for the college considering the fiscal crisis. It was a stressful time for faculty across the campus, especially for PRS as rumors of consolidation or elimination spread, and PRS' only untenured Assistant Professor, María Pérez y González, was susceptible to retrenchment. Seizing the opportunity to showcase its numerous accomplishments, PRS readied itself for the scrutiny of its academic publications, achievements, and events by committee members, some of whom had voiced support for its merging. In military-like fashion, Sánchez Korrol and the faculty marched into the meeting venue with publications and event flyers from 1993-95, spreading the contents on tables for the committee's review. The material represented 25 works highlighting the numerous contributions of five full-time faculty.

Simultaneously, to the Department's credit, President Vernon Lattin co-hosted two of a five-day major international conference on Public Policy in Higher Education: Puerto Rico, Cuba, Dominican Republic, and NYC, which included administrators from CUNY, State University of New York, State University of New Jersey, and the Spanish-speaking Caribbean. The students rallied in support of PRS via silent protests, petitions, and vociferous demonstrations. At a widely attended academic presentation on campus, at which the work of Sánchez Korrol was being shared, PRA President Juan Ocasio and students from the various Latinx student organizations carried signs supporting PRS as they silently processed through the aisles and filed along the walls of the auditorium for the duration of the event. When the final retrenchment decisions were made, PRS was spared. The faculty would continue making advances in research and scholarship while practicing its student-centered educational philosophy and strengthening its community and political alliances.

In 1998, after a ten-year practice of including the various Latino/a[33] communities in the content of the PRS courses and the large influx of Dominican students resulting from changing NYC demographics (Department of Puerto Rican and Latino Studies Self Study Report 1999, 3),[34] the Department renamed itself Puerto Rican and Latino Studies (PRLS).[35] In the spring of 1993, soon after the first Dominican Studies Institute in the U.S. was established at City College of NY, PRS created, among the first Dominican Studies courses in CUNY, a seminar titled "Puerto Ricans and Dominicans: Comparative Perspectives and Contemporary Issues."[36] U.S. Cuban and Mexican studies courses were created to boost the formation of the PRLS and Business major in 2001. Additionally, beginning in 1993, the goal of obtaining permanency for an innovative Latino Culture Media Studies Program was proposed in consultation with the Department of Television and Radio (TVR). In 1999, D. Irene Sosa, a filmmaker, was hired in TVR and assigned one course per semester in PRLS.[37] With the support of the Department of Political Science, a five-year CUNY Distinguished Lecturer position was secured in 2004 to launch the program. Unfortunately, the distinguished individual selected to lead the initiative did not ultimately assume the position.[38]

Fiscal battles continued to overshadow PRLS, but there was some comfort in the knowledge and lessons learned during its first 20 years of navigating academic structures and avoiding or outwitting some of its pitfalls, creating top-notch events on a shoestring budget, forging alliances, and strategic planning. This was doable through the experience of the faculty. Antonio Nadal[39] became a key faculty member in the PRLS-Bilingual Education concentration. He served as a confidant and political advisor to the chairpersons, occupying the role of PRLS' long-standing Deputy Chairperson plus two years as Acting Chairperson. As a pillar of unyielding commitment and continuity with an unparalleled institutional memory, Nadal remained indispensable to Sánchez, Sánchez Korrol and her successor, Pérez y González, until his retirement in 2015 after 44 years in PRLS.[40]

PRLS housed several illustrious visiting faculty,[41] garnered competitive external research grants, and gained international academic and news recognition. Sánchez Korrol secured grants from the Ford Foundation, Wells Fargo, and the National Endowment for the Humanities for the development of the award-winning co-edited three-volume *Latinas in the U.S.: A Historical Encyclopedia* (2006) and accompanying CD-ROM and On-line resource. As a writer, she gained much acclaim with at least 16 books and numerous journal and news articles. Her expertise was sought by the U.S. Department of the Interior, the NY State Department of Education, and various prestigious museums and historical societies.[42] Stevens-Arroyo received much-coveted funding from the Ford Foundation, The Lilly Endowment, Louisville Institute, Henry Luce Foundation, and Anne E. Casey Foundation for the Program for the Analysis of Religion Among Latinos (PARAL) National Survey of Latino Parishes and Congregations, and for establishing the Office of Religion in Society and Culture at BC. As co-founder of PARAL, he brought together international multi-disciplinary scholars of religion to collaborate on research focused on Latin@s. These expansive undertakings resulted in a four-book series and numerous publications on the Latin@ religious experience—Roman Catholic; Protestant; Pentecostal; African, Indigenous, and European-based ancestral and popular practices, including

Discovering Latino Religion: A Comprehensive Social Science Bibliography (Stevens-Arroyo with Pantoja 1995).

PRLS maintained its connections to student organizations with Carrasquillo and Nadal as the faculty liaisons for Familia Latina—the conglomerate of Latinx clubs, including Puerto Rican Alliance, Movimiento Estudiantil Dominicano, Hispanic Society, Panamanian Student Organization, Latin Women, Student Union for Bilingual Education, South American Student Association, Graduate Association for Bilingual Education, and, occasionally, the Graduate Student Organization when the board members were PRLS alumni. The students served as the engine for PRLS faculty to thrive as educators, scholars, and practitioners. It was in the late 1990s, under the presidency of Vanessa Santiago, that PRA began its annual Day of Dignity protest regarding Columbus Day with a silent demonstration to honor and mourn the Indigenous lives lost to conquest in the Americas. About a hundred students came together marching through the quad lifting signs, waving Caribbean/Latin American flags, and donning black armbands while they were spat upon and called racist slurs by onlookers. It was often a contentious event, particularly since Christopher Columbus is revered in U.S. history books. Santiago also spearheaded its annual *Areyto*[43] ceremonial rite of passage where executive board officers are inaugurated, candles are lit, and new members recite an oath.

Overall, during this stage, a small yet productive team of PRS faculty and staff,[44] with the support of students, expanded into Latinx Studies despite persistent financial woes to build a strong foundation of academic achievements and laudable recognitions. Sánchez Korrol recalls Chairperson Sánchez telling her, "You've got to put this Department on the map!" (Virginia Sánchez Korrol 2020, pers. comm.). By the time Sánchez Korrol retired, PRLS had solidified its place in the academy.

YEARS OF THE PHOENIX (2004-2020)

In Spring 1992, María Pérez y González[45] interviewed for an adjunct lecturer position with no college teaching experience. She was coaxed by a recommendation from Carrasquillo and interviewed by a somewhat skeptical Sánchez Korrol. As Nadal exited the interview to meet with students, he said, "Virginia, hire her already—she speaks Spanglish like we do and has to start somewhere!" Upon completing the doctorate, a year later, Pérez y González was hired on a tenure-track position. Hired at BC during a time when positions were scarce, it came unexpectedly when Sánchez Korrol asked her to serve as Acting Chairperson in Fall 2001, a time of crisis for the nation, especially New York City. Accepting the position, Pérez y González again served as Acting Chairperson from 2002-03 and was subsequently elected Chairperson in 2004, beginning a new era in PRLS.

A year earlier, Sánchez Korrol had been approached by a member of the Faculty Council Steering Committee (Executive Board),[46] about authorizing Pérez y González's nomination to serve as a member. Astutely, Sánchez Korrol inquired about who else was being nominated; she negotiated, insisting that she would only authorize the nomination if Pérez y González was the sole nominee. They agreed, and she was elected with broad support. It was the first time PRLS had ever reached that position of influence at BC; it was a strategic move that would help PRLS prepare for and weather many turbulent situations regarding the Core Curriculum, creation of the five-school structure with deans, CUNY Pathways general education curriculum, faculty lines, student concerns, and college-wide policy.

In the academic year 2006-07, three esteemed senior faculty members retired—Sánchez Korrol and Carrasquillo in Fall 2006 and Stevens-Arroyo in Spring 2007. Anticipating this with a plan in hand, PRLS prepared by meeting with the administration to discuss the future. The retirements represented 75 percent of the faculty, instantly making PRLS more vulnerable than ever, yet Provost Roberta Matthews and President Christoph Kimmich saw the significance of immediately restoring PRLS to a minimum of five full-time faculty (tenure-track), commonly accepted as the minimum for any department to fulfill its main functions. PRLS successfully hired three faculty members in Fall 2007—Alan Aja, trained in public and urban policy, had served as an adjunct lecturer since 2004; Miranda Martínez,[47] a sociologist; and Vanessa Pérez Rosario, trained in comparative literature (Spanish) with a background in second language acquisition. Due to the failure of a counteroffer from the BC administration, Martínez left in 2013. This was followed by the retirement of Nadal in 2015 and the unexpected administrative transfer of Pérez Rosario to the Department of Modern Languages and Literatures in 2018. This drastically reduced PRLS' teaching power and increased its need for adjuncts and a reliance on external faculty members to fulfill its obligations.[48]

In 2016, Reynaldo Ortiz Minaya was hired as an Assistant Professor on a tenure-track line; a socio-historian, his hiring was enabled through faculty, student, and alumni advocacy—letters, petitions, demonstrations, and many meetings. Upon his arrival, Ortíz Minaya organized two townhall events on immigration in response to anti-immigrant executive orders from the White House, a critical time for many of our students. He founded and organized the PRLS Faculty Speaker Series, where faculty shared their life-career trajectory and research; spearheaded the November 2017 day-long conference on the effects of and responses to Hurricanes Irma and María, "Weathering the Storm: The Caribbean, Puerto Rico, and the Diasporic Communities," bringing esteemed guests to our campus, such as then Mayor of San Juan, Puerto Rico, Carmen Yulín Cruz Soto, as the keynote speaker.[49] He further promoted the interdisciplinary, inter-school eight-event semester-long collaborative project with multiple speakers and community members as a kickoff to the 50th anniversary of PRLS featuring the work of social documentary photographer, Máximo Rafael Colón, "Puerto Rican Migration Then and Now Through the Lens of Contemporary Art, 1950-2019." Each of these initiatives garnered much positive exposure for PRLS and showcased Ortíz Minaya's networking, mentoring, and organizing skills.

In 2017, after Hurricanes Irma and María ravaged Puerto Rico and the Caribbean, PRLS filed a grievance with the Professional Staff Congress-CUNY union (PSC-CUNY) stating that "there was a failure to act pursuant to the CUNY Policy on Equal Opportunity and Non-Discrimination, and contractual workload provisions," the result of being kept under five full-time faculty for four years, unlike any other senior department and while other departments/programs and the School of Business were receiving faculty lines for newly created departments. President Michelle Anderson never responded to the grievance, and it automatically went to the CUNY Central office where the previous BC head of Human Resources and Legal Services, under which the grievance was filed, had recently been hired.

Ironically, BC's representative countering PRLS was the recently hired Chief Diversity Officer, a person of color, whose office collaborated with

PRLS annually to sponsor its major event, The Possible Dream Encuentro (Encounter). PRLS was not successful in its grievance. Meanwhile, various intense demonstrations, protests, media coverage, and direct challenges to the administration by students from PRA, MEDo, Mexican Heritage Student Association, BC Dreamers, Students for Justice in Palestine, and Young Progressives of America took place around various social justice issues, including the understaffing of PRLS and Africana Studies, NYPD surveillance of Muslim students, and inflammatory statements made by BC professors.[50] There was an online open letter and meeting with President Anderson by the Alliance for Puerto Rican Education and Empowerment (APREE), an organization of mostly BC alumni and founding members of PRA and PRS. A line allocated in Spring of 2018 was cancelled that summer due to a CUNY hiatus on faculty hires and a line was transferred from PRLS to another department. Allied faculty independently created and signed a petition with various large departments also signing on, inclusive of union leaders, calling the administration to task at Faculty Council regarding the case of PRLS. This led to a successful search in 2019 allowing for the return of a former popular outstanding adjunct/substitute instructor, Carla Santamaría, with expertise in Spanish and Latin American, Caribbean, and Latinx Studies. Santamaría came to PRLS as a tenure-track Assistant Professor with community college teaching and administrative experience to fill the most enrolled program in PRLS—the Bilingual Education sequence.

While diversity remains at the forefront of the BC Strategic Plan, as of 2021, the situation remains dire for PRLS. Since 2014, the Faculty Council Committee on Master Planning, Education Policy, and Budget had prioritized PRLS to restore it to five full-time faculty. Although PRLS more than doubled its seat enrollment from 2013 to 2016, reaching 800 per semester, suggestive conversations with administrators about departmental consolidations are often revisited. Additionally, austerity measures, worsened by the current pandemic, are creating a vicious cycle of enrollment suppression that works against the formulae used to determine faculty lines. In the summer of 2021, a tenure-track line was finally approved for PRLS; simultaneously, Ortiz Minaya resigned to take a faculty position at another university.

During this stage, PRLS faculty began participating in specialized areas of the academy, such as teaching at the CUNY Graduate Center, CUNY

Macaulay Honors College, and the Universitat de Barcelona, Catalunya, Spain. They received numerous awards/grants/fellowships—from among, the Fulbright Scholar Core Research/Teaching Grant, Whiting Fellowship for Outstanding Teaching in the Humanities, Instituto de Puerto Rico-NY, Woodrow Wilson Career Enhancement Fellowship, Phi Beta Kappa honorary membership, Harvard Management Development Program, Scholar-in-Residence at New York University, Mellon Transfer Student Research Program, Kellogg Foundation for Leadership Alliance, CUNY Academy for the Humanities and Social Sciences, Feliks Gross Award, National Endowment for the Humanities, and CUNY Mellon Faculty Diversity Career Enhancement Initiative. PRLS also received national recognition through Aja's public intellectual work via television and print news outlets, including his highly acclaimed race-economics policy reports; his role as Production Assistant on the Emmy-award winning documentary, *The Sentence* (Valdéz 2018); Miami's Forgotten Cubans: Race, Racialization, and the Miami Afro-Cuban Experience (2016) was mentioned in a review of the Academy Award winning film *Moonlight* (2016); and his work used as part of the U.S. Congressional legislation on African-American slavery reparations and the Green New Deal. In 2020, Sánchez Korrol received the prestigious Herbert H. Lehman Prize for Distinguished Service in New York History awarded by the New York Academy of History while serving as historical consultant for the 2021 remake film *West Side Story* co-produced by the legendary Puerto Rican actress, Rita Moreno, Steven Spielberg, and Tony Kushner, making use of her broad expertise on the Puerto Rican diaspora in the early to mid-twentieth century.

PRLS successfully shepherded three junior faculty members through tenure and promotion to Associate and Full Professor ranks; completed seven searches; hired the first Cuban- and Dominican-Americans as tenure-track faculty; undertook a departmental self-study; became an integral part of the college body politic; and resisted the pressure to eliminate "Puerto Rican" from its title. Despite setbacks regarding understaffing, PRLS grew in enrollment and engaged in curricular revisions, such as new PRLS-Education majors and courses on Dominicans, Afro-Latinxs, and digital humanities.[51] Additionally, a first for PRLS, D. Irene Sosa produced digitized short documentaries about the mission of the Department upon its 35th

(2004) and 40th (2010) anniversaries, and via supervision of a short film that includes student testimonials by then undergraduate Tanya Mercado, *Empowering a Community* (2011).[52]

Multiple PRLS majors made advancements in academia. In 2015, Reubén Pérez became the first PRLS major to be inducted into Phi Beta Kappa[53] Rho of New York chapter, followed by Maya García Fisher and Daniel Vázquez Sanabria (President of PRA[54]). Pérez is now doing a Ph.D. in Sociology at University of California, Berkeley. That same year Gisely Colón López became the first Puerto Rican/Latinx salutatorian in the history of BC and is now in a Ph.D. program in Urban Education at the CUNY Graduate Center (see Colón López in this volume). PRLS students have earned the Mellon Mays Undergraduate Fellowship, entered the CUNY Pipeline Program for Careers in College Teaching and Research, received a Hispanic Association of Colleges and Universities National Internship, were inducted into the Chi Alpha Epsilon SEEK National Honor Society, and earned numerous graduate degrees.

Under the leadership of Pérez y González, PRLS undertook several important initiatives to concretize its service to students and create visibility. In 2005, BC celebrated its 75th anniversary, and the Latino Faculty and Staff Organization (LFSO)[55] decided it would participate by highlighting the Latinx alumni of BC in a Latino Showcase event and a commemorative booklet. Its momentum led the way to the yearly celebration of The Possible Dream: Latin@ Arts, Communities, and Leadership Encuentro by the BC Comité Noviembre—a planning committee consisting of PRLS, the Latinx student organizations, LFSO, alumni, and a coordinator.[56] It became a multi-day event featuring academic and student panels; alumni-led career sessions; distinguished keynote speakers; a Latin American music recital; an art exhibit, and other cultural activities, culminating with a Don Quijote Leadership Awards Reception.[57]

A key question asked by students time and again over the years was, "What can I do with a degree in PRLS?" Yader Alfredo Bravo, then President of Puerto Rican Alliance, also asked Pérez y González the question, which prompted a direct response in the form of the *PRLS Career Booklet: What Can You Do With a Major, Concentration, or Minor in PRLS?* (2008, 2010, and 2015) that provided a comprehensive look at PRLS curricular offerings, resources, career skills and trajectories, faculty, and alumni.[58]

While serving on the Faculty Council (FC) Steering Committee, Pérez y González was elected to serve on the Presidential Search Committee and unanimously elected FC Chairperson, becoming the first Puerto Rican/Latinx person to occupy the post.[59] It was a long way from the time of the 1970s; now, instead of being at the fringes of BC, PRLS was at its core. One major challenge BC and PRLS faced was how to deal with the Pathways Curriculum general education mandate passed by the CUNY Board of Trustees (BOT). Initially, there was great resistance to its implementation, but BC eventually adopted its own version by 2013. PRLS favored one aspect of Pathways—its inclusion for every student to take at least one course in the U.S. Experience in its Diversity category, for which PRLS and others had long advocated. With access to first-year students, PRLS would finally be able to grow its enrollment numbers and cultivate new majors. Membership on the Steering Committee provided PRLS with access to critical information and the administration.

With the election of Alan Aja in May 2019, PRLS took a historical half century turn. The first male chairperson-elect, Aja is the first Cuban-American to head the Department. In 2020, he became the first PRLS faculty member since 2007 to become a Full Professor.

The future seemed more promising until the COVID-19 pandemic took center stage in mid-March of 2020; all instruction and work quickly went virtual. Some economic austerity measures had already been put into place at BC and CUNY before the pandemic hit due to NY State's $15 billion budget shortfall. Governor Andrew Cuomo's decision to reduce CUNY's funding and the BC administration's fiscal restraints resulted in PRLS spearheading a Declaration of Equity for Diversity letter addressed to BC and CUNY administrations advocating no further budgetary reductions.[60] The Department became a part of the BC Anti-Racist Coalition (ARC) of students, faculty, and staff formed out of a common struggle to establish a Black life-affirming and anti-racist campus agenda. PRLS is bracing for the looming economic challenges resulting from the pandemic that threatens to change CUNY, and Ethnic Studies in particular, in very uncertain ways.

LEGACY OF PRS

Puerto Rican Studies at Brooklyn College accomplished much over half a century, through positively affecting students' lives via teaching, retention, and graduation rates, as well as leadership and public engagement skills; producing excellent scholarship in the fields of humanities and social sciences; and making significant inroads in all aspects of college life involving students, faculty, staff, and, occasionally, administration. Advocacy for Latinxs on campus and creativity in multiplying extremely limited institutional resources into effective programming remain strong components of its activities. Its linkages to student organizations are critical for ensuring accountability and continuity for future generations.

The far-reaching impact of PRS began from the conviction of a few first-generation Puerto Rican college students that their history, culture, and experience were just as worthy of study as that of their Euro-American/ Anglo counterparts.[61] Their joint struggle alongside largely non-Latinx Black, Latinx, and white radical students literally changed the face of BC and CUNY[62] overall and helped to influence academia in general (Arenson 1996; Biondi 2013, 178).

Upon the 50th anniversary of the Department of Puerto Rican and Latino Studies in 2020, some of its founders and activists have documented its history in an APREE-commissioned film,[63] *Making the Impossible Possible: The Story of Puerto Rican Studies in Brooklyn College* (Colón López, Gold, and Sporn 2020). The legacy of Puerto Rican Studies at Brooklyn College reflects the tenacity, perseverance, and accomplishments of Puerto Rican students, professors, and allies responsible for transforming an educational environment and creating a Department that, while its mission is more expansive today, continues to affirm the history, culture, and scholarship of the Puerto Rican diaspora. It was no easy feat, but Brooklyn College became a more inclusive place, all because a few Puerto Rican students dared to transform the ivory tower.

NOTES

[1] The "ivory tower" refers to an attitude of aloofness from practical affairs, usually used in regard to the university.

[2] The "x" denotes gender neutrality and inclusivity.

[3] The BC Department of PRS is the third in the nation, established after Lehman College's Department of PRS (approved by the CUNY Board of Higher Education [BHE] on June 30, 1969) and Hunter College's Department of Black and Puerto Rican Studies (approved on July 22, 1969). The BC Department of PRS is one of only two CUNY Departments that continues to retain "Puerto Rican" in its title; the other is Hunter College's Department of Africana and Puerto Rican/Latino Studies. Reconfigurations, beginning in the 1990s, turned PRS academic units into varying combinations of Latinx, Caribbean, Latin American, and Ethnic Studies (see Pedro Cabán's essay in this volume).

[4] The BC Institute of PRS is the first of its kind in the nation, approved by the BHE on July 22, 1969.

[5] This was a chapter of the mostly Black national youth organization sponsored by the Communist Party U.S.A.

[6] BLAC was homegrown and coined by a student named Peter Sherwood (Pile 2019).

[7] The author acknowledges that the term Black can also refer to Puerto Ricans, but as it is commonly used in the U.S. to refer to a non-Latinx Black person, that will be its usage herein unless otherwise indicated.

[8] Other Puerto Rican members of BLAC were Maxine Rodríguez (Treasurer), Radames Aviles, and María Vargas (Pile 2019).

[9] They ranged from the specific, such as the admission of all Black and Puerto Rican student applicants and the recruitment of 25 Black and 25 Puerto Rican teachers beyond those to be hired in the newly approved Afro-American and Puerto Rican Studies Institutes, to freedom for the 21 Black Panthers who were arrested.

[10] Peck was referred to by protesters as "Pig Peck" (Horowitz 1981, p. 156).

[11] They were as follows: Ray Aviles, BLAC and PRA; Ed Bradly, BLAC; Cassandra Chisholm, BLAC; Bennet Cook, BLAC; Askia Davis, Sr., BLAC; Frank Fernández, PRA President; Sherman Fogg, BLAC; Linda Freeman Williams, BLAC; Cynthia Gumbs (Umakhair Muhammed), BLAC; Clyde Johnson, BLAC; Bruce La Roche (Wali), BLAC; John Lee (Dubaca), BLAC; Cy McClean, BLAC; Larry Murphy, BLAC; Antonio Nieves, BLAC and PRA; Ronald Outlaw, BLAC; Orlando Pile, BLAC President; David Powell, BLAC; and Larry Sparks, BLAC.

[12] Several CUNY colleges suspended commencement exercises in response to nationwide large-scale anti-Vietnam War and human rights protests; these included student strikes involving over 450 colleges, universities, and high schools. At CUNY, the BC situation was deemed the worst in that classes were disrupted from May 5th through the end of the school year (Horowitz 1981, 189).

[13] The *Revista* included editorial staff, José Hamid Rivera and Marie Ferrer Iturrino, and authors, such as Frank Bonilla, Billy Cajigas, Américo Casiano, Enid J.

Cruz, Emilio Díaz Valcárcel, Loida Figueroa, Michael Godreau, Wilfredo González, Víctor Hernández Cruz, Alfredo Matilla Rivas, Etnairis Rivera, Francisco Matos Paoli, Angel Luis Méndez, Pablo Navarro, Luis Nieves Falcón, Pedro Pietri, Juan Rivero, Rafael Rodríguez, Iván Silén, Juan Angel Silén, and Iris Zavala.

[14] This theater group was revived in the late 2000s by Vargas and performed at the 2009 *Possible Dream Encuentro* at BC, where they received the Don Quijote Leadership Award.

[15] On February 24, 1970, the BHE approved the creation of the Cultural Puerto Rican Center at Lehman College effective fall of that year to serve educational programs that teach Puerto Rican-focused courses, to translate materials from Spanish to English, and develop curricular materials. It is unclear whether this came to fruition; however, Aquino-Bermúdez states that at a special meeting of the Lehman College Faculty Council on March 21, 1969, it approved a University Puerto Rican Research Center, which he indicates is what led to the CUNY Center for Puerto Rican Studies in 1973 (1975, 123, 337–9).

[16] Various activist movements, with differing ideologies and priorities, publicly presented a united front to establish PRS. But in private, there were significant differences among the groups. Some were politically ideological in terms of bringing about a revolution and identifying cohorts instrumental in that change; others were concerned about strategies in dealing with an administration that fostered high levels of mistrust and suspicion; still others prioritized a focus on women's issues and the lesbian and gay community, which many felt warranted a separation of the Institute from the Department in order to work independently and expediently.

[17] Among her laudable contributions to PRS, Nieves wrote a seminal Puerto Rican Studies Task Force Centro report *Puerto Ricans in United States Higher Education* (1979) focusing on Puerto Ricans in U.S. higher education, PRS as a new discipline, and how to survive in institutions such as CUNY.

[18] Julio Morales did not serve in this capacity because of a planned special leave from 1973-75 to complete his doctoral studies.

[19] He was commonly known as Richie Pérez.

[20] This information is in the BC Department of PRLS Archives under Roseann González Ramírez, who served as PRS Provisional College Secretarial Assistant, but was among the many who did not acknowledge the legitimacy of Lugo de Luis Deza as PRS Chairperson, and eventually resigned in protest on October 27, 1975.

[21] He was commonly known as Charlie and Indio.

[22] Sánchez was enrolled in the doctoral program at Fordham University at the time.

[23] The PSP established chapters on various CUNY campuses and major cities (Velázquez, Rivera and Torres 2020).

[24] The students were: Charlie Alezandro, Joe Alvarez, Felicita Andino, William Arroyo, Raul Ayala, Sean Breslin, Carmin Camacho, Pablo Cassale, Kevin David, Edgar DeJesus, Joseph Dorta, Arthur Dunn, Linda Elsaieh, Julia Fisher, Henry Garcia, Edward Gillespie, Gloria and Sandra González, Nolda Hernandez, Victor

Maldonado, Montero Martinez, Paul Massas, Jessie Matthew, Cresencio Morales, Joe Morales, Ms. Elainie, Angel Muniz, Beladee Nahem, Gregory Nahen, Violet Nieves, Jose Ojeda, Gerardo Perez, Nydia Quinones, Antonio Ramos, Victoria and Mario Rivera, Ramon Riveria, William Rodriguez, Anthony Sabino, Gilbert Salgado, Joseph Sexton, Daniel Siegel, Mimie Smith, Ricardo Soler, and Jose Torres. The three faculty members were Antonio Nadal, Sonia Nieto, and Herminio Vargas. Note: There were several names repeated, in differing forms, and some were misspelled; the author kept the original spelling that appears on the legal document. Also, Pablo "Paul" Massas was the first Puerto Rican to be elected Student Government President in the spring 1972; he was a candidate of the Third World Federation student group.

[25] These demands included immediate restoration of funds for Africana, Italian, and PRS Institutes (including those promised in the April 1975 Agreement) and the Women's Center; no cutbacks to the Department of Educational Services, including continuous support for Open Admissions and the SEEK program; implementation of all demands made by the Committee for Justice; no tuition; and no financial aid cuts (Brooklyn College Department of Puerto Rican and Latino Studies Archives 1975d).

[26] An overwhelming majority of white middle-class students were the beneficiaries of Open Admissions at BC, and CUNY in general (Horowitz 1981, 166-167).

[27] The Departments of History and Political Science formed part of its initial curricular offerings.

[28] As a result of the fiscal difficulties experienced by CUNY, it converted all institutes to centers, which would be locally supported by the campuses. In 1986, the Department decided to rename its Institute of Puerto Rican Studies. In 2008, PRLS renamed it the María E. Sánchez Center for Latino Studies (MESCLS) in honor of its former Chairperson. It continues to sponsor special lectures and houses a library with archival materials. In 2008 and 2015, materials were received from Donald Watkins, BC Professor Emeritus, who served on CUNY's Affirmative Action Committee and was active in NYC Puerto Rican community circles. In 2018, a book collection was received from Samuel René Quiñones, a poet and journalist with *El Diario-La Prensa*. The MESCLS would go on to host the Undergraduate Latin@ Research Assistantships with grants from the CUNY Diversity Program Development Fund for several years to work on PRLS faculty research projects.

[29] Carrasquillo also initiated and coordinated the Brooklyn Borough President Howard Golden's Hispanic Advisory Council co-chaired by Golden and President Vernon Lattin, who was the first and, thus far, only Mexican American/Latinx President of BC (1992-2000). Carrasquillo remained actively involved in community and religious affairs as well as campus service, receiving the Brooklyn College Award for College Citizenship and Murray Koppelman Professorship.

[30] Key members included Angel Delíz, Herminia Ramos Donovan, and Joaquín Denis Rosa.

[31] Letters from Dennis Spinninger (Chairperson of Comparative Literature);

Chrysie Costantakos (Home Economics and Consumer Studies); Herminia Ramos Donovan (President, PRS Alumni Association); Osman David Mat (President, BC Graduate Student Organization); Lourdes R. Torres Sánchez (Coordinator, Puerto Rican Council on Higher Education—later known as the CUNY Discipline Council of Puerto Rican, Latino, and Latin American Studies); Sonia Nieto (faculty, University of Massachusetts-Amherst); and Josephine Nieves (Director, Department of Community Development, Community Service Society) are in the PRLS Archives.

[32] She was a BC alumna of the Class of 1960.

[33] This essay will use various era-appropriate terms to reference the group that is currently known as Latinx: Hispanic, Latino, Latino/a or Latina(o), Latin@, Latine, and Latinx.

[34] Initially, the proposed renaming was the Department of Puerto Rican, Latino, and Latin American Studies to provide a home base for the floating set of Latin American Studies (LAS) courses. There were several traditional, large departments that offered courses in LAS, and thus a titular and academic turf battle ensued led by the Modern Languages and Literatures Department. PRS eventually withdrew "Latin American" from its proposed title; in 2006, it created an interdisciplinary social science-based Latin American Studies minor, which continues to date.

[35] Faculty Council approved the name change on February 3, 1998.

[36] The course was created by then-adjunct María Pérez y González.

[37] Meetings with Acting Provost Laura Kitch resulted in support for the concept; the faculty line was granted to TVR to diversify its predominately white and male faculty.

[38] Juan González, the co-founder of the New York chapter of the Young Lords and renowned *NY Daily News* journalist, was the selectee.

[39] He was an alumnus of the Classes of 1968 and 1972.

[40] Beloved by students, he was voted favorite professor of the year numerous times over the decades and was recipient of Brooklyn College's Tow Award for Excellence in Teaching and the Eric M. Steinberg Award for College Citizenship.

[41] The exchange faculty from the University of Puerto Rico were Linda Colón, Facultad de Ciencias Sociales; Carlos Alá Santiago, Facultad de Planificación; and Norma Rodríguez Roldán, School of Social Work. Other faculty included Bettina Schmidt from Phillipps-Universitat Marburg in Germany, Juan González while he served as the 2000-02 Belle Zeller Professor in Political Science, and David Badillo who went to the University of Notre Dame.

[42] She would gain local and international recognition for leadership and academic work, such as the 2005 "21 Leaders for the 21st Century" from *Women's E-News*; the 2018 naming of the Puerto Rican Studies Association Virginia Sánchez Korrol Dissertation Award; the 2018 National Puerto Rican Day Parade Lifetime Achievement Award; and the 2020 Herbert H. Lehman Prize for Distinguished Contributions to New York History.

[43] An *areyto* is a religious dance and song ceremony used as a form of communal

education and oral history among the Indigenous Taín@s of Puerto Rico and the Caribbean.

[44] The College Office Assistant, Mildred Nieves Rivera (alumna of the Classes of 1998 and 2001), served from 1980-2000 in PRS/PRLS and was indispensable to Sánchez, Sánchez Korrol, and the faculty. She also initiated the annual PRLS/Familia Latina Commencement/Awards Reception, which continued for 35 years through 2015, ending when tax levy monies could no longer be used for this purpose.

[45] At the time, she was a 26-year-old ABD doctoral candidate with a National Institute of Mental Health Fellowship in Sociology.

[46] The member was Bill Gargan (Library).

[47] Her father, Ernesto Martínez Sierra, was an activist in East Harlem and founder of Casabe Houses for the Elderly as well as Taíno Towers and worked on the Lower East Side's Pedro Albizu Campos Plaza and Mariana Bracetti Houses.

[48] Since 2006, external faculty members have formed part of the departmental personnel action committees due to restrictions placed on non-tenured faculty. Faculty who have served are Gastón Alonso (Political Science), D. Irene Sosa (Television, Radio, and Emerging Media and PRLS), Peter Weston (Psychology), and Carolina Bank Muñoz (Sociology). Also, Alonso, Tomás López Pumarejo (Economics, now Business Management), Joseph Entin (English), and Bank Muñoz served as the Promotion and Tenure Divisional/School-wide PRLS representatives. Recently, on a couple of occasions, external members constituted the committees' majority, putting at risk departmental autonomy were it not for their commitment to the mission of PRLS. All who committed their time and energy to ensure PRLS could move forward, except one, were faculty of color, and all required authorization from their respective chairpersons. Support from allies is essential to understaffed and under-resourced departments.

[49] It also featured panelists such as Jodie Roure from the Department of Latin American and Latinx Studies at John Jay College of Criminal Justice (CUNY) who founded the humanitarian aid medical relief effort Hurricane María Assistance & Relief Institutional Alliance, Inc.

[50] The statements regarding Latinxs and women were posted on the web and featured in BC student newspapers, *Kingsman* and *Excelsior*, and in news outlets such as the *New York Times, Inside Higher Ed*, ABC-News, Telemundo, and CNN in October 2018.

[51] This was possible due to Nadal; PRLS and allied faculty; College Office Assistant Matilda Nistal; Sánchez Korrol; Puerto Rican Alliance and the Latinx student organizations; and APREE, the founders' intent on protecting their legacy.

[52] Sosa is an internationally known Fulbright Scholar with documentaries including *Sexual Exiles* (1999) <http://irenesosa.org/sexual-exiles-1999>, *Shopping to Belong* (2007) <http://irenesosa.org/shopping-to-belong-2007>, and *Vertical Slum* (2016) <http://irenesosa.org/vertical-slum-2016-50-min>. Mercado's film can be found at <https://www.youtube.com/watch?v=sIMKdC3t-tA>.

[53] Phi Beta Kappa, the oldest academic honor and first Greek-lettered society in the

USA, was founded on December 5, 1776.

[54] Puerto Rican Alliance is the oldest, continuous student organization of its kind in CUNY. Vázquez Sanabria graduated in 2021 earning the Donald D. Harrington Ph.D. Fellowship at the University of Texas, Austin, the most prestigious fellowship offered to any student enrolled therein.

[55] It was previously the Puerto Rican Staff and Faculty Organization established around the time of the Department of PRS. LFSO was headed by Nadal and Anselma Rodríguez (alumna of the Classes of 1973 and 1985, staff member).

[56] The coordinators included mostly students, some faculty, and staff: Lenina Nadal; Sonia Valentín; María Pérez y González, Antonio Nadal, and Anselma Rodríguez; Barbara Pimentel; Gisely Colón López; Angélica Lima; Tabatha López; Julia Fernández; Nicole Rojas; Daniel Vázquez Sanabria; and Matilda Nistal as general supervisor.

[57] César Reyes (alum) led the Latin American music recital; María Catalano Rand curated the art exhibit. Active staff members were from the Graduate Dean's Office, Veterans' Affairs and Counseling Center, Center for Academic Advisement and Student Success, and the Office of the Vice President of Student Affairs. Attendance ranges from 400-600 participants; it is primarily sponsored by the Office of Diversity and Equity Programs, the Magner Career Center, Core Curriculum, and BC Alumni Association.

[58] Funding was secured from the administration, career assistance from Natalia Guarín Klein in the Magner Career Center, and editorial support from College Office Assistant Matilda Nistal, Marylu Espinosa, and Gisely Colón López.

[59] She served from 2009-12 and then resumed her position as an at-large member through 2017. The current Chairperson of PRLS, Alan Aja, serves as a member.

[60] Africana and Judaic Studies Departments as well as the interdisciplinary programs of American Studies, Caribbean Studies, Women's and Gender Studies, and Studies in Religion were signatories. Over 40 departments, programs, faculty, professors emeriti, the PSC-CUNY union chapter, and the Latinx student organizations—PRA, MEDo, and MeHSA also supported it.

[61] Among the students were Yvette Aguirre, Ray Aviles, Frank Fernández, Natalie Martínez, Cresencio "Joey" Morales, Milga Morales, Antonio Nieves, Irma Ortíz, Felipe Pedraza, Juan Pérez, Rosario Román, Joaquín Denis Rosa, Federico "Freddie" Vélez, and José Villegas.

[62] CUNY is the nation's largest urban public university system.

[63] Alliance for Puerto Rican Education and Empowerment (alumni group).

REFERENCES

Aja, Alan. 2016. *Miami's Forgotten Cubans: Race, Racialization, and the Miami Afro-Cuban Experience*. New York: Palgrave MacMillan.

Aquino-Bermúdez, Federico. 1975. Growth and Development of Puerto Rican Studies Departments: A Case Study of Two Departments at the City University of New York. Ph.D. dissertation, University of Massachusetts.

Arenson, Karen W. 1996. Study Details CUNY Successes from Open-Admissions Policy. *New York Times* 7 May.

Auster, Elizabeth. 1975. Se Habla Español in City Public Schools: Can Bilingual Program Solve Students' Plight? *Kingsman* 9 May.

Biondi, Martha. 2013. 'Brooklyn College Belongs to Us': Black Students and the Transformation of Public Higher Education in New York City. In *Civil Rights in New York City: From World War II to the Giuliani Era*, ed. Clarence Taylor. 161–81. New York: Fordham University Press.

Brooklyn College. 1970. Kneller Urges Dropping Charges Against '19'. Brooklyn College Department of Puerto Rican and Latino Studies Archives. 20 February.

Brooklyn College Department of Puerto Rican and Latino Studies Archives. [circa 1969]. Demands.

_____. n.d. Background and Detailed Plan--The Beginning: The Institute for Puerto Rican Studies.

_____. 1974. Student Rights and Academic Appointments Have Been Joined Together by Racial Overtones. WBCR-Brooklyn College Radio Statement. 24 October.

_____. 1975a. Agreement Between Dr. John W. Kneller, President, Brooklyn College, and the Committee for Self-Determination of the Department and Institute of Puerto Rican Studies, in Response to Their Demands. 18 April.

_____. 1975b. Open Letter to CUNY Board of Higher Education signed by Sonia Nieto on behalf of the Department of Puerto Rican Studies. 28 April.

_____. 1975c. Letter from CUNY Vice Chancellor David Newton directed to the PSC-CUNY union representative Daniel Kaminker and María E. Sánchez regarding Sánchez v. President (Brooklyn College). 2 July.

_____. 1975d. Letter from Puerto Rican Studies Department to President Kneller. 2 October.

_____. 1975e. The Fight to Defend PRS at BC, flyer. 29 October.

_____. 1975f. BC Veterans Organization Urges You to Demonstrate, flyer. 29 October.

Brooklyn College Faculty Council Minutes. 1970. 17 March.

Brooklyn College: Puerto Rican Students Fight for Self-Determination. 1974. *City Star*. December.

Colón López, Gisely. 2019. A Legacy of Achievement: Puerto Rican Studies at Brooklyn College-CUNY. M.A. thesis, University of Connecticut-Storrs.

Colón López, Gisely, Tami Gold, and Pam Sporn, Producers. 2020. *Making the Impossible Possible: The Story of Puerto Rican Studies in Brooklyn College*. Directed by Tami Gold and Pam Sporn. Alliance for Puerto Rican Education and Empowerment. Third World Newsreel. Documentary. 30 minutes.

CUNY Board of Higher Education Minutes. 1969a. 5 May.

CUNY Board of Higher Education Minutes. 1969b. 9 July.

CUNY Board of Higher Education Minutes. 1970. 22 June.

Department of Puerto Rican Studies Self Study Report. 1988. Brooklyn College of the City University of New York. Prepared for an External Evaluation, 26-27 April. February.

Department of Puerto Rican and Latino Studies Self Study Report. 1999. Brooklyn College of the City University of New York. April.

Dinos, Carmen, Ricardo Pérez, and Sonia Nieto. 1974. Letter addressed to President Kneller in María E. Sánchez's file. Brooklyn College Department of Puerto Rican and Latino Studies Archives. 8 July.

Fiske, Edward B. 1975. City University Rethinks Goals. *New York Times* 19 October. Accessed 23 March 2020. <https://www.nytimes.com/1975/10/19/archives/city-university-rethinks-goals-city-university-rethinking-its-goals.html>.

Gil de la Madrid, Antonio. 1970. Estudiantes Boricuas Logran Brooklyn College Cree Departamento Estudios Puertorriqueños. *El Diario-La Prensa* 26 March.

Horowitz, Murray M. 1981. *Brooklyn College: The First Half Century*. New York: Brooklyn College Press.

Kalech, Mark. 1974. New Sit-In on Campus in B'klyn. *New York Post* 18 October.

Kihss, Peter. 1968. Brooklyn College Defends Actions: School Says It Is Already Meeting Student Demands. *New York Times* 23 May.

Kline, Polly and Steven Matthews. 1974. Delay Decision on Baruch As Downtown Showpiece. *Daily News* 26 November.

Nadal, Antonio. 2014. Interviewed by Gisely Colón López. 27 February.

Nieves, Antonio. 2019. Alliance for Puerto Rican Education and Empowerment (APREE) Interview. November.

Nieves, Josephine. 1979. Puerto Ricans in United States Higher Education. Puerto Rican Studies Task Force, Centro Working Paper 2. New York: Centro de Estudios Puertorriqueños.

Pérez y González, María E. 2000. *Puerto Ricans in the United States*. Westport, CT: Greenwood Press.

Pile, Orlando. 2019. Alliance for Puerto Rican Education and Empowerment (APREE) Interview. 8 November.

Proposal for Caribbean Studies Program. 1982. Brooklyn College Department of Puerto Rican and Latino Studies Archives. 24 May.

Puerto Rican Alliance. [circa 1970]. The Puerto Rican Alliance. Brooklyn College, City University of New York.

Rodríguez, Guillermo, ed. 1974. Turning Point. *Brooklyn College Africana and Puerto Rican Studies Department Bi-monthly Newsletter* 1(2). Department of Puerto Rican and Latino Studies Archives. 22 November.

Ruíz, Vicki L. and Virginia Sánchez Korrol, eds. 2006. *Latinas in the U.S.: A Historical Encyclopedia*. Bloomington: Indiana University Press.

Sánchez, María E., and Antonio M. Stevens-Arroyo, eds. 1987. *Toward a Renaissance of Puerto Rican Studies: Ethnic and Area Studies in University Education.*

Highland Lakes, NJ: Atlantic Research and Publications.

Sánchez Korrol, Virginia. 1983. *From Colonia to Community: The History of Puerto Ricans in New York City, 1917-1948.* Westport, CT Greenwood Press. [Second edition 1994 by University of California.]

_____. 1990. Department of Puerto Rican Studies Annual Report 1989-1990. Brooklyn College, CUNY.

Siegel, Daniel. 1974. Where the Struggle's At: The Dope on Elba Lugo. *Spigot Magazine.* Brooklyn College Student Government—CLAS. 12 December.

_____. 1975. Latest Developments: Puerto Rican Studies Embroiled and Unified. *Spigot Magazine.* Brooklyn College Student Government—CLAS. 17 April.

Slater, Andrew and Ronnie Scalf. 1974. Student Strike Fails to Materialize. *Spigot Magazine.* Brooklyn College Student Government—CLAS. 31 October.

Steier, Richard. 1975a. Protesters Vacate Registrar's office; Kneller's Concessions Cut Lugo's Power. *Kingsman.* Brooklyn College Student Newspaper. 25 April.

_____. 1975b. Kneller Unyielding on Lugo: Protesters Continue Registrar Takeover. *Kingsman.* Brooklyn College Student Newspaper. 18 April.

Stevens-Arroyo, Anthony, with Segundo Pantoja, eds. 1995. *Discovering Latino Religion: A Comprehensive Social Science Bibliography.* New York: Bildner Center for Western Hemisphere Studies, City University of New York.

Valdéz, Rudy. 2018. *The Sentence.* HBO documentary. 1 hour, 27 minutes.

Velázquez, José E., Carmen V. Rivera, and Andrés Torres, eds. 2020. *Revolution Around the Corner: Voices from the Puerto Rican Socialist Party in the United States.* Philadelphia: Temple University Press.

Wallis, Jim. 2017. Truth that Bears Repeating: A Budget is a Moral Document. *Sojourners* 30 March. Accessed 26 October 2020. <https://sojo.net/articles/truth-bears-repeating-budget-moral-document>.

CHAPTER 7

PUERTO RICAN STUDIES: TRANSITIONS, RECONFIGURATIONS, AND PROGRAMS OUTSIDE THE CUNY SYSTEM

Edna Acosta-Belén

At the dawn of the ethnic studies movement, Chicano/a Studies were mostly associated with the Southwest, the state of California being the leader in establishing the first programs. Education-based claims for these programs made by East Los Angeles Mexican-American public school student activists and those at East Los Angeles Community College in 1968, and the founding of United Mexican American Students (UMAS), later to become Movimiento Estudiantil Chicano de Aztlán/MEChA in 1969, were instrumental in organizing protests against systemic inequalities in education, in what is known as the East Los Angeles Walkouts (or Blowouts). Two other institutions, San Fernando Valley State College (California State University at Northridge since 1972) and San Francisco State University were among the first to establish programs, followed in later years by several other campuses of the California State and University of California systems (Acuña 2011; Hu-DeHart 2006). Before long, the educational blaze for change was evident throughout the Southwest and Midwest, and among Puerto Ricans and other populations of color in the Northeast and other parts of the country. For Puerto Ricans, about a dozen campuses of the City University of New York (CUNY) were at the forefront, and most of the early programs that are still active eventually expanded their scope and were reconfigured to include Latina/o Studies and Latin American and Caribbean area studies. Less attention has been given to Puerto Rican Studies programs/departments at other public and private universities in New York, New Jersey, and Connecticut, or the work of Puerto Rican Studies scholars at universities in Chicago, at the time the city with the second largest Puerto Rican population. This chapter highlights most of these programs, and the faculty and student organizations that participated in their founding and early development.

For these pioneers, it meant being part of a relatively small Puerto Rican Studies faculty (on average, three to four full-time tenure-track individuals and a few adjuncts), involved in the development of a newly established non-traditional field of inquiry that emerged from student and community demands seeking to achieve intellectual legitimacy in less than supportive academic environments, and establishing their own research and teaching records required for promotion and tenure. For many, early responses to our campus presence ranged from indifference or lukewarm acceptance, to condescending and, at times, contentious attitudes. Despite their uninvited incursion into the academy, by the early 1990s, there were over seven hundred ethnic and racial studies programs in the country (Butler 1991, 30). A prominent Chicano/a Studies pioneer describes the battles to build and defend the survival of these programs as akin to being "in the trenches of academe" (Acuña 2011), a suitable metaphor to describe past and more recent battles.

For most Puerto Rican Studies pioneer academics and activists, this part of our history was not totally unexpected, considering the surrounding national political, racial, and social unrest, and the insurgent educational objectives behind the origins of ethnic and racial studies programs. Even so, it presented some unique challenges in terms of balancing research, teaching, and service endeavors for incipient programs, in carrying out their respective missions, and also meeting external institutional norms and expectations. Moreover, recruitment of tenure-track faculty with the expertise to teach Puerto Rican Studies courses was an often challenging and conflict-ridden undertaking. First, the number of Puerto Ricans and other Latinas/os with doctoral degrees at U.S. universities was relatively low during those years, which meant there was a small pool of candidates for faculty recruitment and a very competitive environment for hiring the most qualified ones with the appropriate expertise to design and teach courses about Puerto Ricans, especially for tenure-track and tenured senior positions. Both recognized scholars and candidates in the early stages of their careers were frequently apprehensive about faculty employment in small newly established Puerto Rican Studies departments/programs. Candidates being considered to teach in those programs that did not have their own Puerto Rican Studies core faculty were based, by and large, in parochial disciplinary departments with faculty members who were, at times, either unenthusiastic, tacitly or outright racist or sexist, far from supportive of any of the new interdisciplinary fields, and less than welcoming of new hires to be shared with another unit. They were also generally critical of the quality of the scholarship of Puerto Rican Studies recruitment candidates who had published in interdisciplinary journals and favored those in the traditional disciplines, which back then had a poor record of publishing research on Puerto Ricans or other U.S. populations of color. They undervalued journals published outside the United States, and even more so, if they were in Spanish (an exception were Spanish language and literature journals based in the United States). Another factor was that in 1970, stateside Puerto Ricans represented slightly over 2 percent of those completing college degrees or more, a figure that increased to 5.6 percent in 1980 and to 10 percent by 1990; continuing a steady pattern of growth in the new millennium that eventually reached almost 19 percent in 2015 (Acosta-Belén and Santiago 2018, 148–9).

An obvious recruitment alternative during the first decade of Puerto Rican Studies was to hire tenure-track or visiting faculty with Ph.D.'s from various universities in Puerto Rico, primarily from the social sciences, the humanities, and education, who could teach courses on Puerto Rican culture, literature and language, politics, migration, ethnicity and race, public policy, bilingual education, and other pertinent topics. Faculty imported from the island did not necessarily share an understanding of the wide-ranging conditions, experiences, and struggles of stateside Puerto Ricans or about the history of their presence in U.S. society, albeit some of them held doctoral degrees from U.S. institutions. More than a few island hires also showed condescending or elitist attitudes toward the migrant community or viewed younger generations of stateside Puerto Ricans as acculturated or assimilated versions of more "authentic" island Puerto Ricans. Such views led to numerous debates about "the question of identity" or "the identity in question" of the diaspora and what it meant to be Puerto Rican within this context (Acosta-Belén 1992; Flores 1993; Sandoval-Sánchez 1992, 1997). In some ways, the subordinate "otherness" attributed by some island Puerto Ricans to their stateside countrymen/women were influenced by the stereotypes propagated in the U.S. media, which mostly blamed them for their widespread poverty conditions and the numerous problems that afflicted their segregated communities (e.g., poverty, gangs, crime, drugs, idleness, high school dropout rates, and rundown neighborhoods). Underlining this generalized portrait of the community was the belief that, when compared to the island, stateside Puerto Ricans had a weak record of leadership and socioeconomic and cultural achievements in U.S. society. For all purposes, up to that point, they remained mostly invisible or ignored in the nation's history and that of Puerto Rico. Some of these negative views were reiterated by the island's intellectual elites and the general population. Stateside Puerto Ricans were at times criticized for ostensibly being too "Americanized," not knowing Spanish or speaking "Spanglish" and thus, in need of "reverse acculturation" into the island's culture (Seda-Bonilla 1977). Those opinions rarely considered the lingering effects of dominant Anglo-conforming "melting pot" ideologies and practices in schools, aimed at demeaning and suppressing the cultures and languages of (im)migrant students, and their negative internalized effects on those generations of Puerto Ricans born or raised in the United States. Along with the already mentioned hurdles, Puerto Rican Studies faculty had to deal with the scarcity of English-language texts for the classroom and other adequate sources on the migrant communities in New York and other cities, or Puerto Rican history and culture. During those years, most of the major studies about the diaspora were written by U.S. and other foreign scholars who generally relied on stereotypes or biased perceptions of the poor, rather than offering more balanced analyses of the various structural and racial barriers that perpetuate poverty and inequalities intrinsic to capitalist economies. Few of these studies validated the histories, survival struggles, and contributions to the economy of their communities and states, nor the various ways in which Puerto Ricans express their ideas, experiences, and emotions, both culturally and creatively, and their relations with U.S. society.

Along with the numerous hurdles to overcome and battles to carry out—occasionally within the programs/departments themselves, but more frequently at the institutional level—came high levels of commitment, resilience, and renewal.[1] The achievements of the new interdisciplinary programs against these odds are a testament to the pioneering efforts of most Puerto Rican Studies faculty and students, and the communities that supported them. Not surprisingly, many of those faculty members played a prominent role in forging intellectual, pedagogical, and advocacy legacies that brought some degree of legitimacy and continuity to the field. Others based in disciplinary departments contributed by producing new research and scholarship focused on stateside Puerto Rican communities in their respective areas of expertise.

In New Jersey, Rutgers State University's Livingston College, a coeducational experimental college that captured the essence of its mission with its logo "Strength Through Diversity" and its claim to being an institution that "embodied the social and cultural awareness demanded by students at the time," established the first Puerto Rican Studies program outside of New York City. The first class of Puerto Rican students at the college founded the Unión Estudiantil Puertorriqueña (United Puerto Rican Student Organization) that same year and with a dozen or so other Puerto Rican students from Douglas and Rutgers Colleges became fervent advocates for the establishment of Puerto Rican Studies. The Puerto Rican Studies program at Livingston College was founded in 1970 under the leadership of María Josefa Canino Arroyo, a specialist in social and educational policy, social work, and community advocacy. Historian Paul G.E. Clemens writes: "Within a year, the new program was offering courses in Puerto Rican history, migration, art and music, and politics, and students, who were full members of its curriculum committee, helped to plan for the future" (2015, 175). Because of her expertise in the field of education and her record of activism in the Puerto Rican community, Canino Arroyo was the youngest member to be appointed to CUNY's Board of Trustees, a position she held from 1969-1974 and, again, from 1985-1990. At Livingston College, Canino Arroyo directed the program's transition into a department three years after its founding. Her department team included history instructor Carlos Piñeiro, executive secretary Vilma Pérez, and a graduate student. Some of the main aims of the new Puerto Rican Studies concentration were "to recover cultural identity, language and heritage, thereby affirming Puerto Rican consciousness from a sound knowledge base"—Memorandum of April 11, 1972 (Canino Arroyo 2013, 8), and to offer field experiences that connected research and learning to issues and challenges of poor Puerto Rican communities.

Out of the first class of five student graduates in Puerto Rican Studies at Livingston College, four pursued advanced degrees in law and other professional areas, and the fifth was employed by a Puerto Rican educational organization. This became a common pattern among Puerto Rican Studies undergraduate majors at other institutions: to pursue a Master's or doctoral degree, join the teaching profession, or work for a community organization or public service agency; clear examples of students using their education and professional training to improve the lives of their communities.

During the early years of the Livingston College program, Puerto Rican affiliate faculty from other units were involved in its founding and development. Among them were Ralph Ortiz of the Art Department, and Hilda Hidalgo and Edward Ortíz from the Department of Community Development and Urban Studies. Hidalgo was a well-known community activist in Newark. She was a co-founder of the National Puerto Rican Congress of New Jersey and of ASPIRA of New Jersey, as well as appointed Assistant Commissioner of Education for the State of New Jersey, among several other grassroots and professional organizations. She also was an early advocate of gay and lesbian rights. Edward Ortíz had been involved in the founding and development of Livingston College and had a prior strong record of involvement in New York City's community development and housing projects as well as in public service. Among other affiliates were Suni Paz Johnson, a leading children's musician and activist singer-songwriter; Miguel Algarín, an accomplished poet and playwright, and founder of the Nuyorican Poets' Cafe (1973) from the English Department; and Víctor Fernández Fragoso, also a gifted poet and playwright, from the Comparative Literature Program.

In response to the increased migration and presence of Dominicans and Cubans in New Jersey, in the mid-1980s, and under the chairmanship of Miguel Algarín, the unit changed its name to the Department of Puerto Rican and Hispanic Caribbean Studies. In 1990, Pedro Cabán, a prominent specialist in the political economy of Puerto Rico and on Latina/o race and ethnic studies, and a prior faculty member in Puerto Rican Studies at Fordham University, was hired to chair the department. Under his administration, the department was able to expand its Puerto Rican Studies faculty. Some key hires during his term included historian Carmen Teresa Whalen, known for her valuable research on Puerto Ricans in Philadelphia and currently a Professor at Williams College; creative writer, performer, and pioneer scholar in LGBTQ studies, Larry La Fountain-Stokes, now professor of Spanish at the University of Michigan; and anthropologist Ana Ramos-Zayas, known for her ethnographic work on Puerto Ricans and Mexicans in Chicago, and other studies dealing with the intersectionalities and politics of class, race, and ethnicity, and issues of social justice. Ramos-Zayas is currently professor of American Studies, Women's, Gender, and Sexuality Studies, and Ethnicity, Race, and Migration at Yale University. From 2000-2010, Cabán served as Vice Chancellor of the Office of Diversity, Equity, and Inclusion for the State University of New York (SUNY) central system. A few years after his return to faculty life, he served as chair of the Department of Latin American, Caribbean, and U.S. Latino Studies (LACS) at the University at Albany (SUNY) until the Spring of 2020.

Less supportive administrative changes at Rutgers University accounted for diminished faculty resources and a decline in the number of Puerto Rican Studies specialists in subsequent years. In 2005, under the departmental stewardship of Aldo Lauria-Santiago, the Department of Puerto Rican and Hispanic Studies was renamed Department of Latino and Hispanic Caribbean Studies. A well-known historian specializing in Central America and the Hispanic Caribbean, Lauria-Santiago is co-author (with Lorrin Thomas) of the book, *Rethinking the Struggle for Puerto Rican Rights* (2019). More than a decade and a half later, under current chair Carlos Decena, the department's name was changed, again, to Latino and Caribbean Studies (LACS). Carlos Decena is an interdisciplinary researcher whose work spans ethnic, queer, and feminist studies, social justice, and public health. LACS currently has 14 core faculty with joint appointments in other departments, and a dynamic and diverse group of instructors. In 2007, Livingston College was merged into the School of Arts and Sciences and known only as part of the Rutgers-New Brunswick/Piscataway campus. Current faculty there include established Puerto Rican Studies researchers, among whom are former LACS chair (2012-2015) and president of the Caribbean Philosophical Association, Nelson Maldonado Torres, a renowned theorist and author on decolonial thought; sociologist Zaire Dinzey-Flores, author of *Locked In, Locked Out: Gated Communities in a Puerto Rican City* (2013); and historian Lilia Fernández, author of *Brown in the Windy City: Mexicans and Puerto Ricans in Postwar Chicago* (2012), along with other members whose research and teaching interests are on Cubans, Dominicans, U.S. Latinas/os, and other Caribbean areas and specialties.

Through the years, departmental name changes were influenced partly by faculty departures and new hires in different specialty areas, which often required revisions to the curriculum and academic scope of the program or a reconceptualization of its mission. At times, these changes were part of broader administrative consolidations or reconfigurations of campuses, colleges, departments, and programs at Rutgers and other U.S. institutions, usually in response to decreasing institutional budgets and an overall U.S. decline in supporting public higher education (Cabán 2011-2012, 2009).

The Rutgers University campus at Newark started a Puerto Rican Studies program in 1977, as an outcome of student support through the Puerto Rican Organization (PRO) and efforts of Puerto Rican faculty member Olga Jiménez de Wagenheim. She wrote the original proposal in 1973 and became the program's coordinator when it finally was approved by the administration four years later. The program did not sponsor a major, nor have a regular budget or core faculty, but offered a minor with a small number of interdisciplinary courses on Puerto Rican, Latin American, and Caribbean topics. As coordinator, Jiménez de Wagenheim was able to secure a few grants to support program activities and new courses, such as Oral History, which sustained student training and field experiences in the surrounding communities. Today, the campus still offers a Latin American Studies minor, supported by faculty in disciplinary departments, which includes a few courses focusing on Puerto Ricans and U.S. Latinas/os, and broader offerings focusing on Latin America and the Caribbean in history, literature and language, political science, English, and sociology and anthropology.

Jiménez de Wagenheim is known for her invaluable historical study, *Puerto Rico's Revolt for Independence: El Grito de Lares* (1993), the volume *The Puerto Ricans: A Documentary History* (with Kal Wagenheim, 1993), and other books and scholarly articles dealing with women in nineteenth century Puerto Rican history, the Puerto Rican community in Morris County, New Jersey, and other topics. Her most recent work includes the book *Nationalist Heroines: The Women Puerto Rican History Forgot, 1930s-1950s* (2019). Among the program's supporting faculty was Asela Rodríguez de Laguna, a scholar of Spanish language and literary studies, and editor of the volumes, *Imágenes e identidades: el puertorriqueño en la literatura* (1983) and *Images and Identities: The Puerto Rican in Two World Contexts* (1987). Both volumes were outcomes of a major conference Rodríguez de Laguna organized in the spring of 1983 at Rutgers University. This conference brought a large number of prominent stateside and island Puerto Rican writers and critics to share their artistic work and engage in discussions about the different social, cultural, and linguistic environments that shape their respective creative expressions. Other supporting faculty included Hilda Hidalgo, previously mentioned for her contributions to the Livingston College department; and Elpidio Laguna-Díaz, another prominent Spanish language and peninsular literature scholar, also known for his campus and community leadership in promoting and expanding the study of Spanish and Portuguese languages and cultures.

The campuses of SUNY at Albany, Buffalo, and Stony Brook followed the CUNY and Livingston College programs and also started Puerto Rican Studies programs in 1970. The Albany program was initially directed by Antonio Pérez, back then a doctoral student in education and a counselor at the University's Educational Opportunity Program (EOP). In later years, Pérez was to serve as President of the Borough of Manhattan Community College (BMCC); a position he held for over two decades (1998-2018).

During those early years, the majority of Puerto Rican students at the Albany campus were recruited by the EOP program, which had been established in 1968. Their initial interest in course offerings focused on Puerto Ricans was supported by EOP teaching faculty and other professional staff, who were able to secure administrative support for the first few Puerto Rican Studies course offerings, planting the seed for developing an undergraduate major and establishing a department four years later. Black students and faculty on campus also were engaged in similar efforts to start a program and subsequently created a department of African-American Studies (today's

Africana Studies). In 1971, Puerto Rican students founded the organization Puerto Ricans Organized for Liberation and Education (PROLE; today's Fuerza Latina). Up to that point, the white student leadership of the officially elected Student Association (SA) on the campus had done very little to engage students of color or international students in governance, or to seek their involvement in the various annual student-organized celebrations and academic events. This organization had a substantial annual budget for programming events coming from mandatory student fees and was in charge of approving and allocating funds for any new student-initiated projects, but most of its programming had been primarily aimed at the majority white student population. In response to campus pressures, the SA approved the proposals submitted by Puerto Rican and African-American students who joined together to create their separate student organizations and sponsor their own activities, as they had done in their demands for establishing the initial Puerto Rican and African-American Studies programs the previous year. A year later, the Dean of the Division of Social and Behavioral Sciences appointed a committee to hold discussions about expanding the program. As a result, the proposal for a major and the establishment of a Department of Puerto Rican Studies was submitted to the administration in the Fall of 1972.

After Pérez left the University at Albany in the spring of 1973, Edna Acosta-Belén, a faculty member in Puerto Rican Studies since its inception, and at the time a Ph.D. student at Columbia University, was appointed director. Her doctoral work at Columbia University, research interests in colonialism and feminist movements, and subsequent experience as part of a team of EOP's instructional staff and student advisors at the University at Albany, coupled with previous community work with the Neighborhood Association for Puerto Rican Affairs (NAPRA) in the Bronx, were key to her involvement in the founding of the Puerto Rican Studies program. As director, she steered the process of establishing the department, getting courses for the major approved by the various levels of university governance, and implementing the new curriculum as well as the final registration of the undergraduate degree by the SUNY-Central administration that certified the program's eventual transition into a department in 1974. Acosta-Belén was the department's first chair; a position she held again for four non-consecutive terms. This was the beginning of a four-decade career in research, teaching, and service endeavors to the field, the institution, and the profession. She is now a Distinguished Professor Emerita and remains involved in scholarly pursuits.

The installation of a new Albany campus president and severe state cuts to the university's operating budget prompted the retrenchment of several university programs the following year. Because of the threat of cutting approved recruitment lines and reducing the new department's resources, PROLE students held a two-day sit-in at the campus president's office. Alongside faculty negotiations with the administration, their combined interventions mitigated the full implementation of the proposed cuts. During this period, the Department of Puerto Rican Studies (PRS) worked closely with the Bilingual Education Project in securing a major Title VII grant from the U.S. Department of Education, by participating in the proposal writing process during its early years, and by offering instructional support to the newly established program. Under the leadership of Puerto Rican educator Carmen Pérez, Title VII graduate fellowships that supported teacher training in bilingual education allowed for the recruitment of about a dozen students annually for almost a decade. Pérez left the University a few years later to lead the Bilingual Education Bureau of the New York State Department of Education, a position she held for over three decades. The Department of PRS also contributed to the creation and editing of *New Horizons*, the first newsletter of the New York State Association for Bilingual Education (NYSABE), published a year after the organization's founding (1976). Over four decades later, the organization is still a major advocate in promoting multilingual education.

Elia Hidalgo-Christensen, a former psychology professor at the University of Puerto Rico-Río Piedras, was also part of the original core faculty and served as chair of the department in the late 1970s. Her professional activities were strongly connected with the local community, as were those of her sister, Hilda Hidalgo at Livingston College and the City of Newark. Hidalgo-Christensen coordinated community outreach service internships and field experiences for department majors, including a census of the Capital District Hispanic population, organizations, and services. In addition, she played a key role in the founding of Albany's Centro Cívico Hispanoamericano (now Centro Cívico, Inc.), which, almost five decades after its creation, remains active in servicing the community. Heidi Dulay, a

linguist and specialist on second language acquisition and bilingual education, was also part of the core faculty. She taught courses on Puerto Rican
children in U.S. schools, bilingual education, and a research seminar for
department majors. She is co-author of *Language Two* (1982) and co-editor
of the volume *New Directions in Second Language Learning, Teaching, and
Bilingual Education* (1975). Two other core faculty members during this
early period: Juan Ángel Silén, a visiting associate professor and author of
Hacia una visión positiva del puertorriqueño (1970) [*We, the Puerto Rican
People: A Story of Oppression and Resistance*, 1971], and several other books
on different aspects of Puerto Rican history and politics; and historian José
Enrique Irizarry, an assistant professor, who had previously taught Puerto
Rican Studies courses at City College (CUNY).[2]

In the 1980s, other Puerto Rican Studies scholars joined the University
at Albany faculty. These included anthropologist James Wessman, economist Carlos E. Santiago, counseling psychologist Azara Santiago-Rivera,
and political scientist José E. Cruz. Wessman was author of *Anthropology
and Marxism* (1981) and editor of the Caribbean Studies Association (CSA)
newsletter for several years. Santiago was chair of LACS for several years
and later served as Associate Vice President of Academic Affairs and Provost
at the University at Albany. He is one of a select group of Puerto Rican
presidents at U.S. higher education institutions. He left the University at
Albany to serve as Chancellor of the University of Wisconsin-Milwaukee
for several years and is presently Commissioner of Higher Education for
the State of Massachusetts. A prominent scholar, Santiago is author of *Labor
in the Puerto Rican Economy: Postwar Development and Stagnation* (1992),
and co-author of *Puerto Ricans in the United States: A Changing Reality*
(1994) and *Puerto Ricans in the United States: A Contemporary Portrait*
(2018). Santiago-Rivera, a former professor of Counseling Psychology at
the University at Albany, the University of Wisconsin-Milwaukee, and the
Chicago School of Professional Psychology, is also a former Director of
the Clinical Mental Health Program at Merrimack College in Boston, and
currently Coordinator of the Master of Arts in Counseling Psychology at
Felician University in New Jersey. She is co-author of the book *Counseling
Latinos and la Familia: A Practical Guide* (2002) and a founding Editor of
the *Journal of Latina/o Psychology* (now *Journal of Latinx Psychology*) of the

American Psychological Association (APA). She has served as President of the National Latina/o Psychological Association and was a recipient of an APA Presidential Citation for outstanding contributions to the profession. Cruz is a professor of Political Science and Latino Studies, and author of the first major study of Hartford's Puerto Rican community (1998). His latest books are *Puerto Rican Identity, Political Development, and Democracy in New York, 1960-1990* (2017) and *Liberalism and Identity Politics: Puerto Rican Community Organizations and Collective Action in New York City* (2019). Most of these Puerto Rican and Latina/o studies faculty were part of a team of scholars involved in the writing of English and Spanish volumes, *"Adiós, Borinquen querida: The Puerto Rican Diaspora, Its History, and Contributions* (Acosta-Belén, et al. 2000), sponsored by the Comisión 2000 de San Juan, an initiative of the capital city mayor's office, to introduce island and stateside readers to the neglected historical and cultural legacies of Puerto Ricans in the United States.

Three main factors contributed to the reconceptualization and reconfigurations of ethnic and racial studies, and area studies interdisciplinary fields in the 1980s and beyond. First, many institutions that created these programs and departments in the early 1970s were already offering more established area studies specialties focusing on Latin America, the Caribbean, and/or other world regions. Second, the dramatic increase in the U.S. Latina/o populations that began in the 1980s continued growing at a rapid pace during the following decades. This was due primarily to (im)migration and the younger median age of these populations (when compared to the U.S. white population). Furthermore, U.S. Census data projected that by the dawn of the new millennium Latinas/os would become the largest population of color in U.S. society, which officially occurred in 2003. Third, Census projections showed that by the middle of the 21st century, populations of color will constitute nearly half of the U.S. population.

The presence of area studies programs and centers dates back to the late 1950s and early '60s, when numerous higher education institutions throughout the United States began to establish such programs, significantly focusing on Latin America and the Caribbean. The Rockefeller Foundation had taken the lead in offering grant opportunities to create such programs, along with federal funding authorized by the Title VI National Defense

Education Act (NDEA) of 1958. Propelled by these funding opportunities during the Cold War years, higher education institutions responded by creating new interdisciplinary programs on various world regions, aimed at providing specialized knowledge and training, and a broader understanding of different regional areas and countries, most notably developing areas vulnerable to political unrest and the spread of communism. The ultimate goal was to create a stronger knowledge base for the formulation of U.S. foreign policy, strengthening relations and alliances with other countries, and safeguarding national interests. Area studies programs included interdisciplinary training in the social sciences, foreign policy, diplomacy, and a few other fields, along with foreign language training. For the United States, intelligence about Northern and Southern neighbors meant area studies programs focusing on Canada and the Latin American and Caribbean regions. Other regions of the world also came into play, but the emergence of some of the major Latin American Studies centers at U.S. universities paved the way for the development of the interdisciplinary field of Latin American Studies and the founding of the Latin American Studies Association (LASA) in 1962.

However, for almost two decades after their inception, Latin American and other area studies programs were dominated by white male scholars and remained largely disconnected from the study of Puerto Ricans or any of the various other Latin American and Caribbean origin populations living in the United States (today's U.S. Latinas/os). Back then, these populations included descendants from early Spanish and Mexican settlers of the Southwest, a territory that was originally part of the Spanish empire until the conclusion of Mexico's War of Independence (1810-1821) when Mexico became a sovereign nation. This territory was later annexed by the United States as a result of the Mexican-American War (1846-1848). Afterward, the Mexican populations also included several generations of immigrants and contract or undocumented workers. Puerto Rican émigrés began to arrive during the mid-nineteenth century when Puerto Rico was still a Spanish colony. Along with political expatriates, there was a considerable flow of tobacco workers from Puerto Rico seeking employment in the expanding U.S. cigar manufacturing factories. The majority settled in New York City and continued coming until the 1920s. In general, Puerto Rican migration began to increase in more significant numbers after Congress passed legislation to grant U.S. citizenship to the citizens of Puerto Rico in 1917 and reached its largest peak during the post-World War II Great Migration (mid-1940s-1960s). It was not until the New Millennium Migration of the last three decades that Puerto Rican migration reached levels comparable to those of the Great Migration (Acosta-Belén and Santiago 2018; Meléndez and Vargas-Ramos 2014). Cuban immigrants and political refugees, who had been settling in the United States since the 1820s, began to arrive in larger numbers during the second half of the nineteenth century and early decades of the twentieth century, with the largest waves coming after the Cuban Revolution of 1959 and the Mariel boatlift of 1980. For over six decades, about two dozen national Latin American Studies centers have been or still are being partially funded by Title VI grants. Even now, that grant competition does not fund any centers or departments whose primary focus is U.S. Latina/o Studies; although some of these centers have added some Latina/o Studies courses to their curricular offerings during the last two decades. Nonetheless, it was the Chicano/a and Puerto Rican Studies programs that initially paved the way for the field of Latina/o Studies and for inserting U.S. Latinas/os into Latin American and Caribbean area studies (Acosta-Belén 1993, 1991, 2001).

Prior to the early 1980s, area studies and Puerto Rican or other ethnic and racial studies programs that emerged in the late 1960s and 1970s continued to function as two separate spheres, despite their obvious focus on numerous overlapping issues and topics (e.g., race, ethnicity, colonialism, imperialism, poverty, inequality, (im)migration, diasporas, economic development, the study of the histories, cultures, and languages of other countries). In addition to these shared interests, ongoing transnational connections that stateside Puerto Ricans and other U.S. Latina/o national groups maintained with their respective countries of ancestry, provided fertile ground for conceptualizing new hemispheric approaches to the study of their (im)migrant experiences, and for comparative studies of the diverse conditions that prompted them to leave their particular Latin American and Caribbean countries to settle in a wide range of U.S. cities and states.

Furthermore, the significant growth of the Latina/o populations and future projections indicating they were to become the largest U.S. minority by the dawn of the new millennium, was an important factor in the push to explore the porous boundaries between the fields of area and ethnic and racial studies of the mid-1980s. By looking at Latina/o experiences and conditions North and South, the more encompassing hemispheric critical approaches were further stimulated in later decades by the frequent merging of programs at institutions where they had previously co-existed. Although these hemispheric approaches attenuated some of the ethnic nationalistic tenor of the early stages of Chicano/a and Puerto Rican Studies programs, they also invited a closer look at other individual nationalities (e.g., Cubans, Dominicans, and Central and South Americans), and the broader diasporic and transnational experiences of previously colonized and enslaved populations of color in the Americas, now racialized (im)migrants living and working in numerous urban and rural areas throughout the United States.

In 1984, the Department of Puerto Rican Studies at the University at Albany (SUNY) merged with the Latin American Studies Program, originally established in the early 1960s with affiliate faculty based in various disciplinary departments (mostly history, anthropology, political science, and languages and literatures). Faculty interests and expertise in other parts of the Caribbean or Mexico and Central America were revitalized in the 1980s by the increasing immigration to the United States of populations from countries in these regions, such as the Dominican Republic and Haiti in the 1970s and later years, and over a decade of political unrest, government persecution, civil wars, and economic stagnation in various Central and South American countries that started in the late 1970s and continued throughout most of the 1980s.

The latter conditions brought numerous political refugees and other documented and undocumented immigrants, mostly from Colombia, Nicaragua, El Salvador, Guatemala, and Honduras, to the United States and opened up new research and teaching pursuits, providing an opportunity to widen the scope of the department's original mission and curriculum.[3] Out of this merger came a reconstituted Department of Puerto Rican, Latin American, and Caribbean Studies (PRLACS), offering undergraduate majors in Puerto Rican Studies and Latin American Studies and minors in Caribbean Studies and Latino Studies. In addition to a few of the original Puerto Rican Studies courses (e.g., Puerto Rican History and Culture, Puerto Rican Literature, Puerto Rican Politics, Puerto Rico and the Caribbean), some of which had been part of the institution's General Education offerings for years, new courses focusing on the histories and cultures of rapidly growing U.S. Latina/o populations and on the Hispanic and non-Hispanic Caribbean were also added to the curriculum (e.g., Latino USA; Latino Politics; Latino Cultures and Literatures; Introduction to Caribbean History; The Caribbean: Peoples, Histories, and Cultures; and Literature of the Hispanic Caribbean).

The mission of PRLACS was to foster transnational hemispheric approaches to research and teaching endeavors about Puerto Ricans and other U.S. Latinas/os, and their heritage nations, and more comparative perspectives regarding the experiences of Puerto Ricans and other Latinas/os. Back then, the University at Albany and the University of California at Santa Cruz were among the first to pursue these approaches, which also motivated the founding of the Latino Studies section of the Latin American Studies Association (LASA) in 1992, and the *Latino Review of Books* in 1994 (subsequently, *Latino(a) Research Review*, 1997-2012), published by the Center for Latino, Latin American, and Caribbean Studies (CELAC) at the University at Albany. The journal involved the efforts of several Puerto Rican, Chicano/a, Cuban, and Dominican Studies scholars.

One of the main outcomes of the merger of ethnic and area studies at the University at Albany was an overall increase in undergraduate enrollment and the development of a Master's program. A written M.A. research project (equivalent to a thesis) was a degree requirement, and some of these projects focused on Puerto Rican topics. Efforts to expand the graduate program continued, and, in the late 1990s, the department developed a doctoral track in Latin American, Caribbean, and U.S. Latino Cultural Studies, with the collaboration of the Spanish doctoral program, a relationship that continues to this day. Again, the opportunity for doctoral research generated a number of dissertations focused on Puerto Rican topics.

A Puerto Rican Studies Program at what was then the State University of New York at Buffalo (now University at Buffalo, SUNY), was founded in the early 1970s initiated by the activism of the Puerto Rican student organization PODER (Puerto Rican Dignity, Elevation, and Responsibility), originally founded by Alberto O. Cappas and other students, and still active on the campus. In later years, Cappas authored several poetry books and is currently co-publisher and editor of the community newspaper *Buffalo Latino Village*. PODER was involved in campus struggles for more opportunities and an inclusive academic experience for Puerto Rican and other students of color. Thus, since the late 1960s their activist efforts and those of some campus faculty, were instrumental in the founding of the Center for Puerto Rican Studies, a student and community support services office, directed by Francisco Pabón, who also had been involved during those years in Spanish-English developmental and bilingual education programs in some Buffalo schools. These programs were aimed at serving the needs and English language skills of Spanish-speaking children of growing Latina/o populations in New York State's second largest city. Alfredo Matilla, a well-known poet, playwright, and novelist, was hired in 1972 to administer the nascent PRS Program housed in the Department of American Studies. The Department offered a Master's degree with a concentration in PRS, in addition to an undergraduate major. In later years, Matilla also directed the American Studies graduate program and continued to be part of the Buffalo faculty for over two decades. He was the Spanish translator of Pedro Pietri's *Puerto Rican Obituary* (1977), published by the Instituto de Cultura Puertorriqueña in Puerto Rico, and a promoter of the work of the Nuyorican poets in Puerto Rico's literary circles. During those early years, prominent writer Pedro Juan Soto, author of the collection of short stories and a novel about the lives and experiences of New York Puerto Ricans in the late 1950s and early 60s, was a visiting professor and part of the PRS faculty.

The SUNY-Stony Brook (now Stony Brook University) PRS program was initially directed by Juan E. Mestas (1974-1976), a Stony Brook doctoral recipient in Hispanic Languages and Literature. In later years, he was deputy chair of the National Endowment for the Humanities and Chancellor of the University of Michigan-Flint. Olga Aran Méndez, who in 1978 became the first Puerto Rican woman to serve in the New York State Senate, and Iris M. Zavala, a well-known Puerto Rican and Spanish literature scholar, were also part of the program, which was active for most of the 1970s. Zavala co-edited with Rafael Rodríguez, then director of PRS at Queens College, the volumes *Libertad y crítica en el ensayo político puertorriqueño* (1973) [*The Intellectual Roots of Independence: An Anthology of Puerto Rican Political Essays,* 1980], widely used in some of the early PRS courses. In 1995, Stony Brook established a Latin American and Caribbean Studies Center that houses an undergraduate minor and an internship program and offers

Tinker Foundation research grants for graduate students from a wide range of disciplines doing fieldwork in those regions.

In 1994, more than two decades after the inception of the aforementioned New York and New Jersey-based programs, the University of Connecticut-Storrs (UConn) founded the Institute of Puerto Rican and Latino Studies (IPRLS); a recent administrative configuration transformed it into El Instituto: Institute for Latino/a, Caribbean, and Latin American Studies. The founding of the IPRLS was reflective of the growing Puerto Rican and Latino/a populations in the cities of Hartford and Willimantic, as well as the bordering state of Massachusetts, and the increased presence of Puerto Rican Studies faculty and professional staff at UConn and a few other nearby universities and colleges in the New England region. Historian Luis A. Figueroa, currently an associate professor at Trinity College, and Ino Ríos, campus Director of the Puerto Rican/Latin American Cultural Center at UConn during those years, were instrumental in the initial faculty, student, and community efforts to create IPRLS. Appointed as the Institute's first director, Edgardo Meléndez, a prominent scholar of Puerto Rican politics and migration (Meléndez 2017, 2020), now Professor of Africana and Puerto Rican/Latino Studies at Hunter College (CUNY), initiated the process of recruiting new faculty and developing the program during its early years. The fact that most of the faculty hiring positions were administratively shared with parochial disciplinary departments and not core faculty appointments in Puerto Rican Studies initially slowed the recruitment of new faculty. Institute faculty affiliates in later years included prominent historian Blanca Silvestrini, known for her work in Puerto Rico's labor history, women workers, colonial medicine, and law and society, and Guillermo Irizarry, a specialist in Latin American, Caribbean and U.S. Latina/o literature and culture, and author of the award-winning book *José Luis González: el intelectual nómada* (2006). Both are former Institute directors. In 2012, the original Institute merged with the Center for Latin American and Caribbean Studies (CLACS), a unit originally established in 1974.

A few Puerto Rican Studies scholars are among the current faculty. These include Charles Robert Venator-Santiago, a specialist in Puerto Rican and Latina/o politics, political theory, and public law and author of *Puerto Rico and the Origins of US Global Empire: The Disembodied Shade* (2015) and *Hostages of Empire: A Short History of the Extension of US Citizenship to Puerto Rico, 1898-Present* (2018); sociologist Marysol Asencio, editor of *Latina/o Sexualities: Probing Powers, Passions, Practices, and Policies* (2010), whose work focuses on Latina/o sexuality and reproductive issues, and community education advocacy; and historian Emma Amador, whose research interests include Puerto Rican and Latina gender and sexuality studies, race and ethnicity, labor studies, migration, and social welfare and policy. UConn librarian Marisol Ramos, a former M.A. graduate from the University at Albany's LACS program, has been in charge of digitizing books and other archival materials from UConn's well-known Puerto Rican Collection (former Géigel Family Collection).

Among private universities, Fordham University was the only one to create a Puerto Rican Studies program in response to the takeover of the university president's office by a group of activist students in 1970. According to Arnaldo Cruz-Malavé (2018), an associate professor and former director of the current Latin American and Latinx Studies Institute (LALSI), the presence of Jesuit priest-scholar Joseph Fitzpatrick in supporting students and mediating the negotiations between them and the campus administration on their demands for a Puerto Rican Studies program, facilitated its founding. As Fitzpatrick was scheduled to teach a newly created Puerto Rican history course, he was recruited by another institution but, before his departure, reached out to Fernando Picó, a Puerto Rican, who he knew from seminary studies at the Woodstock Jesuit College. Picó had received an M.A. from Fordham a few years earlier and was finishing a doctoral degree in history at Johns Hopkins University in an area far removed from Puerto Rican history. This opportunity was an ironic twist that partly motivated him to significantly shift his original scholarship and teaching interests in subsequent years. Despite Picó's initial misgivings about teaching in an area outside his historical training, but out of consideration and respect for the efforts that Fitzpatrick and the students had invested in persuading the administration to offer a Puerto Rican history course, he accepted the faculty position at Fordham.

The enthusiasm and desire expressed by Puerto Rican students for learning about their historical and cultural roots and about the reasons and conditions that drove their families to leave the island and settle in New York, along with his compelled self-training in Puerto Rican history, would eventually redefine Picó's whole intellectual career. After returning to

Puerto Rico in 1972, he joined the Department of History at the University of Puerto Rico-Río Piedras (UPR) and remained there until his death in 2017. He became a leading authority in Puerto Rican historical studies, publishing over a dozen books and making significant contributions to the new historiography that flourished in the 1970s and following decades. Picó published a prominent Puerto Rican history textbook in Spanish (1988), also translated into English (2006), which is still widely used in Puerto Rico and stateside. Among Puerto Ricans, Fitzpatrick, who returned to have a long career at Fordham, is remembered primarily for his book, *Puerto Rican-Americans: The Meaning of Migration to the Mainland* (1971), which broke away from some of the most obvious deficiencies of prior studies about Puerto Rican migrants available in English. During those early years, this book was required reading in Puerto Rican Studies courses and became one of the most popular and informed sources dealing with migration and Puerto Rican adaptation to U.S. society.

Limited budgetary resources and internal administrative issues slowed the growth of Puerto Rican Studies at Fordham. A broad institutional reorganization in 1995 consolidated some of Fordham University's programs, including Puerto Rican Studies. Course offerings focused on Puerto Ricans and other Latinas/os are now part of the Latin America and Latinx Studies Institute (LALSI). LALSI's academic endeavors emphasize the study of "Latin America in relation to its diasporic communities in the United States, and especially New York, connecting thus the local with the global in organic and non-hegemonic ways" (Cruz-Malavé 2018, 31). Other accomplished Fordham scholars connected to Puerto Rican Studies at different times include Lloyd Rogler Canino, Pedro Cabán, and Clara Rodríguez—all known for their substantive research on Puerto Ricans and in Latina/o Studies. Before joining the Fordham faculty, Rodríguez was a faculty member and former chair of the Department of PRS at Lehman College (CUNY).

In the late 1990s and early 2000s, Cornell University offered PRS courses under its Latino Studies Program and hired a few tenure-track and visiting Puerto Rican Studies faculty. Three former presidents of the Puerto Rican Studies Association (PRSA) have been part of Cornell's Latino Studies Program faculty—Vilma Santiago-Irizarry, an associate professor in the Department of Anthropology and a former faculty member in Puerto Rican

Studies at John Jay College (CUNY), and Pedro Cabán in the Department of Government, both former directors of the program; and Edna Acosta-Belén, a Visiting Professor in the fall of 1998. Héctor Vélez, a sociologist and professor of Latin American Studies at Ithaca College, was a founding member of Cornell's Latino Studies program, and also taught courses on Latinas/os and race and ethnicity at both institutions for many years.

A few public and private universities in the city of Chicago have been offering courses focused on Puerto Ricans for many decades. This effort was influenced, in part, by the community civil rights and Puerto Rican nationalist activism during the 1960s, the emergence and activism of the Young Lords (1968), the founding of Street Sounds (1971), a popular music and spoken word group initiated by Puerto Rican poets and graphic artists, and the launch of *The Rican: Journal of Contemporary Puerto Rican Thought* (1971-1974) by a group of Puerto Rican academics, poets, and artists. The publisher of *The Rican* was Samuel Betances, then a professor of sociology at Northeastern Illinois University and, in later years, cofounder of Souder, Betances & Associates, Inc. (1990), a group of diversity trainers and consultants. Betances' early work focused on racial prejudice in Puerto Rico. In recent years, he has published the books *Winning the Future With Education: One Step at a Time* (2013), and *Communicating Diversity: Powerful, Practical, Persuasive Pointers to Get the Job Done* (2000). The journal's editor was Abdín Noboa-Ríos, an educator in the field of research and social action programs, author of numerous national case studies and ethnographic studies, and founder of Innovative Consultants International in 1992, a firm that provides research and evaluation services. During the last few years of its relatively brief publication life, *The Rican* was edited by Ricardo R. Fernández, at the time based at the University of Wisconsin-Milwaukee, who later established a prominent administrative career in higher education. He served as the second president of Lehman College (CUNY) for twenty-six years (1990-2016). *The Rican* also engaged the collaboration of faculty members affiliated with the University of Illinois-Chicago (UIC; former Chicago Circle Campus) and DePaul University. One of them was the well-known anthropologist and geographer, James M. Blaut, who had previously taught at the University of Puerto Rico in the early 1960s. Both UIC and DePaul are known for their engagement with the city's Puerto Rican, Mexican, and other Latina/o communities during the 1970s. UIC offers a Latin American and Latino Studies (LALS) program that dates back to 1974 and established a Latino Cultural Center in 1976 focused on student services and community outreach. Prominent Puerto Rican/Latina/o Studies specialist, Frances Aparicio, is a former professor and director of the UIC's LALS program. A specialist in cultural and literary studies, and Latina/o Studies, she is the author of *Listening to Salsa: Gender, Latin Popular Music, and Puerto Rican Cultures* (1998) and *Negotiating Latinidad: Intralatina/o Lives in Chicago* (2019), among several other works. Another UIC/LALS professor during this period was Marc Zimmerman, author of a book on U.S. Puerto Rican art, film, and literature, where he includes some of the leading Chicago writers and artists. DePaul University established a Latin American Studies program in the late 1970s that expanded into the current Department of Latin American and Latino Studies (LALS) in the mid-1990s and instituted a Center for Latino Research (CLR) in 1985. Among CLR directors were leading Puerto Rican sociologist, Félix Padilla, and Cuban Studies specialist, Félix Masud-Piloto.

In the late 1990s, the LALS faculty expanded under the leadership of Lourdes Torres, and both LALS and CLR established a closer relationship, sharing physical space and staff resources, and strengthening the programming and research endeavors of both units. One of CLR's major research projects was a series of oral histories of Chicago's Young Lords, which are now part of the university's Latin American and Latino Archives. Torres is a DePaul Professor and editor of the *Latino Studies* journal, a specialist in sociolinguistics, queer Latina/o literature, and Puerto Rican lesbian culture and literature. Also part of the faculty are professor, poet, translator, and essayist, Juana Iris Goergen, who has published on various Puerto Rican topics through the years; and Puerto Rican artist Bibiana Suárez, a DePaul Professor of Art, with numerous solo exhibitions in the United States, Puerto Rico, and Mexico, such as *Memoria (Memory)*, *Island Adrift: The Puerto Rican Identity in Exile*, and *In Search of an Island*. Among the affiliated faculty are Marixsa Alicea, professor in DePaul's School of Continuing and Professional Studies, and author of numerous publications on Puerto Rican women, transnational migration, U.S. Latina experiences, and women and drug use, as well as co-editor (with Maura Toro-Morn) of the volume *Migration and Immigration: A Global View* (2004); and Jacqueline Lazú, associate professor and Associate

Dean of the College of Liberal Arts and Social Sciences, and a specialist on Puerto Rican and other Hispanic Caribbean literatures, and Latina/o theater and performance studies. Another Chicago-based contributor to Puerto Rican and Latina/o Studies scholarship in the areas of gender and immigration is sociology professor Maura Toro-Morn at Illinois State University.

As time progressed, many universities saw the merging of Puerto Rican Studies with Latin American and Caribbean area studies programs, or their expansion into Latina/o Studies, as a way to justify a reduction of faculty resources by tapping into existing faculty in the institution's area studies and language programs. These administrative decisions were often prompted by the premise that the U.S. Latina/o experiences were similar enough to be lumped together (as the U.S. Census has been doing since the 1970s), and by the flawed assumption that the Spanish language and the histories and cultures of the twenty different nationalities that the Census includes under the Hispanic/Latino label are unifying factors that justify their consolidation into a single academic unit. It was common for university administrators to see these mergers as an opportunity to combine resources that, in practice, generally meant a reduction of tenure-track core faculty and operating budgets, and more reliance on affiliated faculty from other departments and part-time lecturers. But, some administrators and faculty also shared the view that the shift from the single national group focus of PRS to the broader pan-ethnic Latina/o Studies umbrella had the potential for appealing to a wider audience of students and thus increasing course and program enrollments.

A number of Puerto Rican Studies faculty members, however, were also concerned about not losing the essence of what gave origin and continuity to the field in the first place, especially in view of the progress made in debunking the myths of prior scholarship and producing new decolonized knowledge and pedagogy about the Puerto Rican people. Due to compelled mergers, faculty were confronted with the challenge of developing new, and not always the most coherent, curriculum and revising degree requirements in order to make them congruent with their particular research and teaching expertise. Yet, for the most part, faculty remained open to the new intellectual possibilities afforded by the Latina/o Studies field and the reconfigurations of the mission of the original Puerto Rican Studies and Latin American and Caribbean area studies programs/departments.

For many Puerto Rican Studies academic units, transitioning into Latin American and Caribbean area studies and Latina/o Studies has had mixed results. Among the most positive outcomes were increased course enrollments and majors, and a more diverse student audience; a broader mix of Latina/o ethnicities, but also a wider range of students of other ethnic and racial backgrounds taking these courses. Courses became more inclusive of the study of the histories, conditions, and experiences of island and stateside Puerto Ricans, as well as other Latinas/os, and introduced more comparative approaches to research and teaching about these populations. At some of the institutions, this meant the eventual elimination of a Puerto Rican Studies major and less regular course offerings focusing primarily on Puerto Ricans. Graduate programs helped mitigate some of the effects of the latter, since graduate seminars allowed faculty to focus on a variety of Puerto Rican issues and thus create opportunities for graduate students to choose Puerto Rican-focused research topics for their M.A. projects or doctoral dissertations. However, only a small portion of these programs, namely those located at research institutions, offer graduate degree programs. Despite that being the case, in the last five decades there has been a notable increase in the number of doctoral dissertations at U.S. universities and in published books and journal articles in the social sciences, the humanities, and the professional fields, dealing with topics related to stateside Puerto Ricans.

More than half of the early Puerto Rican Studies programs and departments are still active and have been able to maintain some degree of balance between their Puerto Rican Studies origins and their voluntary or compelled co-existence with Latin American and Caribbean area studies and U.S. Latina/o Studies. The growth of Latina/o Studies programs and departments persisted, especially after Latinas/os became the country's largest U.S. population of color. It is reasonable to assume that because of their estimated pattern of population growth during the first half of the new millennium, the number of Latina/o Studies programs will continue to expand, if the racist U.S. political environment changes from what it is at this writing and if, as a result, support for public education increases at the state and national levels. However, it is also clear that, historically and in general, support for Puerto Rican and Latina/o Studies programs/departments has been modest at best during periods of institutional bud-

getary constraints and, at worst, these cutbacks prompted the retrenchment of departments, loss of departmental status, or consolidation with
other programs at some of those institutions.

Regarding the influence of Puerto Rican and other ethnic and racial
studies interdisciplinary fields, it is worth mentioning that these new areas of
academic inquiry eventually had an impact through exposing the biases and
shortcomings of the traditional disciplines regarding the study of U.S. populations of color and their mostly neglected histories, cultures, and multiple
contributions to U.S. society. Such was the case with the field of American
Studies, which originated in the 1930s. The few early programs were aimed at
advancing the notion of an American civilization and thought, which would
be a central component to the curriculum at universities and schools, and
shared basic knowledge for the nation's population. The most established
American Studies programs in the country date back to the 1950s and, in
subsequent decades, the orientation of those programs was far from reflecting the multicultural and racial realities and complexities of U.S. society or
the nation's history. According to Christopher Moses' review of the evolution
of American Studies, the field underwent a crisis in the 1960s and early '70s:

Having focused on a canon of "dead white men" and "high" cultural history, the
discipline was very much shaken by the social and cultural revolution, ushered in with
the civil rights movement (...). Scholars and activists alike called for an examination
of America's "denied" past, including slavery, colonialism, and immigration, and for a
reorientation towards popular culture, feminist, and minority studies. (n.d., 19)

As the various Puerto Rican and other ethnic and racial studies interdisciplinary fields began to stabilize and achieve academic recognition, the
field of American Studies gradually transcended its white Anglocentric and
American exceptionalism tenets. Up to the 1970s, these underlying ideologies had dominated the study of U.S. history, society, and culture. The field's
compelled "reorientation" and efforts gradually made American Studies
more critical of Anglocentric mainstream national narratives and tenets,
and more cognizant of the multicultural and multiracial realities of the
U.S. nation, including its previously neglected history of racial violence and
unequal treatment endured by its populations of color. What made these

new inroads possible was the restorative and reframing research being carried out by scholars of color.

CONCLUDING REMARKS

Regardless of their contentious origins, past and current challenges, and half-hearted support by university administrators and other campus faculty, the establishment and development of Puerto Rican Studies, part of a vanguard of interdisciplinary fields of academic inquiry, have managed to survive and achieve a suitable degree of institutional stability. Worthy of notice is the fact that these academic areas continue to generate levels of scholarship comparable to those of faculty in other fields, engage in more inclusive teaching and curricular innovation, foster community service and advocacy work, and play a vital role in efforts to diversify the faculty, staff, and administration of their respective institutions. It is both telling and ironic that the levels of progress of many higher education institutions to create more diverse and inclusive academic environments heavily relies on the commitment and service of faculty affiliated with PRS. However, the service activities of faculty in these areas are often undervalued or taken for granted to a great extent by their departments and institutions, and, at times, even viewed unfavorably in tenure and promotion decisions, or often perceived as a distraction from a faculty member's research and publication record. Other times, the scholarship of Puerto Rican faculty located in some disciplinary departments tends to be undervalued because of its critical view of racism, sexism, heterosexism, and other manifestations of unequal treatment, or unfairly characterized as less objective or too political or biased when compared to the research being done by white male colleagues. In contrast, any issues related to implicit or explicit biases in the traditional scholarship are rarely raised.

Moreover, neither the dedicated efforts of many academics and activists, nor official federal regulations and institutional policies favorable to creating more equitable access and increased diversity in higher education, nor the changing U.S. demographics projecting that by the middle of the 21st century populations of color will constitute close to half of the U.S. population, have been able to deter the upsurge of nativism, white nationalism, vilifying of immigrants, and the amplified racial and gender bigotry and violence of the last few years. Well before the current environment of political polarization, tribalism, and unbridled hatred against populations of color, which at some time in the future might be known as the ignominious "Era of Trumpism," the emergence of ethnic and racial studies was already facing concerted efforts to discredit both their educational value and their critiques of the implicit biases of the bodies of knowledge and analytical paradigms of the traditional academic disciplines. To a large degree, these backlashes were trying to diminish the significance and contributions of these fields, and the scholarship of faculty of color in exposing the nation's enduring educational, social, and racial divides. The new interdisciplinary fields, along with other multicultural and bilingual education endeavors, were repeatedly branded and dismissed as outcomes of "political correctness." A stream of highly publicized book publications decried "the decomposition of the university" and "the closing of the American mind" (Bloom 1987); declared a state of "culture wars" (Hunter 1991) and the rise of "illiberal education" (D'Souza 1991); or viewed multiculturalism as the main culprit to "the disuniting of America" (Schlesinger 1991). On the other hand, this critical onslaught made it patently clear that the entrenched American exceptionalism narrative was still in denial and avoiding or obfuscating the historical weight of slavery, racism, segregation, and racial violence, behind enduring inequalities and injustices faced by the nation's populations of color. In this regard, the late Toni Morrison succinctly captured the essence of this historical denial when she stated that, "in the construction of Americanness" and its national identity, "American" means being "white" (1992, 47). Thus, surmounting that deeply ingrained idea, expanding its meaning, and putting an end to the whitewashing of populations of color in U.S. history will remain an essential part of current and future educational agendas for Puerto Ricans and other excluded groups. For academics, other educators, and activists, it means that our work goes on.

Old and new cycles of these counterattacks indicate that efforts to advance equal representation of Puerto Ricans, and other previously excluded people of color, women, and LGBTQ populations in the academy and other spheres of U.S. society, continue to be a work in progress. Valuable lessons from the past also indicate that the battles for educational equity remain contested terrain that will be dealt with effectively only when institutions are more receptive to implementing multiple mechanisms to periodically monitor their progress in these areas. That in itself could not happen without the continuous collective engagement and advocacy of their Puerto Rican (and Latina/o) Studies faculties, students, and communities in keeping these issues on the front burner.

NOTES

1 Different degrees of internal strife experienced by some Puerto Rican Studies programs/departments during the early years was usually caused by ideological differences or factionalism among faculty members; different faculty opinions on how to deal with the lack of support from university administrators; disagreements on chair appointments, faculty hiring, or promotion and tenure decisions; professional petty jealousies; attempts at getting students involved in faculty disputes; or divisive agendas of individual faculty members.

2 Other part-time or visiting Puerto Rican Studies faculty at the University at Albany during the early years included Antonio Díaz-Royo, Raúl Mayo Santana, and Robert Anderson, members of the University of Puerto Rico-Río Piedras faculty back then or in later years. Other U.S. visiting lecturers were Samuel Betances, founder and publisher of the journal *The Rican*; poet and literature scholar, Myrna Nieves (currently at Boricua College); and visual artist Rafael Colón Morales, at the time affiliated with Taller Boricua.

3 In the 1980s, the Anthropology Department had a strong contingent of archeologists and cultural anthropologists of the Mesoamerican region. Since 1975, the University has housed an Institute of Mesoamerican Studies.

REFERENCES

Acosta-Belén, Edna. 1992. Beyond Island Boundaries: Ethnicity, Gender, and Cultural Revitalization in Nuyorican Literature. *Callaloo* 15(4), 979–98.

———. 1993. Defining a Common Ground: The Theoretical Meeting of Women's, Ethnic, and Area Studies. In *Researching Women in Latin American and the Caribbean*, eds. Edna Acosta-Belén and Christine E. Bose. 175–86. Boulder: Westview Press.

———. 1999. Hemispheric Remappings: Revisiting the Concept of *Nuestra América*. In *Identities in the Move: Transnational Processes in North America and the Caribbean Basin*, ed. Lilianan R. Goldin. 81–106. Austin: University of Texas Press.

———. 2001. Reimagining Borders: A Hemispheric Approach to Latin American and US Latino and Latina Studies. In *Color-Line to Borderlands: The Matrix of American Ethnic Studies*, ed. Johnnella E. Butler. 240–64. Seattle: University of Washington Press.

Acosta-Belén, Edna, et al. 2000. *"Adiós, Borinquen querida": The Puerto Rican Diaspora, Its History, and Contributions.* Albany: CELAC.

Acosta-Belén, Edna and Carlos E. Santiago. 2018. *Puerto Ricans in the United States: A Contemporary Portrait.* First edition 2006. Boulder: Lynne Rienner Publishers.

Acuña, Rodolfo. 2011. *The Making of Chicano Studies: In the Trenches of Academe.* New Brunswick, NJ: Rutgers University Press.

Aparicio, Frances. 1998. *Listening to Salsa: Latin Popular Music and Puerto Rican Cultures.* Middletown, CT: Wesleyan University Press.

_____. 2019. *Negotiating Latinidad: Interlatina/o Lives in Chicago.* Champaign: University of Illinois Press.

Asencio, Marysol. 2010. *Latina/o Sexualities: Probing Powers, Passions, Practices, and Policies.* 2010. New Brunswick, NJ: Rutgers University Press.

Betances, Samuel. 2000. *Communicating Diversity: Powerful, Practical, Persuasive Pointers to Get the Job Done.* Chicago: New Century Forum.

_____. 2013. *Winning the Future with Education: One Step at a Time.* Chicago: New Century Forum.

Bloom, Allan. 1987. *The Closing of the American Mind.* New York: Simon & Schuster.

Butler, Johnnella E. 1991. Ethnic Studies: A Matrix Model for the Major. *Liberal Education* 77(2), 26–32.

Cabán , Pedro. 2009. Puerto Rican Studies: Changing Islands of Knowledge. *CENTRO: Journal of the Center for Puerto Rican Studies* 21(2), 257–81.

_____. 2011-2012. Critical Junctures and Puerto Rican Studies. *Latino(a) Research Review* 8(1-2), 25–41.

Canino Arroyo, María Josefa. 2013. The 40th Anniversary of the Department of Hispanic Caribbean Studies. Unpublished draft of speech at Rutgers University.

Clemens, Paul G.E. 2015. *Rutgers Since 1945: A History of the State University of New Jersey.* New Brunswick, NJ: Rutgers University Press.

Cruz, José E. 1998. *Identity and Power: Puerto Rican Politics and the Challenges of Ethnicity.* Philadelphia: Temple University Press.

_____. 2017. *Puerto Rican Identity: Political Development and Democracy in New York, 1960-1990.* Lanham, MD: Lexington Books.

_____. 2019. *Liberalism and Identity Politics: Puerto Rican Community Organizations and Collective Action in New York City.* New York: Centro Press.

Cruz-Malavé, Arnaldo. 2018. The Founding of Latin American and Latinx at Fordham. *El Boletín* 23, 28–31.

Dinzey-Flores, Zaire. 2013. *Locked In, Locked Out: Gated Communities in a Puerto Rican City.* Philadelphia: University of Pennsylvania Press.

D'Souza, Dinesh. 1991. *Illiberal Education: The Politics of Race and Sex on Campus.* New York: The Free Press.

Dulay, Heidi, Marina Burt and Stephen Krashen. 1975. *Language Two.* New York: Oxford University Press.

Dulay, Heidi and Marina Burt, eds. 1975. *New Directions in Language, Teaching, Learning, and Bilingual Education*. TESOL.

Fernández, Lilia. 2012. *Brown in the Windy City: Mexicans and Puerto Ricans in in Postwar Chicago*. Chicago: University of Chicago Press.

Flores, Juan. 1993. 'Qué assimilated, brother, yo soy asimilao': The Structuring of Puerto Rican Identity. In *Divided Borders: Essays on Puerto Rican Identity*. 182–95. Houston: Arte Público Press.

Fitzpatrick, Joseph P. 1971. *Puerto Rican Americans: The Meaning of Migration to the Mainland*. Englewood Cliffs, NJ: Prentice-Hall.

Hu-Dehart, Evelyn. 1993. The History, Development, and Future of Ethnic Studies. *Phi Delta Kappan* September, 50–4.

Hunter, James Davison. 1991 *Culture Wars: The Struggle to Define America*. New York: Basic Books.

Irizarry, Guillermo. 2006. *José Luis González: el intelectual nómada*. San Juan: Editorial Callejón.

Jiménez de Wagenheim, Olga. 1993. *Puerto Rico's Revolt for Independence: El Grito de Lares*. Princeton, NJ: Markus Weiner Publishers.

———. 2017. *Nationalist Heroines: Puerto Rican Women History Forgot*. Princeton, NJ: Markus Weiner Publishers.

Jiménez de Wagenheim, Olga and Kal Wagenheim, eds. 1993. *The Puerto Ricans: A Documentary History*. Princeton, NJ: Markus Weiner Publishers.

Maldonado-Torres, Nelson. 2008. *Against War: Views from the Underside of Modernity*. Durham, NC: Duke University Press.

Matilla, Alfredo. 1977. *Obituario Puertorriqueño*. San Juan: Instituto de Cultura Puertorriqueña.

Meléndez, Edgardo. 2017. *Sponsored Migration: The State and Puerto Rican Postwar Migration to the United States*. Columbus: Ohio State University.

———. 2020. *Patria: Puerto Rican Revolutionary Exiles in Late Nineteenth Century New York*. New York: Centro Press.

Meléndez, Edwin and Carlos Vargas-Ramos. 2014. *Puerto Ricans at the Dawn of the New Millennium*. New York: Centro Press.

Morrison, Toni. 1992. *Playing in the Dark: Whiteness and the Literary Imagination*. Cambridge, MA: Harvard University Press.

Moses, Christopher. n.d. American Studies: An Annotated Bibliography. <http://academic.reed.edu/am_studies/resources/AmStudBibF00.pdf>.

Picó Fernando. 1988. *Historia general de Puerto Rico*. Río Piedras, PR: Ediciones Huracán.

———. 2006. *History of Puerto Rico: A Panorama of its People*. Princeton, NJ: Markus Wiener Publishers.

Rodríguez de Laguna, Asela, ed. 1983. *Imágenes e identidades: el puertorriqueño en la literatura*. Río Piedras, PR: Ediciones Huracán.

———. 1987. *Images and Identities: The Puerto Rican in Two World Contexts*. New

York: Routledge.

Rivera-Batiz, Francisco and Carlos E. Santiago. 1994. *Puerto Ricans in the United States: A Changing Reality*. Washington, DC: National Puerto Rican Coalition.

Santiago, Carlos E. 1992. *Labor in the Puerto Rican Economy: Postwar Development and Stagnation*. New York: Praeger Publishers.

Santiago-Rivera, Azara and Patricia Arredondo. 2002. *Counseling Latinos and la Familia: A Practical Guide*. Thousand Oaks, CA: Sage Publications.

Sandoval-Sánchez, Alberto. 1992. "La identidad especular del allá y del acá: Nuestra propia imagen puertorriqueña en cuestión." *CENTRO: Journal of the Center for Puerto Rican Studies* 4(2), 28–43.

_____. 1997. Mira que vienen los nuyoricans: El temor de la otredad en la literatura nacionalista puertorriqueña. *Revista de crítica literaria hispanoamericana* 23 (45), 307–25.

Schlesinger, Jr., Arthur M. 1991. *The Disuniting of America: Reflections on a Multicultural Society*. New York: W.W. Norton.

Seda-Bonilla, Eduardo, 1977. Who is a Puerto Rican? Problems of Socio-Cultural Identity in Puerto Rico. *Caribbean Studies* 17(1-2), 105–21.

Silén, Juan A. 1970. *Hacia una visión del puertorriqueño*. Río Piedras, PR: Editorial Edil.

_____. 1971. *We, the Puerto Rican People: A Story of Oppression and Resistance*. New York: Monthly Review Press.

Toro-Morn, Maura I. and Marixsa Alicea, eds. 2004. *Migration and Immigration: A Global View*. Westport, CT: Greenwood Press.

Venator-Santiago, Charles R. 2015. *Puerto Rico and the Origins of US Global Empire: The Disembodied Shade*. New York: Routledge.

_____. 2018. *Hostages of Empire: A Short History of the Extension of US Citizenship to Puerto Rico, 1898*. New York: Routledge.

Wessman, James. 1981. *Anthropology and Marxism*. Cambridge, MA: Schenkman Publishing.

Zavala, Iris M. and Rafael Rodríguez, eds. 1973. *Libertad y crítica en el ensayo político puertorriqueño*. San Juan: Ediciones Puerto.

_____. 1980. *The Intellectual Roots of Independence: An Anthology of Puerto Rican Political Essays*. New York: Monthly Review Press.

CHAPTER 8

SO MUCH KNOWLEDGE AND WE STILL AIN'T FREE: PUERTO RICAN STUDIES FIFTY YEARS LATER

Juan González

Just over fifty years ago, an extraordinary effort began to establish Puerto Rican Studies as a distinct new field of interdisciplinary research and teaching at U.S. colleges and universities. That effort formed part of a broader radical movement during the late 1960s that forced open the doors of higher education to social and racial groups long excluded and oppressed by the dominant society (Vázquez 1988; Rodríguez 1990; Ortíz Márquez 2009; Cabán 2009). We who participated in the formative years of that experiment always regarded the preservation of our community's history not simply as a means to expand the elite lexicon of higher education; we saw it as a weapon for anti-colonial liberation, as a means to achieve a more democratic and economically just world. This was, after all, still the era following World War II, when many long-subjugated peoples of Africa and Asia wrested independence from their European colonizers. The speeches and writings of Frantz Fanon, Amílcar Cabral, and Kwame Nkrumah, revolutionaries barely known at the time to the general public in the U.S., began to reach us and fired our imagination. In particular, Fanon's insights on the Algerian struggle for independence seemed to perfectly capture the Puerto Rican reality:

Colonialism is not satisfied merely with holding a people in its grip and emptying the native's brain of all form and content. By a kind of perverted logic, it turns to the past of the oppressed people, and distorts, disfigures, and destroys it. (1963, 210–1)

Half a century later, it is worthwhile to evaluate both the enormous achievements and persistent shortcomings of the movement for Puerto Rican Studies and, more important, to speculate about its future. Such an appraisal is especially timely given that economic and racial inequalities have worsened both in the U.S. and across the globe, that Puerto Rico under a U.S.-imposed control board is more obviously a colony than it has been in over a hundred years, and that our system of higher education is more dominated than ever by neoliberal corporate policies.

How do we reconcile, for example, the glaring contradiction that despite decades of steady production of scholarly literature on the country's Puerto Rican population, huge swaths of the American public remain woefully misinformed about the Island and its people? During the aftermath of Hurricane María, a national poll found nearly half of Americans did not know Puerto Ricans are U.S. citizens (Dropp and Nyhan 2017). Or, how do we countenance the reality that all three branches of the federal government have shown even greater willingness in the wake of Puerto Rico's financial collapse to run roughshod over the limited autonomy Island residents were granted back in 1952? In two pivotal Supreme Court decisions issued only days apart in June 2016, for example, *Puerto Rico v. California Franklin Tax-Free Trust* and *Puerto Rico v. Sánchez-Valle,* the Court once again reinforced the infamous Insular Cases, maintaining that Puerto Rico enjoys only as much sovereignty as Congress is willing to grant it under the territorial clause of the Constitution. In a subsequent decision issued in 2020 in *Financial Oversight and Management Board for Puerto Rico v. Aurelius Investments, LLC et al,* the Court ruled PROMESA board members had been properly appointed because they were not federal officers but were instead "territorial officers" of the Puerto Rican government. Only Justice Sotomayor joined in eloquent dissents in both of the first two cases, and while she concurred in the Court's unanimous decision in the *Aurelius* case, Sotomayor's stinging separate opinion left no doubt that she believes the creation of the board violated Puerto Rico's autonomy. "The Board members, tasked with determining the financial fate of a self-governing Territory, exist in a twilight zone of accountability," Sotomayor wrote, "neither selected by Puerto Rico itself nor subject to the strictures of the Appointments Clause. I am skeptical that the Constitution countenances this freewheeling exercise of control over a population that the Federal Government has explicitly agreed to recognize as operating under a government of their own choosing, pursuant to a constitution of their own choosing" (U.S. Supreme Court 2020, 24).

Continued paternalism toward Puerto Rico at the highest levels of government in Washington, together with persistent public ignorance about the Island and its people, should prompt us to ask why all the "knowledge" accumulated by Puerto Rican Studies has somehow failed to move beyond the university campuses to engender greater understanding about Puerto Ricans among a broader sector of the U.S. population.

This essay will not attempt to explore the many disputes among scholars in the past decades over evolving trends in the field about whether ethnic vs. area studies, Puerto Rican vs. Latinx, and multiculturalism vs. cultural pluralism better describe this collective intellectual undertaking. My connection to this educational movement, after all, did not originate as a scholar but as an activist and radical community organizer, one who advocated for and was an eyewitness to the birth of Puerto Rican Studies, thus others who have dedicated their entire careers to building the discipline are more capable than I to explore the intricacies of such debates–as many excellent essays in this volume do, and as other retrospectives have done in prior years. In the many decades since the birth of Puerto Rican Studies, I had the privilege as a working journalist to produce thousands of news stories in both print and broadcast media, a significant percentage of which chronicled the exponential spread of the Puerto Rican and broader Latin American diaspora throughout the United States. Along the way, I combined my empirical reporting with archival research in an attempt to document how racial and ethnic narratives have always been central to the evolution of the American media system (González and Torres 2011). It is from the vantage point of an organizer, a journalist and a researcher that I share some conclusions on concrete ways that Puerto Rican Studies and the individuals forged by that movement helped to transform reigning narratives within the university and the mass media about the Island and its diaspora. In addition, I will offer some frank observations on where, in my opinion, things have gone off-course. A few of those observations may provoke disquiet among some scholars or be ascribed by others to be the musings of someone out-of-touch with the times. But, then, why bother to delve into the history of any subject if not to draw lessons for the present?

EARLY PERIOD, 1968-1973

It was the spring of 1968, my final year of undergraduate study at Columbia University, where I was on a full scholarship, the first person in my extended working-class family to attend college, and one of the few New York-raised Puerto Ricans in the school at that time. As a leader of that year's historic Columbia student strike against the Vietnam War and university racism, I was suspended a few days before graduation. A few months later, my fellow Students for a Democratic Society (SDS) members elected me a co-chair of the group's campus chapter, and I ended up helping to organize Black and Puerto Rican high school students from Harriman High School on Manhattan's upper West Side and from Benjamin Franklin High School in East Harlem, who marched in April 1969 to the university's Morningside Heights campus, briefly occupied one of its buildings, and demanded open admissions to Columbia for graduates of four local public high schools (U.S. Senate 1969, 5310). Only a few weeks later, Black, Puerto Rican, Dominican, and Panamanian students at both Brooklyn College and City College launched their own sit-ins and occupations demanding open admissions and funding for new ethnic studies programs, as well as increased hiring of faculty of color (Serrano 1998, 126–7). We in Columbia SDS visited those campuses to express our solidarity, met some of their leaders, and briefly joined in their sit-ins. Such massive pressure from minority students and the community led directly to the first CUNY Ethnic Studies department at CCNY in 1969, the first nationwide Puerto Rican Studies Department at Lehman (Aquino-Bermúdez 1974, 122–3), the first Black and Puerto Rican Studies Department at Hunter, the first Puerto Rican Studies Institute at Brooklyn, and to a policy of Open Admissions at the City University of NY, all approved that same year. Brooklyn College's Department of Puerto Rican Studies was established a year later, and a few others followed in subsequent years. All of these reforms, along with the new Black, Chicano, and Women's Studies programs across the nation represented a seismic shock to the academic world.

Many of us, however, soon abandoned the university campuses, intent on spreading our freshly minted conviction of an imminent revolution to a broader audience. I returned to East Harlem in the summer of 1969 and quickly formed part of the leadership of the New York Young Lords Organization, along with Pablo "Yoruba" Guzmán, Felipe Luciano, David Pérez, Juan "Fi" Ortíz, Denise Oliver, Sonia Ivany, and others. As the Young Lords minister of education, part of my job became to set up programs in Puerto Rican history and culture and radical politics for both our growing membership and community residents. Our newspaper, *Palante* (*Palante, n.d.*; *Palante* 1970-1976), would feature lengthy articles on the Cuban revolution and a continuing series on the history of Puerto Rico and on the Island's movement for independence, which we cobbled together in primitive fashion from whatever literature we could find. On hot summer nights, we would often set up a 16-milimeter projector in an empty lot and stage instant neighborhood film screenings against a tenement wall—precursors of today's "pop-up" events—except ours featured the "Battle of Algiers," or "Night and Fog" or films about the victories of the Vietnamese in their war against U.S. occupation. We constantly talked about Puerto Rico, whose history and culture none of us had ever been taught in school. Iris Morales and Carlos Aponte, the two most knowledgeable members of the Lords on those subjects, became the star teachers in our peoples' education campaign. As Carlos Aponte wrote in an early issue of *Palante*:

When the Amerikkkan [sic] army landed in Guanica in 1898, they brought with them not only soldiers, but teachers, administrators, geologists, biologists, etc. When they got there, they threw away history books written by Puerto Ricans, our culture, language (they also changed the official language to English in the schools), history and our collective understanding of what we are, a nation. (Enck-Wanzer 2010, 125–6)

The Lords were convening education classes every Tuesday evening at 7:30 in East Harlem and the South Bronx, Aponte wrote, "to prepare our brothers and sisters to deal with the society in which we live. That society is racist and capitalistic and has as its desire a world empire (imperialism) built on the backs of Puerto Ricans and other Third World people" (Enck-Wanzer 2010, 125–6).

Two seminal events marked that early period: the Young Lords occupation of the First Spanish Methodist Church in December 1969, and the first Puerto Rican Student Conference, held in September 1970 by the nascent Puerto Rican Student Union (PRSU) and the Young Lords at Columbia University. The church takeover turned into a national news story when police ended the 11-day protest by breaking down the barricades and arresting more than 100 of us. But, during its brief existence, the People's Church, as we christened it, galvanized Puerto Rican youth to political activity like no other event of its era, igniting a cultural revival for an entire generation. It was at the church, for instance, that the great Pedro Pietri first performed in public his epic poem *Puerto Rican Obituary* (Fernández 2020, 180–8). As for the student conference, it attracted more than 1,000 youths from around the East Coast and spurred the creation of Liberate Puerto Rico Now committees at dozens of campuses (Serrano 1998, 132–4). Both events helped forge the cadre of activists who would become the shock troops of this new militant movement.

The fight for Puerto Rican Studies, in short, literally began in the streets of New York, spearheaded by the children of those working-class Puerto Ricans who comprised the Great Migration from the Island in the aftermath of World War II. It directly challenged not only the existing Euro-centric canon of higher education, but the social role of universities in promoting the U.S. imperial project. Long before "decoloniality" became a popular school of thought in academia, we were talking about the "colonized mentality" in El Barrio. "We can only unchain our minds from this colonized mentality if we learn our true history, understand our culture, and work towards unity," Denise Oliver, a member of our central committee, described in a Young Lords pamphlet (Oliver 1972, 28).

The initial movement to reclaim that history culminated with the formation of the Center for Puerto Rican Studies (Centro) in 1973, a remarkable achievement made possible in part by PRSU activists like Hildamar Ortíz and Emilio González who joined with Frank Bonilla, Josephine Nieves, and a handful of scholars from an earlier generation to found it. Bonilla, in fact, had been initially recruited to City College from Stanford as a consultant specifically to help design a Puerto Rican Studies department at CCNY in response to continued protests by PRSU for such a separate department (Serrano 1998, 136–7; Fitzpatrick 1996, 77–8; Aquino-Bermúdez 1974, 333).

He quickly became the most eloquent and respected advocate in academia for Puerto Rican Studies (Ortíz Márquez 2009, 180–1). No one understood the political dimension of this project better than Frank, who would later write: "We have set out to contest effectively those visions of the world that assume or take for granted the inevitability and indefinite duration of the class and colonial oppression that has marked Puerto Rico's history" (Sánchez and Stevens-Arroyo 1987, 17).

THE INVENTION OF THE PUERTO RICAN "PROBLEM"

Today's students and young professors should understand that virtually none of the literature and university courses currently available about Puerto Ricans existed fifty years ago. Very little had been produced by the Island's own scholars back then, certainly not any that dared to directly question the status quo of U.S. control. The celebrated historian Lidio Cruz Monclava, for instance, focused his early research on the period of Spanish rule, while many liberal Puerto Rican intellectuals of the mid-twentieth century had gravitated toward a "literature of docility" that effectively accepted and rationalized the Island's dependence on the U.S. (Silén 1970, 49–64). But, just as Puerto Rican youth on the Island and in U.S. barrios started to rebel, a modern, independent scholarship emerged in Puerto Rico from figures such as Loida Figueroa (1968) and Arturo Morales Carrión (1968). Then in 1970, two radical anti-colonial classics appeared that deeply influenced us in the Young Lords–Juan Angel Silén's *Hacia una visión positiva del puertorriqueño* (1970) and Ramón Medina Ramírez's *El movimiento libertador en la historia de Puerto Rico* (1970), both of which were soon translated into English. The period 1968-1973, in retrospect, signaled not simply the birth of Puerto Rican Studies in the United States, it marked a virtual renaissance in Puerto Rico itself of a truly national scholarship at the universities.

Until then, research about the Island and especially about the growing Puerto Rican diaspora had been dominated by Anglo-American anthropologists or sociologists, usually with the help of young assistants from Puerto Rico's elite who had been sent to study at American universities.[1] Such scholarship became quite popular in the late 1940s and 1950s when the Island suddenly mushroomed into a "social laboratory" for liberal North American social scientists who worked in tandem with the centrist intellectuals and political leaders from Puerto Rico's governing Popular Democratic Party (known in Spanish as PPD) to shape a New Deal version of modernization based on technical expertise and centralized planning. Much of that scholarship was centered at the newly formed Social Science Research Center (Centro de Investigaciones Sociales) at the University of Puerto Rico, which promoted studies on mass migration and population control to alleviate the Island's economic problems. As Michael Lapp and others have noted, Clarence Senior, an American demographer and one-time U.S. Socialist Party leader, would not only fashion the early PPD policies for promoting mass migration, he went on to become the first director of the Office of Migration for the Puerto Rico Department of Labor (Lapp 1995, 178–84; Thomas 2010, 168–70). By the 1950s, research on migrants to the U.S. proliferated as well, but it largely focused on cultural and social life, rather than on politics, economics, or history. Among the most influential of those early works that come to mind are Mills, Senior, and Goldsen (1950); Steward (1956); Padilla (1958); Handlin (1959); Wakefield (1959); Senior (1961); Lewis (1963); Glazer and Moynihan (1963); and Lewis (1966). The only one that dealt extensively with politics and economics on the Island was the classic tome by Gordon Lewis (1963). There was also a raft of studies about Puerto Rican migrants by government agencies in New York City during this period. At first, a liberal and sympathetic perspective infused that research, but following the Nationalist Party uprisings of the 1950s and the wholesale repression of the independence movement, it soon gave way to theories of an intractable Puerto Rican "culture of poverty," and to the creation of a concept, as Laura Briggs has brilliantly documented, of "the poor" as a racialized class. "Centrist, middle-class 'experts'–mostly but not exclusively North Americans–emerged as the interpreters of the Puerto Rican experience in *Nueva York*," Briggs notes (2002a, 83), with influential sociologists such as Oscar Handlin, Daniel Patrick Moynihan, and Nathan Glazer linking Puerto Ricans and African Americans as "different groups exhibiting more or less the same features, particularly disorganized families" (2002b, 175–7). Even the early Puerto Rican organizations in the U.S. "stressed the politics of respectability and found working-class people to be something of a scandal, much as they had on the island" (Briggs 2002a, 80–6). Increasingly, the researchers focused on cultural factors fueling dependency, lack of assimilation, or social maladjustment among Puerto Ricans. Little wonder that Bonilla would later state:

> All the disciplines that we are most directly drawing upon—history, economics, sociology, anthropology, literature, psychology, pedagogy—as they are practiced in the United States are deeply implicated in the construction of that vision of Puerto Ricans as an inferior, submissive people, trapped on the underside of relations from which there is no foreseeable exit. (Sánchez and Stevens-Arroyo 1987, 17)

HALLMARKS OF EARLY PUERTO RICAN STUDIES

From the beginning, Puerto Rican Studies programs at the City University, and the Centro in particular, proclaimed a different approach to higher education. Both early Chicano and Puerto Rican Studies were "founded upon an understanding of institutionalized structural inequalities, dynamics of colonialism, and racialized expressions of class" (Córdova 2016, 56). Most important was the purpose of that structural analysis: "To create new knowledge and quickly and comprehensively transfer it to a long-denied community is the principal goal of all of our efforts," declared Centro's founding statement (cited in Córdova 2005). Those early Puerto Rican Studies programs sought to train students "not as intellectual elites, but as university-based, intellectual workers" (Rodríguez 1990, 2). The offices and library of Centro, for example, were always open to the community, with security guards at Hunter College, which became its home in 1983, specifically instructed not to impede the general public seeking admission to the center's offices and library.

The emphasis by Bonilla and his colleagues on documenting Puerto Rican labor migration as a direct result of the evolution of capitalist market forces and of the needs of an empire for cheap labor directly challenged those scholars who had been content for so many decades to fish in the "culture of poverty" pond. In contrast, the pages of the *CENTRO Journal* constantly explored the rich and complex aspects of the migration. For more than 30 years, the journal has been the premiere venue not only for critical research and analysis by the best scholars in the discipline, but also the place where the foremost pioneers of the broader Puerto Rican diaspora were welcomed to document and analyze their lived experiences, thus exemplifying what Cristina Pérez Jiménez terms the "marriage of scholarship and activism" that was part of *Centro's* orientation from the start (2017, 35).

At CUNY campuses like CCNY, Brooklyn, Queens, and Lehman, and more distant locales such as SUNY Albany and Rutgers, Puerto Rican Studies programs consistently emerged as centers for community engagement and advocacy.

IMPACT ON JOURNALISM AND MEDIA

The early newspapers of the Puerto Rican radical left—*Palante, Maceta, Unidad Latina, Claridad*—were critical advocates for what would become Puerto Rican Studies. Several individuals who wrote for or edited those political papers went on to play key roles in creating the first such programs within the CUNY system. Others devoted themselves to transforming the distorted narratives about Puerto Ricans and other people of color that had dominated the mass media for so long.

A seminal achievement on the media front during those early years was the creation of *Realidades* at WNET/Channel 13 in 1972. The first public television series to focus on the Puerto Rican and Latino community, and the first of its kind to become a nationwide show, *Realidades* was made possible only by community pressure and direct action–specifically, a sit-in and protest during a live Channel 13 pledge drive, one that forced the station to temporarily go off the air and that elicited a commitment from the station executives to fund the new program. That unprecedented victory was spearheaded by the Puerto Rican Education and Action Media Council, a coalition that included veteran community leaders such as Gilberto Gerena Valentín and Julio Rodríguez, pioneer filmmaker José García Torres, best-selling author Piri Thomas, several younger activists from El Comité, among them Federico Lora, Lillian Jiménez, Eulogio Ortíz, and Esperanza Martell, and Diana Caballero from the Lords. During the few years of its existence, *Realidades* produced documentaries of unrivaled quality and it launched the careers of many of this country's finest Latinx filmmakers (Jiménez 1990, 31–9; Rodríguez 1997, 190–2; Noriega 2000, 148–52; Muzio 2017, 71).

Public television, however, was not the only part of the media forced to change; so were commercial television stations and newspapers. Between 1971 and 1973, Black and Latino community organizations filed more than

340 challenges at the Federal Communications Commission against radio and television licenses of stations in virtually every major city in America, all demanding that people of color be hired in greater numbers and that programming better reflect the composition of the communities those stations served. A succession of racial discrimination lawsuits roiled major news organizations such as the *Washington Post*, the *New York Times*, the Associated Press and *The Daily News*. The result was the first great democratic revolution in the American media, with a sudden influx of young black and brown journalists into the nation's newsrooms who posed the first significant challenge to the reigning narratives about Puerto Ricans, Chicanos and other people of color (González and Torres 2011, 306–27).

After the Lords disintegrated, several of us in the organization's original leadership drifted toward careers in the media, the reasons for which are better left to another day. I ended up being hired as a young reporter at the *Philadelphia Daily News* in 1978. At the time, I was the only Latino journalist with a full-time job in the city's mainstream media–including all the radio and television stations and four daily newspapers (the long-running *Puerto Rican Panorama* public affairs show, hosted on a part-time basis by Diego Castellano, had already been available for years at an ungodly hour every Sunday morning on WPVI-TV). A few more Puerto Ricans began appearing shortly afterward, including Vicente Juarbe and Tony León as the first local television producers, and José Santiago as the city's first on-air television reporter, followed by Patrisia Gonzales as the first Latina on the *Philadelphia Inquirer*. Each of those early journalists fought to challenge and correct stereotypical perceptions of the Puerto Rican community. By the early 1980s, for instance, Juarbe and León began producing reports for local TV, as did I in the newspaper, on the resistance by the fisherman's association of Vieques to the U.S. Navy bombing of their Island. Such stories would never have made the news back then were it not for that handful of journalists who were cognizant of Puerto Rico's history and understood their responsibility to assure a new kind of coverage.

My most vivid recollection in that regard came in January 1981, with the campaign against the racist Hollywood movie, *Fort Apache: The Bronx*. Richie Pérez, an old comrade from Young Lords days and later to be a fellow member of the National Congress for Puerto Rican Rights, was then leading the Committee Against Fort Apache in a militant boycott movement against the film that had spread across the country. The editor-in-chief at the *Philadelphia Daily News*, well aware of my history as an activist, insisted I had to view the film before daring to criticize it in print, so he assigned me to attend an invitation-only press junket and screening that Time-Life Films, the production company, had quietly scheduled for the nation's movie critics. The film's producer, David Susskind, its director, Dan Petrie, and its two main actors, Paul Newman and Ed Asner, all enjoyed reputations at the time as Hollywood liberals. Petrie and Newman were scheduled to participate in a Q&A with the press during the event. I immediately telephoned Richie Pérez and alerted him to the date and place of the screening at a hotel in Atlanta, a city apparently chosen by *Time-Life* to avoid any possible protests. Richie purchased an airplane ticket and booked a room at the same hotel. Once we arrived in Atlanta, I shared with him a copy of the agenda for the two days. It called for a luxurious reception the first evening, after which the reporters would board a bus in front of the hotel for a ride to a nearby movie theater for the screening. When the reporters filed into the buses, however, they encountered Pérez, standing at the door in a suit and tie and handing out glossy press packets. Except the packets were not touting the film; they contained literature against it from the Committee Against Fort Apache and press clippings of all the protests. Before *Time-Life* security guards even became aware of what was happening, Richie had boarded the bus, introduced himself, and made a quick speech to the assembled critics about the campaign. He then announced a hospitality suite in his hotel room after the screening to further discuss the racist, anti-Puerto Rican nature of the film. More than a dozen of the reporters subsequently took him up on his invitation. The following morning, at the press conference with Newman and Petrie, Pérez was outside the conference room, again distributing literature. Hotel security guards attempted to remove him, whereupon a short scuffle ensued, with Richie insisting that, as a paying guest at the hotel he had every right to be in the hallway. During the actual press conference, Newman and Petrie were visibly shaken by the unexpected commotion. There is no doubt in my mind that the generally negative reviews of *Fort Apache* that subsequently appeared in the nation's newspapers when the film opened the following month were due, in no small part, to the massive community opposition to the film and to that contentious press junket in Atlanta that Richie had crashed (Pérez 1985). For one brief moment, the distorted narrative about Puerto Ricans in America had not simply been challenged, it was de-legitimized.

THE NEOLIBERAL TURN

The 1980s and 1990s, of course, marked a dramatically different era. As socialist economies in one country after another gradually collapsed or proved profoundly disappointing, as post-liberation governments in the former colonial nations became riven with rising class conflicts and persistent corruption, and as monopoly capital moved to privatize public services and penetrate every corner of the globe under the banner of free trade, neoliberalism grew more ascendant. At the universities, that meant dismantling or defanging the democratic revolution in access to knowledge. Governments sharply disinvested in public education, with fiscal crises and budgetary cuts at CUNY and other schools turning into an annual ritual. Corporate accounting methods rapidly dominated policy, with every unit inside a university designated a cost center and ordered to generate sufficient revenue to justify its existence. "The traditional academic imperative to 'publish or perish,'" Giroux observes, "is now supplemented with the neoliberal mantra 'privatize or perish' as everyone in the university is transformed into an entrepreneur, customer, or client, and every relationship is ultimately judged in bottom-line, cost-effective terms," and with universities effectively turned into "licensed storefronts" (2009, 673–4).

Under such conditions, ethnic studies programs were forced to adapt or wither away. "The 1990s," notes Pedro Cabán, was "a period of consolidation of ethnic studies units, reworking of their academic mission, and adoption of new curriculum on the history of new Latin American and Caribbean populations in New York" (1990, 263). For even as traditional neoconservative intellectuals sought to rescue the canon of white privilege in higher education, the globalized neoliberal elite took to promoting cultural pluralism and multiculturalism to "co-opt some of the more socially and politically palatable aspects of the ethnic studies movement of the late 1960s and early 1970s," notes Jesse Vázquez (1988, 23) [see also Frances Aparicio 1994, 576–8]. This "new fuzzier multiculturalism, unlike race and ethnic studies, did not engage the analysis of the racial dimensions of power and conflict in the United States" (Cabán 1990, 267). Unfortunately, some of our most esteemed leaders and intellectuals, among them Antonia Pantoja, had by then begun to situate the Puerto Rican diaspora within a theory of cultural pluralism that did not distinguish the particular colonial roots of the migration (Pantoja 1976). Others, including Josie Nieves, María Canino, and Sherry Gorelick, would warn years later that "the new 'cultural pluralist' philosophy is now being used to submerge and deflect the most critical and fundamental concerns of our community: its economic, cultural and political survival" (Nieves et al. 1987, 10).

CULTURE, CLASS, AND BRANDING: WHAT HAS GONE WRONG?

By the first decade of the 21st century, Puerto Rican studies had largely turned into a subset at most universities of a broader Latino, and subsequently Latinx, program or department. This no doubt reflected the determination by neoliberal administrators to keep all ethnic studies at their institutions pigeonholed and marginalized, but it also was influenced by growing diversity in the demographics of those college students who traced their heritage to Latin America. At CUNY, which has historically produced the most Puerto Rican graduates of any U.S. university, a significant decline in Puerto Rican admissions reduced the pressure on administrators for distinctly Puerto Rican Studies courses. Between 1999 and 2012, for example, Puerto Rican enrollment declined from 28 percent to 11 percent at CUNY (Falcón 2012)—a far greater reduction than the overall decline in the city's Puerto Rican population. Yes, the Puerto Rican diaspora in the U.S. kept growing in size, but it also became more dispersed to the South and to smaller cities in the Northeast and Midwest, away from the big Northern cities.

This was also the period when I started combining my journalism work with stints in academia, as visiting professor first at Brooklyn College, then a few years later at New York University, and finally, after my retirement from New York's *Daily News* in 2016, as a full-time professor of journalism and media studies at Rutgers University. But, after spending decades in both for-profit and non-profit media, it rapidly became clear to me that the content and character of Latinx research and curriculum at public and "non-profit" universities had dramatically changed during the neoliberal era. As Teresa Córdova describes it, "the general trend in Latino studies over the last twenty to thirty years, particularly among emerging scholars, is to focus on issues related to culture and identity, detached from a political economy analysis" (2016, 59). Cabán likewise discusses the current field as "characterized by a virtual absence of Neo-Marxist analysis of the political economy of colonialism, nor does it sustain the dynamic relationship with communities that was a key element of the 1960s student movement" (2009, 275).

A good number of senior scholars, it seems to me, have unwittingly fallen prey to the trend of the corporate university, increasingly vying to head their own institutes or fiefdoms, or zealously battling for one or two additional faculty lines, or publicly decrying the racism of an elite institution for failing to grant someone tenure, yet they often are removed from actual teaching, and they enjoy relatively comfortable incomes compared to the overall Puerto Rican population. On occasion, rifts have erupted between them and younger scholars who are intent on broadening and diversifying Puerto Rican Studies research into areas of race, gender and sexuality, but who feel blocked and marginalized by an older, male gate-keeper generation. Such disputes among academics, we should not forget, pale in comparison to the plight of more than three million Latinx students at U.S. colleges and universities. Many of those students are forced to burden themselves with ever-growing debt while receiving instruction largely from part-time, poorly compensated, and contingent lecturers, who themselves face little job security and inadequate working conditions. Quite simply, the inconveniences and injustices of academia do not compare to the magnitude of social and economic problems confronting more than 60 million people of Latinx descent in the U.S.

As for the younger scholars, too many have sought to establish themselves with research into areas of racial or gender identity or cultural inquiry so esoteric, marginal, or non-threatening, that they would befit any of the old canon's medieval scholars. As Emilio Pantojas García observed a generation ago, "the average Puerto Rican does not share the obsession of the political and intellectual elites with defining Puerto Rican identity" (2000, 235). Some scholars have even embraced the notion that the more inscrutable and impenetrable their writing is to the average reader, the more subversive and transformative it becomes. It is as if those venerable but still vital lessons of Marxist economic theory had never existed, as when Engels observed in 1878:

the final causes of all social changes and political revolutions are to be sought, not in men's [sic] brains, not in man's [sic] better insight into eternal truth and justice, but in changes in the modes of production and exchange. They are to be sought, not in the *philosophy*, but in the *economics* of each particular epoch. (1969, 316)

An increasing number of academics have opted instead to fashion their own personal "brand" as experts on the Puerto Rican experience, not through the painstaking work of ongoing research that actually empowers the community they study, but through accumulating the most media interviews or opinion pieces in the daily newspapers or the greatest number of Twitter and Instagram followers and Facebook friends or by churning out instant on-demand thought pieces on the trending issues of the day. As Giroux warned more than a decade ago:

the understanding of faculty as a 'brand name' and the university as a new marketplace of commerce is not a line drawn from a gag offered up by Jon Stewart on the Comedy Channel. Instead, it has become one of the dominant views of the purpose and meaning of higher education. (2009, 670–1)

What does all of this portend, given that most Puerto Rican and Latino studies scholars still routinely pepper their writings and their teaching with references to "colonialism," "racial oppression," "social justice," and "intersectionality"? It suggests that scholarly production has become increasingly divorced from the original social justice and political liberation impulses that first animated ethnic studies as a solution to real world oppression inside the world's most powerful imperial state, from the very impulses that cracked open those doors of higher education in the first place. As we used to say in the Young Lords, the national struggle increasingly confronts the class struggle. Identity and culture, after all, are phenomena that all members of an ethnic group or nationality experience–no matter their economic position–vis-à-vis the dominant group in any society. But, class differences still remain most powerful in shaping a worldview, and such differences do not magically disappear within national groupings. Rather, they have only intensified in recent decades for the broader society in general, and for Puerto Rican and other ethnic studies at the universities in particular.

Conceivably, this is a consequence of a changing composition in the class origins of the faculty compared to the 1970s, or simply of more professors, no matter their original intentions, being co-opted by the lure of fame, academic prestige, or increased compensation. And, while these differences should not be regarded as antagonistic, they need to be addressed if Puerto Rican Studies is to remain a force for real change over the next fifty years.

These matters do not simply affect research on the Puerto Rican diaspora. They also shape how scholars approach real-world solutions to Puerto Rico's colonial condition, especially in the wake of the debt crisis, PROMESA, Hurricane María, and a series of earthquakes, all of which have combined to bring unprecedented calamity to the Island's residents. As I have urged repeatedly for years, there is an urgent need for more anti-imperialist scholars to dedicate themselves to analyzing how changes in the world capitalist economy have manifested themselves in Puerto Rico over the past twenty or thirty years. It is time we acknowledge that globalization has rendered historic concepts of national independence almost meaningless. You no longer need foreign armies to control a population when you can read everyone's email, tap everyone's phone, empty a country's coffers, and paralyze its economy from afar through satellites, instant wire transfers, and simple cancellations of bank credit lines. Today, small nations need more creative and flexible tactics to defend themselves from bullying by larger ones, to assert national sovereignty in an increasingly interdependent world, and Puerto Rican Studies cannot tackle such problems with rote references to conditions fifty years ago.

The difference between the pioneering Puerto Rican Studies programs from decades ago and those of today became clear to me in early 2020 in New Brunswick, the city where the main campus of Rutgers University is located–a town where about fifty percent of residents are Hispanic. That population, however, is largely Mexican and Central American, since the city's historic Puerto Rican community declined decades ago due to previous waves of gentrification and out-migration. The Latino and Caribbean Studies Department at Rutgers, however, has remained an acclaimed center for research and teaching, especially on the Puerto Rican and Dominican diaspora and the Caribbean region, and its faculty members are largely of Puerto Rican and Dominican ancestry. In late 2019, my wife and I became involved in a major community struggle against displacement of low-income Latino families. Neighborhood parents were determined to prevent Robert Wood Johnson University Hospital and the Rutgers Cancer Institute from purchasing and demolishing one of the city's best performing public schools, Lincoln Annex, to make way for a huge new joint hospital expansion. Of the school's 750 pupils, 94 percent are Latinx, mostly from immigrant Mexican and Central American families, with many of the parents unable to vote, so the city's political elite figured it would be easy to remove them from the rapidly gentrifying downtown area around the hospital. A broad coalition arose of community residents, progressive Rutgers faculty, and students to oppose the sale. The movement spearheaded repeated militant protests and rallies by hundreds of people, social media campaigns, and several lawsuits led by Latino Justice/PRLDEF. It quickly emerged as a textbook example of oppressed working-class Latinos demanding basic respect and of a university community opposing injustice from its own hierarchy. In the midst of the campaign, the coronavirus pandemic erupted, followed by the national economic shutdown, all of which forced the Coalition to Defend Lincoln Annex to adopt new tactics of resistance. Since the city's immigrant households had been devastated by the pandemic and were receiving no governmental assistance, we in the Coalition launched a GoFundMe page and mutual aid effort to help those families.

We managed within a few short weeks to raise more than $23,000 and to rapidly distribute cash grants of $300 to $500 to nearly 70 families. It was a remarkable show of grassroots perseverance and unity in the face of a public health crisis and economic collapse. What struck me most in this battle, however, was that the Coalition attracted greater participation from the university's white and African-American progressive faculty and students than it did—with a handful of notable exceptions—from the faculty and students of the Latino Studies program, who in prior decades would have been at the forefront of such a struggle. And, my fear is that this is no anomaly. Across the country, academic departments born out of community activism, which championed publicly engaged scholarship, and which still claim to be the voice of the marginalized and the oppressed, are increasingly disconnected from working-class Latino populations that often reside just steps from their ivy-covered walls. I say this not to needlessly cast fault, but to emphasize that the crucial test of our ideas and research, no matter how high-sounding the words, comes in the crucible of popular struggle, especially when that struggle is directed against your own university's actions. That is how it was when Puerto Rican Studies began over fifty years ago and–judging by the widespread youth rebellions across the nation in recent years, such as Black Lives Matter and the movement for immigrant rights– that is how it will continue to be in the future, because all this accumulated knowledge means nothing unless it leads to a freer and more just world.

NOTES

[1] The best-known Puerto Rican scholar in the group, Elena Padilla, was, as Mérida Rúa and Arlene Torres (2010) have noted, the youngest of a handful of graduate students from the Island who were sent by University of Puerto Rico Chancellor Jaime Benítez in 1944 to study in the U.S., where she worked as a researcher first at the University of Chicago and later with Julian Steward and C.W. Mills and Clarence Senior at Columbia University.

REFERENCES

Aquino-Bermúdez, Federico. 1974. Growth and Development of Puerto Rican Studies Departments: A Case Study of Two Departments at the City University of New York. Ph.D. dissertation, University of Massachusetts Amherst. Accessed 11 August 2020. <https://scholarworks.umass.edu/dissertations_1/2924>.

Aparicio, Frances R. 1994. On Multiculturalism and Privilege: A Latina Perspective. *American Quarterly* 46(4), 575–88.

Briggs, Laura. 2002a. La Vida, Moynihan, and Other Libels: Migration, Social Science, and the Making of the Puerto Rican Welfare Queen. *CENTRO: Journal of the Center for Puerto Rican Studies* 14(1), 75–101.

_____. 2002b. *Reproducing Empire: Race, Sex, Science, and U.S. Imperialism in Puerto Rico.* Berkeley: University of California Press.

Cabán, Pedro. 2009. Puerto Rican Studies: Changing Islands of Knowledge. *CENTRO: Journal of the Center for Puerto Rican Studies* 21(2), 256–81.

Córdova, Teresa. 2005. Agency, Commitment and Connection: Embracing the Roots of Chicano and Chicana Studies. *International Journal of Qualitative Studies in Education* 18(2), 221–33.

_____. 2016. The Neoliberal Policy Regime and Implications for Latino Studies Scholarship. *Aztlán* 41(1), 55–84.

Dropp, Kyle and Brendan Nyhan. 2017. Nearly Half of Americans Don't Know Puerto Ricans are Fellow Citizens. *The New York Times* 26 September. Accessed 27 July 2020. <https://www.nytimes.com/2017/09/26/upshot/

nearly-half-of-americans-dont-know-people-in-puerto-ricoans-are-fel-low-citizens.html>.

Enck-Wanzer, Darrel. 2010. *The Young Lords: A Reader*. New York: New York University Press.

Engels, Frederick. 1969 [1878]. *Anti-Dühring: Herr Eugen Dühring's Revolution in Science*. Moscow: Progress Publishers.

Falcón, Angelo. 2012. The Vanishing Puerto Rican Student at the City University of New York (CUNY). *Latino Policy iReport* 14 August. National Institute for Latino Policy. Accessed 26 July 2020. <http://www.publicscienceproject. org/files/2013/04/NiLP-iReport-The-Vanishing-Puerto-Rican-Student-in-CUNY-2012.pdf>.

Fanon, Frantz. 1963. *The Wretched of the Earth*. Pref. by Jean-Paul Sartre. New York: Grove Press.

Fernández, Johanna. 2020. *The Young Lords: A Radical History*. Chapel Hill: The University of North Carolina Press.

Figueroa, Loida. 1968. *Breve historia de Puerto Rico*. Río Piedras, PR: Editorial Edil.

Fitzpatrick, Joseph P. 1996. *The Stranger is Our Own: Reflections on the Journey of Puerto Rican Migrants*. Kansas City, MO: Sheed & Ward.

Giroux H.A. 2009. Democracy's Nemesis: The Rise of the Corporate University. *Cultural Studies – Critical Methodologies* 9(5), 669–95.

Glazer, Nathan, and Daniel P. Moynihan. 1963. *Beyond the Melting Pot*. Cambridge, MA: MIT Press.

González, Juan and Joseph Torres. 2011. *News for All the People: The Epic Story of Race and the American Media*. London: Verso.

Handlin, Oscar. 1959. *The Newcomers: Negroes and Puerto Ricans in a Changing Metropolis*. Cambridge, MA: Harvard University Press.

Jiménez, Lillian. 1990. From the Margin to the Center: Puerto Rican Cinema in New York. *CENTRO: Journal of the Center for Puerto Rican Studies* 2(8), 28–43.

Lapp, Michael. 1995. The Rise and Fall of Puerto Rico as a Social Laboratory, 1945-1965. *Social Science History* 19(2), 169–99.

Lewis, Gordon K. 1963. *Puerto Rico: Freedom and Power in the Caribbean*. New York: Harper & Row.

Lewis, Oscar. 1966. *La Vida: a Puerto Rican Family in the Culture of Poverty-San Juan and New York*. New York: Vintage Books.

Medina Ramírez, Ramón. 1970. *El movimiento libertador en la historia de Puerto Rico*. San Juan: Ediciones Puerto.

Mills, C. Wright, Clarence Senior and Rose Kohn Goldsen. 1950. *The Puerto Rican Journey: New York's Newest Migrants*. New York: Harper & Bros.

Morales Carrión, Arturo. 1968. *Historia del pueblo de Puerto Rico: desde sus orígenes hasta el siglo XVIII*. San Juan: Editorial del Departamento de Instrucción Pública.

Muzio, Rose. 2017. *Radical Imagination, Radical Humanity: Puerto Rican Political Activism in New York*. Albany: State University of New York Press.

Nieves, Josephine et al. 1987. Puerto Rican Studies: Roots and Challenges. In
     *Toward a Renaissance of Puerto Rican Studies: Ethnic and Areas Studies
     in University Education*, eds. María E. Sánchez and Antonio M. Stevens
     Arroyo. 3–12. Highland Lakes, NJ: Atlantic Research and Publications,
     Inc.

Noriega, Chon A. 2000. *Shot in America: Television, the State and the Rise of
     Chicano Cinema*. Minneapolis: University of Minnesota Press.

Noriega, Chon A. and Ana M. López. 2004. *The Ethnic Eye: Latino Media Arts*.
     Minneapolis: University of Minnesota Press.

Oliver, Denise. 1972. Colonized Mentality & Non-Conscious Ideology. In *The Ideology
     of the Young Lords Party*. New York: Young Lords Party. Accessed 15 July
     2020. <https://www.marxists.org/history/erol/ncm-1/ylp-ideology.pdf>.

Ortíz Márquez, Maribel. 2009. Beginnings: Puerto Rican Studies Revisited. *CENTRO:
     Journal of the Center for Puerto Rican Studies* 21(2), 176–97.

Padilla, Elena. 1958. *Up From Puerto Rico*. New York: Columbia University Press.

Palante, n.d. Young Lords Party. (Publications and Pamphlets) Microfilm
     Collection. Center for Puerto Rican Studies Library & Archives, Hunter
     College, CUNY.

Palante. 1970-1976. Young Lords Party. Organización Obrera Revolucionaria
     Puertorriqueña. Bronx, New York. New York University Bobst Tamiment/
     Wagner Archives. <http://dlib.nyu.edu/palante/>.

Pantoja, Antonia, Wilhemina Perry and Barbara Bluerock. 1976. Toward the
     Development of Theory: Cultural Pluralism Redefined. *Journal of
     Sociology and Social Welfare* 4(1), 125–46.

Pantojas García, Emilio. 2000. End-of-the-Century Studies of Puerto Rico's Economy,
     Politics, and Culture. *Latin American Research Review* 35(3), 227–40.

Pérez, Richie. 1985. Committee Against Fort Apache. In *Cultures in Contention*, eds.
     Judith Francisca Baca and Douglas Kahn. Seattle: Real Comet Press.

_____. 1990. From Assimilation to Annihilation: Puerto Rican Images in U.S. Films.
     CENTRO: Journal of the Center for Puerto Rican Studies 2(8), 8–27.

Pérez Jiménez, Cristina. 2017. *CENTRO Journal*: Three Decades of Struggle and
     Scholarship in Support of Puerto Rican Studies. *Diálogo* 20(2), 33-45.

Rodríguez, Clara E. 1990. Puerto Rican Studies. *American Quarterly* 42(3), 437–55.

_____. 1997. *Latin looks: Images of Latinas and Latinos in the U.S. Media*. Boulder:
     Westview Press.

Rúa, Mérida M. and Arlene Torres. 2010. At the Crossroads of Urban Ethnography
     and Urban Latinidad. In *Latino Urban Ethnography and the Work of Elena
     Padilla*, ed. Mérida Rúa. 1–22. Urbana: University of Illinois Press.

Sánchez, María E. and Antonio M. Stevens-Arroyo, eds. 1987. *Toward a Renaissance
     of Puerto Rican Studies: Ethnic and Area Studies in University Education*.
     Highland Lakes, NJ: Atlantic Research and Publications, Inc.

Senior, Clarence Olson. 1961. *Strangers—Then Neighbors: From Pilgrims to Puerto*

Ricans. New York: Freedom Books.

Serrano, Basilio. 1998. ¡Rifle, Cañon, y Escopeta!: A Chronicle of the Puerto Rican Student Union. In *The Puerto Rican Movement: Voices from the Diaspora*, eds. Andrés Torres and José E. Velázquez. 124–43. Philadelphia: Temple University Press.

Silén, Juan Angel. 1970. *Hacia una visión positiva del puertorriqueño*. Barcelona: Editorial Edil.

Steward, Julian H., ed. 1956. *The People of Puerto Rico: A Study in Social Anthropology*. Urbana: University of Illinois Press.

Tugwell, Rexford. 1976 [1946]. *The Stricken Land*. New York: Greenwood Press.

Thomas, Lorrin. 2010. *Puerto Rican Citizen: History and Political Identity in Twentieth Century New York City*. Chicago: University of Chicago Press.

U.S. Senate. 1969. *Riots, Civil and Criminal Disorders: Hearings Before U.S. Senate Committee on Government Operations, Permanent Subcommittee on Investigations*. Washington: U.S. Government Printing Office.

U.S. Supreme Court. 2016. *Commonwealth of Puerto Rico et al. v. Franklin California Tax-Free Trust et al.* <https://www.supremecourt.gov/opinions/15pdf/15-233_i42j.pdf>.

_____. 2016. *Commonwealth of Puerto Rico v. Sánchez Valle et al.* <https://www.supremecourt.gov/opinions/15pdf/15-108_k4mp.pdf>.

_____. 2020. *Financial Oversight and Management Board for Puerto Rico v. Aurelius Investments, LLC.* <https://www.supremecourt.gov/opinions/19pdf/18-1334_8m58.pdf>.

Vázquez, Jesse. 1988. The Co-opting of Ethnic Studies in the American University: A Critical View. *Explorations in Ethnic Studies* 11(1), 23–36.

_____. 1989. Puerto Rican Studies in the 1990s: Taking the Next Turn in the Road. *CENTRO: Journal of the Center for Puerto Rican Studies* 2(6), 8–19.

Wakefield, Dan. 1959. *Island in the City: Puerto Ricans in New York*. New York: Corinth Books.

IN RETROSPECT:
Voices from the Field

CHAPTER 9

PAST IS PROLOGUE: A LOOK BACK AT THE EVOLUTION OF PUERTO RICAN STUDIES IN THE ACADEMY

Jesse M. Vázquez

[This excerpt is based on an article by the same title originally published in *Latino(a) Research Review*. Vol. 8, nos. 1-2 (2011-2012): 42–59. Reprinted with permission; editors left references and personal information provided after conclusion as in original.]

The reader should note that this essay is an effort to recapture my own personal experiences and institutional challenges that I and other colleagues encountered along the way. Looking back from this vantage point, over the last forty years, one can see a considerable body of literature that focused on the content, structure, and curriculum in Puerto Rican Studies. One of the earliest organized efforts at taking a collective look at the state of Puerto Rican Studies came with the first publication of a collection of conference papers delivered at the First International Conference for Puerto Rican Studies convened at Brooklyn College, CUNY, on April 3, 1981. The publication of a select number of conference presentations gathered into one volume, followed this gathering by almost six years. But that collection, published under the title *Towards a Renaissance of Puerto Rican Studies* (Sánchez and Stevens-Arroyo

1987), provides students wanting to learn about the history of this field with a very accurate reading of what we were thinking and doing after the first decade of Puerto Rican Studies. This collection is a very interesting snapshot of what was happening in the field thirty years ago.

After that publication, many of us continued to examine the ongoing development of the field in a variety of publications and conference venues. The Puerto Rican Studies conferences always seemed to make room for a "state of the field" panel, where practitioners would share the latest in their institutions. A number of us were also compelled to provide a counterpoint to the constant sniping at the field of Puerto Rican studies. In later years, my own writings focused on the struggles in academia, and the founding principles that provided a framework for our programs and departments (see Vázquez 1997, 1995, and 1992).

In part, a polemic against ethnic studies, Allan Bloom's book—*The Closing of the American Mind* (1987)—also was published at the same time as the Renaissance volume. Bloom's assault on ethnic studies in that book became legend in the cultural skirmishes. Over the next ten years, other similarly inclined scholars along the way joined Bloom, and the public assault on ethnic studies continued unabated until the late 1990s. It is interesting to ponder that while Bloom was busy formulating his opening salvo on ethnic studies, a group of Puerto Rican Studies scholars had met in Brooklyn, New York and committed themselves to moving forward in the area of Puerto Rican Studies.

For many, it was a year-to-year struggle to stay alive and resist the nay-sayers. This essay is an attempt to try and recapture the tenor of the times and document some of that history as "embattled scholars" in the academy.

PUERTO RICAN STUDIES' FIRST STEPS OF UNCERTAINTY

On the whole, my recollection of that period of Puerto Rican Studies is that many of us were quite uncertain as to the eventual outcome of our struggles to get programs or departments started and institutionalized. Despite a certain level of uncertainty, our confidence came from knowing that we wanted this outcome for the field and for the community, and for changing the traditional academic discourse. And perhaps naively, we also believed that this new academic initiative would be good for the nation.

Unlike other new academic programs fighting to get into the academy, we had a community base behind us that wanted to see us prevail. While emerging academic newcomers were mostly disconnected from a community movement or base, Puerto Rican and other ethnic studies were not. This was something that we fully recognized and acknowledged as we shaped Puerto Rican Studies programs and their curriculum.

This link to community was not only a part of the struggle for Puerto Rican Studies, but if one looks back one can see that the efforts of African American Studies also were propelled by a great push from the larger African American community. The awakenings growing out of the Civil Rights era demanded that educators create places in the schools and universities that would address the heretofore untold stories of marginalized communities. After so many years of scholarly neglect by mainstream scholars, there was so much that needed to be told, recorded, and shared, and this grassroots push for recognition was repeated in the struggles of Chicano, Native American, and Asian/American Studies, and those of other similarly positioned ethnic communities.

What we needed to demonstrate precisely was how these various ethnic communities were a distinct part of the greater American story–not a separate reality or a minor footnote in American history. Without question, expanding the conversation in the community was an important part of our mandate.

What is also interesting to note is that the findings of the early research studies conducted by Kenneth B. Clark (the famous Doll Tests) were used as a key part of the evidence in the *Brown v. the Board of Education* Supreme Court case. As most would recall, the data from Clark's studies were used to support the case for school desegregation.

One could easily argue that the earlier Clark studies became the prototype for so many countless other educational, community and psychological studies examining the impact of racism and segregation in America—not only in schools but in a variety of settings. The legacy of those early studies is reflected in the excellent work that is now being done today in psychology, education, health, and environment studies. That foundational knowledge needed to be produced, shared and applied. And those interested in ethnic studies in our universities needed to have a place/space in the academy that allowed for these kinds of explorations and teachings. This link to community best characterizes that early period in our development.

Social and Institutional Climate

For those involved in education, the stage was set as a result of the earlier social and political struggles, and entry into the university was the next phase in our efforts to empower our communities. In those early days, many were unprepared to fully understand and appreciate the complexity and the degree of resistance that we faced as we struggled to make Puerto Rican Studies a legitimate part of the academic community. It seems to me that the most challenging aspect was how to go about creating a new course of study that might stand alone as a program or department alongside traditional disciplines. To be certain, this was a different kind of border crossing.

In fact, while we had a sense of where we were headed and what we wanted to accomplish, many of us could not, with any degree of accuracy, predict the outcome of our struggles. As noted above, we just never knew when the obstacles and challenges presented would effectively close us down-and indeed some programs were limited, closed down, or sidelined along the way.

We had to quickly learn the rules of the academy (administrative, divisional, and departmental structures) when it came to looking for ways of introducing ethnic studies programs into the existing academic structures. How does a group begin to establish a course of study in an academy? How does one enter an established culture and begin to change that same culture from within? Looking back, we should appreciate that up to that time, the university culture was quite tone deaf to the realities and histories of certain ethnic communities. Learning to navigate the academic labyrinth in order to make those changes presented a major challenge to us personally and institutionally.

The sequence of events that allowed us to make any kind of advancements in the academy on behalf of ethnic studies seemed to receive support from the particular "zeitgeist" in the U.S. political and cultural landscape of that era. Individuals and groups within and beyond the university were beginning to challenge the established order in communities and in other institutions all over this nation. The Civil Rights and other social and political struggles, such as the anti-Vietnam War Movement, the women's movement, the gay and lesbian movement, and the emergence of greater opportunities for open admissions, all contributed to the opportunities we seized at the time. Shifts in the language, culture, and politics were all an integral part of what we were experiencing in academia at the time. From this perspective, the time was ripe for establishing a formal presence in the academy and move toward institutionalization.

On the way to accomplishing some form of institutionalization, we had to answer questions as to whether or not we wanted or needed a program of study (interdisciplinary in nature) or a freestanding department in its own right, making the claim that Puerto Rican Studies was a discipline in its own right; wondering, in some cases, if college structures would allow for the establishment of a division dedicated to the study of ethnicity and race in US society. In order to create these kinds of changes in our respective institutions, we need to have a firm grasp of how they worked and how they were structured both formally and informally.

Most of those involved in the Puerto Rican Studies struggles fought battles that were in large measure defined by the academic rules and the realities of specific campuses and universities. Some institutions did not go beyond creating a loosely strung series of courses offered throughout existing departments, while other places were able to mount fully formed departments or programs, with chairs or directors heading them.

Many of us became quite skilled at working the systems to our advantage. We created alliances with other like-minded departments and faculty and staff supporters across our campuses. Although many of us imported ideas and conceptual frameworks for course offerings and program configurations from other sister institutions, we needed first and foremost to see how these ideas might or might not work at our own institutions. But, what were the prospects for a sustained presence of that program for the long haul? The winner takes all approach that characterized the earliest tumultuous campus uprisings and confrontations ushering in these programs gradually gave away to a kind of academic pragmatism and greater sophistication, as well as a willingness to work with and at times confront others in order to protect our programs.

For the most part, however, our folks were uncompromising, yet at the same time quite skilled at moving within, around, and through the academic weeds that led to solidifying gains for our programs. It should not be forgotten that these programs were all in very vulnerable positions for a very long time, and some still are. In some cases, and far too often, the life and death of a program relied on the unswerving commitment of one lonely faculty member, perhaps a pre-tenured assistant professor, who was new to academia and who sometimes placed the life of the program ahead of his/her survival as a tenured junior professor. These were not easy choices for many.

Most scholars of the Puerto Rican Studies movement point to the 1969 campus occupations at the City College of New York (CCNY) of CUNY as a catalyst that contributed to the establishment of Puerto Rican Studies and Black Studies on that campus, but also propelled other campus movements in other public and private colleges and universities around the New York region and beyond. Those campus "occupations" opened the door for many other ethnic studies programs beyond the CCNY Harlem campus.

This writer remembers the audacity of that time when so much depended on so few individuals putting so much on the line. These were confrontations that many of us were not prepared for; nor did we know what these embattled institutions were willing to do to keep us out, and at the margins of academia. Very angry and combative students and faculty pushed some administrators into negotiations, while other administrators simply called the police. Sadly, by 1999, CCNY, the campus that served as a model and trailblazer for so many ethnic studies programs around the region, found its own departments under attack and eventually reduced to program status with its faculty dispersed to traditional departments throughout the college.

What we should acknowledge, as we reflect on these earlier confrontations and struggles, is that there were many non-Puerto Rican Studies colleagues who emerged as lifelong allies and friends in our shared efforts and remained so for many years after the dust had settled from those earlier skirmishes. Our accomplishments were made a bit easier by forming solid ties with some progressive colleagues who fully understood what we were trying to do in the academy. Others, however, steadfastly refused to support these programs.

Beyond the determined effort to establish and sustain an academic presence where there was none, many of us were fairly unsophisticated when it came to garnering resources and making inroads into those institutions. After all, we had no family endowments to withhold or offer to the gatekeepers. What we had was only the sheer sense of determination and a moral conviction that these programs needed to be part of a curriculum. Certainly, political pressure and social action brought us to the table, but once there, the few of us trained and with advanced degrees were working as best we could to carve a space for those emerging fields in higher education.

It was an on the job learning process for most of us to make these programs work. What was the difference between having a program vis-à-vis a department? How was the department to be structured, and how were we to establish one in the absence of other models? How were we going to find secure funding for these programs and persuade the institution to provide those funds? How were we to get faculty specialists from other departments within the institutions to help us build our programs? And where were we to find qualified faculty with doctoral degrees and persuade them to join our fledgling programs?

The truth was that when our Puerto Rican Studies programs were first launched, many of the instructors were hired as lecturers because they had not completed their doctoral degrees. While many of the stateside doctoral students were in the process of completing their advanced degrees, some schools recruited island professors with solid paper credentials. Sadly, in some cases these appointments were disastrous and short lived. Yet, a handful of academics from the island understood the realities of the U.S. Puerto Rican community, and were easily able to make a smooth transition into the emerging field of Puerto Rican Studies. However, many island-recruited faculty were unable to adapt and found themselves at odds with our students and community. This is a part of our early history that needs to be understood on many levels.

Having allies serving on curriculum committees was key to some of the success or failures in developing Puerto Rican Studies. Learning how these entities worked was crucial to the early development of these programs. In my opinion, what we were able to accomplish was largely based on our gradual understanding of the culture and rules at our particular institutions. Learning those rules allowed us to create effective programs and curricula for our students. However, even after programs and departments were established, our place at the institution was never fully secure.

Our work, beyond the task of program development, always included alliances with other colleagues in higher education, especially when the educational future of thousands of students of color was threatened. While we were busy establishing a presence in the academy, we also believed that it was important to work collectively to secure a positive educational environment for all students at the university. The Puerto Rican Council on Higher Education (PROCHE), founded in 1979, was one of those umbrella groups that attempted to advance the cause of Latino/a students, faculty, and staff in the New York metropolitan area. Many of us were determined to institutionalize our programs, but we were also actively engaged in broader academic issues as these impacted the lives and welfare of thousands of students. In addition to Puerto Rican Studies, PRCHE was also concerned and involved with Student Access and Retention, Affirmative Action/Faculty Development, and Bilingual Education and English as a Second Language issues.

As I look back at those earlier struggles from this vantage point, it seems that many traditional academic disciplines have gone "cultural" these days. Look at the listings of traditional departments and you will find variations of courses which we introduced, and which some of those same gatekeepers fought tooth and nail to keep out of the curriculum. As pointed out by Pedro Cabán (2009), in his detailed and comprehensive review of the changes in Puerto Rican Studies, he asserts that while our programs may be thinning out, the scholarship that we promoted through Puerto Rican Studies seems to be gaining in acceptance in those key disciplines that once found our scholarship lacking. Some program entities may have perhaps been allowed to languish through neglect and underfunding, but Cabán suggests a Puerto Rican scholarship is in its ascendancy at this point.

BUILDING PROGRAMS, CURRICULUM, AND COLLABORATIVE STRUCTURES IN ACADEMIA: THE CASE OF QUEENS COLLEGE, CUNY

At Queens College, the earliest iteration of the Puerto Rican Studies Program was started by Rafael Rodríguez, a faculty member in the College's Romance Languages Department. Rodriguez, together with a handful of faculty and staff at the time, formed a coalition with a very active group of students determined to establish an academic presence on that campus.

This kind of faculty, student, and staff coalition organizational entity was seen in most, if not all, places where ethnic studies departments were being established. The students always played a key and vital role in the development of these new programs, especially during the early years. The Center for Puerto Rican Studies at Hunter College, CUNY, was no exception to this rule. Students, faculty, and community from around the city and beyond, played a key role in moving the agenda for forming a research center for Puerto Rican Studies in New York.

In those early years of program development, there were some very exciting innovations in the curriculum. When one considers that our programs were very small fledgling academic entities, clearly underfunded, and some were not yet departments, we offered courses on a wide variety of subjects and disciplines. Early on, besides the standard Puerto Rican history courses, a wide range of courses were offered in literature and the arts and other humanities and social science courses as well. At Queens College, we introduced a course in the "Art of Puerto Rico and the Hispanic Caribbean," developed and taught by Isabel Nazario and later picked up by other instructors and reshaped and expanded. I remember trying to get the art department to accept it as a part of their art major or minor sequence, but the chair resisted. Similarly, we pushed the envelope with the development of a music course, taught by musicians and by music theorists. One of the contributors to that course was Juan Flores. These courses covered music history and forms of musical genres from Puerto Rico as well as contemporary musical forms. We also developed a music workshop for musicians.

Recognizing the power of the media to shape public perceptions, we developed a course on "Puerto Ricans and Latinos in the Media." Again, this might have been one of the first of its kind offered at CUNY. This happened well before the field of Media Studies had separated itself from being part of the old Communication Arts and Sciences department configuration. The chair of that department was generous enough to crosslist that course within that department—a plus for our students. We recruited a few filmmakers for this course as well as a media specialist years later—Pedro Angel Rivera and Tomas López Pumarejo. Queens was one of the first to offer a course on the "Puerto Rican and Latin American Woman," most recently offered by María Soledad Romero; and early on, Ana Maria Diaz-Stevens first taught a course on "Caribbean Religions."

For those who have had to face down colleagues from across the college on the matter of curriculum revision and content, I am sure they appreciate the full measure of what this process meant to the health of a department or a program. It was the academic community accepting or rejecting our curriculum offerings. This was the end point in a long struggle to get these courses incorporated into the college community. After overcoming the hurdles, it was "on the books" as we used to say.

Some important considerations when it comes to developing curriculum and institutionalizing any program included the following: Was the course part of another major? Was the course accepted as an elective or requirement?—the latter was an important question for the enrollment sustainability of any program or department.

Under the presidency of Dr. Saul Cohen, Queens College ethnic studies directors were encouraged to hire visiting professors for some of the college's ethnic studies programs. That year, Puerto Rican Studies invited Dr. Neftali Garcia Martinez, who came up from Puerto Rico to offer what might have been the first environmental studies course focused on the island. García Martinez, a well-known environmentalist at the time, engaged the students in their very first experience in trying to understand the nature of the relationships between industrial development on island political realities, and environmental degradation, and the need for greater control of these variables.

As other programs, Puerto Rican Studies was a participant in the college's comprehensive course called, "Six Ethnic Groups in New York City," a comparative ethnic studies course. Drawing, at that time, from the six existing ethnic studies programs that formed an Ethnic Studies Council at the College, this particular course was an effort to bring a cohesiveness to the course offerings. But what was interesting about this Council was that we had sought ways of collaborating with each other and early on organized a course that explored the commonalities and differences in our respective ethnic studies communities.

Many of us, new to academia, learned to do what was needed in order to continue to grow and develop our programs. Queens College and some other CUNY schools joined Education and other departments in the development of bilingual teacher training. Grants were written and received, and the presence of Puerto Rican Studies was felt in other departments and divisions. Most, if not all, of the concentrations in the early bilingual teacher training programs required a sequence of courses, not only languages and linguistics, and methods courses in education, but also in ethnic studies.

These cross-divisional partnerships allowed us to become an integral part of the college in many very important ways. Interestingly, colleagues outside of the area of ethnic studies are now, at least in my experience, more willing to recognize the significance of this work and the contributions to a particular field of study.

Education, of course, was one of the earliest and most frequently studied institutions in terms of how children in the Puerto Rican community fared in U.S. schools. Language transition studies, psychological impact studies, parental involvement, and identity studies became *de rigueur* and of course, the area that seems to have benefited most from these earlier and ongoing studies is bilingual education.

Puerto Rican Studies curriculum insisted on bilingual education methods courses, and pressured education departments to develop bilingual education sequences very early on. Title VII programs supported the establishment of bilingual teacher training programs in US universities across the country. Generally, bilingual education was one of those areas where the work by educational researchers directly benefited the community. An early outcome of that work resulted in the landmark ASPIRA Consent decree (1974) (Reyes 2006). These efforts were also a good example of how the joining of the notion of theory and praxis in ethnic studies could result in significant contributions to community change and advancement.

As programs matured and as the demographics of our cities and universities shifted, there was talk of considering moving away from the exclusivity of Puerto Rican Studies and broadening the umbrella to Latino(a) Studies. As early as 1988-89 some in a group called the Puerto Rican Research Exchange, which met regularly in New York City, discussed this issue at several of its meetings. Was it time to broaden the Puerto Rican base of courses and perhaps focus also on a broader more inclusive Latino population? (see Vázquez 1989). Of course, over the last decade, Puerto Rican Studies and some Chicano Studies programs around the nation have moved to be far more inclusive in curriculum approach, in a direct response to the changing demographics in certain urban university centers.

At Queens College, there had been an earlier abortive and misguided attempt to move the fledgling Puerto Rican Studies Program into Latin American area studies. But the real merger of these two programs came several decades after that earlier attempt under a very different set of circumstances, purposes, and intentions. More than a decade ago, I joined with colleague, George Priestley, Director of Latin American Studies at Queens College, in a process that would eventually lead to a merger of our two programs, with an understanding that we would maintain the ethnic studies component as well as the Latin American area studies sequence, and create a blended program with a more comprehensive approach to understanding Latin America, as well as the Latino(a) immigration and community experience in the United States.

After the untimely passing of Professor Priestley, the new program we had formed as a Latin American and Latino(a) Studies Program had struggled to maintain its direction. What remains of the Latino(a) component of that merged program was difficult to discern from a recent search of that program's webpage. I found no mention or listing of Puerto Rican/Latino courses in the offerings that were supposed to have been a part of that earlier promising merger.

Other programs, as we know, have moved in this direction and changed department or program names, and revised curricular offerings that in some way each has tried to provide continuity for Latino and Puerto Rican Studies. Again, these changes came as a response to the budgetary realities of each of these campuses. It seems to me that changes are still taking place in the ever-unfolding evolution of Puerto Rican and Latino studies, and other ethnic studies programs. One thing is certain, the Latino population will continue to grow, and it remains to be seen how and if this growth will reshape our academic programs.

FINAL REFLECTIONS

There was a shared belief at the time of the founding of our programs that we would eventually raise the hopes and accomplishments of our communities. At least that was one of the objectives shared by many engaged in research and teaching during the early period. We also believed that we would contribute to the discourse and research in a variety of academic disciplines and have moved closer to this goal in the last decade.

The legacy of these early programs can be seen in the enormous production in the research literature that has been generated, in the countless number of students that have benefited from engaging issues of race, ethnic, and gender equality in our classrooms, and hopefully are applying this knowledge to a broad range of fields and venues.

The psychologists, social workers, or counselors who look closely at ethnicity, race, and the cultural dimensions in the lives of their clients have directly benefited from ethnic studies. In a very clear way, these professionals are beholden to those pioneers in ethnic studies that insisted on focusing on these aspects of human behavior and experience. Those who now have a deeper sense of the history and cultural complexity of our distinct communities are also beneficiaries of the work done by some of those early founders as well as those who have followed in their footsteps.

Today's appreciation of the strong legacy in literary and artistic expressions that we value for aesthetic enjoyment and their creative imaginative leaps, are a key part of the spirit and sense of identity of the Puerto Rican community. Undoubtedly, Puerto Rican and other ethnic studies programs played a key role in providing a forum and a creative space at colleges and universities for sharing and preserving the older forms of these artistic expressions, and also encouraging the production of new art forms.

Far from a comprehensive account of my own personal experiences and institutional challenges we encountered in the academy, I would hope that the reader of this very brief essay has gotten a bit of the flavor of some of the issues, obstacles, and successes that we experienced on our way toward institutionalizing Puerto Rican and other ethnic studies in the academy.

REFERENCES

Bloom, Allan. 1987. *The Closing of the American Mind*. New York: A Torchstone Book.

Reyes, Luis O. 2006. The Aspira Consent Decree: A Thirtieth-Anniversary Retrospective of Bilingual Education of New York City. *Harvard Educational Review* 76(3), 369–400.

Sánchez, Maria E. and Antonio M. Stevens-Arroyo, eds. 1987. *Towards a Renaissance of Puerto Rican Studies: Ethnic and Area Studies in University Education*. Boulder: Atlantic Research and Publication.

Vázquez, Jesse M. 1989. Puerto Rican Studies in the 1990s: Taking the Next Turn in the Road. *Centro Bulletin* 11, 8–19.

_____. 1992. Embattled Scholars in the Academy: A Shared Odyssey. *Callaloo* 15(4), 1039–51.

_____. 1995. Ethnic Studies and the New Multiculturalism: The Founding Principles of Puerto Rican Studies Revisited. In *Privileging Positions: The Sites of Asian American Studies*, ed. Gary Y. Okira. 435–46. Pullman: WA: Washington State University Press.

_____. 1997. Letter: Myths and 'Tired Old Cliches' about Ethnic Studies Programs. *The Chronicle of Higher Education* 31 January, B3–B11.

CHAPTER 10

PUERTO RICAN STUDIES AT BARUCH COLLEGE

Regina A. Bernard-Carreño

Growing up in Manhattan at a time when there were several neighborhoods that had pockets of Puerto Rican people, families, shops, and cultural institutions, I was always immersed in what later led to my interest in Puerto Rican writing. One of the first children's books read to me was *Pérez y Martina: Un cuento folkórico puertorriqueño* by Pura Belpré (1966). It was not until much later that I discovered that Belpré was the first Puerto Rican librarian of the New York Public Library, an institution I loved then and now. Digging up a bit of my childhood in literature, I discovered that my beloved *Pérez y Martina* was the first Spanish language children's book published by a mainstream press (Ulaby 2016). Belpré's own story of becoming a writer of Spanish-language children's books because she could not find any was an early imprint of what would later become my intellectual pursuit in the field of Puerto Rican Studies.

The Program of Black and Hispanic Studies at Baruch College, as it was originally named, was formed by 1972 after much racial and political pressure was placed on City University of New York (CUNY) schools to make the courses reflect students of color and to prioritize the hiring of faculty of color. Black and Puerto Rican students across the city demanded the establishment of Black and Puerto Rican studies units in 1969 similar to a few of their Chicano/a West Coast counterparts a year earlier. Baruch's program was brought about due to protest, activism, and heavy student engagement.

Later, in the 1990s, Baruch was met with the same racial issues it had faced in the 1970s: "They want better student services to offset the college's low retention rate for minority students. And, they want courses that better incorporate studies of how non-Europeans have contributed to civilization" (Lee 1990). At the time, students vehemently supported the Black and Latino faculty's outrage by stating, "'Some minority students at Baruch say the environment is chilly. The tension is in the air at Baruch," Tony Medina, a Hispanic literature major, said. "I took a modern short novel class where the whole syllabus consisted of white male writers. The professor asked if anyone had any suggestions for other novels. I said how about Toni Morrison's 'The Bluest Eye'? She said, 'Let me borrow it and see if it's appropriate,' Mr. Medina recalled. 'Appropriate'? Here is an author who has won a Pulitzer Prize" (Lee 1990). Due to the struggle and the tension that the students and faculty were faced with at Baruch College over reasons regarding racial injustices, the Middle States Association of Colleges and Schools did not grant Baruch College its accreditation that year until it addressed and remedied the issues it was being charged with. The air of protest might have been quieter during the 1990s, but it never went completely silent.

Before I began as an adjunct lecturer for Baruch College's Black and Hispanic Studies Department, I was teaching at the Graduate School of Education at Hunter College (CUNY). It was clear that the need for classes dealing specifically with issues facing people of color was imperative but also lacking. Searching across the CUNY schools in 2006, I contacted a few of the Puerto Rican Studies departments and heard from the Department of Black and Hispanic Studies at Baruch College first. I wrote to Dr. Héctor Cordero-Guzmán, chairperson at the time, and shared with him my interest in teaching for the department since my personal as well as academic research focused on Blacks, Latinos, and other people of color. What drew me to the department was that Baruch offered a place for Black Studies and Latino Studies as a joint unit. Generally, schools tended to divide the fields of study and ask that students focus on one or the other instead of considering the history of how both of the disciplines can be studied jointly. My initial belief was that having a graduate degree in one discipline (African American Studies) and pursuing research in Puerto Rican Studies were great opportunities for me to be part of whatever was being produced there. The courses offered to me reflected much of the history behind how the department was developed and teaching them made me feel responsible for continuing to share the history of where we were and how we got there. Though the existing courses were based on Island politics or migration from Puerto Rico to New York or the history of Puerto Rico, there was also a population of Puerto Rican students who felt as though they were straddling identities and often talked about being in cultural limbo. As a direct response to those feelings, I decided to develop a senior seminar on Nuyorican poets and writers, in which we discussed works by Miguel Piñero, Pedro Pietri, Miguel Algarín, and Sandra María Esteves. I also assigned selections from my book *Nuyorganics: Organic Intellectualism, the Search for Racial Identity, and Nuyorican Thought* (2010).

Under Dr. Cordero-Guzmán's leadership, the Department of Black and Hispanic Studies thrived and more than just survived. Understanding the importance and the vital necessity of our department, he helped to mentor young and untenured faculty as we struggled to achieve the requirements of moving forward in the academy. He often alerted us to opportunities outside of the school and helped many faculty gain publishing credits. He also attended every single event faculty in his department organized and managed to stay for the duration of the affair. The one thing we did not have to worry about was the consistency of our teaching and the enrollment of courses by students. We always had students, and there were always classes for us to teach. He gave everyone a chance to get their foot in the door of the department and expected 110 percent out of everyone. It was a fair exchange as we were a solid departmental unit.

It was not long before I realized that Cordero-Guzmán's own professional and research background enabled him to effectively manage the intellectual component of the department's Hispanic Studies. Though he was a strong supporter of Black Studies, Dr. Cordero-Guzmán's endless list of achievements, publications, media appearances, community involvement, and academic work helped to shine a light on our department as being successful in the Hispanic studies field. During his time as chairperson, he consistently secured large grants from prestigious funding sources and institutions for successful research projects dealing with Latinos across the country, low wage workers, immigrant groups, the Dominican Republic's economy, and community-based organizations. His numerous grants brought the department to a higher competitive level within Baruch, and our department flourished with an influx of research participants, assistants, and others working on the projects he spearheaded.

During his leadership, one of my undergraduates, Keith García, who now directs Fraternity and Sorority Life at Northwestern University, helped to make a lasting change for our department. Before his graduation in 2004, Keith asked a simple question as to why our department was still named Black and Hispanic Studies. Keith's personal attachment to the department as a Puerto Rican student from New York City drove him to want an immediate departmental name change. He wanted to be accurately represented and realized that he, and others like him, could not allow being misrepresented at a school he dedicated so much of his time to and identify as an activist while allowing the old fashioned ways of the school to continue. Gathering members of his fraternity alongside Latino students from the general student population, Keith began a petition to have the name of the department changed from Hispanic to Latino. Before the semester was over, he had enough signatures and an overflow of support that led to the departmental name change, which shifted the sociopolitical dynamics of a stronger alliance between Black and Latino Studies. Many of the graduates of our department have gone off to successful careers in law, government, culinary school, entrepreneurship, Latino-specific journalism, doctoral work, public school teaching and administration, advocacy work, and major corporations, where they are tapped for their knowledge and interpersonal skills in diversity. The success of our alumni speaks largely to the impact that our department continues to make on students who not only pursue the courses as part of their degree requirements and personal interest, but who use the academic skills gained to ignite their activist spirits and intellectual curiosities when they leave the university setting.

At this point, as an important act of reckoning, I will include the perspectives of my colleagues who have been long standing members of the department and the field. In the early days of my appointment at the newly renamed Department of Black and Latino Studies, I met an adjunct who was the sole instructor of Latino Studies before I arrived. Professor Lourdes Gil arrived in the department in September 2000 and was the longest member of the department teaching solely in the Latino Studies sequence. In 2020, she retired. When I asked her to share a memory of her entry into the department, she recalled that there was no chairperson or lead administrator. Instead, she was greeted by the administrative assistant who was then the point-person for scheduling adjuncts to teach. At the time of Professor Gil's arrival, there were only two other professors, Dr. Arthur Lewin and the late Dr. Martia Goodson, who were both teaching in the Black Studies sequence.

Professor Gil began her time in the department by teaching the Latino Studies introductory courses, such as Latinos in the U.S., Latin America: An Institutional and Cultural Survey, and Latinos in the U.S.: Culture and Society. The following year, she was offering a course on the Dominican Republic since Dominican students were beginning to make up the majority of the Latino students at the time. The Puerto Rican studies courses were offered by another adjunct that left soon after Professor Gil's arrival. As we reminisced about the days when our offices were filled with students who were interested in the course topics well beyond the office hours, we realized that helped to create a department-student family where potluck lunches were shared, and wedding invitations were common. Although Professor Gil agreed that the number of Latino students had significantly decreased over the years, she began her reflection by saying, "The interest in Latino/a and Latin American studies courses has increased. I find myself teaching all the existing Latino courses as well as having to create new ones" (Gil 2020). Her experience was similar to my own regarding the necessity to create the Nuyorican course and later reactivating and developing a course entitled "Latinas." Among her students, there was a desire to see more world leaders reflected in the syllabus. In my section, the students were still a majority Puerto Rican and wanted to see Puerto Rican women writers in the reading list, but they did not necessarily want fiction or literature; they wanted scholarly articles written about identity and about women, such as the imposition of birth control testing and female sterilizations in Puerto Rico, including the fatalities which resulted (García 1982).

As the Latino courses were rising in popularity, the student demographics began to change, and Professor Gil was faced with several petitions for new courses on Cuba, the U.S.-Mexico border, and Brazil. As the student body continued to change from Puerto Rican and Dominican to Colombian, Ecuadorian, and Mexican, Professor Gil once again created courses that spoke directly to those students. The classes were filling without much need for advertisement. Just before her retirement, she was welcoming the change in student diversity as it brought her deep satisfaction to know what the department can do for a variety of students on campus.

The departmental faculty identified the lack of faculty hiring and retention to be the biggest problem affecting growth and its sustainability. Professor Gil stated, "The main difficulty we encounter if we are to continue doing this is the fact that we don't have enough Latino and Latin American Studies professors to undertake the task in front of us. The second obstacle we face is that the growing interest in Latino-based courses lies with the students but also with the faculty," who may not want to teach courses they deem irrelevant or outdated (Gil 2020). Although our Puerto Rican student population has dramatically decreased and has caused a subsequent thinning in Puerto Rican courses being offered, when Professor Gil has offered the courses, they are usually registered at full capacity. Professor Gil's highly regarded works of poetry, such as her collection entitled, *Empieza la ciudad* (1993) and *Anima vagula: parábolas del amor y del poder* (2013) as well as her involvement in Cuban cultural affairs, has driven up great interest in her courses, particularly those on the Spanish-speaking Caribbean. In 1994, she participated in the historic "First Symposium of Writers from the Inside and Outside of Cuba" sponsored by the Olof Palme International Center in Stockholm; her creative work there was later published as "Bipolaridad de la cultura cubana" in Sweden. She was the recipient of numerous prestigious fellowships as well as writing residencies. The accolades she has earned continue to inspire students who often request to hear her poetry.

The question Professor Gil and I have mulled over has been whether students who are not Puerto Rican are also interested in Puerto Rican Studies as a specific focus within the larger Latino Studies field. The answer seems to be a resounding Yes! Given the department's rich history and the caliber of the faculty who either taught full or part-time even for brief stints, students were inspired by the content in the Puerto Rican Studies courses and wanted to embody what they were learning. They recognize that the early fights for Black Studies and Puerto Rican Studies were the ladder for many of the other ethnic studies courses and programs that were subsequently developed. Despite the dwindling Puerto Rican Studies courses in the department and across the nation, Puerto Rican Studies birthed broader Latino Studies courses and academic units that students and scholars are benefiting from.

A senior colleague and pillar of the department, Dr. Arthur Lewin, author of *Africa Is Not A Country: It's A Continent* (1991), has been a faculty member of Black and Latino Studies since 1979 and has worked without a break in service for eighty-one consecutive semesters. When Dr. Lewin arrived, there were six full-time faculty, including Dr. Harrison Tucker and Dr. Robert Martínez, who were the founding members of the Black and Hispanic Studies program at Baruch College circa 1970. Dr. Lewin recalls that Black and Hispanic Studies was only a program, like several of the other ethnic studies programs within CUNY, and did not become a department until the early 1990s around the time of the Middle States Association scandal.

Dr. Lewin recalls the history of the program and CUNY's cultural and racial climate in the 1970s as follows:

African Americans and Puerto Ricans were instrumental in the establishment of Black and Puerto Rican Studies at City College and throughout City University, and they spearheaded the Open Admissions movement that swept CUNY and the country. However, today the number of Black and Latino Students on the senior college campuses of CUNY has sharply declined and within that reduced number African Americans and Puerto Ricans are a distinct minority. Though both are native sons and daughters, they are treated as outcasts. To wit, their harassment by the police, the neglect of Puerto Rico after the hurricanes, and the dubbing of African Americans fleeing Hurricane Katrina as "refugees," and their treatment as such.

Thus, it would seem Puerto Ricans and African Americans have to choose between two poles: to either assimilate or separate from society. Some are able to, and actually do, pass as "white." Others, though not denying their heritage, fully comply with all the customs and behaviors of this culture and focus sharply on climbing the socio-economic ladder. Still others emphasize and celebrate their heritage and focus on maintaining a grass-roots commonality and communion with others in the community. The two sides can come to see each other in a negative light; the nationalists referring to the assimilationists as "sellouts," while the assimilationists counter that the nationalists are escapists refusing to face reality. Here is the seeming paradox. Puerto Ricans and African Americans can neither become a part of this country, nor can they survive apart from it. This perhaps encapsulates the historic conflict and contradiction between Muñoz Marín and Albizu Campos and that between MLK [Martin Luther King, Jr.] and Malcolm X. And, it finds its way into Black Studies, as exemplified by the disagreements between Henry Louis Gates and Molefi Asante, and the two conflicting schools of Black Studies that they are the foremost champions of. (Lewin 2020)

When I asked Dr. Lewin to describe the political, social and intellectual atmosphere at the time the program was being formed, he immediately responded by stating, "It was eminently logical since it was Black and Puerto Rican students who fought shoulder to shoulder for CUNY's Open Admissions and for departments of Black and Puerto Rican Studies at City College and all across CUNY in 1969" (Lewin 2020). He recalled that while there was, in fact, a battle on all the CUNY grounds, "the hottest was at City College" and, of course, Baruch faced its own long battle during the 1990s. Any time Dr. Lewin shares the details of this important time in our department's history, his eyes light up, and his face moves from serious to smiling and back again to serious. I also remember how pleased he was at my arrival in the department as an adjunct with the ability to teach in both the Black and the Hispanic sequence of courses. His faith in my research and my dedication to the education of young people gave me much needed support as I tried to manage teaching as an adjunct all over the city but really finding comfort among the students of Black and Latino Studies at Baruch. Dr. Lewin took my dissertation and began to share insight on Puerto Rican writers that he either knew, taught, or encountered along the way in his own academic career. These kinds of early interactions with senior colleagues in the department, like Dr. Lewin, who headed the Black and Latino Faculty Association, were important to me as a woman of color, as well as helpful for advancing other junior faculty of color who were in departments across the school.

Soon after I arrived, Dr. Lewin immediately told me the story of the department, and subsequently showed me footage on a VHS in his office of his own political involvement in helping to establish the department. He acknowledges the steady decline of Puerto Rican students and Puerto Rican Studies courses at Baruch but purposely includes a Puerto Rican narrative in his senior seminar as a way to alert the students as to the history of our department and those similar to ours across CUNY. Rather than trying to restructure the department, as so many have suggested, he believes in maintaining and managing the special significance of our joint disciplines under a united front.

"We are unlike any other department in the country," he has said to me on several occasions. "The students keep this place moving, and the most important thing you have to keep doing is teaching, because the students they need us, all of them--black, white, Puerto Rican, Latino, Asian, all of them" (Lewin 2020), has been his mantra. With this understanding, he tries to find materials that bridge the two fields while giving students a bit of history into our department's formation as well as our struggles and challenges. I have often critiqued the requirements for a minor declaration in our department because the richness of the discipline is easily lost with the rapid completion of three courses. However, Dr. Lewin is quick to share examples of why that approach is conducive for students who have a major elsewhere, particularly the part-time working adults who he remembers were predominantly Black and Puerto Rican students back when he first began teaching at Baruch.

It is in the capstone course that he teaches every semester that Dr. Lewin uses *Down These Mean Streets* by Piri Thomas (1991) to illustrate the connection between the two fields in our department. He states, "The key scene, for me, in *Down These Mean Streets,* is when Piri and his brother get into a fight because the brother does not like Piri hanging out with the Black kids at school because that reflects on him, the white-looking brother. The students always side with Piri when we discuss and sometimes have the students themselves act out the scene. Then I ask, 'What if Piri came out looking like his brother and his brother came out looking like him? Would Piri still be Mr. Black Power? Or would he be acting like his brother and vice versa?' This not only illuminates a key aspect of the Puerto Rican identity, it illuminates the North American identity and the human identity" (Lewin 2020). Herein, he bridges the narrative experiences of Blacks and Latinos in New York City by using Thomas's book, facilitating intense discussions, and inviting guest speakers who can directly talk about the experiences of dual cultures and dual identities.

Using Thomas's text "is seminal for issues of identity, culture, and color as it relates to both communities" and has given students an exposure to what he argues are "the cultures merging into their African identities" (Lewin 2020). He suggests that the students who bridge both worlds find refuge in the course, where these topics are often ripe for debate. Dr. Lewin states, "Blacks and Puerto Ricans live in close proximity in many NYC neighborhoods. Also, both cultures are heavily African. African Americans look more phenotypically Black, but Latinos are more culturally Black. However, the rank and file of both groups are not champions of their Black heritage" (Lewin 2020). I have witnessed many such exchanges in my courses where these ideas are shared in class; it usually begins with an observation by students who later erupt into their own lived narratives. They begin to recollect instances in which family members have mistreated them or have embodied racial oppression for generations. Professor Gil's courses also examine the lives of those who consider themselves Afro-Latino and those who reject a dual identity. It is in these very spaces that students are able to begin to uncover their personal stories and reflect in ways that no other set of courses enable them to do because the department centers black and brown lives in the college.

"They don't teach you this in any other course," one of my Puerto Rican students once said. "What do you mean 'teach you'? They don't allow you to talk about this in any other course," another student said, which made the rest of the room explode into laughter. Beneath the humor, there was a painful reality that without places like our department in the academy, we lose a bit of our humanity and become disconnected from our students. Dr. Lewin, who arguably has been the recipient of good will from the majority of the students, has served as an advisor and mentor for many students who are both Black and Puerto Rican alike. When I asked him about his reliance on Piri Thomas's overarching narrative on race, racism and, intra-group racism for discussing dual identities, he stated, "Everything cannot be broken into discrete pieces and examined separately, that is the functionalist method. Everything is in a state of change, and everything is connected. If that is true of all things, then it is also true of the Puerto Rican people's past, present and future and the same can be said of the department" (Lewin 2020).

As I reflected on this piece, I spent a lot of time trying to sort through my memories of working in the department. I pondered about our ever-present, precarious position in the university as we have lost many faculty for various reasons, which administrations throughout the decades have not replaced; this has caused low morale, particularly among faculty of color who wind up with a hidden workload as compared to their white counterparts. Working on this piece, however, reminded me of my early days in the department, of how passionately I felt about the significant impact we can have on students' lives. Writing this during the upsurge in the Black Lives Matter movement was a necessary reminder of where we were at one point and how much we need to return to that kind of urgent call to recreate ourselves within the current social and political milieu as we capitalize on our radical histories and our cultural strengths to center the work we do in order to effectively equip our students to successfully engage in society.

Our department has been graced by prominent leaders who inspired students and made them feel a sense of pride that they were affiliated with our department or were graduating with a minor. Members of the Young Lords Party and the Black Panther Party that played major roles in the social movement and helped inspire ethnic studies have served as guest lecturers. There was also the late Dr. Juan Flores, a pioneering scholar in the fields of Puerto Rican Studies and Cultural Studies, who gave special lectures at Baruch College, and who I had the honor of being mentored by and whom I later befriended. More recently, Dr. Ana Yolanda Ramos-Zayas, who is now Professor of American Studies, Women's, Gender, and Sexuality Studies, and Ethnicity, Race, and Migration as well as Director of Undergraduate Studies at Yale University, served as the department's only endowed chair. She also designed the Black and Latino Studies faculty grant, which was created to support the pedagogical work being conducted in the department through our respective classes. Dr. Ramos-Zayas's third book *Street Therapists: Affect, Race, and Neoliberal Personhood in Latino Newark* (2012) won the Frank Bonilla Book Award given to the best Latino/ Puerto Rican-themed book by the international Puerto Rican Studies Association. Being a seasoned scholar in Puerto Rican Studies, her courses were said to be "intellectual maps"; she built a solid following of undergraduate students across majors as well as students from the CUNY Graduate Center.

Dr. Ramos-Zayas was known by her students for the thoughtful design of the coursework, impactful readings, guest speakers and the visits from community scholars and public intellectuals. She also brought middle school students from underserved schools in the South Bronx to meet her undergraduates in Black and Latino Studies. This exchange was an eye-opening experience for both groups of students and serves as an example of the crucial work we engage in to inspire younger generations and create a space for them in the university. Dr. Ramos-Zayas trained students in ethnographic work and qualitative research, particularly those working on the Honors Thesis in Black and Latino Studies, motivating many students to apply to doctoral programs. Though her time with the department was brief, she made a significant impact, and her absence was felt deeply by us all.

I was drawn to Baruch because of the possibilities reflected in the name of the Department of Black and Latino Studies. Rightly so, it is the combination of both fields that allows me to explore the work and lives of those who identify as Afro-Latino/a, more broadly. As a researcher and professor, I have been able to use my existence in this interdisciplinary department to purposefully guide students on their journey of discoveries. For many, when Afro-Latino/a was not on the table as an identifier, they enjoyed learning about those like them, such as Arturo Schomburg, Nicolás Guillén, Mayra Santos-Febres, and, more recently, Elizabeth Acevedo among others. For the students, these intellectuals are heroes; for me, they are pillars of how we can consider ourselves united while beautifully diverse. I have been fortunate to contribute to this source of knowledge with the following books: *Black and Brown Waves: The Cultural Politics of Young Women of Color and Feminism* (2009), *Nuyorganics: Organic Intellectualism, the Search for Racial Identity, and Nuyorican Thought* (2010), and *Say it Loud: Black Studies, Its Students, and Racialized Collegiate Culture* (2014). What began as a personal journey growing up in Hell's Kitchen, NYC, currently inspires my intellectual exploration that defines my work as an academic.

To conclude, there is still a compelling need for the existence of our department and those like ours across university systems. With adequate and equitable institutional support for our department—faculty and students— we can thrive rather than continue in survival mode with a sense of tokenism for the sake of checking off a diversity box but with no real commitment to the ideals of an anti-racist and inclusive academic setting connected to the real world. It is in these moments of purposeful reflection that one remembers how important and necessary Black and Latino Studies were and still are. While our communities demanded and fought for a place in the academy, history has made it clear that we must continuously struggle to remain here against the odds. Empowering students to see themselves reflected in their academic studies is vital and gratifying for those of us engaged in this mission. Our collective power as educators can continue to grow only if we respect each other's discipline and our work both on campus and in the community as colleagues with similar missions in New York City.

The U.S. is facing major racial challenges that many state have not happened since the 1960s. Numerous Black and Latino lives have been lost to violence and succumbed to the structurally racist inequities revealed by the COVID-19 pandemic. In response to these compounding crises, many institutions, including CUNY, have been called to task on how they will seek to bring about equality for Black people and people of color, and effect lasting change amidst this societal shift in demands. While many institutions and corporations have pledged solidarity, only time will tell if their support translates into equity. In the meantime, one way the federal government, New York State, and CUNY can contribute to an anti-racist agenda in society with a two-fold impact is by adequately investing in Black and Latino Studies for all students—thereby improving the value and quality of a higher education and strengthening ethnic studies units that have been doing this type of work for over 50 years.

ACKNOWLEDGMENTS
Thanks to Dr. Pérez y González, Dr. Sánchez Korrol, and Dr. Cordero-Guzmán for inviting me to be part of this important time in our academic history and in our lives. Special thanks to Dr. Arthur Lewin, Professor Lourdes Gil, and Dr. Ana Y. Ramos-Zayas for allowing me to include your contributions to the Department of Black and Latino Studies at Baruch College.

REFERENCES
Belpré, Pura. 1966. *Pérez y Martina: Un cuento folklórico puertorriqueño.* New York: Viking Kestrel.

Bernard-Carreño, Regina A. 2009. *Black and Brown Waves: The Cultural Politics of Young Women of Color and Feminism.* Leiden, The Netherlands: Brill/Sense.

_____. 2010. *Nuyorganics: Organic Intellectualism, the Search for Racial Identity, and Nuyorican Thought.* New York: Peter Lang.

_____. 2014. *Say it Loud: Black Studies, Its Students, and Racialized Collegiate Culture.* New York: Peter Lang.

García, Ana María. 1982. *La Operación.* Latin American Film Project.

Gil, Lourdes. 1993. *Empieza La Ciudad.* Coral Gables, FL: La Torre De Papel.

_____. 2013. *Anima Vagula: parábolas del amor y del poder.* Madrid: Editorial Verbum.

_____. 2020. Interviewed by Regina A. Bernard-Carreño. 1 September.

Lee, Felicia R. 1990. Minorities at Baruch College Charge Neglect of Ethnicity. *The New York Times* 21 April. <https://www.nytimes.com/1990/04/21/nyregion/minorities-at-baruch-college-charge-neglect-of-ethnicity.html>.

Lewin, Arthur. 1991. *Africa Is Not A Country: It's A Continent*. Oxford: Clarendon Press.
_____. 2020. Interviewed by Regina A. Bernard-Carreño. 20 August.
Ramos-Zayas, Ana Y. 2012. *Street Therapists: Race, Affect, and Neoliberal Personhood in Latino Newark*. Chicago: University of Chicago Press.
_____. 2020. Interviewed by Regina A. Bernard-Carreño. 20 July.
Thomas, Piri. 1991. *Down These Mean Streets*. New York: Vintage Books.
Ulaby, Neda. 2016. How NYC's First Puerto Rican Librarian Brought Spanish to the Shelves. *NPR* 8 September. <https://www.npr.org/2016/09/08/492957864/how-nycs-first-puerto-rican-librarian-brought-spanish-to-the-shelves>.

CHAPTER 11

CAMUYANA EN BROOKLYN: REFLECTING ON MY JOURNEY THROUGH PUERTO RICAN AND LATINO STUDIES

Gisely Colón López

In Spring 2015, I became the first Puerto Rican-Latinx Salutatorian to graduate from Brooklyn College, City University of New York (CUNY). My major was Puerto Rican and Latino Studies (PRLS) with a minor in Cultural Anthropology and a concentration in Bilingual Education. I enrolled in the graduate program at the University of Connecticut-Storrs' El Instituto: Institute of Latina/o, Caribbean and Latin American Studies. As part of my graduate work, I conducted extensive research to understand the pioneering vision, goals, and movement that birthed the field of U.S.-based Puerto Rican Studies (PRS), using archival materials and interviews with several of the student activists that contributed to the creation of the Department of Puerto Rican Studies at Brooklyn College, one of the first in the nation. Based on these experiences and as a result of my interactions with various sites of inquiry for the field of Puerto Rican Studies, I share the following story with you.

AS A STUDENT

My academic story begins at CUNY's Eugenio María de Hostos Community College in the Bronx in 2009. I was enrolled in a certificate program for Youth Studies, and this was my introduction to college. Not only did I like the college experience, it melted away any fears, hesitations, and self-doubts I had about pursuing a college degree. After the certificate program, I jumped between a couple of CUNY institutions and earned an Associate degree from New York City College of Technology before finally being accepted into Brooklyn College (BC).

I began my studies at Brooklyn College in 2012, seeking to become a New York State Certified K-12 Bilingual Education Teacher. When I first looked into programs, BC stood out as one of the few colleges that had a teacher preparation program for aspiring bilingual educators. As a child, I knew I wanted to pursue a career in teaching, often serving as a student teaching assistant in elementary school. My introduction to the Department of PRLS occurred because the School of Education required their courses. Historically, the department created the Bilingual (Spanish-English) Teacher Education program. Co-founded by Professors Carmen Dinos and Sonia Nieto, who developed its specialized courses, the School of Education would focus on pedagogy while the department would focus on bilingual theory, second language acquisition, and social studies content. In addition to courses focused on emergent bilingual[1] students (García 2009; García, Kleifgen and Falchi 2008), we were also required to take several foundational courses in PRLS, building historical knowledge about the Spanish-speaking students we were preparing to teach. One of the first courses I took was a foundational course in theories of bilingualism; it was the first time I had a Puerto Rican woman as an instructor in a college classroom.

It was not until my first semester in fall of 2012 at BC, as an undergraduate student taking PRLS courses, that I realized how many more options were available to me beyond the traditional career trajectory embedded into me as a kid. I remember sitting in the theory of bilingualism course, on the first day, hearing Dr. Vanessa Pérez Rosario introduce herself and identify herself as Puerto Rican. My immediate thoughts were, "You can be a Puerto Rican woman and do this as a job? I want to do that." At that very moment, I felt my life had taken a new path. Those thoughts still follow me to this day; a realization of how far I have come and a constant reminder of the impact departments like, and courses offered by, PRLS could have on a student.

As a student preparing to become a bilingual educator, I imagined I would only be taking courses about teaching styles and curriculum for English as a Second Language (ESL) students. PRLS completely transformed this simplistic idea. Subsequent courses and extracurricular programs with PRLS enhanced my formation as a critically engaged individual and member of society, while also equipping me with the tools and skills to analyze, critique and understand the rotting system of education in this country. I also learned about the army of educators, community members, and leaders contributing to new ideas, and bodies of work for students of all languages, races, ethnicities, religions, and experiences.

Institutional inequity prevented me from graduating Brooklyn College with the necessary requirements to become a certified bilingual educator. As a working college student, I was not able to afford an entire semester away from my work obligations to comply with and complete the required student teaching component of the degree I initially sought at BC. Although the School of Education offered an internship-style program through the NYC Department of Education (DOE), with a financial benefit, I was too late learning about it and missed the opportunity to apply. Because of this, I decided to change my major from education to PRLS, preparing me even further to pursue a lifelong ambition to join a community of educators committed to reversing the dismal outcome for traditionally marginalized students the system produces. PRLS prepared me to begin my journey in researching and developing my own ideologies, practices and curriculum for the diverse populations of students I would encounter.

While I envision that I will always be involved in some way or another teaching in different settings, my experience in PRLS solidified my interest in also pursuing a career conducting research and producing new bodies of knowledge. The bilingualism courses developed my understanding of the intersectionalities of systems of education while other PRLS courses revealed layers of the world that had been hidden from me. Prior to PRLS, I had no idea a Ph.D. even existed; at the time I thought the only type of doctor was the medical one. That first semester at BC also introduced me to another Puerto Rican professor, Dr. Miranda Martínez. Her course, "Latin@ Diasporas," exposed me to the fields of sociology and anthropology. When she introduced her own body of research and taught from the book she wrote, *Power at the Roots: Gentrification, Community Gardens, and the Puerto Ricans of the Lower East Side* (2010), I imagined a blueprint for the type of goals and career I wanted to pursue. It took me a couple of weeks to develop the courage to approach her and ask about the difference between the two fields. I was apprehensive and, quite frankly, embarrassed to be a college student—specifically at BC, the place that denied me admission twice—who did not know the difference between the disciplines. She explained it to me, and I decided to take courses in Cultural Anthropology, which is how I ended up graduating with a minor in the field.

It is hard to believe that my life could have changed any further after profound self-realizations those first couple of weeks during my first semester, but it did. This time the department became a major influence. In 2013, the PRLS/María E. Sánchez Center for Latino Studies Undergraduate Research Assistantship sponsored by the CUNY Diversity Projects Development Fund was announced, and the department was accepting applications. I vividly remember reading what it would entail, and I was very interested, almost excited. But, I was no scholar. I had just learned what a Ph.D. was a few weeks before and had fought so hard to get to where I was; in my mind, there was no way I was prepared or qualified to apply to such an amazing program. I saved the flyer with the announcement and promised myself to pursue something similar during graduate school. After all, I thought the assistantship read like graduate level work. Not more than two weeks went by when Dr. Martínez asked me to stay after class one day; she had something she wanted to discuss with me. She expressed her belief that I would be a strong candidate for a research assistantship opportunity being offered by the department. I had not moved beyond my own self-doubts; I remember feeling my face turn warm as she kept describing the details and I thought to myself, "I can't believe what I am hearing...well, if she feels I am qualified, then I will pursue it." I decided to apply and successfully completed the undergraduate research assistantship. I gained an understanding about the process of conducting research and the experience informed me that I was able to do this kind of work. I had discovered an interest in academic research that I could pursue throughout my life. Dr. Alan Aja exposed me to the significance of conducting interviews as part of the research process while understanding how his research eventually became a published book, *Miami's Forgotten Cubans: Race, Racialization, and the Miami Afro-Cuban Experience* (2016). It was transformative to learn that as a result of this assistantship, I would soon see my name somewhere within the pages of a book that could be found in bookstores. Not long after I completed the assistantship, Dr. María E. Pérez y González informed me about the Mellon Mays Undergraduate Fellowship, an Andrew W. Mellon Foundation initiative to increase diversity in the faculty ranks of institutions of higher learning. I applied, was accepted, and engaged in a rigorous scholar-in-training program during my last semesters at BC. These experiences greatly influenced my decision to pursue ethnographic research methods in graduate school.

Immediately after graduating from BC, I began my graduate studies at the University of Connecticut-Storrs (UConn). In this program, I chose to assess the development of the field of Latino Studies, which eventually led me to the story of student-led activism at one of the first PRS departments within CUNY—Brooklyn College, among the epicenters birthing the later field of Latino Studies. Prior to arriving at UConn, I started to learn about the history of PRLS at BC because it was sustained by intergenerational conversations and dialogues embedded throughout the curriculum, teaching practices of PRLS faculty, and interactions with department staff. I was also fortunate to have been one of the last students to take courses and work alongside one of the former pioneering student-activists, Professor Antonio O. Nadal, the longest-serving faculty member of the department before he retired after 43 years. As a result of my time as an undergraduate student in the department, I became keenly aware of how much was still unknown and missing from scholarship and archives regarding this particular history at CUNY as other campuses took prominence as the center of this bi-coastal movement for transformation, inclusion, and Ethnic Studies. My research at UConn further exposed this glaring omittance from scholarship. I acquired my Master of Arts in International Studies from UConn's El Instituto: Institute of Latina/o, Caribbean and Latin American Studies in 2019.

As I culminated my Master of Arts degree, I realized I still had much more to research, uncover, and write regarding the historical, socio-economic, and political roles departments like PRLS have imprinted within the canon, further fueling my interest to pursue a doctoral degree. Motivated by the existence of the CUNY Digital History Archives, I decided to apply to the CUNY Graduate Center's Urban Education program with the expectation to further develop my Master of Arts thesis and body of research. I applied, was accepted, and in the fall of 2020 commenced my first semester as a doctoral student, a dream I would not have imagined had I not encountered the PRLS Department.

EARLY CAREER

During my transition from undergraduate to graduate studies, I worked for the Centro de Estudios Puertorriqueños/Center for Puerto Rican Studies (Centro) at Hunter College-CUNY as a research assistant, oral historian, and in various capacities on several special projects. My experience at Centro solidified my interest in further developing my skills as an academic while exposing me to a very distinct institution of Puerto Rican Studies. I became acquainted with Puerto Rican history in new ways, often through intimate glimpses into the lives of historical figures; reading and seeing archival materials such as the handwritten work of pioneers like Dr. Antonia Pantoja gave me a new perspective about the history of Puerto Rico and Puerto Ricans and the process women like Pantoja endured while affecting change on a national scale. I conducted oral history interviews with New York-based Puerto Ricans who have contributed to sustainable institutional transformation, such as Luis Garden Acosta and Elba Montalvo—visionaries for Williamsburg, Brooklyn's El Puente organization and El Puente Academy for Leadership and Justice, and The Committee for Hispanic Children and Families, Inc., respectively; both continued to expand the production of knowledge for the field and also preserved stories of victories and possibilities for authentic social change. My community experience resulting from my work with Centro taught me about the enormous responsibility institutions, such as a public university, have for and in partnership with the communities they represent. My work with Centro expanded into the New England area through programming and initiatives, such as the New England Puerto Rico, Puerto Ricans Summit, and the Puerto Rican Heritage Cultural Ambassadors Program, established to extend and teach about the history and culture of Puerto Ricans both in the U.S. and Puerto Rico.

As an adjunct at CUNY since 2018, I have worked for the Department of Latin American and Latino Studies (formerly Latin American, Latino, and Puerto Rican Studies) at Lehman College, PRLS at Brooklyn College, and for the College Now Program, a collaboration between the NYC Department of Education and CUNY for high school students to earn college credits while also preparing for the transition to the university. Through these experiences, I have gained a deeper understanding, appreciation, and intensified motivation to advocate for the expansion and sustainability of the field of Ethnic Studies, particularly Puerto Rican and Latinx Studies. Each teaching experience has been distinct at each campus, primarily because of the unique high school and post-secondary demographic differences of the student populations. What has remained consistent is the vast amount of unknown aspects of history regarding Puerto Ricans and Latinx peoples that students bring to the classroom. It is a delicate balance at the end of the semester between an appreciation that students communicate about how much they have learned and grown in skill set for the many aspects of their lives, and the painful realization that our school systems and curriculums are not yet teaching about these particular historical contributions and their impact on global societies.

Puerto Rican and Latinx Studies as Praxis

My PRLS background was essential when I began working at a middle school with a predominantly Puerto Rican and Latino/a student body in New England, which was vastly different from any classroom in New York City I had experienced as either a student or Department of Education employee. The school made me feel like I was transported to the 1970s and '80s, when the majority of Spanish-speaking students in NYC public schools were Puerto Rican. It reminded me of the school environments I read about in books and articles by educators like Dr. Sonia Nieto and Dr. Luis Reyes. I was grateful PRLS exposed me to that particular aspect of American history because it informed my interactions with the students. The majority of students came from different *pueblos* (towns) in Puerto Rico, and some were second-generation Puerto Ricans. There were also several other nations represented, including the Dominican Republic, Colombia, Guatemala, and Honduras. Most of these students, including several from Puerto Rico, were recent arrivals to the United States. My studies with PRLS prepared me to understand the differences not only among the Puerto Rican student population, but also the students from other parts of the Caribbean and Latin America. I was equipped with the knowledge, understanding, and pedagogical tools to engage students while also facilitating their own placement and consciousness within history and society, for the present time and their future.

269

One particular example of how my PRLS experience became helpful with this population of students was during a math class. One of my responsibilities was to work with the math teacher and the emergent bilingual students in her class. Language varieties matter, and I quickly picked up on the different ways of discussing math in Spanish because the students would teach me the vocabulary they knew from their native *pueblos* (towns). Even though the school policy was to rely on Google Translate as an attempt to bridge the linguistic divide between the majority of staff and students, the translations did not reflect the many variations of Spanish and Indigenous languages spoken by the youth, often stifling student content learning. I remember working with a student from Guatemala: her answers to the math problems were always correct. The issue was the work she produced. Her method of solving math was not the same method the teacher used during the lesson; it was one she learned at school in Guatemala. Although she was reaching the correct answer, systemic pressures forced her to learn the method taught by the math teacher because of the institutional goal of preparing her for the state exams she would have to take in a few years. These exams require you to show your work and are graded based on the method used to solve the problem. This is also an example of how cultural and historic knowledge from non-European methodologies in the United States are often erased and devalued to fit into a system reproducing outcomes primarily benefiting a socio-economic structure designed to make profit for a slim percentage of people harboring wealth resulting from what is often referred to as the "hidden curriculum of work" within systems of education (Anyon 1980). Anyon's study found that students from different social classes are taught differently based on a hidden, often subconscious, curriculum producing occupational goals for a future workforce.

A major takeaway from PRLS courses was how much history and stories of people have been erased from spaces of learning, balanced with the knowledge of agency that multi-ethnic and multi-racial people and their communities possess in enacting authentic, action-based transformative change. Although I was born a Camuyana[2] in Puerto Rico, and grew up in New York City with a vibrant Puerto Rican identity, it was not until my undergraduate tenure with PRLS that I began to learn about Puerto Rico, the Island, its history, its people, and the many facets of the Puerto Rican diaspora. Learning about this particular history enabled me to process and understand my own realities, and those of the communities I am a part of, fortifying stronger bonds and more equitable collaborations. In addition to expanding my understanding of public education, bilingual education and the theories, pedagogies, and ideologies surrounding such topics, I was also exposed to the intersectionality between gender, class, immigration, and social movements.

Learning about the student movement at Brooklyn College during the 1960s and '70s transformed my understanding of what it means to be alive. Inspired by the actions of demonstrations, office takeovers, and organizing within the college and surrounding communities, I became more conscious of my own actions, critically analyzing the ways I had decided to live up until that point in my life. I became more involved on campus and with community initiatives to address systemic inequities and contribute to community building and empowerment. My role as a student and maturing scholar evolved into acts of resistance. As a PRLS student, I learned about theorists and visionaries such as Antonia Pantoja, Paulo Freire, and Gloria Anzaldúa, who continue to inform various aspects of my life, both personally and academically. My research is inextricably linked to this personal growth and development because of the academic gaze used as a tool to research and learn through. As a self-identified community-engaged scholar, I make every effort to be inclusive of and to sustain the groups I choose to work with; my aim is to avoid any academic exploitation of peoples, their communities, intelligence, and assets.

It was because of PRLS courses that I learned about my undocumented, and DACAmented[3] *hermanas* and *hermanos* (sisters and brothers). For instance, as a person born in Puerto Rico, I was not aware of my own citizenship privilege until the day I was in conversation with a friend and impassively responded to their excited announcement that they obtained their green card. My experiences never forced me to question my own constitutional rights, let alone the rights of others who risked their lives for a better and new opportunity in this world. Through PRLS courses and interactions with peers and friends, the enormity of that moment my friend so candidly shared was revealed to me. PRLS also enabled me to learn about my own linguistic biases, an essential mirror to acknowledge and confront as an educator. For instance, prior to my experience in PRLS, I never questioned my use of the term *Amer-*

ican, as a subconscious, monolithic label, ignoring the nations, peoples, and histories north and south of the United States who are also Americans.

My commitment to Puerto Rican and Latino/a studies is strong and exists whether or not I decide to pursue a career within these fields. There is a serious need for these particular bodies of knowledge, along with Africana, Asian, and Indigenous Studies, especially today, more than 50 years after their initial adoption into the academy. It is this very institutionalization of the once grassroots movement that creates a specific need for sustainability and a continued assessment of validity for community integration and impact reminiscent of the original vision and goals for such departments, programs, and production of knowledge. Beyond the consistently proven benefits of student identity development (Sleeter 2011), the fields of Puerto Rican and Latino/a Studies inform our collective today and tomorrows. The Latino/a population in the U.S. continues to grow; between 2010 and 2019, Latinos/as in the U.S. increased from 16 percent to 18 percent, accounting for 52 percent of all U.S. population growth (Noe-Bustamante, López and Krogstad 2020). It is imperative that all sectors of society become familiar with and have a deep understanding of the various sources of knowledge within the fields of Puerto Rican and Latino/a Studies in response to this growing demographic. More specifically, sites of inquiry within the field of Puerto Rican Studies are essential to understanding the 2019 uprising in Puerto Rico against Governor Roselló, as well as the complexities of the disaster response after Hurricanes Irma and María in 2017; both events linked to global issues impacting the lives of people. Puerto Rican Studies reveals aspects of history excluded from traditional academic discourse, such as the complexities of colonization and the anti-colonial struggles for unity and inclusion that have prompted people like me to occupy spaces that were not designed for us. Without Puerto Rican or Latino/a Studies, current and future generations will not know what was possible, or worse, what continues to be possible. Historic examples of this includes Open Admissions at CUNY, when any NYC high school graduate interested in attending the public university was eligible to do so as long as they qualified within the merit-based admissions policy for the four-year colleges (Fabricant and Brier 2016; Okechukwu 2019), or California's AB 2016 bill enabling a model curriculum for Ethnic Studies to be developed and implemented as a graduation requirement for high school students in the state.

CRITIQUES

While I am firm in my advocacy for the fields of Puerto Rican and Latino/a Studies, I am also critical of its shortcomings, including the academic institutionalization that has stripped it from its original goals of community engagement and student decision-making power. An unfortunate reality is that these community and student empowerment goals, fundamental to the original student-activist demands and for the optimal functioning of departments and programs of Puerto Rican Studies, have too often been diminished due to administrative budget cuts and other inadequate bureaucratic policies that stifle their growth and leave little room for a beneficial Puerto Rican Studies and community partnership. Often, community and student collaborations are in the form of internships lasting one semester, void of much-needed time to build up neighborhood resources and are instead designed to accommodate the academic calendar. For instance, staff at local community-based organizations (CBOs) have to reintroduce new college students to their organization and the role they will play during their internship—often every semester or every other semester—while also taking time away from their already overburdened duties as CBOs, to develop a rapport between the student representing the institution and the network within the CBO, inclusive of its stakeholders.

This process usually takes a couple of weeks, and often does not account for the delayed internship placement period that results in even less time for interactions between the student and CBOs, hindering both the student learning experience and the purpose of the internship objective. Through my own experiences, I have become keenly aware of the powered-down voice and loss of decision-making power students possess, even as they are further embedded into institutional co-optation through institutionally monitored student clubs and programs. This is not to critique the existence of such clubs and programs as part of the college experience, as they do contribute to a unique multi-dimensional learning opportunity for students, but rather to question their effectiveness in developing the next generation of leaders, doers, and thinkers away from the constraints of systemic oppression that academia often recycles.

During the early phase of PRS at Brooklyn College, a childcare center was developed as a solution for community members that needed both a culturally and linguistically relevant and reflective educational environment for their families. This childcare center, La Escuelita Bilingüe (The Little Bilingual School), brought together BC students, faculty, staff, and community members as integral agents of change. Other anti-colonial, liberatory strands of PRS engaged students in decision-making processes that impacted policy and practices that directly affected them without having to wait to be invited to some of these select spaces, as is the practice today. Students also helped sustain the department by serving in administrative roles that exposed them to all aspects of the university system, further building their skills set, while also enabling them to make decisions in the best interest of their department.

A Legacy of Achievement

Right before I graduated from Brooklyn College, I learned about a new organization, still in the stage of formation, consisting of many of the pioneering student-activists that were part of the early development of PRS and sister struggles during the 1960s. The Alliance for Puerto Rican Education and Empowerment (APREE) sought to continue the legacy of this action-oriented intergenerational community of people while developing practices and philosophies that further empower and transform the Puerto Rican community. The mission of APREE is to advocate for social transformation through programs focused on education and the advancement of the Puerto Rican community. I dedicated myself to APREE to gain a deeper understanding of the process and intricacies of grassroots community-building, especially because of the more than five decades worth of expertise and experience from the now mostly retired group members.

My commitment to APREE also became a personal endeavor as an opportunity to join the legacy of achievement still growing, as a way to actively give back to the movement that transformed my life. Some of the outcomes APREE has attained include the implementation of a readers theater-style community-building program for NYC high school students; funds for college scholarships; publications focused on asset-based approaches to inform policy and social transformation, and advocacy letters and statements in support of PRLS at BC; hosting cultural events to preserve and celebrate Puerto Rican history and culture; and the production of a short educational film discussing the story about the creation of PRS at BC, *Making the Impossible Possible: The Story of Puerto Rican Studies in Brooklyn College.*

FIVE DECADES OF PUERTO RICAN AND LATINO STUDIES

The 50-year commemoration of the Department of Puerto Rican and Latino Studies at Brooklyn College is coinciding with a national intensity of civil unrest many say has not been felt or seen since the 1960s. The collective *lucha* (struggle) from the mid-20th century peak never stopped, and the current uprisings of 2020 are proof of this. The Ethnic Studies movement and its acts of resistance over the last five decades in the U.S. gave birth to new forms of thought and inquiry, while also opening up spaces for the voices of those historically silenced and omitted over centuries of colonialism in this hemisphere. All of these movements are intertwined, and the legacy of PRS at BC is one of the many survivors of this intergenerational fight. I share this reflection as testament and acknowledgment that I was able to experience this educational transformation because of the visions and revolutionary struggles of those that were deprived of such an opportunity. My work, academically and personally, is directly impacted by this legacy; I make every effort to do my part in keeping the movement alive, whether it is through my teaching philosophy; dedicating time and effort to grassroots, community-oriented initiatives and programs; or acts of self-love and appreciation for who I am and the intergenerational force I continue to be a part of. It is because of movements like the one for U.S.-based Puerto Rican Studies fifty years ago that public education students have better prepared teachers to understand and value the rich and distinct backgrounds and realities of their students. Advocacy for Ethnic Studies curricula continues to emerge, albeit slowly, and be implemented across the nation, reaching new demographics and populations of people under the yoke of institutional structures still driven by a Euro-colonial mode of operation. As an alumna of PRLS, I invite you to join the movement advocating for the growth and sustainability of the fields of Puerto Rican, Latino/a, and all strands of Ethnic Studies because it strengthens and enlightens us as globally interconnected peoples.

NOTES

[1] A more productive, equitable, and asset-based term for English Language Learners.

[2] Camuyana is a term used to refer to people from Camuy, Puerto Rico, my hometown and residence as a toddler.

[3] A term used by formerly undocumented individuals that qualified for the 2012 Deferred Action for Childhood Arrivals (DACA) program, temporarily preventing them from deportation while gaining eligibility for a work permit in the U.S.

REFERENCES

Aja, Alan A. 2016. *Miami's Forgotten Cubans: Race, Racialization, and the Miami Afro-Cuban Experience.* New York: Springer.

Anyon, Jean. 1980. Social Class and the Hidden Curriculum of Work. *Journal of Education* 162 (1), 67–92.

Fabricant, Michael and Stephen Brier. 2016. *Austerity Blues: Fighting for the Soul of Public Higher Education.* Baltimore: Johns Hopkins University Press.

García, Ofelia. 2009. Emergent Bilinguals and TESOL: What's in a Name? *TESOL Quarterly* 43(2), 322–26.

García, Ofelia, Jo Anne Kleifgen and Lorraine Falchi. 2008. From English Language Learners to Emergent Bilinguals. Equity Matters. *Research Review No. 1. Campaign for Educational Equity,* Teachers College, Columbia University.

Martínez, Miranda J. 2010. *Power at the Roots: Gentrification, Community Gardens, and the Puerto Ricans of the Lower East Side.* Lanham, MD: Lexington Books.

Noe-Bustamante, Luis, Mark Hugo López and Jens Manuel Krogstad. 2020. U.S. Hispanic Population Surpassed 60 Million in 2019, but Growth Has Slowed. Pew Research Center 7 July. <https://www.pewresearch.org/fact-tank/2020/07/07/u-s-hispanic-population-surpassed-60-million-in-2019-but-growth-has-slowed>.

Okechukwu, Amaka. 2019. *To Fulfill These Rights: Political Struggle Over Affirmative Action and Open Admissions.* New York: Columbia University Press.

Sleeter, Christine E. 2011. The Academic and Social Value of Ethnic Studies: A Research Review. Washington, DC: National Education Association Research Department.

CHAPTER 12

REFLECTIONS ON A RETURN TO LEHMAN COLLEGE

Andrés Torres

There are special moments in life that return you to past experiences. You encounter episodes of coming "full circle": running into a long-lost friend; happening upon an eatery that once sustained you; coming across a novel buried in the stacks of a second-hand bookstore, a book that changed you forever. In September 2010, I returned to Lehman College (City University of New York—CUNY) as a Distinguished Lecturer in Puerto Rican/Latin@ studies. There I was, once again, in Carman Hall where my career as a college educator began thirty-five years earlier.[1]

In truth, back in the early 1970s I was hardly equipped to teach "History of Puerto Rico." My only knowledge of my parents' homeland came from my activism in Puerto Rican political movements in New York City, primarily as a *militante* of the Puerto Rican Socialist Party (PSP). I had also taught Puerto Rican history in an after-school program operated by Evelina Antonetty's United Bronx Parents (UBP). But, UBP's middle-school youths had not prepared me for Lehman's students. I had a master's degree, but that was in economics.

SOME HISTORICAL NOTES

The first departmental meeting in the fall of 2010 introduced me to faculty colleagues and to the projects and concerns that would absorb my energies in the new decade. In prior years, Puerto Rican Studies (PRS) at Lehman had been merged into a new department, Latin American and Puerto Rican Studies (LAPRS). This was a consequence of the steady erosion of CUNY budget cuts since the 1980s and of Lehman faculty and administrators' response to financial constraints. It was an adaptation distinct from that of other campuses, in which alternative formulas were implemented. Other partners were identified for merger or expansion: Africana Studies, Latino Studies, or Caribbean Studies.

That meeting in the fall of 2010 took up yet a new approach, a proposal to broaden the departmental mission to include Latin@ Studies. In two years, the Department of Latin American, Latino and Puerto Rican Studies (LALPRS) was established. Simultaneously, the idea for housing an Institute for Mexican Studies at the college was broached. This was the result of discussions between some LALPRS faculty, Lehman President Ricardo R. Fernández, the CUNY central office, and the Mexican Consulate. These proposals were taking into account the well-documented changes in the demography of Lehman students and the Bronx communities in which the college was rooted.

Already by the millennium, the most striking change was the rising presence of Dominicans among the Lehman student population. The rate of population growth of Dominican New Yorkers was positioning this group to eventually surpass the population of Puerto Ricans, traditionally the largest Hispanic subgroup. Though the Washington Heights section of Manhattan was viewed as the "home" of the community, it was in the Bronx where the largest number of Dominicans lived. Lehman was, therefore, ideally situated to benefit from rising Dominican enrollment over time. Also, the upper Heights (181st Street) and the Inwood area (around 207th Street) were a bus ride away. For those whose academic credentials fell short of Lehman's entry requirements, there was the option of starting out at Bronx Community or Hostos Community colleges, then transferring to Lehman. In the almost seven years of teaching at the college, the largest single group of students in my classes was Dominican, most of them female.

Mexican-Americans were also a growing force in the city, indeed expanding at a more robust pace than even Dominicans, though not yet attaining the population levels of Puerto Ricans and Dominicans. CUNY's welcoming attitude toward the undocumented, and support for DACA (Deferred Action for Childhood Arrivals), made campuses like Lehman a natural choice for the aspirations of Mexican-Americans. The Bronx was also home to many of these students. Lehman was not the only campus interested in providing a home to the CUNY Institute of Mexican Studies, but Lehman prevailed in the informal competition for that role.[2] The original idea was that the institute would be a place for studying conditions and policies related to Mexico and that the Consulate could be helpful in raising financial support. But, given demographic realities, it was argued and agreed that the institute "should have an actual link to Mexican-Americans living in the New York area and that it should promote both academic and grassroots initiatives" (Fiol-Matta 2010, 2). Eventually, the institute also established a scholarship fund for students across CUNY. The founding director was Alyshia Gálvez, a LALPRS faculty member.

The logic for the departmental name change was obvious, despite misgivings within some circles that including "Latino" confirmed the dwindling profile of Puerto Ricans in CUNY and the City. Still, one could not ignore the fact that the demand for courses addressing the experience of other Latin@ populations was growing, not only for Dominicans and Mexicans, but among non-Latin@ populations as well.

As the years progressed, department meetings took up the need for self-assessment and curriculum change in the face of threatened budget cuts across CUNY and the college. We knew that the majority of our majors were in education-related fields: early childhood education, teacher prep, educational counseling, and bilingual education. Latin@ studies provided a solid background for professionals wanting to serve the booming population of Latin@ students in the city's public school system.

An internal self-study tracked the graduation of LAPRS students (before its change to LALPRS) during the mid-2000s to the early 2010s and found that growth had more than doubled (Torres 2014, 1). The percentage increase of LAPRS students graduating Lehman outpaced the percentage increase of the general student population who graduated over the same time period. Comparison of proportions so widely differentiated in size are extremely problematic. Yet, what was true of combined LAPRS graduation numbers was not true of the PRS graduates among them, which was relatively small and remained so over time. Upon the name change, data on majors and minors similarly showed that enrollments in the LAL component were outpacing those in PRS. Questions regarding course offerings had to be addressed. LALPRS courses registered a good number of Lehman students, typically three hundred each semester, because they satisfied general education requirements. But, institutionally, a department's "value" mirrored the metric of majors and minors, which determines whether faculty lines are allocated, not just total enrollments.

In time, new courses were created shifting from Puerto Rico-focused content to generic Latin@ content or other-Latin@ populations. For example, offerings in "Latino Media," "Religions in Latin America, the Caribbean, and Latin@ U.S.," "Latino New York," "Haitian-Dominican Border Nation," and "Latino Health" were introduced. Classes that for years were under-enrolled were eliminated: "Political Parties in Puerto Rico, 1869 to the Present," "Puerto Rican Literature: Genre Studies," and "Puerto Rican Historiography." Others were restructured or consolidated to appeal to more students: "The Economy of Puerto Rico" and "Variable Topics in Puerto Rican Studies".

In 2010, I was appointed to the department as a Distinguished Lecturer (DL), joining a group of eight full-time faculty.[3] I was given the freedom to teach my interests (what a luxury!); but I understood that to be useful I should not restrict myself to Puerto Rican-focused subjects, an area in which the department was already very strong. This was not an issue for me since my own research and teaching had, since the 1980s, expanded to comparative studies of Puerto Ricans with African Americans and other Latin@ populations.

Increasing the enrollment of majors involved several ideas, which were introduced over the years: diversifying course offerings, mounting a greater profile in the Student Fair (of the School of Arts and Humanities), producing an updated department brochure, creating an active Facebook page, sponsoring an annual Open House and Christmas party, and reaching out to LALPRS alumni.[4] One obstacle to a significant expansion of majors was the perception by pragmatically minded students that career advancement lay in the occupational tracks of nursing, counseling, teaching, etc. One cannot fault them for thinking this way, though this is a sad commentary about the state of affairs in public higher education and the future labor economy. In undervaluing the humanities are we not undermining civil society?

SURVIVAL AND LONGEVITY

Lehman's offerings in Puerto Rican and Latin@ Studies date from the late 1960s. Indeed, the Department of Puerto Rican Studies was the very first one in the CUNY system when the Board of Higher Education approved its creation on June 30, 1969. It was also the only separate Department of Puerto Rican Studies established that year; the other units were either institutes or programs (Brooklyn and Queens Colleges), broad ethnic studies (City and John Jay Colleges) or combined departments (Hunter College) (CUNY Board of Higher Education Minutes, May 9, June 30, and July 22, 1969; Totti 2020). This was in the aftermath of Black and Puerto Rican student mobilizations on campus during that time, involving takeovers of faculty meetings and occupations of campus buildings. These actions were carried out with demands for bringing in more minority students and faculty. November 2019 marked the 50th anniversary of the department, which has survived multiple challenges and changes over the years, involving restructurings, mergers, recasting of mission and at least one repeat wave of student activism in the late 1980s (Lehman Marks 50 Years... 2019).

While there has been drama and contention across the decades, my impression is that the department's longevity is attributable to more mundane factors. Demographic change, political astuteness of faculty and administrator-allies, faculty scholarship, and extra-departmental "activism"—each has contributed to a winning formula for survival. The sheer weight of demographic change has spurred a vibrant and continuing demand for the department's instructional services. That the department was able to adapt to the changing Latin@ ethnic composition of that demand is a testament to the flexibility and creativity that is required for prevailing in the Ivory Tower's bureaucratic infighting.[5] It was advantageous that LALPRS had an unofficial ally in Lehman's top administrator, Dr. Ricardo R. Fernández. Fernández was a nationally recognized university leader and an active public figure in the Bronx and well beyond. Through the years, he created and sustained a climate of relative stability and oversaw construction of new facilities. In 2016, he retired, concluding a tenure of 26 years as Lehman's president, the longest ever to have served in such a position in the CUNY system.

Internally, the department was composed of a solid core of veteran and younger academics, several of whom had extensive administrative experience. Administrative skill is a quality not often in abundance within the professoriate. After what can turn out to be a 10- to 15-year marathon from doctoral studies to a tenure-track position, few are attuned to, much less enthusiastic about, "pushing paper" or dealing with human resource and budgetary issues. It is not why young intellectuals get into the field of higher education. We were a group of experienced and politically savvy educators; some verging on veteran burnout perhaps, but as a whole fully capable of defending our interests and that of our students.[6] During my years, there was one new full-time hire that was authorized for LALPRS, which helped slightly to improve unit diversity by age, race, and ethnicity.

Faculty scholarship is another reason for the long-term continuity of LALPRS. Among the topics addressed in books published by the faculty are the following: Latin@ history, ethnicity, and contributions in New England and Michigan, as well as a case study in a New York City neighborhood; a historical and demographic overview of Hispanics since the 1980s; Latin@ religiosity and the new immigrant church; the end of ideological struggles and the rise of liberalism in Latin America; an assessment of Gabriela Mistral, queer Chilena poet and feminist; a critical analysis of four iconic Puerto Rican women singers (Lucecita Benítez, Mirta Silva, Ruth Fernández, and Ernestina Reyes); politics and spirituality in movements for citizenship among Mexicans in New York City; an examination of the "Latina health paradox" among Mexican immigrant women; and Puerto Rican tobacco farmers in the early 20th century and their challenge to U.S. colonialism. Additional topics include political dynamics of Dominicans in New York City; a treatment of how Dominicans have asserted their African heritage, thereby subverting official history and culture; and a memoir of a hearing son in a New York Puerto Rican deaf family. There are also numerous articles in journals and chapters published in edited volumes that comprise a highly productive level of academic output that has brought prestige to CUNY.[7]

The work spearheaded by Laird Bergad, LALS faculty member and Director of the CUNY Graduate Center's Center for Latin American, Caribbean, and Latino Studies (CLACLS), has created a cadre of reputable resources useful for policy makers, scholars, and the community alike. LALS faculty member Xavier Totti, Editor of *CENTRO Journal* since the early 2000s and concurrently of Centro Press, heads a font of scholarship in Puerto Rican and Latin@ studies.

There is a level of "activism" required if a department is to project its importance to the college. This involves programming campus activities and creating alliances with other units in the campus community. Whether screening films and documentaries, presenting scholars reporting on their research, sponsoring celebrations of Hispanic Heritage Month, organizing special panel discussions on immigration legislation or Puerto Rican history, LALPRS could be counted on for a wide range of offerings to the campus. One of the last events I participated in, on an early November day of 2016, will stay in my mind for a very long time. I was tasked to give welcoming remarks to an LAL-PRS-sponsored conference with the theme "Latinos, National Politics and the 2016 Election." To lighten my delivery, I compared election day to an annual wellness visit. If the doctor's assessment is positive, so is your health status. If the election outcome is positive, so is your subjective feeling about the state of American democracy. The surprising results to come in the following week left me dreading the four years to follow. President Trump's demonization of immigrants, especially Mexican immigrants, and his handling of the economic crisis and Hurricane María in Puerto Rico, to say nothing of his complete inability to promote social harmony, confirmed my worst fears.

LALPRS had numerous linkages with other programs and initiatives in the School of Humanities, the college, across CUNY, and with professional and community associations. Faculty was very active at the (CLACLS). Some professors taught at the Graduate Center (GC), including in its Master's Program in Latino Studies. GC doctoral students were recruited as adjuncts in the department. As previously mentioned, LALPRS was instrumental in the establishment of the CUNY Center for Mexican Studies. There were also initiatives in international programming with Cuba and the Dominican Republic headed by Teresita A. Levy and Milagros Ricourt, respectively. Faculty members assisted as mentors for the Urban Male Leadership Program, closely tied to the Africana Studies Department; and participated in the college-wide Diversity Council and in several faculty governance bodies. LALPRS worked arduously to counter the silo syndrome that pervades many institutions of higher learning. These strategies enabled LALPRS to maintain a vibrant presence in the institution.

BACK IN THE CLASSROOM

During the youthful years when I was pursuing my doctoral degree in economics at the New School for Social Research, I had lectured in private and public colleges, including Lehman, and worked as a Centro researcher, benefitting from then Director Frank Bonilla's mentorship. In the early nineties, I took a position at the University of Massachusetts at Boston (UMB). I became part of the Labor Studies Program at the College of Public and Community Service and taught economics and labor studies in a competency-based curriculum. Later at UMB, I directed the Mauricio Gastón Institute for Latino Community Development and Public Policy. The Institute, now in existence for thirty years, still engages in a wide spectrum of activities: publishing scholarly research on Latin@ conditions in the region, providing student support programs such as the Latino Leadership Opportunity Program, and convening statewide policy conferences. It was during this period that I became Full Professor. The mid-2000s found me back in New York City in research and administrative roles at Centro, including a stint as Interim Director and directing a CUNY faculty diversity project.

I then entered the Distinguished Lecturer phase of my teaching career at Lehman College where I covered several courses: "Latin@s in the U.S.," "Latino Urban Development and Policy Issues," "Latino Political Economy," and "Latino New York." Generally focusing on the history and political economy of the Latin@ experience, I viewed each class as a performance, integrating several modes of education. Aside from direct instruction, I facilitated small-group discussions, devised prompts for in-class unannounced quizzes, had students lead "seminars" on assigned readings, and presented visual media. Rarely did I invite guest lecturers. Why should I? There was a lot of ground to cover, and these were *my* students, *my* responsibility, not to be shared with others. They were a captive audience for a short time, and I was intent on delivering the goods personally. Electronic Blackboard was a convenient technology to store assigned readings and for communication. But, I did not favor PowerPoint presentations. I used the *real* blackboard and chalk. By the time students arrived, I had already outlined my lecture. I resisted teaching online classes, which struck me as a retreat from quality education, except, of course, for those who can only access higher education through distance learning.[8] I suspect that my senior status may have contributed to the respect for "house rules" and to my style of classroom management. In any case, my philosophy was clearly stated in the syllabuses: "Our goal is to create a learning community in which all opinions are welcome. We will observe standard rules for mutual respect and understanding in the classroom." Of course, there were challenges: most students were not oriented toward abstract thinking, so I gradually reduced theoretical content; many students were intimidated by math, so I struggled to make quantitative material accessible and interesting. A full discussion of the challenges and lessons learned in my teaching experience would require a much more extended treatment. These challenges were offset by students' openness to talk about their backgrounds and life stories, and their willingness to share opinions about current policy issues, topics of racial and ethnic identity, and, in general, the state of the world! In the end I received fairly positive evaluations from my students, though there were two things I received complaints about: my lectures could be too long, and I was not the most exciting and dynamic professor to have taught them. I plead guilty. In my defense, I can report their positive feedback: I was very organized, they learned a lot from me, I encouraged their participation, and I graded fairly.

Take-Aways

On Monday evening, December 19, 2016, I left my classroom on the second floor of Carman Hall. In my shoulder bag were bundles of blue books, containing my students' final exams. A week later, I submitted grade rosters for my classes, closing out the semester. Previously that year, having "crunched the numbers" again and again, determining that I could afford to end my teaching career—the third one, that is—I put in my retirement papers. My final semester ended, bringing me full circle as a lecturer at Lehman College.

Among the more gratifying aspects of the Lehman experience is learning the impact I had on my students. Some were simply glad to have had a Puerto Rican/Latin@ at the front of the classroom. To be told that you made them believe they 'too' could achieve a career dream, that you made them feel proud of their history and culture—these are wonderful things. To be thanked for making them aware of Latin@ contributions to U.S. society; for making them aware more fully of American history itself, this is very satisfying. Equally gratifying is having possession of a store of anecdotes and memories shared in student presentations, as mini-essays, or in confidential talks with me. Substituting pseudonyms for my students' names, I will share a few impressionable ones here.

There is Ricardo's account of being arrested at Citi Field in Queens after he ran across the outfield in the middle of a Mets game. With a fellow student, he carried aloft a banner protesting the latest anti-immigrant measure by the U.S. Congress. Ricardo, a Puerto Rican, and his Mexican-American *camarada* (comrade) were activists with the Lehman "Dream Team" organization. As a U.S. citizen by birth, Ricardo's stance had special resonance. He was demonstrating his solidarity across the boundaries of citizenship and Latin@ identity.

Then, there was Xiomára, a young Dominican, who revealed that she had recently learned that *mami*, who raised her, was actually her *tía*; the distant "aunt" who visited occasionally was her blood mother. *Mami* and *Tía* were sisters. She explained how this shocking revelation about her true identity and origins changed her life. Disoriented and distracted from her studies, she dropped out of college. Untangling her past and coming to terms with the meaning of all this was to absorb all of her attention for some time. I learned later that she had entered graduate school for a degree in school counseling.

I always tried to be an open and accessible professor. But, certain situations will deter a student from revealing a personal problem. Margarita, a Central American, had unaccountably disappeared from class toward the end of a semester in which she was doing very well. I had to assign her the grade of "Incomplete." Months later I approached a friend of hers asking if she knew what happened. Margarita wound up homeless, fleeing a household crisis. I wondered aloud why she didn't tell me. We could have worked things out. Her friend responded that she was ashamed.

Manuel was assigned to lead a class discussion on a Pew Foundation research report. The article summarized survey results on the experiences and attitudes among young Latin@s across the country. He argued that the report gave a one-sided interpretation of street gangs. Manuel did not feel negatively about gang members and pushed back when his classmates agreed with the report's anti-gang perspective. He explained that his father had been a principal drug dealer in the area, but the local toughs, instead of recruiting Manuel, actually "got on his case" if he seemed about to fall into their world. On his way to middle school, the guys would salute him with "high fives" and encourage him to do well. They seemed to get a sense of pride that "one of them" was going to succeed in the world outside of the barrio. He may have been the beneficiary of a privileged status, given his father's position (it was not clear what became of his father), and he was not about to publicly reject the street gangs of his youth.

Then, there was Michael, quiet but insightful with his occasional interventions in class. He was a DACA (Deferred Action for Childhood Arrivals)[9] student and a campus leader of the Lehman "Dream Team." He worked in a Bronx non-profit organization that assisted immigrants facing deportation due to incarceration or other interactions with law enforcement. He was also concerned about his mother's legal status. None of these demands stopped him from taking a full-time course load and achieving a high grade point average.

I remember other students, if only in flashes of recollection. The U.S. Army veteran, a Latino immigrant with a heavy accent and right-wing politics. He had no qualms criticizing the liberal leanings of his classmates who tolerated his comments. I wondered whether there was some irony here. Then, the young, white Midwesterner who chose to study at Lehman where a good 80 percent of the students were students of color. Her gentle disposition and friendly manner obliterated barriers of communication. There was the *Boricua* (Puerto Rican) and the Mexican-American couple who met in class and eventually partnered; both smart and struggling financially, and they decided to face the world together. Later, I heard from them that they were doing graduate studies and had a growing family.

A central theme in my courses was the idea that the Latin@ experience involves a reciprocal dynamic: as they are changed by being in the United States of America, Latin@s also help to transform the United States of America. The first part of that equation is taken for granted; the second part is often ignored. Something analogous can be said of the relation between my students and me. From the first day of class it was my goal to change their lives for the better, however slightly. Retrospectively, I perceive certain lessons they conveyed to me; this despite the fact that I was very much like them at their age and a student-activist. The students' stories reveal their sheer determination to succeed in the face of poverty, homelessness, and other obstacles; the high value they attach to family and culture; their intention to give back to the communities they came from; and the commitment to risk-taking solidarity for positive social change. However, I am also aware of the resistance to Latin@ aspirations that persists in large swaths of the U.S. population. Fear, ignorance, and problematic ideologies remain prevalent. Nevertheless, these narratives affirm my sense that Latin@s are on a journey of collective self-uplift and transformation of the society they inhabit.

The enduring change that most affects me is that my students continue to give me hope for the future.

NOTES

[1] This essay is based on personal archives and recollection. It covers the period of my employment at Lehman from 2010-2017. I am deeply appreciative to Carmen Vivian Rivera, María E. Pérez y González, and Virginia E. Sánchez-Korrol for their feedback and suggestions.

[2] It was later renamed the Jaime Lucero Institute for Mexican Studies at CUNY, still located at Lehman. In 1992, at the City College of New York (CUNY), the Dominican Studies Institute (DSI) was established as a home for research, scholarship, and educational opportunities on behalf of the Dominican population. It is also involved in community engagement initiatives.

[3] At the time, DLs were a discretionary non-tenured line made available to campuses at the discretion of the CUNY Chancellor's Office. I am grateful to the following who were instrumental in originally facilitating my appointment: Jay Hershenson, Vita Rabinowitz, Ricardo R. Fernández, Timothy Alborn, Xavier Totti, and David Badillo. My colleagues at LALPRS were: David Badillo, Laird Bergad, Forrest Colburn, Licia Fiol-Matta, Alyshia Gálvez, Teresita Levy, Milagros Ricourt, and Xavier Totti. Before I left, we were joined by Sarah Ohmer. Previously, Fiol-Matta had accepted a position at New York University. Several faculty held joint positions with other departments or units. Lecturers and adjuncts at the time included Magdalena Sagardia, John González, and Gisely Colón López. Not to be overlooked was the department secretary, the ever-loyal Veronica Mason.

[4] At the start of Academic Year 2013-14, my estimate is that there were 73 majors in LALPRS. I am unable to determine the number as of my departure in Academic Year 2016-17.

[5] Since its founding in 1969, there were restructurings that involved other academic units, such as Bilingual Education and Latin American Studies.

[6] I was the oldest member, but my guess is that the average age of department faculty did not drop dramatically upon my retirement.

[7] I refer to books that were published from the early 2000s to 2017. All were released by academic publishers. Some involved co-authorship or co-editorship with others outside of the Department of LALPRS.

[8] These include the disabled, rural residents, etc. I am fully aware that work conditions in my case were privileged compared to those for faculty carrying a 5-5 or 5-4 teaching load, as is the case in many institutions. As of this writing, the USA continues to be affected by COVID-19, and higher education is forced to transition even more rapidly into a world of virtual learning. The unequal distribution of quality education can be expected to intensify further in the absence of a public will to restore fairness in our society, especially given the digital divide.

[9] DACA is an immigration policy, enacted by the Obama administration in 2012, that allows undocumented people, known as Dreamers, brought to the United States as children, to defer deportation and live and work in the U.S. legally. The Trump administration has tried to end it, but as of this writing, it is still in effect.

References

City University of New York (CUNY) Board of Higher Education. 1969. Minutes of 9 May, 30 June, and 22 July.

Fiol-Matta, Licia. 2010. Lehman College (CUNY) Department of Latin American and Puerto Rican Studies. Minutes of 15 September.

Gonzalez, Evelyn. 2004. *The Bronx*. New York: Columbia University Press.

Lehman Marks 50 Years of Latinx and Africana Studies with Stories of Student Activism. 2019. *Lehman News* 6 November. <https://tinyurl.com/y2hrlqzy/> and <https://tmg-web.lehman.edu/news/Lehman-Marks-50-Years-of-Latinx-and-Africana-Studies-with-Stories-of-Student-Activism.php#:~:text=In%20the%201968-1969%20academic%20year%2C%20coalitions%20of%20Puerto,faculty%20would%20be%20brought%20into%20the%20college%20community>.

Torres, Andrés. 2014. Memo to David Badillo, Chair of LALPRS, on Student Success Measures. 5 March.

Totti, Xavier. 2020. Lehman College (CUNY) Department of Latin American and Latino Studies. Information provided via email. 13 July.

West, Melanie Grayce and Mariana Alfaro. 2017. NYC Hispanic Population is Growing. *Wall Street Journal* 22 June.

NOTES ON CONTRIBUTORS

Edna Acosta Belén (eacosta-belen@albany.edu) is Distinguished Professor Emerita of Latin American, Caribbean, and U.S. Latino Studies at the University at Albany, SUNY. Her research areas include Latina/o and Puerto Rican cultural and historical studies. She is coauthor of *Puerto Ricans in the United States: A Contemporary Portrait* (2006, 2018), and numerous other publications on the Puerto Rican diaspora.

Regina A. Bernard-Carreño (Regina.Bernard@cuny.edu) was born and raised in New York City. She holds graduate degrees from Columbia University and The CUNY Graduate Center. Now in the Department of Youth Studies in the CUNY School of Professional Studies, she was previously an Associate Professor of Black and Latino Studies at Baruch College, CUNY. She is the author of three books on race, class, feminism, and engaged activism.

Christine E. Bose (cbose@albany.edu) is a sociologist and Professor Emerita, University at Albany, State University of New York. She has been President of two academic professional associations (Eastern Sociological Society, 2011 and Sociologists for Women in Society, 2006), Editor of the journal *Gender & Society* (2000-03), and is author or editor of eight books. Her interest areas are U.S. and global gender inequalities, labor market issues, migration, and race/ethnicity/class differences.

Pedro Cabán (pcabanmoca@gmail.com) is Professor of Latin American, Caribbean, and U.S. Latino Studies at the University at Albany. His research is on the political economy of colonialism with a focus on Puerto Rico, U.S. Latina/o political engagement, and race and ethnic studies in higher education. He is author of *Constructing a Colonial People: Puerto Rico and the United States, 1898-1932* (1999). He was President of the Puerto Rican Studies Association (2003-2004). In addition to dozens of academic publications, he has recently published essays on Puerto Rico in *Latin American Perspectives, 80grados, Monthly Review Online, Jacobin, Dissent, NACLA, Current History, New Politics, Latino Rebels, the Conversation.com, and Latin American Perspectives Political Reports.*

Gisely Colón López (g.colonlopez@gmail.com) began her doctoral studies in Urban Education at The CUNY Graduate Center in Fall 2020. She has a Master of Arts from University of Connecticut-Storrs in International Studies and previously graduated from Brooklyn College, CUNY, with distinct honors as the college's Salutatorian and a Mellon Mays Undergraduate Fellow.

Juan González González (juan.gonzalez1@rutgers.edu) is Richard D. Heffner Professor of Communications and Public Policy at Rutgers University, State University of New Jersey, and co-host of the TV/radio news show *Democracy Now!* A leader of New York's Young Lords and former *Daily News* award-winning columnist and investigative reporter, he is author of the acclaimed *Harvest of Empire: A History of Latinos in America* (2000, 2011).

Milga Morales Nadal (MMNadal@gmail.com) was born in Guayanilla, Puerto Rico. A product of New York City public schools, her research has centered on second language acquisition and the history of bilingual education. She received her doctoral degree from Yeshiva University's Ferkauf Graduate School of Psychology. She taught for over 20 years and served as Dean of Students and as Vice President for Student Affairs at Brooklyn College, CUNY, before retiring in 2017.

Antonio Nadal (nadalantonio636@gmail.com) retired in 2016 after a 43-year teaching and administrative career in the Department of Puerto Rican and Latino Studies at Brooklyn College, CUNY. He was among the founders and faculty of the Institute of Bilingual Studies at Kingsborough Community College, CUNY (1970) and served as consultant and evaluator for the Institute for Research and Professional Development in the evaluation of bilingual and TESOL programs in several New York City school districts.

María Elizabeth Pérez y González (MariaPG@brooklyn.cuny.edu) is a Puerto Rican born in Brooklyn, New York, and Associate Professor in the Department of Puerto Rican and Latino Studies at Brooklyn College, CUNY, where she has served as faculty for 30 years, with 17 of those years as Chairperson, including two as Acting Chairperson. Her research includes the Puerto Rican diaspora, Latinxs, women in ministry, and Pentecostals. She is the author of *Puerto Ricans in the United States* (2000) and scholarly pieces on Latinas in Christian ministry.

Conor Tomás Reed (conortomasreed@gmail.com) is a Puerto Rican/Irish genderfluid scholar-organizer at Brooklyn College, CUNY, and contributes to *LÁPIZ, Lost & Found,* Free CUNY, and Rank and File Action. Conor's forthcoming book, *New York Liberation School,* chronicles Black, Puerto Rican, and Feminist Studies and movements at City College and in New York City.

Virginia Sánchez Korrol (VSanKorr@brooklyn.cuny.edu) is Professor Emerita at Brooklyn College, CUNY, where she chaired the Department of Puerto Rican and Latino Studies from 1989 to 2004. Her publications include *From Colonia to Community: The History of Puerto Ricans in New York* (1983, 1994), and the three-volume *Latinas in the United States: A Historical Encyclopedia* (2006). She serves on the boards of the New York Historical Society Center for Women's History, Arte Público Recovery Project, and the Latino Expert Panel of the National Park Service. She is a 2020 recipient of the prestigious Herbert H. Lehman Prize awarded by the New York Academy of History.

Andrés Torres (uzibla@aol.com) was Distinguished Lecturer at Lehman College, CUNY. His authored/co-edited works include *Between Melting Pot and Mosaic* (1995); *The Puerto Rican Movement: Voices from the Diaspora* (1998); *Latinos in New England* (2006), and *Signing in Puerto Rican: A Hearing Son and His Deaf Parents* (2009). Most recently he has co-edited *Revolution Around the Corner* (2020).

Jesse M. Vázquez (jessemvz@icloud.com) is Professor Emeritus at Queens College, CUNY, and former Director of the Puerto Rican Studies Program. He has written extensively on Puerto Ricans, identity, multiculturalism, counselor education, bilingualism, and ethnic studies.

PHOTO CREDITS

Cover design by Carmen Iris Santiago

CONTRIBUTORS PHOTO CREDITS

- Edna Acosta Belén, Regina Bernard-Carreño, Christine Bose, Pedro Cabán, Gisely Colón López, Juan González and Andrés Torres provided their photos used in the collage.

- María E. Pérez y González's photograph is courtesy of CUNY-TV.

- Conor Tomás Reed's photograph is courtesy of **María E. Pérez y González.**

- Virginia Sánchez Korrol's photograph is by **Madrigal Studio, Nyack, New York.**

- Photographs of Félix V. Matos Rodríguez, Milga Morales Nadal, Antonio Nadal and Jesse Vázquez were taken by unknown photographers for use at their respective campuses.

OTHER IMAGES USED

- Antonio Nieves provided the black and white images (including the overlay image) taken during the late 1960s and early 70s at Brooklyn College.

- Department of Puerto Rican and Latino Studies Archives, Brooklyn College—student newspapers (*Kingsman, Spigot Magazine*), flyers, departmental records, newspaper clippings (*El Diario, New York Daily News, City Star, Latin NY*).

- April 1969: City College students protest on campus (https://www1.cuny.edu/mu/forum/2019/04/12/50-years-later-ccny-remembers-pivotal-protest/).

- Unknown, "CCNY Protest Flier," CUNY Digital History Archive, accessed March 1, 2021 (https://cdha.cuny.edu/items/show/6962).

- Unknown, "Five Demands," CUNY Digital History Archive, accessed March 1, 2021 (https://cdha.cuny.edu/items/show/6952).

- In 1969, Black and Puerto Rican students demonstrated at City College, protesting what they say was an under-representation of minority students (https://psc-cuny.org/node/11816).

- Queens College: "Other CUNY Schools" From *Knightbeat*, Volume 12, April 22, 1969. (http://qcvoices.qwriting.qc.cuny.edu/files/2018/10/CUNYwide2.png).

- "Prevent A Militant Takeover" cartoon published on *The New York Times* on September 28, 1969, reflecting the militant climate at colleges across the US. Queens College. http://qcvoices.qwriting.qc.cuny.edu/files/2018/10/toon2.png

- *Palante: Latin Revolutionary News Service, Young Lords Party*, Volume 3, No. 3, February 1971. (http://dlib.nyu.edu/palante/). Tamiment Library & Robert F. Wagner Labor Archives at New York University.

- Day of Dignity protest in commemoration of Indigenous Peoples' Day in 2017 hosted by Puerto Rican Alliance Student Organization, Brooklyn College, courtesy of María E. Pérez y González.

INDEX

Made in the USA
Middletown, DE
11 February 2022

60211640R00186